Acclaim for Brenda Wineapple's

White Heat

Winner of the Arts Club of Washington
National Award for Arts Writing

"One of the most astonishing books about poetry I have ever read. It causes us to see Emily Dickinson, perhaps for the first time, as an actual human being of a particular time and place, rather than as a timeless, ghostly, and ethereal instrument of first-rank poetic genius. . . . Irresistibly entertaining." —Franz Wright

"A wonderfully evocative double portrait."
—Joyce Carol Oates, *The New York Review of Books*

"One of the best books of 2008. . . . Wineapple's superb biography of the friendship between Emily Dickinson and her editor, Thomas Wentworth Higginson, complicates our understanding of the Belle of Amherst." —Maureen Corrigan, NPR

"A dual biography of astonishing depth and grace."
—*The Boston Globe*

"A brilliant account of one of the oddest literary friendships in American history." —*Foreign Affairs*

"A prismatic double portrait. Ms. Wineapple specializes in imparting flesh-and-blood substance and narrative thrust to literary biographies." —*The Wall Street Journal*

"Intelligent, delightful. . . . A rich and satisfying journey."
—*The Christian Science Monitor*

"A model biography cum literary study set against an inexhaustibly interesting historical backdrop." —*The Miami Herald*

"Careful research and a lively prose style. . . . A double delight."
—*St. Louis Post-Dispatch*

"In her trenchant, memorable narrative of Dickinson's quarter-century entanglement with Higginson, Wineapple takes us into the "white heat" they generated together, a synergy that made their cold New England souls immeasurably warmer."

—*The Times Literary Supplement* (London)

"This double biography reveals a captivating Dickinson." —*Time*

"Brenda Wineapple, a superb literary critic, has a historian's soul. In *White Heat*, she beautifully describes the quiet drama and elusive tempos of one of the most improbable and fateful authorial friendships in all of American writing. Few contemporary interpreters, if any, could have understood the story in all its richness as Wineapple has—and then related it with such grace as well as authority." —Sean Wilentz

"Wineapple has done an admirable and eloquent job of unraveling this intriguing chapter in Emily Dickinson's story, but always with respect for the mystery of compatibility at its core. No book I know brings us deeper into the inner chambers of this poet's private life." —Billy Collins

"[This] is one of the strangest stories in American literary history—poignant, exasperating, moving—and Wineapple tells it with a rare brio and authority. *White Heat* is biography at its very best. It brings these two to life more exactly, more sympathetically, more vividly than ever before. A triumph!"

—J. D. McClatchy

Brenda Wineapple

White Heat

Brenda Wineapple is the author of *Genêt: A Biography of Janet Flanner; Sister Brother: Gertrude and Leo Stein;* and *Hawthorne: A Life*, winner of the Ambassador Award of the English-Speaking Union for Best Biography of 2003. Her essays and reviews appear in many publications, among them *The New York Times Book Review* and *The Nation*. She has been the recipient of grants from the National Endowment for the Arts and the Guggenheim Foundation. She lives in New York City and teaches creative writing at Columbia University and The New School.

Her website address is www.brendawineapple.com.

White Heat

White Heat

The Friendship of Emily Dickinson and
Thomas Wentworth Higginson

Brenda Wineapple

Anchor Books
A Division of Random House, Inc.
New York

FIRST ANCHOR BOOKS EDITION, DECEMBER 2009

The Library of Congress has cataloged the Knopf edition as follows:
Wineapple, Brenda.
White heat : the friendship of Emily Dickinson and Thomas Wentworth Higginson /
by Brenda Wineapple. —1st ed.
p. cm.
Includes bibliographical references and index.
1. Dickinson, Emily, 1830–1886—Friends and associates. 2. Poets, American—19th century—Biography.
3. Higginson, Thomas Wentworth, 1823–1911. 4. Dickinson, Emily, 1830–1886—Correspondence.
5. Poets, American—19th century—Correspondence. I. Title.
PS1541.Z5W545 2008
811'.4—dc22
[B] 2008011770

Anchor ISBN: 978-0-307-45630-4

Author photograph © Marion Ettlinger
Book design by Iris Weinstein

www.anchorbooks.com

Printed in the United States of America
10 9 8 7 6 5 4 3 2 1

In memory of Sybille Bedford

Contents

Illustrations

Introduction

The Letter

ONE

The Letter

This is my letter to the World
That never wrote to Me —
The simple News that Nature told —
With tender Majesty
Her Message is committed
To Hands I cannot see —
For love of Her — Sweet — countrymen —
Judge tenderly — of Me

Reprinted by Thomas Wentworth Higginson and Mabel
Loomis Todd in Emily Dickinson, Poems *(1890)*

A re you too deeply occupied to say if my Verse is alive?"
Thomas Wentworth Higginson opened the cream-colored envelope as he walked home from the post office, where he had stopped on the mild spring morning of April 17 after watching young women lift dumbbells at the local gymnasium. The year was 1862, a war was raging, and Higginson, at thirty-eight, was the local authority on physical fitness. This was one of his causes, as were women's health and education. His passion, though, was for abolition. But dubious about President Lincoln's intentions—fighting to save the Union was not the same as fighting to abolish slavery— he had not yet put on a blue uniform. Perhaps he should.

Yet he was also a literary man (great consolation for inaction) and frequently published in the cultural magazine of the moment, *The Atlantic Monthly,* where, along with gymnastics, women's rights, and slavery, his subjects were flowers and birds and the changing seasons.

Out fell a letter, scrawled in a looping, difficult hand, as well as four poems and another, smaller envelope. With difficulty he deci-

3

phered the scribble. "Are you too deeply occupied to say if my Verse is alive?"

This is the beginning of a most extraordinary correspondence, which lasts almost a quarter of a century, until Emily Dickinson's death in 1886, and during which time the poet sent Higginson almost one hundred poems, many of her best, their metrical forms jagged, their punctuation unpredictable, their images honed to a fine point, their meaning elliptical, heart-gripping, electric. The poems hit their mark. Poetry torn up by the roots, he later said, that took his breath away.

Today it may seem strange she would entrust them to the man now conventionally regarded as a hidebound reformer with a tin ear. But Dickinson had not picked Higginson at random. Suspecting he would be receptive, she also recognized a sensibility she could trust — that of a brave iconoclast conversant with botany, butterflies, and books and willing to risk everything for what he believed.

At first she knew him only by reputation. His name, opinions, and sheer moxie were the stuff of headlines for years, for as a voluble man of causes, he was on record as loathing capital punishment, child labor, and the unfair laws depriving women of civil rights. An ordained minister, he had officiated at Lucy Stone's wedding, and after reading from a statement prepared by the bride and groom, he distributed it to fellow clergymen as a manual of marital parity.

Above all, he detested slavery. One of the most steadfast and famous abolitionists in New England, he was far more radical than William Lloyd Garrison, if, that is, radicalism is measured by a willingness to entertain violence for the social good. Inequality offended him personally; so did passive resistance. Braced by the righteousness of his cause — the unequivocal emancipation of the slaves — this Massachusetts gentleman of the white and learned class had earned a reputation among his own as a lunatic. In 1854 he had battered down a courthouse door in Boston in an attempt to free the fugitive slave Anthony Burns. In 1856 he helped arm antislavery settlers in Kansas and, a loaded pistol in his belt, admitted almost sheepishly, "I enjoy danger." Afterward he preached sedition while furnishing money and morale to John Brown.

All this had occurred by the time Dickinson asked him if he was too busy to read her poems, as if it were the most reasonable request in the world.

"The Mind is so near itself — it cannot see, distinctly — and I have none to ask—" she politely lied. Her brother, Austin, and his wife, Susan, lived right next door, and with Sue she regularly shared much of her verse. "Could I make you and Austin—proud—some-time—a great way off—'twould give me taller feet—," she con-fided. Yet Dickinson now sought an adviser unconnected to family. "Should you think it breathed—and had you the leisure to tell me," she told Higginson, "I should feel quick gratitude—."

Should you think my poetry *breathed; quick gratitude:* if only he could write like this.

Dickinson had opened her request bluntly. "Mr. Higginson," she scribbled at the top of the page. There was no other salutation. Nor did she provide a closing. Almost thirty years later Higginson still recalled that "the most curious thing about the letter was the total absence of a signature." And he well remembered that smaller sealed envelope, in which she had penciled her name on a card. "I enclose my name—asking you, if you please—Sir—to tell me what is true?" That envelope, discrete and alluring, was a strategy, a plea, a gambit.

Higginson glanced over one of the four poems. "I'll tell you how the Sun rose— / A Ribbon at a time—." Who writes like this? And another: "The nearest Dream recedes—unrealized—." The thrill of discovery still warm three decades later, he recollected that "the impression of a wholly new and original poetic genius was as distinct on my mind at the first reading of these four poems as it is now, after thirty years of further knowledge; and with it came the problem never yet solved, what place ought to be assigned in literature to what is so remarkable, yet so elusive of criticism." This was not the benign public verse of, say, John Greenleaf Whittier. It did not share the metrical perfection of a Longfellow or the tiresome "priapism" (Emerson's word, which Higginson liked to repeat) of Walt Whit-man. It was unique, uncategorizable, itself.

The *Springfield Republican,* a staple in the Dickinson family, regu-larly praised Higginson for his *Atlantic* essays. "I read your Chapters in the Atlantic—" Dickinson would tell him. Perhaps at Dickin-son's behest, her sister-in-law had requested his daguerreotype from the *Republican*'s editor, a family friend. As yet unbearded, his dark, thin hair falling to his ears, Higginson was nice looking; he dressed conventionally, and he had grit.

Dickinson mailed her letter to Worcester, Massachusetts, where he lived and whose environs he had lovingly described: its lily ponds edged in emerald and the shadows of trees falling blue on a winter afternoon. She paid attention.

He read another of the indelible poems she had enclosed.

> *Safe in their Alabaster Chambers —*
> *Untouched by Morning —*
> *And untouched by noon —*
> *Sleep the meek members of the Resurrection,*
> *Rafter of Satin and Roof of Stone —*
>
> *Grand go the Years,*
> *In the Crescent above them —*
> *Worlds scoop their Arcs —*
> *And Firmaments — row —*
> *Diadems — drop —*
> *And Doges — surrender —*
> *Soundless as Dots,*
> *On a Disc of Snow.*

White alabaster chambers melt into snow, vanishing without sound: it's an unnerving image in a poem skeptical about the resurrection it proposes. The rhymes drift and tilt; its meter echoes that of Protestant hymns but derails. Dashes everywhere; caesuras where you least expect them, undeniable melodic control, polysyllabics eerily shifting to monosyllabics. Poor Higginson. Yet he knew he was holding something amazing, dropped from the sky, and he answered her in a way that pleased her.

That he had received poems from an unknown woman did not entirely surprise him. He'd been getting a passel of mail ever since his article "Letter to a Young Contributor" had run earlier in the month. An advice column to readers who wanted to become *Atlantic* contributors, the essay offered some sensible tips for submitting work—use black ink, good pens, white paper—along with some patently didactic advice about writing. Work hard. Practice makes perfect. Press language to the uttermost. "There may be years of crowded passion in a word, and half a life in a sentence," he explained. "A single word may be a window from which one may perceive all the kingdoms of the earth. . . . Charge your style with life." That is just what he himself was trying to do.

The fuzzy instructions set off a huge reaction. "I foresee that 'Young Contributors' will send me worse things than ever now," Higginson boasted to his editor, James T. Fields, whom he wanted to impress. "Two such specimens of verse came yesterday & day before—fortunately *not* to be forwarded for publication!" But writing to his mother, whom he also wanted to impress, Higginson sounded more sympathetic and humble. "Since that Letter to a Young Contributor I have more wonderful expressions than ever sent me to read with request for advice, which is hard to give."

Higginson answered Dickinson right away, asking everything he could think of: the name of her favorite authors, whether she had attended school, if she read Whitman, whether she published, and would she? (Dickinson had not told him that "Safe in their Alabaster Chambers" had appeared in *The Republican* just six weeks earlier.) Unable to stop himself, he made a few editorial suggestions. "I tried a little,—a very little—to lead her in the direction of rules and traditions," he later reminisced. She called this practice "surgery."

"It was not so painful as I supposed," she wrote on April 25, seeming to welcome his comments. "While my thought is undressed— I can make the distinction, but when I put them in the Gown— they look alike, and numb." As to his questions, she answered that she had begun writing poetry only very recently. That was untrue. In fact, she dodged several of his queries, Higginson recalled, "with a naive skill such as the most experienced and worldly coquette might envy." She told him she admired Keats, Ruskin, Sir Thomas Browne, and the Brownings, all names Higginson had mentioned in his various essays. Also, the book of Revelation. Yes, she had gone to school "but in your manner of the phrase—had no education." Like him, she responded intensely to nature. Her companions were the nearby Pelham Hills, the sunset, her big dog, Carlo: "they are better than Beings—because they know—but do not tell."

What strangeness: a woman of secrets who wanted her secrets kept but wanted you to know she had them. "In a Life that stopped guessing," she once told her sister-in-law, "you and I should not feel at home."

Her mother, she confided, "does not care for thought," and although her father has bought her many books, he "begs me not to read them—because he fears they joggle the Mind." She was alone, in other words, and apart. Her family was religious, she continued,

"—except me—and address an Eclipse, every morning—whom they call their 'Father.' " She would require a guidance more perspicacious, more concrete.

As for her poetry, "I sing, as the Boy does by the Burying Ground—because I am afraid." Such a bald statement would be hard to ignore. "When far afterward—a sudden light on Orchards, or a new fashion in the wind troubled my attention—I felt a palsy, here—the Verses just relieve—."

In passing, she dropped an allusion to the two literary editors—she was no novice after all—who "came to my Father's House, this winter—and asked me for my Mind—and when I asked them 'Why,' they said I was penurious—and they, would use it for the World—." It was not worldly approval that she sought; she demanded something different. "I could not weigh myself—Myself," she promptly added, turning slyly to Higginson. This time she signed her letter as "your friend, E— Dickinson."

Bewildered and flattered, he could not help considering that next to such finesse, his tepid tips to a Young Contributor were superfluous. What was an essay, anyway; what, a letter? Her phrases were poems, riddles, lyric apothegms, fleeing with the speed of thought. Her imagination boiled over, spilling onto the page. His did not, no matter how much heat he applied, unless, that is, he lost himself, as he occasionally did in his essays on nature—some are quite magical—or in his writing on behalf of the poor and disenfranchised, when he tackled his subject in clear-eyed prose and did not let it go. Logic and empathy were special gifts. Yet by dispensing pellets of wisdom about how to publish, as he did, in the most prestigious literary journal of the day, he presented himself as a professional man of letters, worth taking seriously, which is just what he hoped to become.

This skilled adviser was not as confident as he tried to appear. Perhaps Dickinson sensed this. In the aftermath of Harpers Ferry, Higginson had more or less packed away his revolver and retired to the lakes around his home, where he scoured the woods after the manner of his favorite author, Henry Thoreau. "I cannot think of a bliss as great as to follow the instinct which leads me thither & to wh. I never yet dared fully to trust myself," Higginson confided to his journals. He wrote all the time—about slave uprisings and Denmark Vesey and Nat Turner and also about boating, snowstorms, woodbines, and exercise. Fields printed whatever Higginson gave him and suggested he gather his nature essays into a book.

But the Confederates had fired on Fort Sumter, and all bets were off. Then thirty-seven years old (Dickinson was thirty), he unsuccessfully tried to organize a military expedition headed by a son of John Brown's, assuming that the mere sound of Brown's name would wreak havoc in the South. He tried to raise a volunteer regiment in Worcester. That, too, failed. "I have thoroughly made up my mind that my present duty lies at home," he rationalized.

By his "present duty" he meant his wife, an invalid who in recent years could not so much as clutch a pen in her gnarled fingers. She needed him. "This war, for which I long and for which I have been training for years, is just as absolutely unobtainable for me as a share in the wars of Napoleon," he confided to his diary. To console himself, he wrote the "Letter to a Young Contributor" in which he declared one need not choose between "a column of newspaper or a column of attack, Wordsworth's 'Lines on Immortality' or Wellington's Lines of Torres Vedras; each is noble, if nobly done, though posterity seems to remember literature the longest." No doubt Dickinson agreed. "The General Rose—decay— / ," she would write, "But this—in Lady's Drawer / Make Summer—When the Lady lie / In Ceaseless Rosemary—."

> South Winds jostle them —
> Bumblebees come
> Hover —Hesitate —Drink — and are gone —
> Butterflies pause — on their passage Cashmere —
> I, softly plucking,
> Present them —Here —

Hover. Hesitate. Drink. Gone: the elusive Dickinson enclosed three more poems in her second letter to Higginson, along with a few pressed flowers. He must have acknowledged the gift quickly, for in early June she wrote him again. "Your letter gave no Drunkenness," she replied, "because I tasted Rum before—Domingo comes but once—yet I have had few pleasures so deep as your opinion."

That initial taste of rum had come from an earlier "tutor," who had said he would like to live long enough to see her a poet but then died young. As for Higginson's opinion of her poetry, she took it under ironic advisement. "You think my gait 'spasmodic'—I am in danger—Sir—," she wrote in June as if with a grin. "You think me 'uncontrolled'—I have no Tribunal." To be sure, Higginson could not have been expected to understand all she meant; who could? No matter. She did not enlist him for that, or at least not for that alone. She wanted understanding and friendship, both of which he offered, all-important to her even if his advice proved superfluous. "The 'hand you stretch me in the Dark,' " she said, "I put mine in."

Nor would she admit to being put off by his apparent suggestion that she "delay" publishing. She smiled archly. " 'To publish'—," she shot back, "that being foreign to my thought, as Firmament to Fin—." Yet "if fame belonged to me," she also observed, "I could not escape her—." Perhaps he had mentioned *The Atlantic Monthly,* where he often recommended new talent—particularly women—to Fields. He need only dispatch one of her poems.

He did not.

That he told her to be patient seems paradoxical. This was the man who urged immediate, even violent action in the political sphere. Yet he did not say she should *never* print her poems. He had said "delay." He needed to find his bearings. Her poetry shocked him, violating as it did the canonical forms of meter and rhyme, and it stunned him with well-shaped insights that thrust him into the very process of writing itself—the difficult transition from idea to page, the repeated attempts to get it right:

> We play at Paste —
> Till qualified, for Pearl —
> Then, drop the Paste —
> And deem ourself a fool —
>
> The Shapes — though — were similar —
> And our new Hands
> Learned Gem-*tactics* —
> Practising Sands—

Having reminisced about her former tutor, Dickinson concluded her third letter with the suggestion that Higginson replace him. "Would you have time to be the 'friend' you should think I need?" she wondered with shy charm. "I have a little shape—it would not crowd your Desk——." And though she did not enclose any poems in this letter, she concluded with a verse:

> *As if I asked a common Alms,*
> *And in my wondering hand*
> *A Stranger pressed a Kingdom,*
> *And I, bewildered, stand —*
> *As if I asked the Orient*
> *Had it for me a Morn —*
> *And it should lift it's purple Dikes,*
> *And shatter Me with Dawn!*

"But, will you be my Preceptor, Mr. Higginson?"
He could not say no.

EARLY IN HIS CAREER, Higginson had planned to write a sermon, "the Dreamer & worker—the day & night of the soul." "The Dreamer shld be worker, & the worker a dreamer," he jotted in his notebook. In a country that measures success in terms of profit rather than poetry, dreamers are an idle lot, inconsequential and neglected. But inside every worker there's a dreamer, Higginson hopefully insisted, and by the same token dreamers can turn their fantasies to Yankee account: "do not throw up yr ideas, but realize them. The boy who never built a castle in the air will never build one on earth."

Fragmentary, incomplete, disconsonant—these terms—dreamer and worker, poet and activist—recur with frequency in his later writing. Back and forth he swerved, between a life devoted to dreams and one committed to practical action. The themes are clear, too, in his "Letter to a Young Contributor," where he incorporated whole sentences from his "Dreamer and Worker" journal to come to a propitious conclusion: "I fancy that in some other realm of existence we may look back with some kind interest on this scene of our earlier life, and say to one another,—'Do you remember yonder planet, where once we went to school?' And whether our elective study here lay chiefly in the fields of action or of thought will matter little to us then, when other schools shall have led us through other disciplines."

Fields of action, fields of thought; the active life or seclusion—twin chambers of a divided American heart. This was Higginson's conflict. He who would risk his life to end chattel slavery nonetheless fantasized about a cabin in the woods where, like his idol Thoreau, he might front only the essential facts of life. But Higginson had already run for Congress, and would later serve in the Massachusetts legislature and co-edit *The Woman's Journal* for the National American Woman Suffrage Association. And he would command the first regular Union army regiment made up exclusively of freed slaves (mustered far earlier than Robert Gould Shaw's fabled Massachusetts Fifty-fourth). You could not do this from a cabin in the woods.

Opting for the seclusion he could not sustain, Dickinson had walked away from public life, informing Higginson that she did not "cross her Father's ground to any House or town," and for many years, as she told him, her lexicon had been her only companion. "The Soul selects her own Society— / Then—shuts the Door—." Yet she did not choose unequivocally. No one can who writes.

Emily Dickinson and Thomas Higginson, seven years apart, had been raised in a climate where old pieties no longer sufficed, the piers of faith were brittle, and God was hard to find. If she sought solace in poetry, a momentary stay against mortality, he found it for a time in activism, and for both friendship was a secular salvation, which, like poetry, reached toward the ineffable. This is why he answered her, pursued her, cultivated her, visited her, and wept at her grave. He was not as bullet-headed as many contemporary critics like to think. Relegated to the dustbin of literary history, a relic of Victoriana cursed with geniality and an elegant prose style, Higginson has been invariably dismissed by critics fundamentally uninterested in his radicalism; after all, not until after Dickinson's death, when the poet's family contacted him, did he consent to reread the poems and edit them for publication, presumably to appeal to popular taste. Yet he tried hard to prepare the public for her—"The Truth must dazzle gradually / Or every man be blind—," as she had written—and in his preface to the 1890 volume frankly compared her to William Blake.

Dickinson responded fully to the man he thought—and she thought—he was: courtly and bold, stuffy and radical, chock-full of contradictions and loving. For not only did she initiate the correspondence, but as far as we know she gave no one except Sue more poems than she sent to him. She trusted him, she liked him, she saw in him what it has become convenient to overlook. And he reciprocated in such a way that she often said he saved her life. "Of our greatest acts," she would later remind him, "we are ignorant—."

To neglect this friendship reduces Dickinson to the frail recluse of Amherst, extraordinary but helpless and victimized by a bourgeois literary establishment best represented by Higginson. Gone is the Dickinson whose flinty perceptions we admire and whose shrewd assessment of people and things informed her witty, half-serious choice of him as Preceptor, a choice she did not regret. Gone is the woman loyal to those elect few whom she truly trusted. Gone is the sphere of action in which she performed, choosing her own messengers. Gone, too, is Higginson.

Sometimes we see better through a single window after all: this book is not a biography of Emily Dickinson, of whom biography gets us nowhere, even though her poems seem to cry out for one. Nor is it a biography of Colonel Higginson. It is not conventional literary criticism. Rather, here Dickinson's poetry speaks largely for itself, as it did to Higginson. And by providing a context for particular poems, this book attempts to throw a small, considered beam onto the lifework of these two unusual, seemingly incompatible friends. It also suggests, however lightly, how this recluse and this activist bear a fraught, collaborative, unbalanced and impossible relation to each other, a relation as symbolic and real in our culture as it was special to them. After all, who they were—the issues they grappled with—shapes the rhetoric of our art and our politics: a country alone, exceptional, at least in its own romantic mythology—even warned by its first president to steer clear of permanent alliances—that regularly intervenes on behalf, or at the expense, of others. The fantasy of isolation, the fantasy of intervention: they create recluses and activists, sometimes both, in us all. "The Soul selects its own Society" is a beloved poem; so, too, the "Battle Hymn of the Republic."

Though Higginson preserved a large number of Dickinson's letters to him, most of his to her have mysteriously vanished. Before she died, in 1886, Emily instructed her sister, Lavinia, to burn her papers, a task Lavinia dutifully performed until, about a week after the funeral, she happened upon a boxful of poems (about eight hundred of them) in a bureau drawer. (It seems Dickinson had not instructed Lavinia to burn these.) Lavinia, who wanted these poems published, suddenly realized the literary significance of her sister's correspondence, but by then she had unthinkingly tossed much of it—Higginson's letters included—into the blaze. That's the standard tale. Yet when Higginson, along with Mabel Loomis Todd, Austin's mistress, was preparing the first edition of Dickinson's poems, Todd noted in her diary that Lavinia had stumbled across Higginson's letters to the poet. "Thank Heaven!" she sighed.

At a later date, however, Todd jotted in the margins of her diary: "Never gave them to me." Today no one knows what became of them: whether Higginson asked that they be destroyed—he seems to have purged as much as he saved—or whether for some inexplicable reason Lavinia intentionally lost them.

Because these letters are missing, one has to infer a good deal: his dependence on her, his infatuation, his downright awe of her strange mind. But not that she sought his friendship.

Yes, she sought him. And the two of them, unlikely pair, drew near to each other with affection as fresh as her poems, as real and as rare.

Part One

Before

TWO

Thomas Wentworth Higginson: Without a Little Crack Somewhere

D on't you think it rather a pity that all the really interesting Americans seem to be dead?" an Englishwoman once asked the aging Colonel Higginson, who, slightly startled by the insult, sadly agreed.

There was a belated quality about Thomas Wentworth Higginson. Born in 1823, almost two decades after Emerson and Garrison and Theodore Parker, he was of a generation fated to admire and emulate but never outshine them. For they were the giants of what Higginson called the sunny side of the transcendental period, spawned by a German philosophical idealism in which the love of nature and humanity routed out the bogey of Puritan gloom, substituting idealism for depravity and sin.

Yet Thomas Wentworth Higginson, their beneficiary, had been at the banquet, unbelievable as that might be to future chroniclers. "It would seem as strange to another generation for me to have sat at the same table with Longfellow or Emerson," Higginson admitted with characteristic modesty, "as it now seems that men shld hv. sat at the table with Wordsworth or with Milton."

Perhaps; but perhaps not.

DESCENDED FROM SEVEN GENERATIONS of Higginsons in America, Thomas Wentworth bore the mixed blessing of a long New England lineage. His ancestor the Reverend Francis Higginson had sailed to the New World from England in the spring of 1629 along with six goats, about two hundred other passengers (not including servants), his eight children (one of whom died during the voyage), and his wife, Higginson's fare on the *Talbot* paid by the Massachusetts Bay Colony. For one hundred acres of land and thirty pounds per annum, Reverend Francis had been commissioned to save souls in Naumkeag, and he would perform so conscientiously—changing the name of the village to Salem and establishing its first church—that Cotton Mather would dub him the Noah of New England.

When the Reverend Higginson died, just a year after setting foot on Massachusetts soil, his son John took up his mantle by promptly banishing Quakers and then signing a nefarious share of arrest warrants during the witchcraft hysteria of 1692. But John's rather lackluster commitment to killing witches compromised his own daughter, who was soon accused of the dark art. Not surprisingly, in later years he apologized in public for the terrible delusion he had helped incite and, always one to admit a mistake, at age ninety backed Judge Samuel Sewall's efforts to abolish slavery and the slave trade, the foundation of much of Salem's wealth. The local historian Charles Upham, who approved of very few, called Higginson a man of sterling character.

Conscience was a Higginson inheritance, or at least the legacy insisted on by its nineteenth-century descendant Thomas Wentworth. Of course the family had by then distinguished itself in commerce. Higginson's paternal grandfather, Stephen, shipowner, merchant, and soldier, was the Massachusetts delegate to the Continental Congress in 1783 and the reputed author of *The Writings of Laco,* published in 1789, which, arguing for freedom of the press, scathingly denounced John Hancock. A member of what was called the Essex Junto, a group of well-to-do Federalist merchants who, despising Jefferson, considered seceding from the United States to protect their interests, he opposed the Embargo Act of 1807, which choked off trade in the port of Salem, but he managed to turn a profit during the War of 1812. No wonder his grandson Wentworth (as Thomas was called) long remembered this imposing specter, attired in black, as wielding a gold-headed cane.

Wentworth Higginson would write laudatory biographies of his ancestor Francis and his grandfather but kept largely silent on the subject of his own father. An improvident investor and lavish spender, Stephen Higginson Jr. had to liquidate most of his colossal library after the War of 1812 and move his family from Boston's fashionable Mount Vernon Street to a sheep farm in Bolton, where they remained until well-placed friends landed him a job as steward of Harvard College. He immediately built a house on Kirkland Street, then a sandy plain, but doubtless the good-hearted profligate was not the best man to guard the Harvard treasury.

By then his family was quite large. After his first wife died, leaving him five children, Stephen wed his daughters' governess, Louisa Storrow, a New England Jane Eyre with a pedigree eminently respectable (Appletons, Wentworths, and Storrows) as well as swashbuckling (she was also descended from an English officer who had been imprisoned in Portsmouth, New Hampshire, during the Revolution). Stephen Higginson's ward since her eleventh year and his wife at nineteen, she bore ten children, six of whom lived to adulthood. Named for her forebears, Thomas Wentworth Storrow Higginson was her last, "the star that gilds the evening of my days—and he must shine bright and clear," she ominously continued, "or my path will be darkened." Later in life, Higginson identified his mother as the woman who influenced him most, particularly since he had been a feeble, sickly infant "half dead," as she had liked to remind him.

Higginson's childhood was comfortable, privileged, and difficult. A charitable man who helped organize the Harvard Divinity School, his father had not mended his ways. "I think sometimes he will offer his wife and children to somebody who has not got any," Mrs. Higginson grumbled, and Wentworth would comment, with some aspersion, that "his hospitality was inconveniently unbounded." When the Republicans in the state legislature (along with Emily Dickinson's grandfather) chartered the Congregationalist Amherst College in protest against Harvard's balmy Unitarianism, Harvard lost its annual appropriation, and Stephen Higginson Jr. faced a crisis he could not contain. (The families of Emily Dickinson and Thomas Higginson were thus linked, and though they sat on different sides of the theological fence, each was intimately connected to the way in which that fence had been built.) The deficit mounted, salaries were cut, students were charged for the wine they drank in chapel, and the college sloop was sold. He resigned his post in disgrace, and the Harvard Corporation held him personally responsible for the bills.

The family crated their household goods, auctioned much of their furniture, and took up residence on the far side of Cambridge Common, where Mrs. Higginson could support her brood with boarders in a house built by her eldest son, Francis, now a physician. Another son began to tutor, and yet Stephen Higginson sank deeper into debt, squandering what remained of his own father's legacy until, at age sixty-four, he suddenly died.

"In works of Love he found his happiness," read his double-edged epitaph, hinting at promises left unfulfilled. By this time, Wentworth was ten.

HIS HEALTH HAD IMPROVED, he learned to read and recite at four, and as a docile child, good-natured and by many accounts good-looking, he soaked up the scholarly, status-minded standards of the neighborhood, which happened to be Harvard College. Boyhood memories were bookish: he recalled a good set of Dr. Johnson's works, an early edition of Boswell, the writing of Fanny Burney, and his mother reading Walter Scott. Harvard professors brought by volumes of Collins, Goldsmith, and Campbell to woo his brilliant aunt, Ann Gilliam Storrow, who lived with them; Jared Sparks, later Harvard's president, entertained the family with portfolios of Washington's letters to his mother; John G. Palfrey, dean of the divinity school and the historian of New England subsequently adored by Henry Adams, recited aloud all of Hawthorne's *Twice-Told Tales*.

At the private school run by William Wells, a place to "fit" for Harvard College, Wentworth hopefully memorized the list of undergraduate classes and at thirteen, well versed in Latin grammar and something of a prodigy, entered the freshman class. "Born in the college, bred to it," as he later said. (His three elder brothers had also attended Harvard, and each remained involved with it during their lives.) But Wentworth was a lonely, awkward boy who had spurted up to six feet and, desperate to excel, worried lest he be fated for second place.

He studied Greek with the poet Jones Very, French literature with Henry Wadsworth Longfellow, and chemistry with John Webster, soon notorious for the gruesome murder of George Parkman. He enrolled in a class in entomology, which he adored, and he helped form a makeshift natural history society. He long remembered Edward Tyrrel Channing's courses in rhetoric. "I rarely write for three hours without half consciously recalling some caution or suggestion of his," Higginson later recollected of Channing, who also taught Emerson, Oliver Wendell Holmes, Charles Sumner, Wendell Phillips, and Charles Eliot Norton.

At Harvard his friend Levi Thaxter (future husband of the poet Celia Laighton Thaxter) introduced him to the writings of Emerson, Browning, and Hazlitt. Another acquaintance, if not quite a friend, was James Russell Lowell, with whom he felt rivalrous, particularly since he adored Lowell's fiancée, Maria White, a grand woman flushed with consumption, poetry, and abolition. (Years later Higginson would print her poems whenever he could.) Mainly, though, in the presence of women outside the family, Wentworth was clumsy and tongue-tied until, fed up, he scribbled out topics of conversation on scraps of paper, which he would pull out of his pocket whenever the banter between him and a pretty young woman lagged. Even in flirtation he was something of a pedant.

Emotionally unprepared for college, in 1841 he was equally unready to leave it. Though he toyed with the idea of growing peaches—the communal living experiment at Brook Farm, then in its halcyon days, stirred his suggestible imagination—he took a job teaching in nearby Jamaica Plain, his mother and two sisters having decamped to Vermont, where his brother Francis had opened a medical practice. Wentworth lasted just six months in Jamaica Plain. Fortunately, a rich older cousin, Stephen Perkins, rescued him with an offer to tutor his three sons, one of whom would be cut down at Cedar Mountain in the summer of 1862.

At the Perkins estate in rural Brookline, Higginson entered a world of cultured, self-conscious wealth. Cousin Perkins owned paintings by Sir Joshua Reynolds and Benjamin West, eventually bequeathed to the Boston Museum of Fine Arts; he avidly read Continental literature and talked volubly about the need for social change. For this was the period of what Higginson would call the Newness, when the skies of New England rained reform. The estimable Ralph Waldo Emerson had himself resigned the pulpit in 1832, yearning for a more humane form of belief, one that squarely put divinity in the soul of the individual. Four years later, when Higginson was an impressionable twelve-year-old, Emerson published the very bible of Newness, *Nature,* which asked, "Why should not we also enjoy an original relation to the universe?" ("God incarnates himself in man," Emerson declared at the Harvard Divinity School in 1838 and was not to be invited back for thirty years.) In

1840, Elizabeth Peabody opened her atom of a foreign bookshop (Higginson's description) on West Street in Boston, where she talked up Brook Farm and in the back room printed the transcendentalist organ, *The Dial,* while so-called transcendentalists—like Emerson and Bronson Alcott—snatched French or German volumes from her shelves. And Higginson's sister Anna was friends with the peerless Margaret Fuller, the bookstore's resident sibyl, who organized a series of "Conversations" for Boston women. Fuller sat on a tripod in a velvet gown, demanding no less of herself than of the women assembled before her: What are we, as women, born to do, she asked, and how do we intend to do it?

James Russell Lowell and William Story quit the legal profession to give their all to art, and women writers from George Sand to Lydia Maria Child sympathized with the downtrodden poor. And the slaves. In 1833, Child published her abolitionist *Appeal in Favor of That Class of Americans Called Africans,* and in 1834, Wentworth's brother Francis published *Remarks on Slavery and Emancipation,* a rational argument demolishing any and all excuses for chattel slavery. In 1841 the courts ruled that the Africans who had staged a revolt aboard the *Amistad* were but kidnapped people unlawfully traded, and Frederick Douglass spoke at the antislavery convention in Nantucket about the abominations he himself had endured.

Buoyed by the Newness, Higginson disdained the predictable professions of law and medicine, and though shaken by the phrenologist who told him he had "splendid talents but no application," he dreamed of the ideal, inchoate as it was. "I feel overflowing with mental energies," he told his mother; "I will be Great if I can." But the only thing he knew how to do was study, so in 1843 he returned to Harvard, where he could dabble in an institutionally sanctioned way, letting greatness find him. (The college permitted resident graduates to take courses without working toward a degree.) "If I have any genius, I *must* have a fair chance to cherish it," he pleaded with his dubious mother. "The point I wish to insist upon about all this you see is that it is sensible & rational—not at all utopia." For money, he applied for a proctorship, and when denied he earned a pittance by tutoring and copying. "I have been brought up poor & am not afraid to continue so," he declared, more vehement than ever, "and certainly I shall be glad to do it, if it is a necessary accompaniment to a life spent as I wish to spend it."

Renting a room with a view on the third floor of the College

House, he could see pigs and cows meandering on the muddy streets. He was nineteen. He was free. Living on his own, he could redo his college years with no mother waiting up nights for the sound of the latch. And he had at last decided on a profession. He would be a poet. There was no higher calling.

The Higginson household had for years consumed Byron with delight, and the great Emerson had himself said that "all the argument and all the wisdom is not in the encyclopaedia, or the treatise on metaphysics, or the Body of Divinity, but in the sonnet or the play." Poets unfix the world, banish our habits, dwell in possibilities of change and daring action. They make the world whole; they allow us to catch what we ordinarily miss. "What I would not give to know whether I really have that in me which will make a poet," he mused, "or whether I deceive myself and only possess a mediocre talent."

But the latter seemed the case. When the boy's verses had been summarily rejected by *The Dial,* Emerson let him down with a thud. "They have truth and earnestness," the Concord philosopher told him, "and a happier hour may add that external perfection which can neither be commanded nor described."

Reading De Quincey and Coleridge, Wentworth experimented with opium, hoping for a New England version of "Kubla Khan," but with no visions forthcoming, he threw himself back into his books, sowing intellectual wild oats, as he later said: Newton, Homer, Hesiod, Chaucer, George Sand, Linnaeus, and more Emerson. He learned German in order to read Jean Paul Richter, whom he worshipped, and Goethe, whom everyone did; he kept up his Greek, and one of his first projects after the Civil War would be a translation of Epictetus, the Stoic philosopher, born a slave, who taught that all souls were equal.

"I did not know exactly what I wished to study in Cambridge," Higginson would later reminisce. "Indeed, I went there to find out." At the time, though, he figured his scheme of promiscuous apprenticeship would take ten to fifteen years. "I think I have a fair right to expect, in the then state of my powers, to make my living as a *literary* man without a profession," he calculated. Yet something was missing. "I cannot live alone," he informed his family. "Solitude may be good for study sometimes, but not solitude in a crowd for a social-hearted person like me."

Actually, with statements like these Wentworth was trying to brace his family for news of his precipitous and wholly unexpected engagement to Mary Channing. A second cousin two years his senior (she was twenty-one) and neither wealthy nor submissive, Miss Channing was not the woman Mrs. Higginson would have chosen for her gilded boy. Intelligent and tart—a real conversational gymnast—she was also pert, churlish, and frequently abrupt. "Whatever be her faults of manner," Higginson gallantly defended her, "I do like her very much."

Perhaps Mary Channing was his first rescue mission. Her mother had died when Mary was two, and though her father, an obstetrician esteemed in Boston, had happily remarried, his second wife died in childbirth when Mary was but twelve. This second loss and her father's inadvertent hand in it devastated her, and as Higginson would later learn, Mary had concluded then and there not to have children herself. The decision predated the onset of a chronic malady that would grip her in her twenties, never to let her go, crippling her limbs and scarring her soul. "Mrs. Higginson is very queer, a great invalid from rheumatism," an acquaintance once remarked, "a perfect mistress in the art of abuse, in which she indulges frequently with peculiar zest & enthusiasm."

If Higginson's mother had not been pleased by her son's precipitous engagement, the name of Channing had calmed her. Channings occupied the upper reaches of Brahmin Boston, their intellectual and cultural influence radiating from the golden dome of the new State House to the clatter at Quincy Market—and this despite their commitment to such outré causes as women's rights, prison reform, and abolition. Mary's own uncle was the celebrated Unitarian preacher William Ellery Channing, who had liberated an entire generation from old-line Congregationalism, and Mary's brother (William) Ellery, the poet with the orange shoes, had married Margaret Fuller's sister. Then there was William Henry Channing (who happened to be Higginson's cousin), the Christian socialist with the honeyed voice who dared scold Emerson for his asocial individualism. (Ironically Channing served as one of the models for Hawthorne's Hollingsworth, the egomaniacal reformer in *The Blithedale Romance.*)

As for Higginson, it was Mary herself and her prickliness that pleased him. Besides, he might help with her grief. Hadn't he lost his own father at a tender age? Certainly both of them were lonely. But Higginson sheepishly admitted that while he could dally at Harvard, picking and choosing courses of study, women were slated for marriage, caretaking, and the so-called domestic arts. Yet his sisters, his mother, and his exceptional aunt demonstrated every day that there was no distinction of sex in intellect, and his sister Anna, as he noted, had written the part of his commencement speech that received the most applause.

"I don't care about outside show, but I do go for the Rights of Women," he bolstered Mary, "as far as an equal education & an equal share in government goes." He meant every word.

He and Mary attended James Freeman Clarke's liberal Church of the Disciples, the ecumenical congregation that she had helped organize, and together they discussed religion and reform. But Higginson referred to Theodore Parker, not Freeman Clarke, as his spiritual guide. A polymath contemptuous of the status quo, a transcendentalist long before the group rated a name, and the most blasphemous of all preachers in the public's eye, Parker had the audacity to doubt miracles and champion the enslaved, a bad combination. "God's fanatic," Higginson later called him, "pompous, annoying, and eminently good." (A book by Parker was given to Emily Dickinson, though not by Higginson, some years after the preacher's untimely death. "I heard that he was 'poison,' " Dickinson thanked her donor. "Then I like poison very well.") In old age, Higginson still dreamed about hearing him preach.

Parker's fire-and-brimstone sermons damning the sin of slavery; William Henry Channing's dulcet oratory sketching out the shape of a better world; Margaret Fuller, intrepidly insisting it belonged to woman; the cantankerous tongue of Mary Channing taking nothing for granted; and in the Concord distance, Emerson counseling self-trust, self-reliance, and the triumph of good—together they swept Higginson forward into the Newness. He might become Great after all.

POETRY ASIDE, he still needed a paying profession.

Maybe he could be a preacher. Yet as one of his biographers observes, though Higginson assumed the goodness of people, he was far less certain about the nature of God. To him Jesus was a brother, the Bible a book, and all religion an activity shared by all humans regardless of creed; the latter belief he traced to an event in his boyhood, when in 1834 he watched flames demolish the Ursuline convent, on Mount Benedict in Charlestown, torched by an anti-Catholic mob. The rioters were acquitted of arson, and the ringleader, also acquitted, later became head of the anti-Catholic Know-Nothing party. Higginson never got over it.

Warmed by an inner light "not infallible but invaluable," Higginson read Emerson as if the Concord sage wrote to him alone, and he staked his future on a democracy of perfectible love, what Emerson had called a "just and even fellowship, or none." "The career of man has grown large, conscious, cultivated, varied, full," Higginson wrote in later years. "He needs India and Judaea, Greece and Rome; he needs all types of spiritual manhood, all teachers."

In 1844 he enrolled halfheartedly in the Harvard Divinity School, a court of last resort, but within months scoffed at his teachers, whose theology he considered as weak as the spines of his fellow students. "Any man with some Yes in him would be a blessing," Higginson loudly complained, feeling belated once again. Gone, he feared, was the heyday of the divinity school, when his father had charge of a crop of superior young men, like Emerson himself.

And besides, events taking place outside the cloistered halls of Harvard concerned him more: Texas, for instance, and its possible admission to the Union as a slave state. "In Cambridge we are in peace," he wrote in some relief, "since the Texas petition—764 names, 13 ft. long, double column—went off." Abolition had rapidly become the focus of his frustration, his sense of injustice, his desire to accomplish something tangible. "I crave action . . . , unbounded action," he burst out. "I love men passionately, I feel intensely their sufferings and short-comings and yearn to make all men brothers."

Years later Higginson traced his abolitionist leanings not just to Emerson or his brother's book (which he hardly mentioned) or Lydia Child's treatise, all formative, but to his mother and an incident in her life, which trifling though it seems, also associates the abolition of slavery with the emancipation of women, as he and many others would do. Mrs. Higginson had visited cousins in Virginia, who provided her with a male slave to drive her about, and as she'd never encountered a slave before, she asked him if he was satisfied with his life, since, it seemed, he was well fed, well treated, well cared for. Life is good, she prompted. Without hesitation he shot back, "Free breath is good." So it was, for her too.

Dissatisfied and impatient, Higginson withdrew from divinity school within a year of his enrollment, for despite his failure at getting *The Dial* to recognize him as a writer, he still guiltily craved literature. "I have repented of many things," he justified himself to his mother, "but I never repented of my first poetical Effusion." Again he presented his verse to various magazines but this time chose more hospitable editors. "La Madonna di San Sisto" went to his activist cousin William Henry Channing, who published it in *The Present* in 1843; Channing then published Wentworth's poem "Tyrtaeus" in his Brook Farm magazine, *The Harbinger.*

Tyrtaeus appealed to Higginson: his martial poems had allegedly inspired Spartan soldiers during the Second Messenian War, and Higginson himself hoped to sing on the barricades:

> *Times change,*
> *And duties with them; now no longer*
> *We summon brothers to take brothers' lives;*
> *But rouse to conflict higher, holier, stronger*
> *. . . Against the seeds of ruin now upsurging*
> *Here in this sunny land we call the Free.*

Poetry: one might take up the pen for a cause and infuse "a higher element" (Higginson's term) into, say, the entire antislavery movement, much as the abolitionist poet John Greenleaf Whittier had done. Isn't this what Emerson meant by a just and even fellowship—though Emerson's antislavery views were as yet ill-formed. And although antislavery verse encumbered Whittier's literary career, at least initially (he was scolded by the important literary magazine *The North American Review*), by lashing poetry to politics, Higginson might still be a poet and yet take action, use himself, say something that could move or change people. In 1846 he dedicated a sonnet to William Lloyd Garrison, abolitionist editor of the staunch antislavery paper *The Liberator,* and composed a hymn for an antislavery picnic in Dedham. "The land our fathers left to us / Is foul with hateful sin," the crowd sang; "When shall, O Lord, this sorrow end, / And hope and joy begin?"

"The idea of poetic genius is now utterly foreign to me," Higginson informed his mother. Instead he had a gospel to sing, its providential ends consistent with his reading of scripture, its goals to be realized on earth. If it brought him some measure of the fame he sought, so much the better.

Higginson applied for readmission to the divinity school in the fall of 1846, oddly explaining his decision in a clumsy third person:

"He has abandoned much that men call belief, but seems to himself to have only won former ground to believe more deeply than ever." That is, he would shuck poetry for the moment but not forgo the brass ring: he intended to reform America to make it, and himself, great.

Mary should be warned. "Setting out, as I do, with an entire resolution never to be intimidated into shutting either my eyes or my mouth," Higginson told her, "it is proper to consider the chance of my falling out with the world."

Mary did not blink. She never would through all the trials ahead, and the couple was married on September 22, 1847, James Freeman Clarke presiding.

IF HIGGINSON DID NOT YET KNOW the extent of his agenda, neither did the congregation of the First Religious Society of Newburyport, thirty-eight miles north of Boston, a staid port community that in its salad days was a hub of maritime trade and shipbuilding. The gracious homes of the old shipowners still lined High Street, the main thoroughfare, but by 1847 only their ghosts strolled on the decaying wharves, where they were joined by the factory workers, mostly women, who kept spindles running dawn to dusk for the rich textile men—a poor match all around.

The Higginsons adjusted slowly. Mary found the congregants dull and uncouth. Wentworth hated their materialism, their intolerance, their complacency. Since he also deplored the Mexican War as a means to extend the reach of slavery, he alienated his conservative parishioners, merchants and bankers mostly, who regarded him as a crank. "There are times and places where Human Feeling is fanaticism," he archly reminded them, "times and places where it seems that a man can only escape the charge of fanaticism by being a moral iceberg."

With human feeling flowing from every principled pore, Higginson lambasted the Whig candidate for president, Zachary Taylor, as a slaveholder; he invited the abolitionist William Wells Brown, a former slave, to speak at his church. He established a newspaper column to agitate for higher wages, and when the town's clergy tried to prevent Emerson from lecturing at the Newburyport Lyceum, Higginson chastised them in print. He argued for women's rights and set up more than one night school for factory workers, particularly women. "Mr. Higginson was like a great archangel to all of us then," recalled the writer Harriet Prescott Spofford, a protégé from those days. "And there were so many of us!"

And he entered politics. Though pledged, at least in his private journal, to disunion—he could not endorse a constitution that sanctioned slavery—in 1850 he ran for Congress as a Free-Soil candidate in this Whig stronghold. "It will hurt my popularity in Newburyport for they will call it ambition &c," he shrugged.

Enthusiastic and naive, Higginson innocently assumed he was invincible. Certainly no harm could come to him for advocating fair wages, literacy, temperance, generosity, and above all, abolition in this, the birthplace of Garrison. "They are so much more dependent on me than I on them that I am in no danger," he informed his family with nonchalance. Yet this was also the town that had clobbered Whittier with sticks, stones, and rotten eggs when the Quaker tried to address an antislavery rally.

Higginson lasted in Newburyport just two years. "My position as an Abolitionist they could not bear," he concluded when his congregation asked him to resign in 1849. "This could not be altered."

He took his dismissal with composure, and years later, when he chalked it up to the inexperience of youth, he also admitted that even if he had been more tactful, "I think I would have come to the same thing in the end."

Leaving Newburyport, he and Mary moved into the home of a relative in nearby Artichoke Mills, a rural retreat deep in the piney woods, and seeking the like-minded, he befriended the gentle Whittier, who lived in Amesbury, just four miles away. For fifteen years, Whittier had been an outspoken abolitionist, publishing (at his own expense) in 1833 the polemical *Justice and Expediency; or, Slavery Considered with a View to Its Rightful and Effectual Remedy, Abolition.* "Slavery has no redeeming qualities, no feature of benevolence, nothing pure, nothing peaceful, nothing just," Whittier said, calling for immediate emancipation. A shy Quaker most comfortable operating behind the scenes, he had helped found the Liberty party (precursor of the Republican party), and it was he who insisted Higginson run for United States Congress. (Higginson lost by a wide margin.)

But Higginson was already growing skeptical about politics. The Free-Soilers mainly wanted to keep slavery out of the territories, not abolish it altogether, as he did. And the Fugitive Slave Act, recently passed, permitted slave catchers to pursue escaped slaves into the free states—all the way to Massachusetts, for instance. Plus, the reprehensible law was a rider to the Compromise of 1850, which presumably maintained a balance between slave and free states—and in so doing preserved the status quo, which was slavery itself. "There are always men," Higginson observed with disgust, "who if anyone claims that two and two make six, will find it absolutely necessary to go half way, and admit that two and two make five."

To Higginson, armed resistance, not civil disobedience, more and more seemed the only alternative to such legalized inhumanity, and his increasingly militant rhetoric was put to the test when a seventeen-year-old black man, Thomas Sims, was arrested in Boston in the spring of 1851.

Higginson rushed to the city. As a member of the Vigilance Committee, an organization of blacks and whites established several years earlier to assist fugitive slaves, he went straight to the grimy offices of Garrison's *Liberator* for a meeting but found to his dismay that only he and two other men—Lewis Hayden and Leonard Grimes, black community leaders—advocated taking action on Sims's behalf. (Hayden had famously hidden Ellen and William Craft, two fugitive slaves, in his home on Phillips Street, threatening to blow it up rather than surrender the couple.) Garrison, a committed pacifist whose preferred weapon was moral suasion, typically disputed the long-term results of overt action, or violence; his reasoning, Higginson later recalled, "marched like an army without banners." Others wanted to argue the case in court. This seemed to Higginson to legitimate the very system he believed perfidious: in fact the gloomy granite Court House in which Sims now sat, manacled, was itself a symbol of judicial failure.

Arguing for legal redress, the political abolitionists won the day, and while the case dragged on, Higginson addressed a massive crowd gathered to protest at the Tremont Temple, urging them to do something. No one did. Discouraged, Higginson and his two co-conspirators hatched a plot: Sims would leap out of the third-floor Court House window onto a mattress, placed below, and then jump into a carriage waiting to whisk him to the docks, where a sloop stood ready to take him to Canada. But someone must have leaked the plans because on the evening of the intended rescue, fierce iron gratings were installed in the windows of the Court House.

Higginson was livid.

On April 13, Thomas Sims, in tears, was paraded through Boston in chains. Placed on the brig *Acorn,* he was deported to Savannah, where he was publicly whipped until he bled. Two hundred fifty armed federal deputies had stood at the Boston wharves, their faces impassive, while witnesses chanted "Shame! Shame!"—themselves ashamed for not having done more.

WITH MERRY CONDESCENSION, Henry James once said that Thomas Wentworth Higginson reflected almost everything in the New England air—those agitations, that is, "on behalf of everything, almost, but especially of the negroes and the ladies." Yet it would be a mistake to dismiss Higginson's commitment to abolition or woman suffrage as faddishness—or, equally, to disparage it as a calculated scramble for *la gloire* once he realized poetry was not his métier. Of course reform was in the New England air. Of course Higginson was ambitious. He sought approval, no doubt. He liked to move large audiences. And he was in awe of men like Emerson, Parker, and Channing, who, commanding platform, pulpit, and pen, swayed minds and warmed hearts: what better way to satisfy personal vanity and at the same time salve one's own conscience for being vain in the first place.

But Higginson was also a true believer and, to put it in unfashionable terms, a very good man.

It would also be a mistake to ignore the sacrifice a man like Higginson was willing to make for his convictions. "Remember that to us, Anti-Slavery is a matter of deadly earnest, which costs us our reputations today, and may cost our lives tomorrow," he told a friend less exercised about the issue than he. This was not braggadocio. Abraham Lincoln, the most successful antislavery politician of his day, regarded the word *abolitionist* as odious. At best an abolitionist was a foggy-headed dreamer; at worst, a zealot rabble-rouser, even an atheist willing to abolish churches, the Bible, Christianity. ("Assent—and you are sane— / ," Dickinson would write. "Demur—you're straightway dangerous— / And handled with a Chain—.")

"Without a little crack somewhere," Higginson sharply agreed, "a man could hardly do his duty to the times."

Lacking a formal pulpit once he lost his Newburyport congregation, Higginson frequently traveled whatever distance it took to speak at abolitionist or women's rights or Free-Soil rallies. Committed to all three often-overlapping movements, he was still uncertain about the efficacy of Free-Soil. Politics was a stopgap measure more than a real solution to the problem of slavery, he reasoned. And in 1850, when the Whigs split over slavery, he was particularly chary of a proposed Free-Soil coalition with Democrats, which meant to him compromising the party's antislavery platform. "I hope, however, that there is less real danger of our being corrupted than of our being *deluded;* deluded by too sanguine hopes of a sudden regeneration of the Democratic Party," he wrote to a Free-Soil newspaper. When the editor refused to publish his letter, calling it impolitic, Higginson brought it to *The Liberator,* which did print it. He would not be silent. He would not be silenced. He had joined the Free-Soilers because he thought there he could speak his mind. Now, he noted with contempt, it was said he "'might damage the cause.'"

At home in Artichoke Falls, his life veered in a different direction. He was quiet, helpful, considerate, and depressed, for Mary was slowly losing control of her muscles. She sat in a special chair and walked with such difficulty that in later years Higginson had to carry her up and down the stairs. Today a diagnosis might reveal rheumatoid arthritis or multiple sclerosis; then, there was nothing known, nothing to do. And though her symptoms occasionally remitted, as is the case with multiple sclerosis, their recurrence left her weaker and more querulous than ever.

But it wasn't illness alone that tugged at her husband's heart. The couple had no children, a cruel blow to Higginson, who loved them so unabashedly that he was constantly on the lookout for excuses to bring them into his home. For many years the couple took care of Mary's niece, a daughter of Ellery and Ellen Fuller Channing, after Ellen Channing died. Mary, however, preferred to avoid children—and, it seems, sex with her husband.

He bore the rebuff with outward equanimity, assuming he had been asked to renounce that which he had no right to claim. For he believed a woman should be able to choose to live as she wished. Mainly, of course, he referred (at least in public) not to sex, though he hinted as much, but to a woman's right to educational and professional opportunities, signing (along with Mary) the petition for the first national women's rights convention and urging the Massachusetts Constitutional Convention to reform qualifications for voting. "If Maria Mitchell can discover comets, and Harriet Hosmer carve

statues; if Appolonia Jagiello can fight in European revolution . . . ,"
he insisted, "then the case is settled so far— . . . Nor can any one of
these be set aside as an exceptional case, until it is shown that it is
not, on the other hand, a *test* case; each person being a possible spec-
imen of a large class who would, with a little less discouragement,
have done the same things."

In his address to that convention, Higginson eloquently spoke on
behalf of suffrage and professional opportunities for women: A
woman "must be a slave or an equal; there is no middle ground," he
bluntly declared. "If it is plainly reasonable that the two sexes shall
study together in the same high school, then it cannot be hopelessly
ridiculous that they should study together in college also. If it is
common sense to make a woman deputy postmaster, then it cannot
be the climax of absurdity to make her postmaster general, or even
the higher officer who is the postmaster's master." And what of the
men who stand in her way? They are primarily anxious, he said,
about whether an educated woman, happy and productive, would
still make them dinner.

"I, too, wish to save the dinner," he concluded. "Yet it seems more
important, after all, to save the soul."

Printed as a pamphlet, the speech was considered so alarming that
Harper's New Monthly Magazine immediately ran a rebuttal. "A
woman such as you would make, her teaching, preaching, voting,
judging, commanding a man-of-war, and charging at the head of a
battalion would be simply an amorphous monster not worth the little finger of the wife we would all secure if we could." Higginson, as
usual, was unperturbed. He continued to support the rights of
women, his enthusiasm tempered by good humor and rational argument. For like a carefully swept and sunlit room, Higginson's mind
was free of cobwebs and clutter, and while he was heir to the
Enlightenment in his thought, his heart throbbed with the idealism
of the New. In his superb "Ought Women to Learn the Alphabet?"
an article printed in 1859 in *The Atlantic,* he summarized his argument with characteristic and unassailable intelligence: "What sort of
philosophy is that which says, 'John is a fool; Jane is a genius: nevertheless, John, being a man, shall learn, lead, make laws, make
money; Jane, being a woman, shall be ignorant, dependent, disfran-
chised, underpaid'?" James Russell Lowell, then editor of *The
Atlantic,* shuddered.

When Isabelle Beecher Hooker wrote to Higginson to praise his stand, he answered with some annoyance: "Nothing makes me more indignant than to be thanked by women for telling the truth— thanked as a man—when those same persons are recreant to the women who, at infinitely greater cost, have said the same thing. It costs a man nothing to defend woman—a few sneers, a few jokes, that is all—but for women to defend themselves, have in times past cost almost everything. Without the personal knowledge & influence of such women as Lucretia Mott, Lucy Stone, and Antoinette Brown, I should be nothing."

Some might say he spoke more truly than he knew, for the most amazing of them all, Emily Dickinson, was not yet on his horizon.

THREE

Emily Dickinson:
If I Live, I Will Go to Amherst

Biography first convinces us of the fleeing of the Biographied—," Emily Dickinson would tell Thomas Wentworth Higginson, as if already flouting the scholars—and busybodies—who might in future years try to dig beneath the surface of her life. For of all people, she is the biographied par excellence: elusive, inexplicable, inscrutable, like the light that exists in spring: "It passes and we stay—."

Even so, one can't help pummeling her with questions: Why retire so completely from the public world, never even to cross her father's lawn, as she told Higginson? Why dress in white? Not want her poems published? And why write to Thomas Wentworth Higginson, of all people, when she could have contacted any number of the luminaries she admired: Emerson, Hawthorne, Dickens, the Brownings, George Eliot?

Yet she did confide in Higginson, and we are grateful—or should be—for only to him, outside her family, did she reveal herself, sharing with him revelations that still puzzle and intrigue us. Coy but not capricious, she was the "only Kangaroo among the Beauty," as she told him, referring not so much to her looks as to her work, and then purposely warning us, again by means of Higginson, that "when I state myself, as the Representative of the Verse—it does not mean—me—but a supposed person."

Convinced regardless that the key to her poetry lies in her life, generations of biographer-critics have scurried to their desks, her cryptic letters in hand. The best of these is Richard Sewall, whose scrupulous and standard two-volume biography of Dickinson appeared in 1974. Amassing a huge archive on the poet's family and friends in order to glimpse her, as he says, through Jamesian reflectors, Sewall handles her reticence by circumventing it; as a matter of fact, the poet herself isn't born until the first chapter of his second volume. The result is astonishing and reliably balanced in all things—except the matter of Higginson, whom Sewall unfailingly dismisses with a presumption typical of his generation.

Since Sewall's biographical feat appeared, scholars as talented or dogged as Cynthia Griffin Wolff, Polly Longsworth, Vivian Pollak, Susan Howe, Judith Farr, Christopher Benfey, and Alfred Habegger—to name a very few—have probed Dickinson's religiosity, her family, her artistry, and her ravishing, often blistering verse. Yet Dickinson teases us, winks at us, and escapes, leaving us begging for more.

What, then, is known of her, particularly in the days before she wrote to Thomas Higginson? Like him, she was the beneficiary of a long line, her paternal ancestor having arrived on one of John Winthrop's vessels in the port of Salem in 1630. But the Dickinsons settled in the fertile Connecticut River Valley, not in the bustling suburbs of Boston or Cambridge, and, mostly farmers, they did not own ships or command markets or aspire to adventure on high seas and to the gratifications of high office—except in the case of the poet's grandfather, Samuel Fowler Dickinson, a man well educated, devout, and long remembered in his native village of Amherst as a leading citizen of "unflagging zeal." That was an understatement.

Samuel was a generous, idealistic, and prominent attorney with a flair for civil service, Calvinism, windy speeches, and debt. Educated at Dartmouth, admitted to the Massachusetts bar, a member of the legislature (both branches), he was also ordained a deacon and remained a deacon for forty years, his deeply religious vision woven into the founding of Amherst College. For without an orthodox institution of higher education in their own backyard, he and his cohorts fretted lest their children slide into that pool of watery theology preached at Harvard and known as Unitarianism.

And with Harvard Unitarians disdaining what they called a new "priest factory," Squire Dickinson redoubled his efforts. Lobbying to win a charter from the Massachusetts legislature—the same charter that, decreasing Harvard's stipend, precipitated the ignominious fall of Higginson's father—Dickinson argued that the new college be located in Amherst. To this end he pledged his own property to defray costs, and paying out of pocket, he depleted so much of his savings that, as his wife reported, "they have compleated the College our affairs are still in a crazy situation."

But it wasn't the college that ruined Dickinson. A litigious man, he sued far too often, liquefying great sums; crisis followed financial crisis. Yanked out of Yale, his eldest son, Edward (Emily's father), was forced to take classes at the Amherst Collegiate Charity Institution, as the college was at first known, until he could go back to New Haven. Then his father hauled him out again. It could not have been easy. Edward, managing finally to graduate from Yale in 1823, desired above all to be free of his father's embarrassing affairs. "My life," he sternly warned the woman he loved, "must be a life of business—of laborious application to the study of my profession."

After studying law in his father's office and at the Northampton Law School, Edward opened his own practice in Amherst in 1826, the very same year he proposed marriage by mail to Emily Norcross, whom he met in nearby Monson during a lecture on chemistry. But though he plotted his romantic course with the precision of a watchmaker, the two-year courtship lasted far longer than he intended, and despite her poet-daughter's later characterization of her mother as possessing "unobtrusive faculties," Emily Norcross was as stubborn as Edward, pulling when he pushed. If he pelted her with letters, she replied infrequently, sometimes not at all. "There is a vast field for enterprise open before us, and all that can excite the ambitious—kindle the zeal—rouse to emulation, & urge us on to glorious deeds is presented to view," he tried wooing her with his prospects. "A man's success must depend on *himself*," he said over and over, trotting out his attributes—diligence, industry, loyalty, rectitude—so regularly one wonders about the untold depth of the man's insecurities. And flinging out the last arrow in his odd quiver, he suggested Norcross examine his references.

Norcross delayed answering Edward's offer of marriage with her roundabout reply: "Your proposals are what I would wish to comply with, but without the advise and consent of my father I cannot consistantly [sic] do it." Edward duly wrote to her father, a prosperous farmer and entrepreneur in Monson. Again he heard nothing. Ambivalent about marriage, about Edward, about leaving her home, the poet's mother exercised power in refusal, as her daughter later would; she hardly visited Amherst and did not explain her behavior or her silences. That, too, would become a family trait.

As for Edward, his references were good. A chip off the Puritan block, he neither drank nor smoked nor swore but beat his horse when it displeased him; daughter Emily screamed in protest. Yet he

Edward Dickinson,
1853.
"His Heart was pure
and terrible."

Emily Norcross
Dickinson.
"We were never
intimate Mother and
Children."

rang the village bell so everyone in town might see the northern lights, and though he read the Bible every morning to his assembled family, he easily laughed at the tedious sermon. Still, he was exacting and cranky, and he typically exempted himself from the rules he made, whether at home or in government. A good temperance man, he backed strict prohibitions against the sale of liquor, but when he asked the apothecary to fill his flask with brandy—though he didn't have the necessary prescription for it—the shopkeeper reminded him of the regulation. "That rule was not made for me," Dickinson presumably thundered, adding that he would send to Northampton for his drink.

Raw emotion displeased him. He rarely smiled, and though he read Shakespeare, he frowned at poetry, preferring, as his daughter Emily noted, actualities. "Fathers real life and mine sometimes come into collision," she would tell her brother, "but as yet, escape unhurt!" An oft-repeated anecdote (likely apocryphal) reveals his histrionic need for control—and affords a glimpse into his daughter Emily's equally dramatic response to him. At dinner one day, when Edward sputtered about a nicked plate at his setting, Emily sprang from the table, grabbed the offending dish, and marched to the garden, where she smashed it on a stone, saying she was reminding herself not to give it to her father ever again.

But Higginson would find Edward more remote than harsh, and Emily agreed. "Father was very severe to me," she would typically chuckle to Austin. "He gave me quite a trimming about 'Uncle Tom' and 'Charles Dickens' and these 'modern Literati' who he says are *nothing,* compared to past generations, who flourished when *he was a boy.*" Deftly outmaneuvering him, or so the incident of the plate suggests, she similarly humored him when, deciding she was spiritually deficient, he asked the Reverend Jonathan Jenkins to interview her. Emily was by that time in her early forties, and outwardly compliant, sat in the parlor with the fidgeting reverend, a good friend of Austin's and not much older than she. "There must have lurked in her expressive face a faint suggestion of amusement at the utter incongruity of the situation," the reverend's son recalled many years later, "but she was far too urbane a person to have betrayed it." Jenkins pronounced her "sound," and that was the end of that.

Edward also huffed and puffed about the education of women, although, as with many things, his timing was slightly off. While courting his reluctant fiancée, he had unsentimentally pontificated about what sort of education women should have, writing under the pseudonym Coelebs (bachelor) in the *New-England Inquirer,* a short-lived local newspaper. "They do not need a severe course of mathe-matical discipline," he claimed. "They are not improved by a minute acquaintance with foreign languages; it is of no use that they are instructed in the laws of mechanical Philosophy. Their sphere is dif-ferent. They were intended for *wives*—for *mothers.*"

The unsettling prospect of marriage evidently inspired a diatribe so anachronistic even one of Edward's sisters objected. Still, his fiancée's grammatical infelicities troubled him. "How does it affect us," he disingenuously wondered, "to receive an epistle from a val-ued friend, with half the words mis-spelled—in which capitals & small letters have changed positions—where a plural noun is fol-lowed by a singular verb?" (He might have been forecasting his daughter's orthographic style.) Though Emily Norcross's father had funded the local academy, where she was educated (she also briefly attended the Reverend Claudius Herrick's school in New Haven), she remained stubbornly unlettered. Her spelling *is* atrocious. Edward thus plied his fiancée with copies of *The Spectator* (on which he based his Coelebs essays), as well as several novels by women, noting he admired America's female literati even though, of course, education was of no great concern to females. It diverted them from their duties as wives and mothers or, worse yet, made them think such duties didn't matter.

Stuffy, yes, and thoroughly conservative, the Janus-faced Edward actually did value education—the raison d'être of his own hapless father—and made certain his daughters had one. "We are warranted in presuming that," he relented, "if they [women] had opportunities equal to their talents, they would not be inferior to our own sex in improving in the sciences." A literary career was acceptable to him, too, if, that is, women were willing to abjure domestic happiness for the sake of it: "Let them bend all their energies to attain that object, and when we bid them farewell, on their departure from society, we shall most cheerfully give them a passport to the honors of literary distinction, & joyfully participate with them in the rewards which await their approach to the portals of the temples of Minerva." He may well have meant what he said.

· · ·

TODAY LITERARY PILGRIMS by the thousands flock to the hip-roofed house on Amherst's Main Street, but once there they step into an empty nest. The place familiarly known as the Homestead—reputed to be Amherst's first brick residence—is spare of furniture; the unhaunted rooms are cold, and though the docents are helpful, the poet has fled.

Yet that the place is a shrine would doubtless strike Emily Dickinson's grandfather Samuel as vindication, for though built by him in 1813 as a monument to his significance, for many years the Homestead instead memorialized his failure, which loomed very large in the Dickinson psyche.

After Edward Dickinson and Emily Norcross married, in 1828, they separated themselves from the Homestead, or thought they had, by moving into the widow Jemima Montague's place, also owned by Samuel. Edward had overseen everything, even the installation of the window blinds, for his laconic bride; the closets were painted red, the rooms white, the floors slate—or yellow, he nervously added, if she would like that better. She preferred the color of lead. But unbeknownst to Edward, his father's insolvency would soon necessitate the sale of all his property, including the Montague place and half the Homestead itself. Edward negotiated with the purchasers of the Montague house so he could remain there, but when the arrangement fell apart two years later—one can imagine Edward's chagrin—he was at least able to put a four-hundred-dollar down payment on the Homestead's western half.

By then the Mansion, as it was also called, had been partitioned into two dwellings with a common kitchen. Samuel Dickinson, his wife, Lucretia Gunn Dickinson, and their unmarried children were occupying the eastern half when Edward bought the western side. There Emily Elizabeth Dickinson was born at five in the morning on December 10, 1830; there she later quarantined herself; there she wrote most of her poetry; there she would die.

But living and dying in the family manse was not inevitable. In 1833, the year her sister, Lavinia (called Vinnie), was born, the Homestead, along with eleven acres of land, went on the block. The mortgage on Samuel's half had been foreclosed, and Edward, whose income was less than he had hoped, had to sell his share of the place. Samuel left Amherst for a position under Lyman Beecher at the Lane Theological Seminary in Cincinnati, where, just five years later, at the age of sixty-three, he died of cholera in what seemed to be the Wild West.

Edward had stayed behind, and though the Homestead's new proprietor permitted—noblesse oblige—Edward's family to rent the east side of the house, the transaction dealt another blow to Edward's fragile pride. Nothing was going well. Weakened by Vinnie's birth—and, no doubt, her husband's rage at his father—Mrs. Dickinson dispatched the two-year-old Emily to her sister, Lavinia Norcross, in Monson.

If at this time Emily missed her mother or felt as forsaken and bereft as biographers speculate, or if her childhood curdled into pain from the separation, nothing in her aunt's letters suggest it. According to Lavinia Norcross, Emily was an affectionate, inquisitive, and happy child with reddish curly hair. "She dont appear at all as she does at home—, & she does not make but very little trouble." Of course every childhood has its secret sorrows. "They shut me up in Prose— / ," she later wrote, "As when a little Girl / They put me in the Closet— / Because they liked me 'still'—."

It's tempting to read those lines literally: frustrated parents lock their precocious child in the closet; she never forgets and never forgives. But we know little about specific childhood trials, and in any case Dickinson herself warned us not to take her poems autobiographically. Yet we also know that as an adult Dickinson tended to idealize childhood: "Bliss is the sceptre of the child." When she was but twenty, she would plaintively tell a friend, "I so love to be a child," and to her brother, Austin, she lamented in 1853—she was then twenty-two—"I wish we were children now. I wish we were *always* children, how to grow up I don't know."

"Two things I have lost with Childhood—," she once remarked, "the rapture of losing my shoe in the Mud and going Home barefoot, wading for Cardinal flowers and the mothers reproof which was more for my sake than her weary own for she frowned with a smile." Then, too, there is a late poem:

> The Things that never can come back, are several —
> Childhood — some forms of Hope — the Dead —

She was not posturing. As an adult, she played games with children in ways only they fathomed; she baked them tasty treats and seemed to participate wholly in their fantasies, lowering down from her room on the second floor baskets of long, oval cakes of gingerbread, decorated with a small flower. One of the young boys in the neighborhood affectionately remembered her as lavish, and her niece idealized her: "The realization of our vivid fancy, the confederate in every contraband desire," this niece recalled, "the very Spirit of the 'Never Never Land' . . . there was nothing forbidden us by her."

Perhaps Emily sought to re-create a moment when all Dickinsons seemed happy, even her father, who was still plotting his illustrious career, dreaming not just of his children's success but of his own, imagining himself idolized for doing good like men no less stalwart than Jefferson and Adams, whose almost simultaneous deaths caused him to cry, "How enviable their fame! To be the authors of happiness to millions—and constantly increasing millions of people! This affords a spectacle at which even fancy wonders—Ambition bows before it!" Himself unbowed, Edward bought a pew in church, earned an appointment as Amherst College's treasurer, and ran for a seat in the state legislature. Hardworking, reliable, punctilious, he would fulfill his promise to Emily Norcross and install himself in the Amherst constellation of important gentlemen. "What man has done, man can do," he declared more than once.

In 1840, the year his daughter Emily turned ten, Edward finally managed to quit the cramped scene of Samuel's disgrace ("half a

North Pleasant Street home, Amherst, Massachusetts, 1840–1855.
Photograph ca. 1870.

house, & a rod square for a garden," he sputtered) and buy a spacious white clapboard place on West Street (now North Pleasant Street), right next to the village cemetery. For though he traveled to New York or Boston or Northampton on business, allegiance to home— for Edward no less than for Emily Norcross and later their children— was ironclad. This was true even when he served in the Massachusetts House of Representatives in 1838 and 1839. "It does seem to me," he assured his wife from Boston, "that if I once more get home, I can not consent ever to leave you & the little children again to spend another winter here. The sacrifice is too much for me to make, & too much for you to suffer. . . . Home is the place for me—and where my family are, is home."

Had Mrs. Dickinson been willing to relocate, or if he had married a different woman, as it was later said, Edward might have re-created himself elsewhere, but she was not, and he did not, so he packed up his ambition, or so he thought, and made Amherst a bulwark against the miserable world of politics and petty men. He thus strikes us as a disappointed, implacable, and provincial man, dreams denied, who once in a rare moment confessed to daughter Emily that he felt his life had passed in a wilderness or on an island. Perhaps he never truly admitted what he wanted, a friend would write in his obituary. "His failing was he did not understand himself; consequently his misfortune was that others did not understand him."

His daughter Emily did. When Edward was a delegate to the 1852 Whig convention in Baltimore, she told her brother, Austin, "I think it will do him the very most good of anything in the world, and I do feel happy to have father at last, among men who sympathize with him, and know what he really is." She was correct. The next year, when he was elected to the United States House of Representatives from Massachusetts's Tenth Congressional District, he was so pleased with himself that he strutted down Washington's muddy streets, a volume from the congressional library under his arm— proof positive that he was the man he thought he was. It did not last.

The American party, or nativist Know-Nothings, put him out of office, not hard to do since he had also lost regional support by insisting the federal armories at Springfield and Harpers Ferry (of all places) be staffed with military men and civil servants, not local residents. Yet his last hurrah as congressman was not without its moments of valor: he presented Congress with a petition on behalf of Amherst citizens to repeal the Fugitive Slave Act and in 1854 fought against the Kansas-Nebraska bill, which would allow the inhabitants of the Nebraska and Kansas territories to decide for or against slavery by popular vote. In so doing, the bill would effectively repeal the Missouri Compromise of 1820 while extending the reach of slavery into territories previously considered untouchable. When it passed at the end of May, Dickinson entertained a group of thirty members of Congress in his Washington rooms to help establish the Republican party, although an old-line Whig to the bitter end, he declined to join it.

But in Amherst, Edward was a very big fish. As patriarch of the town's first family, he lived in a commodious home with gorgeous gardens satisfyingly admired, particularly when the college commencement festivities took place there. "Our house is crowded daily with the members of this world, the high and the low, the bond and the free, the 'poor in this world's goods,' and the 'almighty dollar,' " Emily Dickinson sarcastically noted in 1853. Her mother arranged the parties, set out the dark blue china, oversaw the refreshments, made certain that the linens were clean, the tables set, the guests comfortably seated. Vinnie remembered after her mother's death how fond she was "of every bird & flower & so full of pity for every grief."

And Dickinsons participated in civic events such as the annual cattle show, an agricultural fair of community importance, where Emily was celebrated for her Indian and rye bread, her father for his fine horses, her mother for her manners. That was not all: still striving, in 1855, when the poet was twenty-four, Edward was finally able to buy back the celebrated Homestead, victorious at last over the indigence of his father.

That site was the home of Dickinsons until there were none. Neither Emily nor Vinnie left the old Mansion for places of their own; Emily ventured no farther than the Dickinson meadow, and when her brother, Austin, married, he moved right next door, into the Italianate villa that Edward had built for him.

As for Edward Dickinson, attorney, he would never again countenance the loss of the Homestead. He did not even countenance the loss of his own life. When he died, he died intestate.

THE DICKINSON FIRSTBORN, William Austin (known as Austin) was the apple of his father's eye, and his sister Emily adored him. Close in age—just a year apart—and in temperament, Austin and Emily considered themselves unlike everyone else and particularly their parents, those "ancient people," as they laughingly called them, whom at least in the case of their father, they loved, obeyed, sidestepped, and indulged.

His hair a coppery red, like his sister's, his deep-set blue eyes lighting an angular, almost anguished face, the handsome Austin liked a high-stepping horse, and, adventurous, he went so far as to sample dangerous Unitarian services while he was a law student. But moody and reflective, he was the self-dramatizing incarnation of the inhibited Edward, a doomed romantic hero in search of the ideal. Like his father and doubtless like his sister Emily, he craved attention though it left him queasy with guilt. At times he considered leaving Amherst. He stayed, however, frequently assailed by doubt and the desperate sense that all things come to naught. "I look around me, to see what others are doing," he wailed, "whether *they* too are suffering in the same anxious suspense, or whether it is to me alone Life is a sealed book."

For his peers, religion promised to open that book. Not for Austin. "I ask myself, Is it possible that God, all powerful, all wise, all benevolent, as I must believe him, *could* have created all these millions upon millions of human souls, only to destroy them?" he agonized, all the while veering, insofar as he could, away from the orthodoxies of his cloistered world. He did not wander far. Graduating from Amherst College in 1850, he taught near Amherst and in Boston and read law in his father's office in the intervals between jobs. In 1854 he received his degree from the Harvard Law School and, after passing the bar, entered his father's practice but avoided trials. Professing his faith in Christ (a stipulation imposed by his fiancée), he then married, sired three children, buried one of them, moderated at town meetings, organized the Wildwood Cemetery, took over his father's position as treasurer of Amherst College, supervised the draining of the town common, monitored the landscaping of the college grounds, and was a very unhappy man.

Besides Austin, there was Vinnie, the youngest, less literary than her siblings and not as pressed as they by religious doubts or angst. Or if she was, she resolved them in more traditional ways than did sister Emily. Neither introspective nor inhibited, with large wide eyes and a soft, brooding mouth, Vinnie was pretty, plump, warm, and cheeky. She entertained a number of suitors, among them

William Austin
Dickinson, 27 years
old, 1856.
"We're all unlike
most everyone."

Lavinia Dickinson
at 19, in 1852.
"The tie is quite
vital."

Austin's roommate at Williston Seminary, Joseph Lyman, whose affection waned after he moved to New Orleans—and when Vinnie's parents stiffly rejected him, apparently because of his Southern sympathies. There were other men, other interdictions; she received at least one offer of marriage. Edward, though he liked the young man, seems to have disapproved. A dutiful daughter, Vinnie trembled before her father even after he died and resented him a very long time. In later years, after Emily's death, she eagerly recounted tales of their father's tyrannies, unbottling years of pent-up rage.

Mostly, and like all Dickinsons, she did not publicize regret. Instead she grew tarter, meaner, slyer. Born sickly, Vinnie was the Dickinson child closest to Mrs. Dickinson, the one most spoiled by her. Emily, in the middle, knocked against the sainted Austin on one side and her babied sister on the other. Yet her bond with Vinnie was, as she would say, "early, earnest, indissoluble. Without her Life were fear, and Paradise a cowardice, except for her inciting voice." Vinnie bucked up her siblings. "I, you must know," a friend recalled her saying, "am the family inflator. One by one the members of my household go down, and I must inflate them." Her loyalties were ferocious. "Vinnie is full of Wrath," Emily would remark, "and vicious as Saul—toward the Holy Ghost, in whatever form."

Their being unlike each other kept the sisters close. "The tie is quite vital," Emily acknowledged. "Yet if we had come up for the first time from two wells where we had hitherto been bred her astonishment would not be greater at some things I say."

"A dire person!" an acquaintance of Vinnie's declared. "Perhaps she partly explains her sister."

ALTHOUGH THOMAS WENTWORTH HIGGINSON'S father helped organize the Harvard Divinity School, his religious upbringing was tolerant and mild. True, the pretty Mrs. Higginson allowed only sacred music played on the Sabbath, but she considered all good music holy, and despite his family's regular attendance at Sunday church, Higginson claimed that as a boy he never heard of hell, never read the Old Testament, never professed his faith, and, most remarkable in a man headed to the ministry, never experienced religion.

If Higginson slipped free from the cold clutches of New England Calvinism, Emily Dickinson decidedly did not. Sin, death, and the frailty of humankind were kith and kin to Amherst, where the old orthodoxy had not lost its grip. And Dickinsons were good evangelical Christians. Grandmother Lucretia Gunn Dickinson never tired of warning her children to improve the hour by declaring publicly their love of their Savior, and the younger Mrs. Dickinson professed her allegiance to Jesus Christ in 1831, when daughter Emily was but a year old.

Evangelical Christians, then as now, demand a conscious experience of conversion in order to receive God's love. Frequently inspecting their souls for sin—in England the evangelical Protestant William Wilberforce, member of Parliament, presumably kept a pebble in his shoe to remind himself of his imperfections—they also commit themselves to preaching the Gospel with the hope of enlisting more converts. Mrs. Dickinson, however, confined her vocation to her husband, a worldly man who desired worldly things, albeit with a measure of guilt. Not by nature a believer though plagued by the demon of doubt, Edward hewed to the orthodox theology of his rigorous parents, his rigorous community, his father's college, and his resolute and religious wife. "Were I a christian, my dear," he told her early on with deep regret, "it would give me great pleasure in anticipating the happy times, when you and I should be spending that eternal sabbath of enjoyment, in company, which is possible to all who are redeemed."

He would try. He launched each Dickinson day with group prayer, led by him—"with a militant Accent," observed daughter Emily—along with a reading from the King James Bible. Still, he tarried two more decades before he embraced his Savior in an act of contrition and love. The year was 1850, the same year Vinnie, too, converted and the year that the revivalist Protestantism known as the Second Great Awakening, in its last phase, blazed through Amherst, setting souls afire. Edward, then forty-seven, said that at last he felt "the working of God's spirit among us." Others, however, remembered his conversion as typical of his parched character: the pastor had to remind him to come to Christ as a humble sinner, not as an attorney arguing a case.

But in 1850, Edward's nineteen-year-old daughter Emily was resisting the imprecations of the saved. "Christ is calling everyone here," she cried; "all my companions have answered, even my darling Vinnie believes she loves." Not she.

She had been resisting for a while, though she was not at all indifferent to the spiritual thirst her elders and friends slaked in conventional ways. As early as her fifteenth year, when the eminent scientist-theologian Edward Hitchcock, recently installed as college president, held weekly prayer meetings at his home, Emily avoided them lest she be "deceived" by the passions of the moment. The excuse sounds flimsy until one remembers how seriously she regarded the apostasy. "I feel that I am sailing upon the brink of an awful precipice, from which I cannot escape & over which I fear my tiny boat will soon glide if I do not receive help from above," she told her friend Abiah Root. "I feel sad that one should be taken and the others left."

Faith came hard. "I was almost persuaded to be a christian . . . ," she again confided to Abiah, "and I can say that I never enjoyed such perfect peace and happiness as the short time in which I felt I had found my savior." But too honest to mistake a mere mood for a conversion, she admitted that she soon forgot her morning prayer, "or else it was irksome to me. One by one my old habits returned and I cared less for religion than ever."

And so she stood alone, tentative, jittery, unable to find grace. That she considered herself one of the "lingering *bad* ones" did not change her mind. "The shore is safer, Abiah, but I love to buffet the sea—I can count the bitter wrecks here in these pleasant waters, and hear the murmuring winds, but oh, I love the danger!" Higginson would seek danger on the plains of Kansas, she in the confines of her room.

Later, to Higginson, she explained her recalcitrance by noting that as a child "I was taken to a Funeral which I now know was of peculiar distress, and the Clergyman asked 'Is the Arm of the Lord shortened that it cannot save?'

"He italicized the 'cannot,' " she continued. "I mistook the accent for a doubt of Immortality and not daring to ask, it besets me still." Her temperament nuancing, interrogative, unshuttered, she strove for the spiritual certitudes that her agile mind discounted. "Sermons on unbelief ever did attract me," she said. Paradox was her forte. " 'We thank thee Oh Father,' for these strange Minds, that enamor us against thee," she would tell Higginson, grateful to whatever higher power produced a consciousness capable of doubting it.

Birds, flowers, the shifting quality of light and of mind thus constitute her faith. Personal, pantheistic, and paradoxical, it was seldom tranquil: "Doubts of all things earthly, and intuitions of some things heavenly"; as Melville explained, "this combination makes neither believer nor infidel, but makes a man who regards them both with equal eye."

FROM THE AGE OF NINE until the age of sixteen, Emily Dickinson attended Amherst Academy. Her attendance was sporadic; coughs, influenza, or "general debility" often kept her at home. One teacher remembered the girl as slight and diffident but intelligent. "Her compositions were strikingly original," he reminisced, "and in both thought and style seemed beyond her years, and always attracted much attention in the school and, I am afraid, excited not a little envy."

Operating in theological concert with the college, the academy offered first-rate teaching and, despite its pietism, a humanistic smorgasbord of courses: foreign languages, geology, botany, history, natural philosophy, grammar, arithmetic, music, even gymnastic exercises. (Higginson would have been pleased.) Regardless, religion underlay it all: instructors shall be "firmly established in the faith of the Christian religion," parents were told, "the doctrines and duties of which they shall inculcate as well by example as precept."

"We have a very fine school," Emily bragged to Abiah Root, no longer at the academy. On the surface she appears a typical teenager: roguish, affectionate, energetically devoted to her circle. And good-looking, or at least self-conscious about her looks: "I am growing handsome very fast indeed!" she joked. "I shall be the belle of Amherst when I reach my 17th year." (When Higginson requested a picture, she said she had none and went on to describe herself rather seductively as "small, like the Wren, and my Hair is bold, like the Chestnut Bur—and my eyes, like the Sherry in the Glass, that the Guest leaves.")

Actually, there is one known image of her; a daguerreotype taken around that time. She is young, seated, solemn, and secretive. She faces front, unafraid, her eyes wide and clear, her lips slightly parted, her hair drawn back. She neither smiles nor frowns. She waits. She looks. And except for that expectant glance, she seems a creature of the stolid bourgeois world. Her dress is dark and well made, with dropped shoulders and tucks about the waist. She wears a ribbon around her neck clasped with a small brooch. Otherwise, she is unadorned except for the book near her elbow and the flowers in her hand, a symbol of her beloved herbarium.

The herbarium was a green album containing 424 specimens of dried plants and flowers and finished by her when she was about fourteen years old, her passion for botany as intense as Higginson's. Perhaps we should consider this her first book even though keeping a herbarium was the pastime of many a schoolgirl or New England dame. But how to separate the typical from the singular? This is the question underneath those well-worn anecdotes about Dickinson's refractory nature, stories that would be fragrant with forgettable petty rebellions if, that is, they didn't involve Emily Dickinson. Recalled her niece, Emily once "put four superfluous kittens on the fire-shovel and dropped them into the first convenient jar the cellar offered, her family being in church—her chosen time for iniquity."

This startling story likely contains a germ of truth even if the circumstances surrounding it have long vanished, and the real point of it may lie in her family's sense of Emily as unruly, hostile, possibly cruel if she did not get her own way. More credible is the story about Edward Dickinson's hustling his children off to Sunday school, insisting they leave the house immediately. Emily was nowhere to be found. After church, when the Dickinsons returned home, they discovered Emily in the cellar, quietly reading. Technically speaking, she had obeyed her father by "leaving" the house.

And more verifiable are those spasms of worrisome sadness. After one, precipitated by the death of her friend Sophia Holland in 1844, her parents sent her to relatives in Boston for a few weeks. That was like her too: to form heated, ravening attachments and to grieve inconsolably when, for whatever reason, the friendships faded. Early on these attachments were to schoolmates like Abiah Root; then, to Sue Gilbert; and still later, to Sue's friend Catherine Scott Turner Anthon. So fierce was this connection that a scholar, writing in 1951, prematurely nominated Kate Anthon as the love of Dickinson's life. ("That her thesis is partially true," Elizabeth Bishop observed, "might have occurred to any reader of Emily Dickinson's poetry—occurred on one page to be contradicted on the next, that is.") Today Sue Gilbert is considered the prime recipient of Dickinson's erotic outpourings, but there were doubtless other loves as well, female and male, most of whom we do not know.

Chatty, affectionate, and hyperbolic, she was also competitive. In

Emily Dickinson, 17 years old, daguerreotype, 1847.

later years she was said to confide to a visitor that, on hearing Rubinstein play in Boston, she had abandoned her piano completely. This too may be apocryphal, but as her father's daughter she judged herself harshly, it seems, and despite her self-assurance did in fact ask Wentworth Higginson if her verse was alive when she clearly suspected it was. At the Mount Holyoke Seminary, in South Hadley, in the fall of 1847, she was frantic about her initial exams, which she handily passed—many did not—and despite the victory soon doubled over with homesickness, crying, "Home was always dear to me & dearer still the friends around it, but never did it seem so dear as now." Perhaps competition produced too much anxiety. Yet Emily could hold her own.

And she did when assailed by the proselytizers clucking over her spiritual health. "There is a great deal of religious interest here and many are flocking to the ark of safety," she told Abiah. "I have not yet given up to the claims of Christ, but trust I am not entirely thoughtless on so important & serious a subject."

Founded by Mary Lyon, Mount Holyoke was conceived by her as a place to save the spotted souls of young girls. An intelligent woman, formidably devout, Lyon intended not just to educate her students but to prevail on them to embrace their Savior and appreciate—especially the truculent ones—their awful sinfulness. Once they accepted their Savior with love, they too would save other impenitents from perdition. To that end, Miss Lyon held meetings, private and public, lots of them, meetings for the converted, meetings for those who hoped for conversion, meetings for the unconverted.

According to Vinnie, "There were real ogres at South Hadley then."

Dickinson's roommate was her cousin, one of the "established Christians." Not Emily. A tale from these days, credible and certainly suggestive of how others viewed her, was later recounted by another cousin. Emily said that when Miss Lyon asked all students who wanted to be a Christian to stand, she sat stock-still. "They thought it queer I didn't rise," she quipped. "I thought a lie would be queerer."

But that was after the fact. "I have neglected the *one thing needful*," she moaned at the time to Abiah Root, "when all were obtaining it, and I may never, never again pass through such a season as was

Dickinson family silhouette, 1848.

granted us last winter." Again she had resisted, completing the school year as a "no-hoper"—one with no hope of conversion.

Then again, there was another place of needful comfort, where she could be herself, where grapes grew purple and peaches fat and pink, where the autumn smelled of sweet, wet leaves, and rich brown bread, freshly baked, came smoking onto the table, where the hay scented the meadow and cherry trees blossomed in spring. "Home," she would write, "is the definition of God."

SHE WAS ALLOWED TO RETURN, and the rest is history—or, since history depends on a historical record, speculation.

During her first year at Holyoke, her father determined, for reasons unknown to us, that there would be no second, and if Dickinson went back to boarding school, which she thought she might, it would have to be somewhere else. There was nowhere else.

In the summer of 1848, she was seventeen, impassioned, smart, and increasingly strange. For years she had outwardly fulfilled all the ritual functions of girlhood: she sewed, learned to bake (her mother had a reputation for custards and crullers). She practiced the piano, went to parties, entertained the family's guests, and exchanged breezy letters with friends; she attended lectures, sermons, and concerts, and she presumably walked out of the Shakespeare club when its young men threatened to censor the bard's crudeness for the sake of the young ladies. In winter she tapped the maple trees for sap; in summer there were picnics. She gossiped, read German plays, and visited relatives in Worcester and Boston. Of all their social group, said Austin, she was the one always sought for her brilliance, originality, and wit.

But her friends were whispering. It wasn't just her willfulness at Holyoke but her indifference to social duties, the Sewing Circle, for instance. "Sewing Society has commenced again—and held its first meeting last week—now all the poor will be helped—the cold warmed—the warm cooled—the hungry fed—the thirsty attended to—the ragged clothed—and this suffering—tumbled down world be helped to it's feet again," she jibed. "I don't attend—notwithstanding my approbation—which must puzzle the public exceedingly. I am already set down as one of those brands almost consumed—and my hardheartedness gets me many prayers," she coolly concluded, her condescension laced with hostility and a modicum of guilt.

She was firm. And firmly ensconced in her prodigious reading: Longfellow's *Kavanagh,* Emerson's essays, Dickens, the beloved Elizabeth Barrett Browning, the Brontës, Shakespeare, Tennyson, George Herbert, Robert Burns, Keats, popular novels. Soon her father's library would contain such items as Elisha Kent Kane's bestselling *Arctic Explorations,* the work of the historians Motley, George Bancroft, and Prescott, alongside all of Addison's writing and all of Washington Irving's, and the poetry of Byron and William Cowper. She read and used what she learned. Inventive situations, whimsical and parodic, some nonsensical, all bright and effervescent, spill out of her early letters: "vain imaginations," as she jested, "to lead astray foolish young women. They are flowers of speech, they both *make,* and *tell* deliberate falsehoods, avoid them as the snake." Yet she also complained of an excruciating melancholy that refused to let go. "Pain—has an Element of Blank— / " she would later write; "It cannot recollect / When it begun—Or if there were / A time when it was not—."

If we in the twenty-first century admire Emily Dickinson for her staunch individualism and her catlike ability, as James said of

Hawthorne, to see in the dark, we need also consider the cost of originality in a sleepy village where comings, goings, and the least sign of deviance were of public note. "She was full of courage," Austin recalled, "but always had a peculiar personal sensitiveness." The price of nonconformity was loneliness. And yet one could manage nonconformity—and loneliness, too, in certain ways. Despite the pressures of convention, upper-class women were frequently permitted eccentricity. They might live alone or with one another, not marry, or achieve the acceptable status of a talented maiden sister or dotty old aunt. These women—Higginson's Aunt Storrow, Emerson's Aunt Mary—were moral touchstones who roamed without a pack.

One cannot know to what extent Dickinson chose her nonconformity or to what extent it chose her, but over time her commitment to independence, poetry, and a handful of soul mates comes into clearer focus. Early on there was one special person, the young man she called her "first" male friend, Benjamin Franklin Newton. They met in 1847, after he, at twenty-five, had come to Amherst to study law in her father's office. Emily was sixteen and likely awed as well as flattered by his interest, for she considered his intellect as "far surpassing" her own (evidently she did not think many exceeded hers). He taught her what to read, she said, "and that sublimer lesson, a faith in things unseen, and in a life again, nobler, and much more blessed—." He was her gentle, grave Preceptor, the title she would confer on Higginson.

When his apprenticeship to Edward Dickinson ended two years later, Newton corresponded with Emily from Worcester—unfortunately these letters do not survive—where he had likely heard of Wentworth Higginson, soon to take over the city's Free Church, a congregation far more radical than that of Newburyport. Higginson's flaming abolitionism and his incendiary preaching were by now matters of public record and, in the Free-Soil city of Worcester, approbation; his home was a well-known stop on the Underground Railroad. But whether or not Newton mentioned Higginson to Emily, she herself probably made the connection, for in her second letter to Higginson, plausibly referring to Newton, she mentioned the "friend who taught me Immortality—but venturing too near himself—he never returned—." She was alluding to his untimely death, in 1853, not long after he was appointed Worcester's district attorney, a position in which he was bound to encounter, or prosecute, Higginson.

Like Higginson, who was a year younger, Preceptor Newton was a freethinker, though a milder one, who had grown up in the brave new world of transcendentalism, where there were no sinners, everyone was saved, and God was neither angry nor intemperate. Like Higginson, too, he seemed to contemplate perfectibility, goodness, and the indwelling divinity of all living things. And he loved poetry. Shortly after leaving Amherst, he sent Emily a volume of Emerson's verse, which taught her, as she said, what was "most grand or beautiful in nature."

This was her conversion: beauty, its own excuse for being. "When half-gods go, / the gods arrive," wrote Emerson in "Give All to Love," a poem close to Higginson's heart. "My dying Tutor," she would tell Higginson, "told me that he would like to live till I had been a poet." Higginson should know that Newton believed in her. "My earliest friend wrote me the week before he died," she added. " 'If I live, I will go to Amherst—if I die, I certainly will.' "

THERE WERE OTHER FRIENDS of course, chiefly Susan Gilbert, the temperamental beauty who married Austin and dwelled next to the Dickinsons for the rest of her life, outliving them all save her own daughter. Just nine days younger than Emily, Sue was dark haired, discontented, clever, and complex. Time and tragedy would harden her into the distant, stately woman swathed in black whom Vinnie, among others, hated and feared.

That would be much later. Born in Deerfield, Massachusetts, the youngest of seven children, she was orphaned by the age of eleven and taken in, along with a sister, by an aunt in Geneva, New York. Educated at the Utica Female Academy and for a term at the Amherst Academy, she went to live in Amherst with another sister and, resentful, never felt she had a permanent home or stable toehold in the social world. But she believed that in her marriage to Austin she had found security and position. She was wrong, but that realization would come later.

Sue was intelligent, self-possessed, and volatile, just the sort of woman to impress both Austin and Emily. Emily showed or gave Sue over two hundred poems, sharing more, it seems, of her private life with her than with any other relative. "We are the only poets," she would exclaim, "and everyone else is *prose.*"

Susan Gilbert.
"Everyone else
is *prose.*"

For a time Sue Gilbert might well have been the center of Emily Dickinson's erotic imaginings. "Oh Susie, I would nestle close to your warm heart, and never hear the wind blow, or the storm beat, again," Dickinson wrote to her in 1852. *yet "literary" female-female eroticism not atypical, and a convention of the period.*

> Is there any room there for me, darling, and will you "love me more if ever you come home"?—it is enough, dear Susie, I know I shall be satisfied. But what can I do towards you?—dearer you cannot be, for I love you so already, that it almost breaks my heart—perhaps I can love you anew, every day of my life, every morning and evening—Oh if you will let me, how happy I shall be!

Certainly Dickinson loved a number of her female friends—Abiah Root, Jane Humphrey, Emily Fowler—with a passion so startling it may have pushed some of them away. For, as a child wedged between Austin and Lavinia, Emily demanded of her friends that which she could never have from her family: unqualified approval.

Sue seemed to provide it, if temporarily. And Sue had earned the family's endorsement, for Edward liked her, perhaps or particularly because she professed herself, and was admitted, to the First Church of Amherst on the same day as he. Soon Sue was occupying a place of honor in the exclusive Dickinson household. And there was Austin, too, the most eligible bachelor in the village, asking her to ride with him, if she thought it proper, the same summer one of her sisters died in childbirth. She dressed in mourning for the next three years—but the Dickinsons beckoned, and Austin was fervently tender. Soon she and he were vowing to think of each other at the first strike of the vesper bell when they would both eat a commemorative chestnut.

The Dickinsons would have approved of Austin's clandestine engagement had they known of it, but Austin kept mum, and anyway Sue was dragging her heels. She was teaching school in Baltimore, he in Boston, and in the fall of 1852, when Austin went to Harvard to study law, he barraged her with letters much as Edward had Emily Norcross, but Austin's were overwrought, clamorous, more plainly needy. His gnawing uncertainty caused him to worry that Sue did not love him as he loved her or misunderstood him or mistook him or regarded him amiss, particularly when he confided—he could not help himself—that though he had prayed and prayed, he could not ignore his physical desire for her. "Is there anything debasing in human love—does it rather not exalt & refine & purify our nature above all else," he desperately asked in one of the many drafts he made of his letters to her. "Has not God planted it in us—" [Crossed out: "Did not Christ teach that the love of a man for his wife should be paramount."]

As ardent and insatiable as Emily, Sue frequently fortified herself against the demands of others. Nor was she a woman to be trifled with. Over the years she would prove a mercurial friend, lover, and wife: unpredictable, hurtful, arrogant. Austin sensed as much early on. "It seems strange to me, too . . . ," he unburdened himself to Sue's sister Martha, "that just such characters should have chosen each other to love, that two so tall, proud, stiff people, so easily miffed,—so apt to be pert . . . —that two who could love so well, or hate so well—that two just such *could* not choose but love each other!—but we could not." Later these two would just as ineluctably choose hate.

But the Dickinsons loved with greedy ardor, each in his or her own individual way, each an absolute monarch overseeing an intensely private kingdom, as Vinnie would one day remark. Together they were unified against the hoi polloi, with whom they believed they shared little. It was a matter of class, intellect, and rampant insecurity. "We're all unlike most everyone," Emily remarked to Austin, "and are therefore more dependent on each other for delight." That would remain more or less true even when, as in the case of Austin and Sue, they were indissolubly bound by antipathy, disappointment, and self-loathing.

When Sue devised a clandestine visit to Boston to meet Austin, Emily, learning of the assignation, offered to help out. And when Austin disappointed his fiancée, she consoled him: "I guess we both love Sue just as well as we can." Soon she was putting a bit of distance between herself and Sue, "a dear child to us all," she observed with defensive condescension or self-protection. For Emily's passion—for physical love, for spiritual connectedness—palpably suffused her body and her imagination. "I feel as if love sat upon my heart, and flapped it with his wings": she marked those lines in her father's copy of the novel *Thaddeus of Warsaw.* In Austin's copy of *Lalla Rookh,* by Thomas Moore, she noted these: "I knew, I knew it *could* not last— / 'Twas bright, 'twas heavenly, but 'tis past! / O! ever thus, from childhood's hour, / I've seen my fondest hopes decay."

Pining for Sue, she yearned, albeit with ambivalence, for the same physical love, vehement and consuming, that her brother longed for.

> Those unions, my dear Susie, by which two lives are one, this sweet and strange adoption wherein we can but look, and are not yet admitted, how it can fill the heart, and make it gang wildly beating, how it will take *us* one day, and make us all it's own, and we shall not run away from it, but lie still and be happy!

She continued:

> How dull our lives must seem to the bride, and the plighted maiden, whose days are fed with gold, and who gathers pearls every evening; but to the *wife,* Susie, sometimes the *wife forgotten,* our lives perhaps seem dearer than all the others in the world; you have seen flowers at morning, *satisfied* with the dew, and those same sweet flowers at noon with their heads bowed in anguish before the mighty sun; think you these thirsty blossoms will *now* need naught but—*dew?* No, they will cry for sunlight, and pine for the burning noon, tho' it scorches them, scathes them; they have got through with peace—they know that the man of noon, is *mightier* than the morning and their life is

henceforth to him. Oh, Susie, it is dangerous, and it is all too dear, these simple trusting spirits, and the spirits mightier, which we cannot resist! It does so rend me, Susie, the thought of it when it comes, that I tremble lest at sometime I, too, am yielded up.

Yet she could resist and she could yield, both simultaneously and, more and more, in her own way. She would not be caught or confined. "Captivity is Consciousness— / ," she wrote, "So's Liberty—."

FOUR

Emily Dickinson: Write!
Comrade, Write!

lthough undergraduates from Amherst still came to call and she still rode out with them or chattered sociably, although the family still fed guests and coddled dignitaries as before, Emily Dickinson was gradually, imperceptibly, absenting herself from all forms of public life. She did not welcome strangers. They inhabited a marketplace of vanity and grime: the endless clack of the dirty horsecars, the slop on the cobblestones, the poverty, the crime, the pain, the jockeying and the mealymouthed palaver of Boston that, as Austin reported after Emily's visit, confirmed his sister's "opinion of the hollowness & awfulness of the *world*."

Home was different. "As the great world goes on and one another forsake, in whom you place your trust," Emily told Austin, "here seems indeed to be a bit of Eden which not the sin of *any* can utterly destroy." Neither gritty streets nor smutty gardens spoiled the view of the meadow from her bedroom window. No skies streaked with a mouse-colored gray, no rattling carts, no hollow, spinning world. Here was quiet, even if it was, some days, the quiet of emptiness: "And I, and Silence, some strange Race / Wrecked, solitary, here—."

Her retirement—what else to call it, even if the word is harsh— mingled passion with conviction and impudence with dread. She possessed an originality that pleased. It made her special. Yet withdrawal also springs from fear—the fear of losing or having lost. "I'm afraid I'm growing *selfish* in my dear home, but I do love it so," tellingly she warned her old school chum Jane Humphrey, "and when some pleasant friend invites me to pass a week with her, I look at my father and mother and Vinnie, and all my friends, and I say no—no, cant leave them, what if they die when I'm gone." Dickinson clung to their physical presence; proximity was her defense against disruption, change, calamity, loss and the threat of it. When invited to visit her friend Abiah in Springfield in 1854, she again declined, carefully explaining, "I don't go from home, unless emergency leads me by the hand, and then I do it obstinately, and draw back if I can. Should I ever leave home, which is improbable, I will with much delight, accept your invitation; . . . but don't expect me. I'm so old fashioned, Darling, that all your friends would stare."

Deliberate, gracious, and self-deprecating, Dickinson filed her renunciatory rhetoric to a razor's edge, her weapon, words, charming and implacable. Otherwise, she darkly hinted, there were consequences. Going to church by herself, she had to rush to her seat and, terrified, wondered why she trembled so, why the aisle seemed so wide and broad, why it took almost half an hour afterward to catch her breath. Yet knowing when and how to protect herself, she managed her fear, and evidently her family cosseted her. When her father suggested they come to Washington in 1853, he did not insist that Emily join them. Instead, she stayed at home with Sue and a cousin, John Graves, who later remembered Emily improvising on the piano late at night: he was invited to sit in the next room while she mesmerizingly played.

In 1855, when Edward Dickinson was a lame-duck congressman, Emily agreed to visit him in Washington. She and Vinnie stayed at the smart new Willard Hotel on Pennsylvania Avenue, just two blocks from the White House. The sisters threaded their way through the crowded streets, wandering in new ways, as Emily put it, greeting silken ladies and high-hatted gentlemen and by all indications enjoying themselves in a city where, as a future friend would quip, "everybody knows everybody and the nobodies are the most clamorous of all." She took it in stride, confounding a Supreme Court justice, according to family legend. When a flambé was served for dessert, she turned to him sweetly and asked, "Oh Sir, may one eat of hell fire with impunity, here?"

True to form, she refused a number of social engagements, pleading illness. Washington, Boston — it made little difference. Even Amherst grew too wide. Home was best. "I fear I grow incongruous," she said with a shrug.

THE TIME HAD COME for the Dickinsons to reoccupy the Homestead. Measured against the grandeur, the psychological satisfaction, and the conspicuous prominence of the family mansion, the

Dickinson Homestead, 1858.

comforts of West Street—where Austin would say he had spent the best years of his life—meant nothing to Edward. Until he could regain the Homestead, it would stand—just blocks away—a souvenir of his misfortune.

In the spring of 1855, Edward paid six thousand dollars for the place—a bargain, he reckoned—and then forked over almost the same amount, it was rumored, for renovations. He needed to leave his own mark on the wainscoting and balustrades, and after overseeing six months of hauling, nailing, plastering, and painting, he had a conservatory, servants' quarters, a cupola, and a new east wing, which opened onto a magnificent garden. To the west a veranda faced the Evergreens, the home he built, on his land, for Austin and Sue, married in July of the following year. And he planted a hedge of cedar trees to the front of the Homestead, as if to seal off the place from the street.

Though important for Edward, moving proved hard on the family. "I am out with lanterns," Emily bleakly remarked, "looking for myself." Displacement shook the myth of home at its very foundation. Mrs. Dickinson sank into a lingering depression and seldom left her chair for long during the next four years. "I cannot tell you how we moved," Emily wrote, recounting the upheaval to her friend

Elizabeth Holland. "I had rather not remember. I believe my 'effects' were brought in a bandbox, and the 'deathless me,' on foot, not many moments after. . . . It is a kind of *gone-to-Kansas* feeling," she concluded, "and if I sat in a long wagon, with my family tied behind, I should suppose without doubt I was a party of emigrants."

For Higginson, the settlement of Kansas as a free state would be a political necessity, invigorating and imperative; for Dickinson, a horror: families dislodged, their earthly possessions crammed into packing crates, things and people displaced, confused, stranded.

She continued to withdraw.

> *To put this World down, like a Bundle —*
> *And walk steady, away,*
> *Requires Energy — possibly Agony —*
> *'Tis the Scarlet way*

Emily might tiptoe across the grass to visit Austin and Sue at the Evergreens, but if a guest should pull the bell, she would run back. "In such a porcelain life, one likes to be *sure* that all is well, lest one stumble upon one's hopes in a pile of broken crockery," she wryly noted.

With Mrs. Dickinson incapacitated, Vinnie assumed her role, offering Emily the protection she needed more than ever. "I would like more sisters," she sighed when Vinnie left to tend an ailing aunt, "that the taking out of one, might not leave such stillness."

To Vinnie, Emily's withdrawal was nothing special and implied nothing morbid. Emily simply got in the habit of staying home, Vinnie later explained—"and finding the life with her books and nature so congenial, continued to live it, always seeing her chosen friends and doing her part for the happiness of others." Perhaps Vinnie also suspected that if her sister was becoming less interested in setting foot past the front gate, she was exploring recesses of feeling, thought, and imagination—what Dickinson later called a "route of evanescence"—that made contact with the humdrum world superfluous. Emily told Abiah Root and Jane Humphrey that she was undertaking "strange things—bold things"—poems probably— and like the exceptional women of her time, mainly but not always poets (Elizabeth Whittier, Christina Rossetti, the Brontës, Margaret Fuller), she was choosing her own society, then shutting the door.

That door, in fact, appears over and over in her poetry as an image of protection, solitude, and exits and entrances: "The Heart has many Doors—" but "Doom is the House without the Door—."

And as was the case when she played the piano for John Graves, she nudged the door slightly open.

> *So we must meet apart —*
> *You there — I — here —*
> *With just the Door ajar*

NO ONE KNOWS EXACTLY when Dickinson started composing poetry, especially since after 1855 the record of her daily life grows thinner. There was no need to write to Austin anymore because he lived just beyond the hedge. Ditto Sue, and overall many letters to Dickinson's friends have not survived. And those extant few, though charged with meaning, are often disconcertingly oblique. Yet they do tell us something. "We used to think, Joseph, when I was an unsifted girl and you so scholarly," she half-explained to Joseph Lyman, "that words were cheap & weak. Now I don't know of anything so mighty. . . . Sometimes I write one, and look at his outlines till he glows as no sapphire."

The power of words: assuming several voices, she used them to speak her life—as penitent young woman in search of divine assistance, as impenitent rebel unable to believe, as coy mistress indulging flights of fancy, as good daughter, smart-aleck sister, as lover. She traveled far, and like Virginia Woolf's Orlando years later her personae leaped across time and sex and culture. A Valentine's Day spoof, in a way her first publication, appeared in 1850 in a college paper, *The Indicator,* and it bursts with "what they call a metaphor in our country. Don't be afraid of it, sir, it won't bite!"

> But the world is sleeping in ignorance and error, sir, and we must be crowing-cocks, and singing-larks, and a rising sun to awake her; or else we'll pull society up to the roots, and plant it in a different place. We'll build Alms-houses, and transcendental State prisons, and scaffolds—we will blow out the sun, and the moon, and encourage invention. Alpha shall kiss Omega—we will ride up the hill of glory—Hallelujah, all hail!

The hill of glory shall be made of metaphors far-flung, blowing out the sun. Her rhythmic sentences swing and fold, and though she did not imagine herself battering down courthouse doors, as Higginson would do, she declares that we can change the world through language.

Yet world there was, with real almshouses and scaffolds and auction blocks: while at Holyoke she had dreamed the family field had been mortgaged to the local postmaster, a Democrat derisively called a Locofoco (after the matches a group of anti-Tammany Democrats used in 1835 when the gaslights had been turned off). " 'I should expire with mortification' to have our rye field mortgaged, to say nothing of it's falling into the merciless hands of a loco!!" she wrote Austin, doubtless mimicking her father. But who was the presidential candidate? she asked in mock consternation. "I have been trying to find out ever since I came here & have not yet succeeded. I don't know anything more about affairs in the world, than if I was in a trance. . . . Has the Mexican war terminated yet & how? Are we beat? Do you know of any nation about to besiege South Hadley? If so do inform me of it, for I would be glad of a chance to escape." Leaping from the stuff of the world to the stuff of fancy, from concern to comedy, Dickinson was very much aware of the political life around her. One detaches from something, after all; for it was this world, steeped in ignorance and error, that she affected to spurn but could never forget, no matter what we might like to believe about her vaunted reclusiveness.

But her real domain—her huge gift—lay elsewhere. "*Write! Comrade, write!*" she commanded Sue. That was in 1853. And when Austin picked up a pen, she put him straight. "I've been in the habit *myself* of writing some few things," she swiftly told him, "and it rather appears to me that you're getting away my patent, so you'd better be somewhat careful, or I'll call the police!"

Writing demanded commitment. Her frolicsome Valentines anticipated the witty irreverence of her poems; she told Higginson that "Some keep the Sabbath going to Church— / I keep it, staying at Home— / With a Bobolink for a Chorister— / And an Orchard, for a Dome—." She kept the Sabbath by writing poetry, in fact, and pledged herself to a life of it: "I'm ceded—I've stopped being Their's— / The name They dropped upon my face," she exclaimed in one of her many declarations of independence. And since poetry implied freedom as well as commitment, in one way the critic R. P. Blackmur was partially right when he said Dickinson married herself; her point of view hers alone, she played off big and small, near and far, high and low: "When we stand on the tops of Things— / And like the Trees, look down," she wrote, altering perspective at will and, taking up the imperative, snapping out orders: "If your Nerve, deny you— / Go above your Nerve—."

Poetry also offered a form of grace:

> *I reckon — When I count at all —*
> *First — Poets — Then the Sun —*
> *Then Summer — Then the Heaven of God —*
> *And then — the List is done —*
>
> *But, looking back — the First so seems*
> *To Comprehend the Whole —*
> *The Others look a needless Show —*
> *So I write — Poets — All —*

Sly humor, poetic declamations, and peremptory commands aside, she also worked hard to be incongruous, her analogies bold and startling and composed with the technical precision of a Donne or a Herbert or a Vaughan, her images violent, corporeal, sexual:

> *He fumbles at your Soul*
> *As Players at the Keys*
> *Before they drop full Music on —*
> *He stuns you by degrees —*
> *Prepares your brittle nature*
> *For the Etherial Blow*
> *By fainter Hammers — further heard —*
> *Then nearer — Then so slow*
> *Your Breath has time to straighten —*
> *Your Brain — to bubble Cool —*
> *Deals — One — imperial — Thunderbolt —*
> *That scalps your naked Soul —*
>
> *When Winds take Forests in their Paws —*
> *The Universe — is still —*

These were strange and wondrous lines: the musicality of "fainter Hammers—further heard"; the unabashed brutality of verbs like "fumbles," "stuns," "scalps"; the anthropomorphizing of "wind," giving it "paws." And these together create—with terrifying faith, angry passivity, and sheer ingenuity—a spectacularly original poem.

And while writing verse like that, she fell upon Thomas Higginson.

"Literature is attar of roses, one distilled drop from a million blossoms," Higginson wrote in his "Letter to a Young Contributor," words that Dickinson heeded well.

"This was a Poet—," she wrote as if in reply,

> It is That
> Distills amazing sense
> From Ordinary Meanings —
> And Attar so immense
>
> From the familiar species
> That perished by the Door —
> We wonder it was not Ourselves
> Arrested it — before —

WHEN DICKINSON SHOWED SUE "Safe in their Alabaster Chambers—," Sue criticized the second stanza. The two friends went back and forth. "Your praise is good—to me—," Emily replied, because I *know* it *knows*—and *suppose*—it *means*—."

If writing demanded commitment, it also required a recipient. There were Newton and other friends, like Joseph Lyman, George Gould, Perez Cowan, and Henry Vaughan Emmons, to whom she seems to have shown some of her early work; there was Sue, there was Higginson himself, who loved language and the outdoors, as she did, and whom, despite his "surgery," she trusted. One need not understand everything.

Her most perplexing connection was to the unknown person she addressed as Master in three letters probably composed in the late 1850s. Undiscovered until her death—and they were found in draft form only—these letters contain no clues to the recipient's identity. No one even knows if Dickinson actually mailed final copies of the letters, and as in most things Dickinson, much about their origin is guesswork. The reigning hypothesis is that the Master was the Reverend Charles Wadsworth, moody minister of Philadelphia's Arch Street Presbyterian Church, whom Dickinson apparently met while visiting that city en route from Washington in March of 1855.

The Reverend Wadsworth, an oddball of the first order, thrilled parishioners with his overheated theatrics: he had a trapdoor cut into the pulpit floor so he might appear and disappear without having to mingle with the congregation, and a poet in his younger days, or so he had hoped, he was an ace performer, the religious thespian with brimming eyes, quivering cheeks, heaving chest, a "man of God of the old school, . . . a tower of strength to the wavering and distressed." He reveled in the theology of John Calvin, calling it the single philosophical defense against blank atheism, and his sermons were said to rival Henry Beecher's. "And the Church below, Christ's witness unto the world, in all her ordinances and utterances, cries, 'Come, come!' And the Church above, with the resulting of white robes, and the sweeping of golden harps, cries, 'Come, come!' " Though one reviewer found his published sermons florid, he admitted not having seen the eminent Wadsworth preach, which Mark Twain had. "But every now and then, with an admirable assumption of not being aware of it," Twain reported, "he will get off a first-rate joke and then frown severely at any one who is surprised into smiling at it."

Likely Dickinson's visit to her Philadelphia cousins included a Sunday sermon by the preacher she later called a Man of Sorrow. Was this Man of Sorrow the Master to whom Dickinson addressed her love letters? Jay Leyda, Dickinson sleuth supreme, doubted it though he conjectured that Dickinson initiated a correspondence with Wadsworth shortly after the move to the Homestead and about the time her mother fell ill. Dickinson did contact Wadsworth about something troubling her, for he answered kindly, referring to "the affliction which has befallen, or is now befalling you." And in 1860 he called at the Dickinson home, "Black with his Hat," as the poet later recalled, telling her "My Life is full of dark Secrets." We don't know much more than this, but it does seem that Dickinson turned to Wadsworth, seeking relief for an affliction that likely had nothing to do with him. And if the affliction refers to a romance with the Master, then the Master is someone else.

Other candidates for the Master include the family friend Samuel Bowles, editor of the *Springfield Republican,* or someone whose identity has not yet surfaced. After her death, Austin concluded that Emily had been "several times in love, in her own way," and years later Dickinson's niece insisted that "my Aunt had lovers, like Browning's roses, 'all the way' to the end—men of varied profession and attainment who wrote to her and came to see her, and whose letters she burnt with a chivalry not all of them requited in kind." (The last remark is a posthumous jab at Higginson, who allowed the publication of his stash of Dickinson letters.)

The specific identity of the Master matters less than the letters she intended for him. There we overhear the "afflicted" Dickinson, alternately passive and brash, pleading and adamant, violent, poetic, secretive, and exposed. "I've got a cough as big as a thimble—but I don't care for that—I've got a Tomahawk in my side but that don't humor me much, Her Master stabs her more—Wont he come to her—," she asks in the second letter, possibly written as many as two years later. Raging, scathing, self-destructive, she was very much aware of what she was writing.

Evidently the relationship had progressed, at least in her mind. "Open your life wide, and take me in forever, I will never be tired— I will never be noisy when you want to be still—I will be your best little girl—nobody else will see me, but you—but that is enough—I shall not want any more—."

And there is the third letter, written near the date of the second (or so it seems.) Its masochism is harrowing, its initial image of violence almost vindictive:

> Master.
>   If you saw a bullet
> hit a Bird — and he told you
> he was'nt shot — you might weep
> at his courtesy, but you would
> certainly doubt his word —
> One drop more from the gash
> that stains your Daisy's
> bosom — then would you believe?
>
> . . . .
>
> I am older — tonight, Master —
> but the love is the same —
> so are the moon and the
> crescent —

. . . .
— but if I had the Beard on my cheek — like you — and you — had
Daisy's petals — and you cared so for me — what would become of you?
Could you forget me in fight, or flight — or the foreign land?
Couldn't Carlo {her dog}, and you and I
walk in the meadows an hour —
and nobody care but the Bobolink —
and his—a silver scruple?

. . . .
I waited a long time — Master —
but I can wait more — wait
till my hazel hair is dappled —
and you carry the cane —
then I can look at my
watch — and if the Day is
too far declined — we can take
the chances for Heaven —
What would you do with me
if I came "in white"?
I want to see you more — Sir —
than all I wish for in
this world — and the wish —
altered a little — will be my
only one — for the skies —
Could you come to New England —
Would you come
to Amherst — Would you like
to come — Master?

If the master letters are aggressive, sexy, and an amalgam of fury, doubt, pride, and supplication, they also reveal a Dickinson in complete command of herself, despite protestations to the contrary.

This is how she loved.

> *Perhaps you think me* stooping!
> *I'm not ashamed — of that!*
> *Christ—stooped — until he touched the Grave!*
> *Do those at* Sacrament—
> *Commemorate* dishonor—
> *Or love — annealed of love —*

Until it bend — as low as Death
Re-royalized—above?

BY 1858, DICKINSON WAS FASTENING GROUPS of her
poems together into small hand-sewn packets, each of which contained as many as twenty poems. She sent a number of these poems
to friends; others she kept and reworked. And even after she entered
them into booklets, she continued to alter them, dividing long stanzas, for instance, into quatrains, or shifting some of the punctuation,
or substituting words. Later called fascicles by one of her first editors, these packets survive, all forty of them, and though they cannot
be dated with precision, they reveal a self-conscious poet, never satisfied with the work at hand. " 'It is finished,' " she would say, "can
never be said of us."

Though publication was "foreign to my thought, as Firmament to
Fin—," as she had told Higginson, she obviously considered her
verse, as she famously wrote, her letter to the World. Naturally she
sought recognition, though that was not her primary aim. "It's a
great thing to be 'great,' Loo," she told her cousin Louise Norcross,
"and you and I might tug for a life, and never accomplish it, but no
one can stop our looking on, and you know some cannot sing, but
the orchard is full of birds, and we all can listen What if we learn,
ourselves, some day!"

Yet if she could learn to be a singer, to whom would she sing?
Audience is one of the great mysteries vexing Dickinson scholars,
who variously infer that she devised an alternative form of publication by addressing herself mainly to family and select friends. But
readers then and now also feel that she speaks to them alone; her
verse is intimate, private. Higginson would classify it with what
Emerson called the poetry of the portfolio, something produced
without thought of publication, solely to express the writer's own
mind. But this is only partly true and reflects more of Higginson's
prejudice than Dickinson's intention. For she spoke of her writing
with increasing if comically humble confidence, hesitancy growing
to assertion:

> *My Splendors, are Menagerie —*
> *But their Competeless Show*
> *Will entertain the Centuries*
> *When I, am long ago,*

> *An Island in dishonored Grass —*
> *Whom none but Daisies, know —*

Deliberately she defied the conventional, the sentimental, the predictable: birds gossip, roads wrinkle, suns stoop, skies pout, and daffodils untie their bonnets. Emotionally raw and intellectually dense, her poems divide nouns from verbs, past from present ("When I, am long ago, / An Island in dishonored Grass—"), only to reunite them. Ditto pronouns: they lose case or reference and yet stay what they are. Fantastically, she transforms life and death, speaking after death ("Because I could not stop for Death—") or at the moment of its onset ("I heard a Fly buzz—when I died—"), and in many poems, with color and delight she embraces sensually the things of this world ("We like March—his Shoes are Purple—"), the change of seasons and their recurrence, as in this early example:

> *An altered look about the hills —*
> *A Tyrian light the village fills —*
> *A wider sunrise in the morn —*
> *A deeper twilight on the lawn —*
> *A print of a vermillion foot —*
> *A purple finger on the slope —*
> *A flippant fly opon the pane —*
> *A spider at his trade again —*
> *An added strut in Chanticleer —*
> *A flower expected everywhere —*
> *An axe shrill singing in the woods —*
> *Fern odors on untravelled roads —*
> *All this and more I cannot tell —*
> *A furtive look you know as well —*
> *And Nicodemus' Mystery*
> *Receives it's annual reply!*

She can tilt her rhyme; she'll use an off rhyme or an eye rhyme: "Power is only Pain— / Stranded—thro' Discipline." She shuns full stops: "First—Chill—then Stupor—then the letting go—." The open-ended dash, breathless, was her pause of choice, dashes in all sizes and shapes: short, long, slant, each prying the door ajar. Nouns stand at attention, capitalized and substantive. "Narcotics cannot still the Tooth / ," she writes, "That nibbles at the soul—."

Invoking the Bible, blaspheming, misquoting, and subverting the expected, she tests the idea of God, rails at his distance. She suffers, she sees; she suffers because she sees:

> I had some things that I called mine —
> And God, that he called his —
> Till recently a rival claim
> Disturbed these amities.
>
> The property, my garden,
> Which having sown with care —
> He claims the pretty acre —
> And sends a Bailiff there.

"On subjects of which we know nothing," she once said, "we both believe, and disbelieve a hundred times an Hour, which keeps Believing nimble."

> Some things that fly there be —
> Birds — Hours — the Bumblebee —
> Of these no Elegy.
>
> Some things that stay there be —
> Grief — Hills — Eternity —
> Nor this behooveth me.
>
> There are that resting, rise.
> Can I expound the skies?
> How still the Riddle lies!

"Can I expound the skies?" If not, why not? Though church doctrine might annoy her, she never tires of its human side: "When Jesus tells us about his Father, we distrust him. When he shows us his Home, we turn away, but when he confides to us that he is 'acquainted with Grief,' we listen," she says, "for that also is an Acquaintance of our own." Sorrow touches sorrow, offering the comfort of the unknown: "This World is not conclusion." Like her poetry, the wounded deer leaps highest. ("I sing," as she had told Higginson, "as the Boy does by the Burying Ground — because I am afraid.") A poet of incalculable loss, infinite compassion, she speaks urgently, intimately, frugally, of the unspeakable. The space between us and her melts away.

She employs the common folk measure of Protestant hymns, writing in six- and eight-syllable lines, in order to unbalance it — no full stops at the end of a stanza, for instance. A miniaturist, she composes poems in brief, most of which fit on a single page. She loves shortcuts. She manages — invents — an economic phrase to express the inexpressible, raiding the unspeakable, cutting to the quick of emotion, all emotion, and dissecting it with such speed we wonder how she can possibly know what she knows:

> *She dealt her pretty words like Blades —*
> *How glittering they shone —*
> *And every One unbared a Nerve*
> *Or wantoned with a Bone —*
>
> *She never deemed — she hurt —*
> *That — is not Steel's Affair —*
> *A vulgar grimace in the Flesh —*
> *How ill the Creatures bear —*
>
> *To Ache is human — not polite —*
> *The Film opon the eye*
> *Mortality's old Custom —*
> *Just locking up — to Die —*

The succinct description of Hawthorne she would later send Higginson — he "appalls, entices" — refers equally to herself. Her pretty words, too, are dealt like blades:

> *Title divine — is mine!*
> *The Wife — without the Sign!*
> *Acute Degree — conferred on me —*
> *Empress of Calvary!*
> *Royal — all but the Crown!*
> *Betrothed — without the swoon*
> *God sends us Women —*

Incomparably modern, the poetry is as ephemeral as experience itself. Sensual, its decided sexuality — whether directed toward the

Master or Susan or Higginson or her own vocation as poet—is expressed in a language compounded of colloquialism and religious reference, aphorism and plaint, statement and plea. Direct, dense, often excruciating, her poetry lies close to the reader and one step beyond, fervently waiting: Because I could not stop.

DICKINSON DISPATCHED POEMS TO FRIENDS, her verse often accompanied by a pressed flower or a leaf. A large number went to Samuel Bowles, the close friend of Susan and Austin's (later it was rumored that Bowles and Susan were uncommonly fond of each other), who visited Amherst often, sometimes with his wife, sometimes not. Owner and editor of the influential *Springfield Republican,* a conservative weekly newspaper founded by his father in 1824, Bowles converted it into a daily, working until he collapsed and then diving back into his work as soon as he recovered. But he managed to produce a newspaper respected nationally for its clarity, its pith, its independence, and its editorials. The Dickinsons were enthusiastic readers.

Liberal, generous, unhappily married, and reputed to be some-

Samuel Bowles, editor
of the *Springfield
Republican.*
"His nature was
Future."

thing of a roué as well as a supporter of women writers—his paper often printed their poetry—Bowles was also a dabbler in national as well as local politics, a diplomat, and a dynamo with real sensitivity and beautiful, seductive eyes, a modern man impatient, canny, and worldly. "His growth was by absorption," said his biographer. "Other people were to him sponges out of which he deftly squeezed whatever knowledge they could yield." His journalistic ear sleeplessly cocked, his politics fresh, his sentiments broad, his pen ready, he was an antislavery man who considered abolitionists to be dangerous extremists. (Most did.) He applauded Edward Dickinson's stand against the Kansas-Nebraska bill and supported the congressman's unsuccessful bid for reelection in 1854 (though it seems he eventually withdrew his support). In 1856 he supported the antislavery Republican John C. Frémont for the presidency, then in 1860 endorsed the rail-splitter Abraham Lincoln, whom he didn't much like, and reluctantly supported the war, which he liked even less.

Radicals like Higginson found the *Republican* too pessimistic for their taste, and Boston salonistas like Annie Adams Fields airily dismissed its publisher: "Mr. Bowles is quite handsome and would be altogether if he had elegance of manner to correspond with what nature has done for him in giving him fine eyes," the Brahmin hostess recorded, "but he is an ambitious man, ambitious to be known as a literary man, but apparently mistaking popularity for fame he has learned to know almost everybody of literary celebrity, to get on the top word continually, to keep open house, to be a general good fellow, which combined with real ability has made him widely liked & given him a brilliant restless way, which makes so many Americans." James Fields, her husband, took Bowles's measure more crisply: heaven forbid the man should start a magazine; it would bury *The Atlantic.*

"His nature was Future": Emily Dickinson grasped him best. But the future was something he never quite reached. A series of ailments, including sciatica and shingles, along with his chronic insomnia and his headaches, all wore him down, and in 1862 he sailed for Europe to rest. When he returned, he picked up exactly where he had left off. The work and the illnesses continued, and he died sixteen years later, at the age of fifty-one.

As early as 1860, Bowles and his wife, Mary, were Dickinson staples. It was Mary who gave Emily an antislavery Christmas parable by Theodore Parker, but it was Samuel, with his "vivid Face and the besetting Accents," with whom the poet shared a special conversation, he ribbing her as "the Queen Recluse" who "has 'overcome the world.' " Bowles appreciated and respected Dickinson's need for solitude. "I have been in a savage, turbulent state for some time —," he confided to Austin, "indulging in a sort of chronic disgust at everything & everybody — I guess a good deal as Emily feels."

Emily trafficked with no movement, no group, no cabal of do-gooders outside the select circle that now included Bowles, with whom she could disagree, particularly about politics. "I am much ashamed Mr. Bowles," she jauntily apologized after one of his visits. "I misbehaved tonight. I would like to sit in the dust. I fear I am your little friend no more, but Mrs Jim Crow." The issue seems to have been women's rights. "I am sorry I smiled at women," she continued. "Indeed, I revere holy ones, like Mrs Fry and Miss Nightingale." She and Bowles treated each other as equals, and when he left for Europe, she deeply missed him. "When the Best is gone — I know that other things are not of consequence —," she explained to his wife. "The Heart wants what it wants — or else it does not care —."

Vinnie once observed that her sister was "always watching for the rewarding person to come." Bowles was one such person.

"I AM SO FAR FROM LAND," Dickinson once told Bowles. One wonders if, this time, he understood her meaning, and it seems he did. She asked him to mail some letters she did not want to post from the gossipy village of Amherst; he could be trusted to be discreet. And if he did not thoroughly understand her poems — his taste in verse hugged the shore — he published several in the *Republican* when his wife or Sue gave them to him: "Nobody knows this little Rose" in 1858, "I taste a liquor never brewed" in the spring of 1861; and on March 1, 1862, "Safe in their Alabaster Chambers."

That last poem was one of the four that Dickinson chose to mail Higginson just six weeks after it had appeared the *Republican.* There it stood, anonymous but hers, in one of the best papers of the day. Pride of publication had nudged the door a bit more ajar, and behind it lay her query to Higginson, another special person: Is my Verse alive?

Of course she knew the answer. That was not the point.

FIVE

Thomas Wentworth Higginson: Liberty Is Aggressive

C ome strong." In the drizzly spring of 1854, three years after the aborted Sims rescue, Higginson received the call from the abolitionist Samuel May Jr., Louisa May Alcott's cousin. Come to Boston right away.

Anthony Burns, a twenty-year-old fugitive slave from Virginia, had been arrested—kidnapped, roared the Boston Vigilance Committee—and imprisoned in the same Court House that had confined the luckless Sims.

Burns had already declined the legal counsel of such patrician notables as Richard Henry Dana, for even if the abolitionists of Boston dreamed otherwise, Burns, no fool, knew where all the commotion was headed. "It is of no use," he told Dana. "They will swear to me & get me back; and if they do, I shall fare worse if I resist." Also aware that a legal wrangle would just delay but not prevent Burns's reenslavement, the Vigilance Committee called for a public meeting at Faneuil Hall on Friday evening, May 26, and asked Higginson, if he could, to bring a posse of Worcester men.

"Give all the notice you can," May had said. What he actually intended—beyond rallying public support—is unclear.

Himself prepared for battle, Higginson stepped off the train in Boston that Friday to find his fellow committee members squabbling over how best to proceed, their debate droning on until one of them, learning the slave catchers were to pass by, suggested they march outdoors and "point the finger of scorn." The finger of scorn? Higginson's mouth fell open. "As if Southern slave-catchers were to be combated by such weapons," he wailed in frustration.

While the committee dithered into the late afternoon, Higginson broke away and bought a dozen hand axes. Martin Stowell, a friend from Worcester, had told him that Burns might be sprung from the

Court House that same night if the abolitionist leaders could channel the anger sure to be unleashed at the rally. Someone could yell
that a mob of black men was at the Court House trying to free
Burns, Stowell continued, and the Faneuil Hall crowd would then
surge into Court Square, where Higginson would be waiting, ready
to pilot the freedom lovers toward the jail and Burns's liberation.

It was a grand plan, bold and dangerous and so enticing that Higginson never stopped to consider its practicality: that it might be
impossible, for instance, to alert the leaders of the rally to the details
of the plot in the din of a roaring crowd, nearly five hundred strong
(mostly men), that crushed into Faneuil Hall that night. And so the
silky-tongued orator Wendell Phillips, key member of the Vigilance
Committee, never heard of the scheme, and it's not clear whether
the other speakers, Samuel Gridley Howe and Theodore Parker,
really understood it even if they had.

Higginson had no choice but to saunter back over to Court
Square, where Stowell had stashed the axes, and affect nonchalance.

"I am a clergyman and a man of peace," Theodore Parker's voice
meantime rang out in the packed and steamy hall. "I love peace. But
there is a means, and there is an end; Liberty is the end, and sometimes peace is not the means towards it." Still, the crowd should
reconvene the next morning, he continued, for a nonviolent protest
against the kidnapping. Wendell Phillips was ready to assent when
someone screamed out that a group of black men were at the Court
House rescuing Burns that very moment. Pandemonium. From
Court Square, Higginson spied in horror a group of men hurrying
up State Street: the "froth and scum of the meeting, the fringe of
idlers on its edge," he later described them, and not the men or at
least not the hundreds he had expected.

Posted near the Court House, Stowell began to hammer its heavy
oak door with one of the axes. Several men threw bricks. Several
other men—Higginson at the front—hoisted a fourteen-foot
wooden beam. Someone inside began ringing the Court House bell.
The men with the battering ram shoved forward; one of the door's
hinges tore; the door tipped to the side. Higginson, at the head of
the beam, elbowed his way into the room, but Lewis Hayden pressed
ahead of him. Unarmed, Higginson fought bare-handed. The police
were swinging swords and billy clubs, and Higginson received a cut,
nothing severe, on his chin. Hayden fired his revolver. Stowell fired

his. Perhaps the guards did too. For many years afterward Higginson supposed, or wanted to believe, the sheriff's deputies would carelessly or drunkenly murder their own.

One man was killed. Special officer James Batchelder, a twenty-four-year-old teamster stationed behind the teetering door, fell backward, moaning "I am stabbed."

Higginson didn't hear Batchelder's cry. Beaten back by the guards, he ran down the passageway and onto the Court House steps, where he saw that the sullen mob was dispersing. "You cowards, will you desert us now?" he shouted. For a moment the crowd didn't move. But it was over. "That meeting at Faneuil Hall was tremendous, I never saw such enthusiasm," Higginson later told a friend, "& (though warned that it would be so) I could not possibly believe that it wd exhale so idly as it did in Court Square."

Just then Bronson Alcott strode up the Court House steps, cane in hand, and paused to ask Higginson why he and his men were not inside. "Because these people will not stand by us," Higginson growled. Alcott continued up the steps, a model of transcendental courage. Another pistol shot rang out. Alcott walked back down the stairs.

With the approval of President Franklin Pierce, Nathaniel Hawthorne's benefactor, the United States marshall in Boston called out federal troops. "The law must be executed," he declared.

Later that night Batchelder died. No one was ever quite sure what had happened, whether Hayden or Stowell had fired the deadly shot, if in fact it was a shot that had killed Batchelder and not a wound from a saber. Unaware of this, Higginson spent the night at a friend's and, lest he be recognized by the police the next day, tied a kerchief around his face when he ventured out. He again met with the Vigilance Committee, but since legal proceedings were now inevitable, there was nothing left for him to do but go back to Worcester on Monday, consoling himself that the rescue's failure would provoke outrage among waffling antislavery people. And it did. "We went to bed one night old fashioned, conservative, Compromise Union Whig," said the textile manufacturer Amos Adams Lawrence, "& waked up stark mad Abolitionists."

The struggle against slavery was now an armed insurrection. "Massachusetts antislavery differs much from New York or Pennsylvania antislavery," one citizen would note in dismay; "it is fanaticism

& radicalism." But Higginson was pleased. "That attack was a great thing for freedom, & will echo all over the country," he told his mother.

As for Batchelder, Higginson informed Samuel May that the Committee should offer to assist his family, "supposing it to be so arranged as to show no contrition on our part, for a thing in which he had no responsibility, but simply to show that we have no war with women and children." Willingly, in other words, Higginson adopted the rationalization of a radical: that the death and suffering of combatants or bystanders are the inevitable if regrettable by-product of the greater struggle. It was a position that in later years he would disavow. For now, though, the customarily compassionate Higginson preferred to see Boston in flames rather than tolerate one person's reenslavement, but he also chafed at the idea, then bruited about, of Burns's being repurchased by New Englanders and set free, which would undermine his effectiveness as a symbol. As it happened, the United States district attorney, a Democratic party operative, delayed the proposed sale and then outlawed it, citing Batchelder's death as his reason.

Not blind to the inherent cruelty of his position, Higginson brooked no qualms about the morality of force. "A revolution is begun!" he shouted in Worcester. "If you take part in politics henceforward, let it be only to bring nearer the crisis which will either save or sunder this nation—or perhaps save in sundering."

A warrant was issued for Higginson's arrest, indicting him for treason or what he scorned as "the crime of a gentleman." An uncle, the businessman George J. Higginson, sent money. "It is the only way you know that we traders dare to show any sympathy," he told Wentworth. Urged to leave the country, Wentworth refused. "My penalty cannot be very severe; & I shall consider it the highest honor ever attained by a Higginson," he explained to his mother. Backing him fully, Mary said that the jail should open an annex for anti-slavery wives, and jesting only by half, Lucy Stone noted that "it would be best for the 'cause' if they should hang you." Higginson granted "that months & years in jail would be well spent as a protest against slavery. The men now arrested are obscure men," he continued; "their sufferings will be of comparatively little service; but I have a name, a profession, & the personal position which make my bonds a lesson & a stimulus to the whole country. What better things could I do for liberty?"

Anthony Burns: broadside depicting the former slave's escape, capture, imprisonment, and, finally, deportation from Boston, 1855.

No doubt wishing to avoid that very showdown, the government reduced the charge to disturbing the peace, and the indictment was quashed.

Yet nothing could rub out the memory of Bad Friday, June 2, 1854. Thousands of faceless troops on horseback patrolled the gray streets, shops closed their doors, women draped dark shawls from upper-story windows, and a small coffin, the word *Liberty* painted on it, hung on State Street. As many as fifty thousand citizens lined the streets to watch Burns, six feet tall, well dressed, and escorted by a martial entourage—the soldiers' bayonets fixed, their swords drawn—make his way down to the docks, where the United States cutter *Morris* placidly waited to ferry him to Virginia.

Burns aboard, the glum crowd grew quieter, its stiff Yankee back broken.

The following Sunday in church, Higginson denounced the whole sorry affair with the resolution of one ready to amputate a gangrenous limb. Invoking the names of the revolutionary heroes of Europe, Giuseppe Mazzini and Lajos Kossuth, in a sermon he called "Massachusetts in Mourning," he exhorted his congregation not to "conceal Fugitives and help them on, but show them and defend them. Let the Underground Railroad stop here! Say to the South that Worcester, though part of a Republic, shall be as free as if ruled by a Queen! Hear, O Richmond! and give ear, O Carolina! henceforth Worcester is Canada to the Slave!"

No longer did he believe the Fugitive Slave Act—or any of the laws supporting slavery—would be repealed. "I am glad of the discovery (no hasty thing, but gradually dawning upon me for ten years) that I live under a despotism," he said. "I am glad to be deceived no longer."

A revolution had begun.

"LIBERTY IS AGGRESSIVE," Emerson wrote in his journals. "It is only they who save others, that can themselves be saved," he added, referring to Higginson, transcendentalist in arms.

"I knew his ardor & courage," Richard Henry Dana remarked, "but I hardly expected a married man, a clergyman, and a man of education to lead the mob."

Thoreau also praised him as "the only Harvard Phi Beta Kappa,

Unitarian minister, and master of seven languages who has led a storming party against a federal bastion with a battering ram in his hands."

Whether or not the failure to save Burns was a national watershed, it was one for Higginson. For as a Higginson scholar commented, his action was the deliberate and strategic culmination of his years of preaching, lecturing, and working for a cause—and of his progressive disillusionment with antislavery politics. Now, as stalwart hero or fanatic or both, Higginson was a staple of New England newspapers, his sermons reprinted or quoted, especially his enraged requiem of the Burns affair. Had Emily Dickinson read those accounts—or the sermon? Doubtless both had been discussed at the Dickinson dining table. Did she know of him, too, from Amherst gossip? After all, it had been a local Baptist clergyman, the Reverend G. S. Stockwell, who, learning the whereabouts of Anthony Burns, had contacted Burns's owner, asking to purchase him with the intention of then letting him go.

And now there was Kansas, the next battleground, where Higginson would be known as the Reverend General and preach at what he called the makeshift Church Militant, a hodgepodge of packing crates covered in buffalo robes. "Ever since the rendition of Anthony Burns, in Boston, I have been looking for men," he said. "I have found them in Kanzas."

After the passage of the Kansas-Nebraska Act in 1854, proslavery men and what were termed border ruffians—violent proslavery mobs mainly from the slave state of Missouri—had armed themselves to fight the antislavery homesteaders sent to the territory by New England emigrant aid societies, a Bible in one hand, a rifle in the other, according to Stephen Douglas, the author of the bill. Douglas wasn't entirely wrong. In Worcester, for instance, Higginson's friend Eli Thayer (a man of more brag than action, Higginson later noted) might have established the New England Emigrant Aid Company to supply Kansas-bound homesteaders with food and clothes, advertising the territory as a good place to live, but Theodore Parker shipped them rifles and six-shooters in boxes labeled "Bibles."

With hundreds of nonregistered voters pouring into Kansas, the proslavery majority swiftly elected a proslavery legislature and passed the so-called bogus laws forbidding antislavery talk of any kind. (David Rice Atchison, proslavery senator from Missouri, encouraged Missourians in Kansas "to kill every God-damned abolitionist in the district.") Free staters countered by setting up their own legislature in Topeka. Violence between the two groups escalated, and in the spring of 1856, a gang of fuming proslavery men mobbed the Free-Soil town of Lawrence, burned the hotel, sacked the governor's house, and demolished two antislavery newspaper offices. Secretary of War Jefferson Davis dispatched federal troops to the territory, and the fifty-six-year-old abolitionist crusader John Brown rounded up four of his sons—he had sired twenty children—along with his son-in-law and two other men and rode out to Pottawatomie County, where they dragged five proslavery settlers from their cabins and hacked them to death with cavalry broadswords.

Appointed unofficial agent of the Massachusetts Kansas Aid Committee in the spring of 1856, Higginson had traveled west briefly to assist a band of what he called bona fide homesteaders (not like those ruffians from Missouri) and equip them with pistols, cartridges, and the cash raised in Boston. "These are times," said Henry Ward Beecher, "when self-defense is a religious duty." The National Kansas Committee then authorized Higginson to buy what he figured the homesteaders needed most: rifles, muskets, pistols (ninety-two of them), knives, and plenty of ammunition—fifty-nine hundred caps for the revolvers alone.

In September he returned to the Plains, hoping to help emigrants cross from Nebraska into Kansas. He found them cold, hungry, beleaguered; for breakfast they ate squash and green corn; for lunch and dinner they ate squash and green corn. In Nebraska City, Higginson purchased them cowhide boots, plaid flannel shirts, and warm blankets before setting off for Topeka, which he reached on September 24, riding with twenty-eight wagons and about 150 people. "Never before in my life," Higginson later remembered with decided pleasure, "had I been outside the world of human law." But he was often discouraged. Settlers herded their wagons in the opposite direction, back toward Iowa—some to avoid arrest, some to avoid starving, some with stolen horses—and in any event away from what many of them, in ignorance, had hoped would be the Promised Land.

Yet to Higginson the mission was clear, as he wrote—ghoulishly—of his Kansas trip in a series of letters to the *New York*

Tribune. "I almost hoped to hear that some . . . lives had been sacrificed," he said, "for it seems as if nothing but that would arouse the Eastern states to act. This seems a terrible thing to say, but these are terrible times."

But late in October, back at home, Higginson slumped into a depression. Although the situation in Kansas was improving, to his mind the clear-headed John Geary, appointed by Pierce as governor of the territory, managed to bring peace only by co-opting the settlers and ignoring the larger struggle against slavery. In addition, that fall, James Buchanan, sympathetic to slaveholders, was elected president of the United States. Then came the Dred Scott decision: the Supreme Court ruled in a stunning 7–2 vote that blacks had no rights of citizenship, that slaves were property, and that all congressional acts excluding slavery from the territories were unconstitutional. Racism was pervasive, north and south. In exasperation, Higginson cried, "Colored men are thrust illegally out of cars in New York, and to take their part is Fanaticism."

Though he continued to vote in national and local elections, he preferred to see the North secede from the South than to submit to the likes of a President Buchanan, and early in 1857 he spearheaded the Worcester Disunion Convention. "We the Undersigned invite the citizens of Massachusetts to meet in Convention at Worcester on Thursday January 15 to consider the practicality, probability and expediency of a separation between the free and slave states," the convention circular proclaimed. "It is written in the laws of nature the two antagonistic nations cannot remain together," Higginson exclaimed to his fretting mother. "Every year is dividing us more & more, & the sooner we see it, the better we can prepare for a perfect & dignified policy."

But in 1857, grain prices were falling, inventories of merchandise languished in warehouses, stocks were plummeting, railroads defaulting, and the land boom collapsing. This was the first and last Disunion Convention.

And that fact made Higginson all the more susceptible to John Brown—"Weird John Brown," as Melville would call him: a folk hero, eloquent and shrewd and already lionized far in excess of his accomplishments. Like many others, Higginson chose to ignore Brown's role in the Pottawatomie massacre, although he later admitted that he had heard of no one who disapproved it. It had the salubrious effect, Higginson coldly added, of restraining the bloody Missourians. For, as he remarked, John Brown "swallows a Missourian whole, and says grace after the meal."

HE DIDN'T REMEMBER SEEING BROWN in Kansas but was interested when Franklin Sanborn, a young schoolmaster in Concord whose students would include two of Henry James's brothers, the Alcott sisters, and Nathaniel Hawthorne's son, suggested they meet. Brown is the "best Disunion champion you can find," Sanborn declared, "and with his hundred men, when he is put where he can use them . . . will do more to split the Union than a list of 5000 names for your convention—good as that is," Sanborn hastily added.

Higginson consented to see Old Brown when the freedom fighter came to Massachusetts to solicit funds from the parlor radicals of Boston. Possessed like Melville's Ahab with one besetting idea, the elimination of slavery, grim Brown glowed with "that religious elevation," Higginson recalled, "which is itself a kind of refinement,— the quality one may see expressed in many a venerable Quaker face at yearly meeting." With Kansas no longer the battle's frontier—its newly appointed governor, Robert Walker, had allowed elections that fall, resulting in a victory for free staters—Brown would take his war elsewhere, with a plan: attack the federal arsenal in Harpers Ferry, Virginia, which in turn would lead to a rebellion of huge proportions, fugitive slaves and free blacks rushing to his side.

Frederick Douglass considered the scheme stupidly suicidal, but Higginson joined the clandestine group soon widely known as the Secret Six. It included Sanborn himself; a self-made financier, George Luther Stearns, who had struck a fortune in lead pipes; the antislavery philanthropist Gerrit Smith of upstate New York, on whose land the Brown family lived; the intransigent Theodore Parker, unfortunately ailing from congenital tuberculosis; and the Byronic Samuel Gridley Howe, founder of the Perkins Institute for the Blind, who in his younger days had fought the Turks in Greece. These men were to finance Brown's plan and ignite, so they initially hoped, an insurrection that would eradicate slavery once and for all.

Higginson resigned from the Free Church. Action mattered. Only action mattered.

Of the Secret Six, Higginson alone would remain loyal to Brown's plan, for good or ill, and was the one who never let fear for his own safety interfere with what he believed to be right. And though he had little cash to give Brown—he himself barely managed to make ends meet—he protested loudly any delay of the plan, correctly sensing ambivalence in two of the six. "I long to see you with adequate funds in your hands, set free from timid advisers, & able to act in your own way," he told Brown. "Did I follow only my own inclinations, without thinking of other ties, I should join you in person if I could not in purse." The tie to Mary—and to his mother—was too strong, particularly since Mary did not approve.

Still, he placed his faith in deeds, however violent or brazen. "The world has always more respect for those who are unwisely zealous," he noted, "than for those who are fastidiously inactive." As it began in blood, he said of slavery, "so to end." He was right, although premature.

For Brown the beginning of the end came on October 16, 1859, in Harpers Ferry when he and twenty-one others, including several of his sons, stormed the federal arsenal, seized a local rifle works, and then took about sixty local citizens as hostages. But rather than strike quickly and escape to the nearby hills, Brown and his men positioned themselves near the arsenal for thirty-six hours, a tremendous strategic blunder. A local militia quickly cut off any escape route, forcing Brown and his gang to retreat into a small firehouse in the armory yard. Brown sent men to negotiate; one was arrested, the others shot. Another of Brown's raiders, having run out of the armory, was killed, his dead body used for target practice by snipers circling the area. Lieutenant Colonel Robert E. Lee and a squadron of twelve marines offered Brown a chance to surrender unconditionally; the next day they bashed the door down. Seventeen people died, including two of Brown's sons, two slaves, a slave owner, a marine, and three residents of Harpers Ferry. Brown, who'd been stabbed with a decorative dress sword, was taken prisoner.

Summarily tried, found guilty, and sentenced to hang, Brown was unrepentant—and he refused to reveal the names of the Six. But the United States Senate issued warrants for the arrest of several of them. Frank Sanborn hid for a night in Concord before taking off for Canada. Gerrit Smith committed himself to an insane asylum in Utica, New York, after he methodically destroyed all incriminating documents. Higginson stood his ground. Along with Howe, the attorney Samuel E. Sewall, and Ralph Waldo Emerson, he signed a circular soliciting funds for Brown's defense and then traveled to the Adirondacks to escort Brown's wife to Boston. He planned to accompany her all the way to Virginia, where he hoped she would urge her jailed husband to escape. This was part of Higginson's plot to rescue Brown and his raiders, but Brown himself was unwilling, having judged himself more effective as martyr than fugitive.

The antiabolition press clamored for more than just Brown's head. Papers had been found in Brown's possession that pointed in the direction of the Secret Six, and with their attorney not sanguine about what they might face in court, Stearns and Howe also fled to Canada, and Sanborn, who had returned, went back. "Sanborn," Higginson asked in disgust, "is there no such thing as *honor* among confederates?" Then Howe published a letter distancing himself from Brown. Higginson was appalled. "Gerrit Smith's insanity— & your letter—," he told Howe, "are to me the all too sad results of the whole affair."

On December 2, 1859, the day of Brown's execution, bells tolled in Boston. "I believe John Brown to be the representative man of this century, as Washington was of the last," said George Stearns, who would soon testify before Congress. Emerson went further. Brown's death, he supposedly said, "will make the gallows as glorious as the cross." Not everyone agreed. "Nobody was ever more justly hanged," said Emerson's neighbor Nathaniel Hawthorne, ". . . if it were only in requital of his preposterous miscalculation of possibilities."

As for Thomas Wentworth Higginson, a Vigilance Committee in Worcester rallied round him, should he be seized by the government. But civil disobedience implied an acceptance of consequences, and he was ready for them. Even eager. "Under a government which imprisons any unjustly," Thoreau had written, "the true place for a just man is also in a prison."

Higginson did not run. He did not burn incriminating evidence. Instead he organized an attempt (unsuccessful) to spring Aaron Stevens and Albert Hazlett, two members of Brown's party, from the Charles Town, Virginia, jail. Aided by the former Kansas guerrilla James Montgomery, Higginson was to lead the attack, but he called it off when Montgomery learned that soldiers were swarming over Charles Town. Stevens and Hazlett were hung. Higginson stood fast. "John Brown is now beyond our reach," he declared, "but the oppressed for whom he died still live."

When the Senate investigated Harpers Ferry, summoning Howe

Thomas Wentworth Higginson, 1857. "He prided himself not a little on his good looks," said Angelina Grimké Weld.

and the others, Higginson was ready, proud to tell all he knew. But the government likely second-guessed his motives once again and decided that of all people, Higginson, capable of making his testimony a cause célèbre, was worth avoiding. He was never called.

THE MINISTERIAL CLOTH was never a comfortable fit, and Higginson had left the church without regret. For though he redeemed himself in his own eyes, he had wondered if there wasn't something unmanly about his calling. "What satirists upon religion are those parents who say of their pallid, puny, sedentary, lifeless, joyless little offspring, 'He is born for a minister'?"

His reference to himself as the sickly, half-dead child he once had been partly accounts for his commitment to forcible political action. It also accounts for his devotion to exercise, bodybuilding, and the nonministerial physical values he touted in such early essays for *The Atlantic Monthly* as "Saints and Their Bodies," "Physical Courage," "Letter to a Dyspeptic," "Barbarism and Civilization," and "Gymnastics." Behind each article lurked Higginson's need to prove himself as strong, fit, virile.

He also admired in fugitive slaves the quality he most desired in himself—physical valor—not because he romanticized them in a typically benighted way, though he was capable of that, but because he genuinely admired their staggering bravery. As he wrote in "Physical Courage," one of his earliest *Atlantic Monthly* essays: "These men and women, who have tested their courage in the lonely swamp against the alligator and the bloodhound, who have starved on prairies, hidden in holds, clung to locomotives, ridden hundreds of miles cramped in boxes, head downward, equally near to death if discovered or deserted,—and who have then, after enduring all this, gone voluntarily back to risk it over again, for the sake of wife or child,—what are we pale faces, that we should claim a rival capacity with theirs for heroic deeds?"

The outlet for Higginson's self-confident, radical prose had become *The Atlantic Monthly*. Initially conceived as an antislavery magazine in 1853, it wasn't truly launched until 1857, when its inaugural editor, James Russell Lowell, put a drawing of Shakespeare on the frontispiece and called *The Atlantic* a magazine of literature, art, and politics; literature would trump current events. Lowell canvassed the historian John Lothrop Motley as well as Nathaniel Hawthorne, Harriet Beecher Stowe, Dante Gabriel Rossetti, John Ruskin, Mrs. Gaskell, and Higginson as early contributors, and Oliver Wendell Holmes (who named the magazine) appeared in the first issue, along with Emerson, Whittier, Lowell himself, and Charles Eliot Norton. Higginson published his first article, "Saints and Their Bodies," about the weakness of civilized (white) men, in its fifth issue.

It was Lowell who reluctantly published Higginson's "Physical Courage" in 1858 and in 1859 his satiric tour de force "Ought Women to Learn the Alphabet?" Higginson tried to push Lowell deeper into politics. "Would you like an article on the Maroons of Jamaica and Surinam, suggested by the last Virginia affair," he queried Lowell in 1859, a week after Harpers Ferry. More hospitable to the antislavery movement than to female suffrage, Lowell acquiesced, and in all, under either Lowell or the next editor of *The Atlantic,* James Fields, Higginson published four essays on slave uprisings, including the tragic tale of Denmark Vesey's failed revolt in Charleston, South Carolina, which warned readers that slaves could and would rebel, and the story of the insurrectionary slave Nat

Turner, whom Higginson compared with John Brown: ordained by Providence, devoted to freedom, baptized in blood.

That Higginson respected these leaders without reservation is consistent with his increasing militancy and his conviction that slavery brutally injured the enslaved. And these pieces also demonstrate Higginson's conviction that despite all, neither the essential humanity of the slaves nor their craving for freedom had been destroyed. Many northerners doubted that the black man would fight for freedom; their stereotype was Stowe's reassuringly gentle Uncle Tom. Higginson laughed. "If it be the normal tendency of bondage to produce saints like Uncle Tom," he sarcastically noted, "let us all offer ourselves at auction immediately."

In 1860, after his unsuccessful attempt to spring two of Brown's cohorts from jail, Higginson started keeping a small journal he called his "Field Book" and on the flyleaf scribbled "Recalled to Life" (from Dickens's *Tale of Two Cities*). "I began this book on returning from an abortive expedition to Pa. in hopes of rescuing Hazlett & Stevens," he later explained; "I had thought it likely that my life might be sacrificed." The truth was more complicated. Documenting Higginson's return to and love of nature in the face of recent failure, the book served as his refuge. "In these unsettled days it is perilous for a writer to commit his self to a course of systematic thought," Higginson had commented as early as 1849, "& better to fall back upon nature."

Inspired by Thoreau's *A Week on the Concord and Merrimack Rivers,* a book he reread every year, Higginson had called on Thoreau in 1850, boarding the Concord train and arriving unannounced at the family pencil factory. There Thoreau sat, a bronzed, spare man, working. "On other days he surveys land," Higginson reported to his mother, "both mathematically & meditatively; lays out houselots in Haverhill & in the moon." If the man was a little dry, his scrupulous love of the natural world and of beauty, his self-containment, even his egotism, redeemed him. "He talks sententiously & originally; his manner is the most unvarying facsimile of Mr. Emerson's, but his thoughts are quite his own," said Higginson. "I find nobody who enjoys his book as I do (this I did not tell him)."

He subsequently followed in Thoreau's footsteps, tentatively publishing his own nature essays in *Putnam's Monthly* in 1853 and 1856. Higginson's "Going to Mount Katahdin" was literally inspired by

Thoreau's Maine climb, although in his account Higginson pretended he was a woman, perhaps to conceal his unmanly love of things natural. No longer—Kansas had changed all that.

Just before the publication of *Walden,* in 1854, Thoreau presented Higginson with a copy of the book, along with his "Slavery in Massachusetts," the lecture on the Burns affair that Higginson had admired. But Higginson had already read *Walden.* Fields had given him the proofs, so eager was he for Thoreau's latest. "Thoreau camps down by Walden Pond and shows us that absolutely nothing in Nature has ever yet been described—," Higginson unstintingly declared, "not a bird nor a berry of the woods, nor a drop of water, nor a spicula of ice, nor summer, nor winter, nor sun, nor star."

Nothing in nature had yet been described, and yet this was the task Higginson now set himself, Thoreau as his guide. Weary and demoralized with the ways of men, he fully indulged his love of nature, swearing he would at last earn his living in the way he had long dreamed. Down the back of the activist was a large reclusive streak.

SINCE CHILDHOOD, Higginson had roamed the outdoors, attentively observing flowers and trees and the varieties of birds. And since college, when he studied natural history and entomology and recorded whatever specimens he found during botanical expeditions (today housed at Harvard's Gray Herbarium), Higginson liked to bathe at dawn in the cold lake water near his home, or skim its surface in a small boat, or search for birds' nests while hiking through the thick woods on long, hot summer afternoons. Animals and plants, he said, were more human than most people, more kind. "The birds are as real and absorbing to me as human beings," he wrote in his journal. "I will trust this butterfly against all the dyspeptic theologians or atheists of the world." He almost sounds like Dickinson.

"I need ask for nothing else when I find myself coming round again into all that old happiness in nature," he confided to his diary, "wh my years of hard labor seemed to have stilled." Writing about nature for *The Atlantic,* he burst with pride when Thoreau praised his essay "Snow." "He was the only critic I should regard as formidable on such a subject." But fan letters about his essays were collecting at the post office. "I had more [mail] about 'April Days' than about anything I have written," he told Harriet Prescott late in 1861. "I am sure I have never come so near to Nature as during the last year," he continued, "and therefore never so truly and deeply lived; and sometimes I feel so Exalted in this nearness that it seems as if I never could sorrow any more."

Although these essays on nature distracted him from the public failures of Free-Soil, Thomas Sims, Anthony Burns, and Harpers Ferry, those were disappointments he still felt compelled to reverse. Yet after Fort Sumter was fired on, he turned down an offer to lead the Fourth Battalion of Infantry, partly for Mary's sake and partly because he was skeptical of Lincoln's commitment to antislavery. Changing his mind in the fall of 1861, he received permission from Governor Andrew to raise a division of troops—the news reached Dickinson's Amherst by means of the *Springfield Republican*—but when the War Department subsequently decided not to authorize another Massachusetts regiment, he figured he was destined to be the chronicler of nature after all. And with the prestigious *Atlantic* beckoning, the tall ex-preacher pitched himself headlong into literature at last.

He entertained few illusions. "I do not find that my facility grows so fast as my fastidiousness," he admitted. And yet he was determined to remake his life, to retire from the fray, to become the writer in repose he had long wanted, or thought he wanted, to be. "The more bent any man is upon action, the more profoundly he needs the calm lessons of Nature to preserve his equilibrium," he said, speaking of himself in the lovely essay "My Out-Door Study." "The radical himself needs nothing so much as fresh air. The world is called conservative; but it is far easier to impress a plausible thought on the complaisance of others than to retain an unfaltering faith in it for ourselves." So he kept a place for himself in the woods, regrets suppressed, notebook in hand, and wrote his lyrical paeans to nature—and art—in "Water-Lilies," "April Days," "My Out-Door Study," "Snow," "The Life of Birds."

> We talk of literature as if it were a mere matter of rule and measurement, a series of processes long since brought to mechanical perfection: but it would be less incorrect to say that it all lies in the future; tried by the outdoor standard, there is as yet no literature, but only glimpses and guideboards; no writer has yet succeeded in sustaining, through more than some single occasional sentence, that fresh and

perfect charm. If by the training of a lifetime one could succeed in producing one continuous page of perfect cadence, it would be a life well spent, and such a literary artist would fall short of Nature's standard in quantity only, not in quality.

Perfecting that cadence and polishing the surface of his prose, eventually he would deplete its strength with prolixity and pedantry. But that was much later, after the war. And even then he was capable of a rousing call to arms or the hushed mellow resonance that stirred his reader in Amherst, for whom literature, too, was not a matter of rule and measurement but of April days and snow and perhaps even insurrection, physical courage, rebellion.

His quiet eloquence heeded by the coruscating poet of inner life—his quiet eloquence touching her—she reached out.

"My size felt small—to me—," Emily Dickinson now told him; "I read your Chapters in the Atlantic—and experienced honor for you." She knew who this man was.

Part Two

During

SIX

Nature Is a Haunted House

I enclose my name — asking you, if you please, Sir — to tell me what is true?

Emily Dickinson stops my narrative. For as the woman in white, *savante* and reclusive, shorn of context, place, and reference, she seems to exist outside of time, untouched by it. And that's unnerving. No wonder we make up stories about her: about her lovers, if any, or how many or why she turned her back on ordinary life and when she knew of the enormity of her own gift (of course she knew) and how she combined words in ways we never imagined and wished we could.

[handwritten margin note: her "timelessness" somewhat oversold?]

And when we turn to her poems, we find that they, too, like her life, stop the narrative. Lyric outbursts, they tell no tales about who did what to whom in the habitable world. Rather, they whisper their wisdom from deep, very deep, within ourselves. And perhaps these poems plunge down so far — perhaps they unsettle us so — because Dickinson writes of experiences that we, who live in time, can barely name.

For like Hawthorne, whom she greatly admired, Dickinson spurned the overtly topical; he sneered at what he called the "damned mob of scribbling women" who wrote of social issues, not timeless truths of the human heart, and Dickinson, who shared his sense of literature's incomparable and universal mission, took literature even further from recognizable person, place, or event. "Is it Intellect that the Patriot means when he speaks of his 'Native Land'?" she would inquire of Higginson.

In a letter he remembered receiving in the summer of 1862, she explained warily what she was after: even if "you smile at me, I could not stop for that —," she told him. "My Business is Circumference." To Dickinson, circumference evidently meant both limits and the transgression of them: the soul selects its own society; the brain is wider than the sky. "St. Augustine described the nature of God as a circle whose center was everywhere and its circumference nowhere," Emerson wrote in his 1841 essay "Circles." "There is no outside, no inclosing wall, no circumference to us."

And thus Dickinson braved the unknown:

> *I saw no Way — The Heavens were stitched —*
> *I felt the Columns close —*
> *The Earth reversed her Hemispheres —*
> *I touched the Universe —*
> *And back it slid — and I alone —*
> *A speck upon a Ball —*
> *Went out upon Circumference —*
> *Beyond the Dip of Bell —*

The poetic "I" is alone in the universe, intrepid though a speck upon a ball. Yet she does see a way (poetry) that extends beyond time (the "Dip of Bell"). For nothing is categorical in Dickinson, whether delight or despair or even time and death. If contentment is ragged, loneliness intolerable, her task was "To learn the Transport by the Pain—."

More down-to-earth when writing her friends Elizabeth and Josiah Holland, she offered them, too, an explanation of her ambitions similar to the one she gave Higginson. "Perhaps you laugh at me! Perhaps the whole United States are laughing at me too!" she cried. "*I* can't stop for that! My business is to love. I found a bird, this morning, down—down—on a little bush at the foot of the garden, and wherefore sing, I said, since nobody *hears*? One sob in the throat, one flutter of bosom—'*My* business is to *sing*—and away she rose!' "

My business is circumference; my business is to love, my business is to sing beyond the dip of bell. By 1862 she had chosen her domain: "I dwell in Possibility— / A fairer House than Prose—." That year she wrote more than ever: approximately 227 poems, including some of her most frequently anthologized, such as " 'Hope' is the thing with feathers—," "I'm Nobody! Who are you?" and "I like to see it lap the Miles—." The sheer quantity of her output far exceeded that of the previous year, when she composed about 88, and a year later, in 1863, she produced even more, at least 295.

Her business had thus become poetry. "Each Life converges to some Centre—," as she wrote circa 1863,

> *Expressed — or still —*
> *Exists in every Human Nature*
> *A Goal —*
>
> *Embodied scarcely to itself — it may be —*
> *Too fair*
> *For Credibility's presumption*
> *To mar —*
>
> *Adored with caution — as a Brittle Heaven —*
> *To reach*
> *Were hopeless, as the Rainbow's Raiment*
> *To touch —*
>
> *Yet persevered toward — surer — for the Distance —*
> *How high —*
> *Unto the Saints' slow diligence —*
> *The Sky —*
>
> *Ungained — it may be — by Life's low Venture —*
> *But then —*
> *Eternity enable the endeavoring*
> *Again.*

When published posthumously, this poem was titled "The Goal," but Dickinson did not use titles; a title, as she obviously sensed, would deprive her first lines of their startling force. Take these: "He put the Belt around my life—," "The Soul has Bandaged moments—," "The Zeros taught Us—Phosphorus—," "Nature—sometimes sears a Sapling—" "Remorse—is Memory—awake—," "Doom is the House without the Door—," "I had been hungry, all the Years—," "One need not be a Chamber—to be Haunted—," and "Crisis is a Hair." One could go on and on.

And there was also, by this time, a range of tone and subject. There are poems of playful doubt—but doubt nonetheless—as in "I reason, Earth is short—." There is the verse of pure elation: "Inebriate of air—am I— / And Debauchee of Dew— / Reeling—thro' end-less summer days— / From inns of molten Blue—." Other poems describe the numbly indescribable, as in "After great pain, a formal feeling comes—," "There's a certain Slant of light," "It was not Death, for I stood up." (Often for Dickinson, death is the mother of beauty.) Still other poems possess a lyrical certainty, lovely and aus-tere, even pietistic after a crooked fashion, as in "God is a distant— stately Lover—." And "The Soul selects her own Society—" would become an equivocal anthem of independence: "I've known her— from an ample nation— / Choose One— / Then—close the Valves of her attention— / Like Stone—."

There is the poetry of raw emotional experience, demanding ruth-less gerunds to describe it: "I felt a Cleaving in my Mind—." Parts of speech, for her, unlock the world: "Breaking in bright Orthogra-phy / On my simple sleep— / Thundering it's Prospective— / Till I stir, and weep—." She sang of extremes and fused them while keeping them distinct—light and dark, frailty and force, silence and noise blazing in gold and quenching in purple. Hers is also a poetry of mood, of change and doubt and temporary rapprochement. Art is all. Is it enough? Possibly:

> *The Martyr Poets — did not tell —*
> *But wrought their Pang in syllable —*
> *That when their mortal name be numb —*
> *Their mortal fate — encourage Some —*

DICKINSON IS ALSO A POET OF LOSS. " 'We take no note of Time, but from its loss,' " Dickinson (like her father) quoted Edward Young's poem "Night Thoughts." And if hyperbolic, she was also deadly earnest; even at the young age of fifteen, she lived in retrospect. Time was fleeting, yes, and a robber too. "I often part with things I fancy I have loved,—sometimes to the grave, and sometimes to an oblivion rather bitterer that [than] death—," she would tell Sue on the occasion of Sue's visit to family in Michi-gan. "Thus my heart bleeds so frequently that I shant mind the hem-orrhage."

"Of nearness to her sundered Things / The Soul has special times—," she wrote circa 1862 in a poem of reversal that anticipates Gerard Manley Hopkins.

. . . .

Bright Knots of Apparitions
Salute us, with their wings —

As we — it were — that perished —
Themself — had just remained till we rejoin them —
And 'twas they, and not ourself
That mourned —

Again, a few years later: "A loss of something ever felt I— / The first
that I could recollect / Bereft I was—of what I knew not / Too
young that any should suspect." Loss, as subject, helped her outline
the painful but perhaps necessary distances that separate us, person
from person and person from nature. "A Light exists in Spring," she
writes, probably in 1865,

> *Not present on the Year*
> *At any other period —*
> *When March is scarcely here*
> *A Color stands abroad*
> *On Solitary Fields*
> *That Science cannot overtake*
> *But Human Nature feels.*
>
> *It waits opon the Lawn,*
> *It shows the furthest Tree*
> *Opon the furthest Slope you know*
> *It almost speaks to you.*
>
> *Then as Horizons step*
> *Or Noons report away*
> *Without the Formula of sound*
> *It passes and we stay —*
>
> *A quality of loss*
> *Affecting our Content*
> *As Trade had suddenly encroached*
> *Opon a Sacrament —*

Loss, true. But March is her season ("Dear March—Come in—"),
a time of transition and renewed hope. For even when the light of

spring passes and we stay, the poet produces a vision "That Science cannot overtake / But Human Nature feels." It almost speaks to you, as she does, without the derivative and predictable "Formula" of conventional verse—or narrative. And it happens in an instant; it's an experience much like that of reading her poems.

Higginson felt this, and she had told him as much when she enclosed this poem in her first letter, postmarked April 15, 1862:

> *The nearest Dream recedes — unrealized —*
> *The Heaven we chase —*
> *Like the June Bee — before the School Boy —*
> *Invites the Race —*
> *Stoops — to an easy Clover —*
> *Dips — evades — teazes — deploys —*
> *Then — to the Royal Clouds*
> *Lifts his light Pinnace —*
> *Heedless of the Boy —*
> *Staring — bewildered — at the mocking sky —*
> *Homesick for steadfast Honey —*
> *Ah — the Bee flies not*
> *That brews that rare variety!*

As the bee is to the boy, the distant "Heaven we chase" tempts, tantalizes, and finally evades us, and we, yearning for "steadfast Honey," never quite attain the things—that paradise of perfection—we most desire ("the nearest Dream recedes—unrealized—"). Yet this is not a poem of despair—far from it, for the poet does in fact "realize" a dream, encapsulating it in a language that calls, dips, and flees from us—true—but that leaves us less alone, less aggrieved, less bereft than we were.

Higginson considered this poem one of her most exquisite.

LOSS: WE KNOW THE QUEST is futile but nonetheless rake over Dickinson's life, hunting for the concrete experiences that might account for her obsession with it, particularly during her most prolific years. Had the birth of Sue and Austin's son Edward (Ned) in 1861 stolen Sue's attention; had the imminent departure of the Reverend Charles Wadsworth for a ministerial post in San Francisco scalded the poet's heart? Is that why she told Higginson, much later, that his friendship had rescued her? Or was she thinking solely of her poems when she approached him, grateful that he responded as he did?

Or was it the war? Certainly the world outside the Homestead was besieged by narrative: each day villagers listened at the telegraph office for the ominous clicks and scanned the newspapers for names of the wounded and dead. "Sorrow seems more general than it did and not the estate of a few persons, since the war began," Dickinson sadly observed. "They dropped like Flakes—," she wrote in a poem Higginson later called "The Battle-Field."

> *They dropped like Flakes —*
> *They dropped like stars —*
> *Like Petals from a Rose —*
> *When suddenly across the June*
> *A Wind with fingers — goes —*
>
> *They perished in the seamless Grass —*
> *No eye could find the place —*
> *But God can summon every face*
> *On his Repealless — List.*

Men disappear into a vast indifference of "seamless Grass"—wonderful image, all the more striking because grass typically reassures; here it cannot. It does not. Frazar Stearns, the twenty-one-year-old son of the Amherst College president, was killed at the Battle of New Bern in North Carolina in March 1862. He had murmured, "My God," Dickinson said, and asked for water twice before he died, "his big heart, shot away by a 'minie ball.'"

"Nobody here could look on Frazar—," she reported to her cousins, "not even his father." The casket, drenched in spring flowers, was uncharacteristically closed, and Austin was devastated, as Emily wrote Samuel Bowles, "says—his Brain keeps saying over 'Frazar is killed'—'Frazer is killed,' just as Father told it—to Him. Two or three words of lead—that dropped so deep, they keep weighing—."

Words of lead: "This is the Hour of Lead— / Remembered, if outlived, / As Freezing persons, recollect the Snow— / First— Chill—then Stupor—then the letting go—." Is the letting go resignation? A deathlike capitulation to despair? In either case, as

Hawthorne bleakly wrote in the July 1862 *Atlantic*, "there is no remoteness of life and thought, no hermetically sealed seclusion, except, possibly, that of the grave, into which the disturbing influences of this war do not penetrate." Yet Higginson was counseling the long view in his "Letter to a Young Contributor," published three months earlier and just as the awful Battle of Shiloh had left twenty thousand casualties in its wake. Remember literature, Higginson wrote: "General Wolfe, on the eve of battle, said of Gray's 'Elegy,' 'Gentlemen, I would rather have written that poem than have taken Quebec.'"

Little wonder that he snagged her attention. Of course she could not know, as he then did not, that his withdrawal from the field of action was not unqualified and never could be.

But neither was hers. "I'm sorry for the Dead—Today—," Dickinson writes in one of her poems, and to her cousins bleakly remarked, "If the anguish of others helped with one's own, now would be many medicines."

"I noticed that Robert Browning had made another poem," she continued, "and was astonished—till I remembered that I, myself, in my smaller way, sang off charnel steps. Every day life feels mightier, and what we have the power to be, more stupendous."

> It dont sound so terrible — quite — as it did —
> I run it over — "Dead", Brain — "Dead".
> Put it in Latin — left of my school —
> Seems it dont shriek so — under rule.

Perhaps under the rule of poetry, the shrieking will stop. "We— tell a Hurt—to cool it—," she writes in another poem, reminding us that she told Higginson she sang to relieve a palsy. Of what she did not say. Yet anguish and bereavement paradoxically toughened her ("An actual suffering strengthens / As Sinews do, with Age—"). As did poetry. In her second letter to him, she sent "Of all the Sounds despatched abroad," ostensibly about the wind but containing an implicit tribute to the poet, whose fingers comb the sky:

> Of all the Sounds despatched abroad,
> There's not a Charge to me
> Like that old measure in the Boughs —
> That phraseless Melody —

> The Wind does — working like a Hand,
> Whose fingers Comb the Sky —
> Then quiver down — with tufts of Tune —
> Permitted Gods, and me —

WHAT DID HIGGINSON really think when he *first* read Dickinson's poetry? "The bee himself did not evade the schoolboy more than she evaded me," he wrote, recalling his bafflement, "and even at this day I still stand somewhat bewildered, like the boy."

This one arrived in the summer of 1862:

> A Bird, came down the Walk —
> He did not know I saw —
> He bit an Angle Worm in halves
> And ate the fellow, raw,
>
> And then, he drank a Dew
> From a convenient Grass —
> And then hopped sidewise to the Wall
> To let a Beetle pass —
>
> He glanced with rapid eyes,
> That hurried all abroad —
> They looked like frightened Beads, I thought,
> He stirred his Velvet Head. —
>
> Like one in danger, Cautious,
> I offered him a Crumb,
> And he unrolled his feathers,
> And rowed him softer Home —
>
> Than Oars divide the Ocean,
> Too silver for a seam,
> Or Butterflies, off Banks of Noon,
> Leap, plashless as they swim.

The poem's surface charm would not be lost on Higginson: a bird, scrupulously observed by the speaker ("rapid eyes . . . like frightened Beads"), takes his morning meal. But there is nothing romantic here:

the bird eats the angleworm raw. And what about the off rhymes (abroad / Head, Crumb / Home)? The collective nouns ("Dew," "Grass") introduced by singular articles ("a Dew," "a . . . Grass")? The dashes? Certainly this looked unlike anything he had ever seen. And who is in danger, who is cautious, the speaker or the bird? Are the two of them forever separate, alien from each other, as the bird's flight at the end of the poem, so meticulously described, suggests?

More easily comprehended, not just by Higginson but by everyone, was Julia Ward Howe's "Battle Hymn of the Republic," published in *The Atlantic* in the winter of 1862 and sung by Union troops to the tune of "John Brown's Body." (Said Ralph Waldo Emerson of Howe, "I could well wish she were a native of Massachusetts. We have no such poetess in New England.") Howe delivered public poetry to an eager audience bred on the verse regularly printed in newspapers and magazines, set to music, or adapted by politicians to their ends. When the Hutchinson Family Singers included one of Whittier's abolitionist poems in their repertoire, set to the melody of Luther's hymn "Ein' feste Burg ist unser Gott," they lost their permit to give concerts because, it was alleged, the Union troops resented their radical politics. But Salmon Chase, secretary of the Treasury, read the poem during a Cabinet meeting, and Lincoln said it was just the thing he wanted the troops to hear. The ban was lifted.

Higginson's friend Whittier was well liked, particularly after the publication of his postwar masterwork, *Snow-Bound* (1866), which sold a whopping twenty thousand copies within months of its appearance. And Higginson's former teacher, the genteel Henry Longfellow, had already been selling poems by the bushel. His first volume, *Voices of the Night* (1839), went through three printings. Here are four lilting stanzas of iambic tetrameter from one of his most beloved works, "A Psalm of Life":

> *Tell me not, in mournful numbers,*
> *Life is but an empty dream! —*
> *For the soul is dead that slumbers,*
> *And things are not what they seem.*

> *Life is real! Life is earnest!*
> *And the grave is not its goal;*
> *Dust thou art, to dust returnest,*
> *Was not spoken of the soul.*

> *Not enjoyment, and not sorrow,*
> *Is our destined end or way;*
> *But to act, that each to-morrow*
> *Find us farther than to-day.*

> *Art is long, and Time is fleeting,*
> *And our hearts, though stout and brave,*
> *Still, like muffled drums, are beating*
> *Funeral marches to the grave.*

The fourth stanza deserves comparison with Dickinson's "I felt a Funeral, in my Brain":

> *I felt a Funeral, in my Brain,*
> *And Mourners to and fro*
> *Kept treading — treading — till it seemed*
> *That Sense was breaking through —*

> *And when they all were seated,*
> *A Service, like a Drum —*
> *Kept beating — beating — till I thought*
> *My mind was going numb —*

> *And then I heard them lift a Box*
> *And creak across my Soul*
> *With those same Boots of Lead, again,*
> *Then Space — began to toll,*

> *As all the Heavens were a Bell,*
> *And Being, but an Ear,*
> *And I, and Silence, some strange Race*
> *Wrecked, solitary, here —*

> *And then a Plank in Reason, broke,*
> *And I dropped down, and down —*
> *And hit a World, at every plunge —*
> *And Finished knowing — then —*

Dickinson's sensibility—never mind her use of form—could not be more different. While the virtuosic bard, a master of several languages and author of the famous *Evangeline* and the equally famous *Courtship of Miles Standish,* stretched himself across poetic genres (ballad, pastoral, folk epic), she did not care about genre or story or about pleasing the average audience. (Longfellow would please even the queen of England, who granted him a private audience.) Where Longfellow aims toward universal uplift, Dickinson stays alone, her tenor somber, her wit quick, her rhymes dissonant, and her images ("Being, but an Ear") typically raucous and strangely splendid. A temperate man who always looked to the horizon, Longfellow aimed to forge a national myth; Dickinson burrowed deep into the individual soul, tapping feelings often suppressed, unacknowledged, recondite, and fearsome.

Dickinson carefully read Browning and Emerson, enthusiasms she shared with Higginson (he adored Emerson's "Days"), and Higginson recommended Browning's *Pippa Passes.* Of women poets they both admired Elizabeth Barrett Browning and Emily Brontë, but Higginson was also promoting the verse of Harriet Spofford. (Spofford's short story "Circumstance," in which a woman calms a hideous forest beast by singing to it, was the only story, said Dickinson, she could not imagine having written herself.) Sue later remembered Spofford's "Pomegranate-Flowers" as a swatch of vivid color in those old sepia-seeming *Atlantic Monthly*s.

> *Now all the swamps are flushed with dower*
> *Of viscid pink, where, hour by hour,*
> *The bees swim amorous, and a shower*
> *Reddens the stream where cardinals tower.*
> *Far lost in fern of fragrant stir*
> *Her fancies roam, for unto her*
> *All Nature came in this one flower.*

Despite its lush decor, the tightly wound Spofford poem is phonically tedious. Dickinson is not. She pauses where we least expect a pause, and she bunches phrases in unusual lyric clusters. Aware of her metrical innovations—and no doubt of her sensuality, too—Higginson in his first letter to her perceptively asked Dickinson what she thought of Walt Whitman. She said she avoided him, having heard he was scandalous. (She also said she'd been so haunted by "Circumstance" she now avoided its author.)

Likely she fibbed. She had told Sue she wanted to read all of Spofford's work—and regarding Whitman, she did know that guardians of high culture like Charles Eliot Norton, a friend of Higginson's, said he'd be sorry to learn that a woman had read beyond the title page of *Leaves of Grass.* "It is no discredit to Walt Whitman that he wrote *Leaves of Grass,*" Higginson himself would say in 1870, "only that he did not burn it afterwards."

Higginson had met Whitman ten years earlier, having bumped into him at the Washington Street offices of the radical Boston publishers William Thayer and Charles Eldridge. Sitting on a counter, the poet had come to read proofs of the third edition of *Leaves of Grass,* and though handsome and burly, he did not look, as Higginson would remember, "to my gymnasium-trained eye, in really good condition for athletic work. I perhaps felt a little prejudiced against him from having read 'Leaves of Grass' on a voyage, in the early stages of seasickness,—a fact which doubtless increased for me the intrinsic unsavoriness of certain passages. But the personal impression made on me by the poet was not so much of manliness as of Boweriness, if I may coin the phrase."

Yet while Whitman stood apart from the pulling and hauling of a commercial America, of all his contemporaries he best bridged the gulf between public and private—and between action and contemplation—which Higginson hoped to do. Like Dickinson, he sang, and he sang of himself, but his inclusive vision celebrated and touched, or aimed to touch, the broad expanse of people and place and preoccupation that made America. Higginson would dismiss this as rank hypocrisy. "We all looked to him as precisely the man to organize a regiment on Broadway," he later said; but Whitman chose "the minor & safe function of a nurse." Higginson thus resented *Drum-Taps* even more than *Leaves of Grass*—war poems written by one who had never carried a drum.

Still, here he was, in 1862, asking Dickinson if she knew of Whitman's work. Whatever his limitations, and despite his queasiness, Higginson could spot and respond to talent.

THE DEATH OF FRAZAR STEARNS, Wadsworth's removal to California, now Samuel Bowles's departure for Europe and Dickinson's unresolved relation to a mysterious Master—these were the circumstances of her life in the spring 1862, when she first wrote to Wentworth Higginson. And here, in a sense, narrative begins. Higginson is narrative. His life proceeds by it; he believes in it. For him there are beginnings and middles, and when it comes to slavery, he is focused on ends.

Yet she wrote to this man of the world not as a bereft lover or plaintive friend, not as a woman besieged by a beast in the woods, not as sister-in-law or sister, not as anything but a poet, sweetly imploring him in her next letter, "Could you tell me how to grow — or is it unconveyed — like Melody — or Witchcraft?"

Flattered by her queries and evidently floored by her poems, he offered some criticism, then worried he had been a touch too harsh. Not at all, she reassured him. She had wanted the truth: "I had rather wince, than die," she explained. "Men do not call the surgeon, to commend — the Bone, but to set it, Sir, and fracture within, is more critical."

In return, though, she flirtatiously promised him obedience and gratitude, intending no doubt to flatter him further. She then sent him another four poems. She had taken none of his advice. "I thanked you for your justice —," she would tell him, "but could not drop the Bells whose jingling cooled my Tramp."

Still, his response to her had been insightful and tender enough to please her, and in a very early letter to him, she had included the poem "Your Riches, taught me, poverty —"

> *Your Riches, taught me, poverty —*
> *Myself a Millionaire —*
> *In little wealths — as Girls could boast —*
> *Till broad as Buenos Ayre —*
> *You drifted your Dominions —*
> *A different Peru —*
> *And I esteemed all poverty —*
> *For Life's Estate, with you —*
>
> *Of Mines, I little know, myself —*
> *But just the names — of Gems —*
> *The Colors of the commonest —*
> *And scarce of Diadems —*
> *So much — that did I meet the Queen —*
> *Her glory — I should know —*
> *But this — must be a different wealth —*
> *To miss it, beggars so —*

> *I'm sure 'tis India — all day —*
> *To those who look on you —*
> *Without a stint — without a blame —*
> *Might I — but be the Jew!*
> *I'm sure it is Golconda —*
> *Beyond my power to deem —*
> *To have a smile for mine, each day —*
> *How better, than a Gem!*
>
> *At least, it solaces to know —*
> *That there exists — a Gold —*
> *Although I prove it just in time*
> *It's distance — to behold!*
> *It's far — far Treasure to surmise —*
> *And estimate the Pearl —*
> *That slipped my simple fingers through —*
> *While just a Girl at school!*

She had already given Sue a version of this poem, which she may have composed in memory of Benjamin Newton; by presenting it to Higginson, she buttressed her request for his friendship: his riches, his worldliness, his fame, his gentility made him exotic, foreign, powerful. And the "Girl at school"? No droopy supplicant, drab and forlorn, she can create her own interlocutor just by imagining him, which she, in part, will do. But he will help.

She also enclosed "Success — is counted sweetest," a poem often reproduced today and that, in this context, spoke to Higginson's dilemma about joining the war effort, for Dickinson knew he was writing essays in Worcester, not shooting at Confederates in Virginia. He need not second-guess his decision not to enlist, she seems to suggest; victory lies in defeat, perhaps even in withdrawal.

> *Success — is counted sweetest*
> *By those who ne'er succeed —*
> *To Comprehend a Nectar —*
> *Requires sorest need —*
> *Not one of all the Purple Host*
> *Who took the Flag — today —*
> *Can tell the Definition — so clear — of Victory —*
> *As He — defeated — dying —*

> *On whose forbidden ear —*
> *The distant strains of Triumph*
> *Burst — agonized — and Clear!*

As for herself, Dickinson was content, or seemed to be, with the paradox of never succeeding. Defeat was specific victory, far better than success.

HE MUST HAVE ANSWERED right away, for their correspondence begins to sound like a conversation. "You say 'Beyond your knowledge,' " she gently chided him in the summer of 1862. "You would not jest with me, because I believe you—but Preceptor—you cannot mean it? All men say 'What' to me, but I thought it a fashion—."

He was unlike all other men. Nor did she believe she was "beyond his knowledge," or at least not completely. And if she was, then his confusion pleased her, his gallantry in the face of what he did not understand, his respect for it.

She teased him with coquettish condescending humor. "I think you called me 'Wayward,' " she reproved him. "Will you help me improve?" She sent him a poem, "Of Tribulation—these are They," with the note "I spelled ancle wrong" but did not correct the spelling.

Again she enclosed poems: along with "A Bird, came down the Walk—," she sent "Before I got my eye put out—," "I cannot dance upon my Toes—," and, it seems, a resplendent "Dare you see a Soul at the 'White Heat'?" Mostly about the act of creation, these poems told Higginson that even if she could not dance upon her toes—"No Man instructed me"—her poems, irreducible, are distinct, self-sufficient, and much more arresting than standard "Ballet knowledge," however graceful or well executed. The soul burns at the white heat. Dare he look? "Are these more orderly?" she asked, tongue in cheek.

> *Dare you see a Soul at the "White Heat"?*
> *Then crouch within the door —*
> *Red — is the Fire's common tint —*
> *But when the vivid Ore*

Has vanquished Flame's conditions —
It quivers from the Forge
Without a color, but the Light
Of unannointed Blaze —

Least Village, boasts it's Blacksmith —
Whose Anvil's even ring
Stands symbol for the finer Forge
That soundless tugs — within —

Refining these impatient Ores
With Hammer, and with Blaze
Until the designated Light
Repudiate the Forge —

Dickinson had thrown down the glove, daring him to watch her perform. But poetry was more than a performance, however incandescent; it was transcendent, white-hot, volcanic. "When I try to organize — my little Force explodes," she told him, "and leaves me bare and charred."

Higginson wanted to meet her, this small, wrenlike correspondent with the sherry-colored eyes and exploding force. Was he conscious of the sexual innuendo? Was she? In either case he would have to wait; he had left his study to drill troops at Camp Wool, near Worcester, and prepare them for battle. She at first said nothing and then responded, "You told me in one letter, you could not come to see me 'now,' and I made no answer, not because I had none, but did not think myself the price that you should come so far —."

She was definitely worth the price. About this both of them tacitly agreed, for they had begun the rare epistolary communication that seems, somehow, more real than bodily contact, with its averted eyes and fidgety hands, its blushes and shuffling feet. "A Letter always feels to me like immortality because it is the mind alone without corporeal friend," she would tell him. "Indebted in our talk to attitude and accent, there seems a spectral power in thought that walks alone." They were able to invent each other, at least in part, as well as speak to each other without bounds. For their link was words — their letters, her poetry, his essays. Words meant everything to her and a great deal to him.

The Evergreens.

"Of our greatest acts we are ignorant—," she told him at a later date, recollecting then what his attention, his courtesy, his comprehension offered her during their first months of correspondence. "You were not aware that you saved my Life."

Perhaps the same was true for him. In any case, he did save almost every letter.

IT WAS A CLEAN, well-lit bedroom in the southwest corner of the Homestead. To the west it faced the Evergreens, and from a set of windows to the south Dickinson could peer across rolling meadows, their color fading from yellow in fall to the glittering bone white of winter. And there was the light: "There's a certain Slant of light, / Winter Afternoons—." Inside, a Franklin stove relieved the chill; her small mahogany sleigh bed was covered with a warm counterpane. Beyond it sat the bureau, in which Lavinia, years later, would find her manuscripts. And slipped into the southwest corner was the small cherry desk (only seventeen and a half inches square) on which she conducted a vast correspondence and composed almost eighteen hundred poems. "Sweet hours have perished here, / This is a timid room—," she wrote. It was not.

No more than five feet tall, she covered her small shoulders with a paisley wool shawl of auburn and orange. Her housedress contained several pockets; supposedly she kept pencil and paper in one of them. In coming years, though, she dressed only in shades of alabaster.

It was the raw November of 1862, and the war dragged on, but the *Springfield Republican* trumpeted Higginson's essay, published in the December *Atlantic,* "an article upon wildflowers as only T. W. Higginson can write, since no other like him explores the sylvan haunts with the foot of a child, the eye of an artist and the heart of a woman."

The *Republican* was referring to Higginson's "Procession of the Flowers," another of his languid nature essays, which concludes, as his essays often do, with a tribute to the art he himself could not produce:

> If, in the simple process of writing, one could physically impart to this page the fragrance of this spray of azalea beside me, what a wonder would it seem!—and yet one ought to be able, by the mere use of language, to supply to every reader the total of that white, honeyed, trailing sweetness, which summer insects haunt and the Spirit of the Universe loves. The defect is not in language, but in men. There is no conceivable beauty of blossom so beautiful as words,—none so graceful, none so perfumed. It is possible to dream of combinations of syllables so delicious that all the dawning and decay of summer cannot rival their perfection, nor winter's stainless white and azure match their purity and their charm. To write them, were it possible, would be to take rank with Nature; nor is there any other method, even by music, for human art to reach so high.

Dickinson would agree with him in that trenchant, pithy way of hers: "Nature is a Haunted House—," she informed him, "but Art—a House that tries to be haunted."

BY THE TIME "Procession of the Flowers" appeared in *The Atlantic,* Higginson had already polished his rifle, packed his duffle, and dispatched a trunk to South Carolina, prompting Dickinson to remark dryly, "I trust the 'Procession of Flowers' was not a premonition—."

SEVEN

Intensely Human

L ike many others, Higginson had not expected a long war, but unlike them he was convinced that its outcome, whoever won, "must put the slavery question in a wholly new aspect." This was the theme of his article "The Ordeal by Battle," published in the July 1861 *Atlantic.* "I have never written any political article there before, because there never has been a time when I could write freely without being too radical," he informed his mother with a certain pride, "so I thought I would use the present opportunity."

Higginson insisted that the war be understood as a conflict between competing principles—slavery versus freedom. "Slavery is the root of the rebellion," he declared, "and so War is proving itself an Abolitionist, whoever else is." For slavery was a hateful institution, pure and simple. In his chilling essay "Nat Turner's Insurrection," he recounted not the insurrection as much as "the far greater horrors of its suppression," and documenting the hysteria that followed the rebellion—the maiming, the burning, the killing of the black population—Higginson chronicled the brutalities without heat, noting, nonetheless, that those summarily executed were not even identified by name. So where he could, he learned their names, recording them with telltale understatement, as in the case of one woman, called Lucy, about whom we know nothing except that "she was a woman, she was a slave, and she died." The sentence, clean and unassuming, clearly influenced Ralph Ellison's elegy for his character Tod Clifton in *Invisible Man,* published almost a century later. And according to the poet Susan Howe, one of Dickinson's most intuitive readers, Higginson's Nat Turner essay may well have inspired the poet's unforgettable "My Life had stood—a Loaded Gun—."

Strangely encouraged by the Union's rout at the First Battle of Bull Run, Higginson calculated that "but for this reverse we never should have the law of Congress emancipating slaves used in rebellion." He referred to the Confiscation Act, passed that summer; the Union's lawful seizure of property used for insurrection, including slaves, had effectively freed them. But this bolder antislavery policy, as Higginson called it, meant he could no longer stay at home writing essays. "No prominent anti-slavery man has yet taken a marked share in the war," he observed in the fall, "and . . . there are a great many in this and other States who would like to go if I do. I have made up my mind to take part in the affair, hoping to aid in settling it the quicker."

Perhaps inflating his own importance, Higginson never betrayed his position of the past several years: abolition or nothing. But until the summer of 1862, nothing happened: emancipation was not forthcoming; recruiting offices were temporarily closed. Then, with casualties mounting, the government called for fresh reserves, and Higginson obtained Governor Andrew's permission to assemble a regiment. As its captain he would finally play a part in the revolution he had called for, fought for, hoped for. All the currents of his life, he hastily scribbled in his journal, had converged. ("Each Life converges to some Centre—," as Dickinson would write.) He put down his pen. "What I could write I have written and should I never write anything more, no matter."

Settling Mary into a parlor and a bedroom in a boardinghouse nearby—he was stationed at Camp John E. Wool, just outside Worcester—he asked Margaret Channing, their niece, to stay with her the days he was gone, Tuesday to Saturday. On Sunday he came home, and on Monday he rejoined his regiment, the Fifty-first Massachusetts, at the barracks. He could not wait to get there and in future years remembered those first heady days "as if one had learned to swim in air, and were striking out for some new planet." The scratchy uniforms, the mindless drills, the marching, the rules—he relished all of it. A military novice, he read handbooks about formation, maneuvers, and the rules of conduct, but what counted most to him were the men; it was as if he was their father. At night he loved to hear them sing in the dark or watch when, bunks moved aside, as they square-danced, their long arms looping in huge arcs, half the men marking themselves as women by tying a handkerchief to their arm. "In each set," he told his mother "there are mingled grim & war-worn faces, looking as old as Waterloo, with merely childish faces from school, & there is such an absorption, such a passionate delight that one would say dancing must be a reminiscence of the felicity of Adam before Eve appeared, never to be seen in its full zest while a woman mingled in it."

Higginson so thoroughly reveled in the maleness of army life that today scholars consider him a "man of somewhat fluid gender identifications," especially since in later years he freely admitted to loving his friend from his seminary days, the charming William H. Hurlburt of Charleston, South Carolina, a true southerner, as Higginson had excitedly told his mother, "slender & graceful, dark with raven eyes & hair," a man charismatic and capacious, who translated South American and West Indian poets and was writing a book on Cuba. Hurlburt eventually moved to New York, where he wrote theater criticism for *The World;* during the Civil War, he was imprisoned as a spy by the Confederacy when he traveled south; and in later years he lived in London, where he was a lesser light in Wilde's circle. "All that my natural fastidiousness and cautious reserve kept from others I poured on him," Higginson would reminisce years later; "to say that I would have died for him was nothing."

Though they drifted apart, he had loved Hurlburt without shame. And he loved male flesh, muscular and lean, whether in the gymnasium or in the barracks, also without shame. Convention allowed him this physical appreciation of men—part erotic, part aesthetic—while at the same time forbidding as salacious the mere glimpse of a woman's ankle. And Higginson was a man of delicacy, which also means, particularly in his case, a repressed blue-blood reared to endure privation without complaint no matter how the limits of his sexual life—with whatever gender—saddened him.

Allowing himself the unself-conscious joy—part sensual, part paternal—of male company, he permitted himself the luxury of looking, watching, savoring, patronizing, and fantasizing, but he remained a spectator. As for women, he discussed them only in cerebral or political terms, though several of his female acquaintances whispered that the handsome Higginson had an eye for the ladies. He definitely liked their attention. Physically fit and slightly vain, he was no longer the gangling boy clutching a pocketful of topics for conversation.

He was, in other words, noticed. People knew of Wentworth Higginson. They recognized him (he was quite tall); they went to hear his speeches. They read his essays. They saw a limerick about him in the local papers:

There was a young curate of Worcester
Who could have a command if he'd choose ter,
  But he said each recruit
  Must be blacker than soot,
Or else he'd go preach where he used ter.

But it wasn't until early November, three months after he had entered the service, that Captain Higginson received a letter from Brigadier General Rufus Saxton, military governor of the United States Volunteers in the Department of the South. (The Department of the South officially included South Carolina, Georgia, and Florida but in practical fact meant just the Sea Islands, captured seven months after Fort Sumter fell.) Promoting Higginson to the rank of colonel, Saxton invited him to lead the First South Carolina Volunteers, the first federally authorized regiment of freed slaves, its mandate issued five full months before Governor Andrew of Massachusetts received permission to recruit the Massachusetts Fifty-fourth.

Though elated, Higginson wanted to talk to Saxton in person before accepting the offer, for he was now reluctant to leave the Massachusetts Fifty-first. So he boarded the railroad to New York and then a steamer to Beaufort, South Carolina, a pretty river town about twelve miles above Hilton Head. A beachhead for Union troops after Hilton Head had been seized in the fall of 1861, Beaufort had been abandoned by its wealthy white residents, who bolted before the thick-booted blue bellies (Union men) came to carve their names on the mahogany mantels. They'd left everything: the cutlery on the table, the linens in the cupboard, the crinolines, the pianos, the livestock—and the slaves. Noisy northerners soon thronged there, mostly abolitionists and teachers intending to educate these former slaves, as well as entrepreneurs and civic minions. "The government sent agents down here, private; so too private philanthropy has sent missionaries, and while the first see that the contrabands [former slaves] earn their bread, the last teach them the alphabet," Charles Francis Adams Jr. noted. "Between the two, I predict divers results, among which are numerous jobs for agents and missionaries, small comfort to the negroes, and heavy loss to the government."

But Rufus Saxton, an obdurate antislavery man, was different

African Americans, Beaufort, South Carolina, from the collection of Rufus Saxton.

from all those. And he was certainly unlike his flamboyant predecessor, Major General David Hunter, a man of impeccable if aggressive abolitionist leanings who on his own initiative had declared the Sea Islands slaves free. Preempting the president's Emancipation Proclamation, Hunter had irritated Lincoln and then everyone else by pulling former slaves, terrified, out of their cabins under the cover of darkness, tearing them from their families and bullying them into uniform. But his brash behavior had one salutary effect in the North: the issue of whether to arm black men was on the table.

Less choleric than Hunter, Rufus Saxton was a practical idealist. Short, compact, with deep-set eyes and curly black side whiskers—and just a year younger than Higginson—he had been a maverick abolitionist among his fellow West Point graduates and so committed to the cause that the strategic-minded Higginson at first worried that he might actually "overlook means in his zeal for ends" (as Hunter had). He did not. Directed to take possession of all plantations previously occupied by rebels and to feed, employ, and govern their inhabitants, whom the army had left without shelter, clothing, provisions, or the wherewithal to buy any, he had charge of the ten thousand or more freed slaves from the Sea Island plantations, knowing that his was an anomalous position, his function straddling that of civilian and soldier, despot and benefactor.

Though Saxton was to report to Hunter, Secretary of War Edwin Stanton had also granted him authority to recruit and train volunteers of African descent as the First South Carolina Volunteers. (According to the author James Branch Cabell, a Virginian who wrote scathingly of the enterprise, the former slaves unshackled themselves "from the dull and tedious drudgery of farm work in favor of a year or two's military service under the more noble excitements of gunfire.") But adamantly believing, like Higginson, that the slaves would fight for their freedom—Higginson's theme in the Denmark Vesey and Nat Turner essays—Saxton felt it would be hypocritical not to allow them to do just that. This was a minority position among the ultras, as radical abolitionists were censoriously called.

Higginson's first conversation with Saxton assured him that he was not being snookered into "a mere plantation-guard or a day-school in uniform." The First South Carolina was the real thing. For with conviction, stubbornness, and unprejudiced empathy, Saxton had won the respect of the African Americans, many of whom Hunter had discouraged, demoralized, and abused, and Higginson soon reported with satisfaction that Saxton could effortlessly silence those pious northerners who pestered him with their elaborate, often insulting inquiries about the freed blacks (whatever were they *like*?) with a terse reply: "Intensely human."

It was settled. "I had been an abolitionist too long, and had known and loved John Brown too well," Higginson later said, "not to feel a thrill of joy at last on finding myself in the position where he only wished to be." It was also vindication—and action—at last.

AT NIGHT THE TANGY SMELL of roasting peanuts wafted through Camp Saxton, where Higginson and his men were billeted, four miles below Beaufort on the sumptuous grounds of the defunct Smith Plantation. The place was beautiful, Higginson thought, overgrown, luxurious, and fragrant with oleander and myrtle. Long tendrils of Spanish moss dropped from the branches of the mammoth live oaks like a misty curtain; roses bloomed in December, gangling palmettos rustled in the damp breeze. Hares and wild pigeon and quail scrambled across the long avenues leading to the ruined estate, on whose grounds 250 army tents shone pearly in the moonlight. Only the pigs running wild in the camp annoyed him.

Emerging from his tent, Higginson would stroll among his six hundred enlisted men without seeing a single white face, hearing only wild curlews, he told Mary, wailing through the night "like vexed ghosts of departed slave-lords." There, standing in the middle of a plantation among freed slaves, hundreds of them, the eagle buttons on his new blue uniform tight and shiny, he prepared to lead their regiment and fight with them for freedom, their freedom: this was a dream come true.

"The first man who organizes & commands a successful black regiment will perform the most important service in the history of the War," he confided to his journal. But he would need to demonstrate to a skeptical North—and a contemptuous South—that a black regiment was as good, as brave, as disciplined, and as dogged as any white one.

He did not lack certain comforts. At mealtime his adjutant, a young bookkeeper from Boston, spread newspapers over the table before serving plates of hominy, hot sweet potato, and oysters or fish. The pork was tasty, and so were those griddle cakes made from corn and pumpkin. His tent contained a bed, two chairs, two pails of water, and a small camp stove. He had a table for writing, on which he placed Hugo's *Les Misérables,* and he carried a small book of Shakespeare's sonnets wherever he went. Wooden planks covered the floor of the tent to prevent dampness. At Christmas he hung a wreath of oranges by the door, and when nights grew chilly, he snuggled beneath the prickly buffalo robe his mother had bought him. He wrote to Fields requesting books. He bathed in the nearby river. He cantered by horseback over roads made of oyster shells, one path passing by an enormous oak that not long before had doubled as a whipping post, the marks of the lash still visible.

The men of the First South, as the regiment was known, were former slaves, mainly from the rice plantations of the Sea Islands. There they had toiled long hours without adequate nourishment, medical care, education, and of course remuneration; here, at Camp Saxton, they were eager, they were free, and Higginson would be damned if they weren't correctly trained; it was the least he could do. Waiting for his regiment to fill (a minimum of 830 was needed for assignments), he relentlessly drilled his young "barbarians," as he affectionately called the black soldiers, while Saxton rallied the troops, telling them about Higginson's courage during the "old dark days" and how he had tried to break Anthony Burns out of jail. You could still see the saber cut on his face.

No black soldier in Higginson's regiment would be treated unjustly, Saxton assured them.

Higginson was pleased. "It needs but a few days to show the absurdity of doubting the equal military availability of these people, as compared with whites," he wrote in his journal.

> There is quite as much average comprehension of the need of the thing, as much courage I doubt not, as much previous knowledge of the gun, & there is a readiness of ear & of imitation which for purposes of drill counterbalances any defect of mental training. They have little to sacrifice, are better fed, housed & clothed than ever before & have few vices such as lead to insubordination. At the same time I think, as I always did, that the sort of paradisiacal innocence, attributed to them by their first teachers were founded on very imperfect observation. They are not truthful, honest or chaste. Why should they be? but they are simple, docile and affectionate. The same men who have stood a fire in open field with perfect coolness, have blubbered in the most irresistibly ludicrous manner on being transferred from one company in the regiment to another.

Though paternalistic, Higginson was more perceptive, effective, and humane than most of his peers, even the self-proclaimed enlightened ones, who still suffered from "colorphobia" (Higginson's word): Emerson, he recalled, had squirmed when Frederick Douglass was proposed for the Town and Country Club. Few white northerners had ever interacted with blacks, free or enslaved, and very few were impatient for the chance. Fewer still were willing to put their lives on the front line for a black regiment. "He will be a marked man," commented Whittier on hearing of Higginson's commission; the Confederacy had vowed to hang all white officers of black troops on capture. But the abolitionist preacher Sojourner Truth, a former slave and a women's rights crusader, declared Higginson appointed by God.

A Boston Brahmin, Higginson was also a progressive whose sense of class was not fixed. That was true of his sense of race as well. He investigated prevailing stereotypes, even his own; this was part of his

Town House, Beaufort, South Carolina, 1862.

task as he defined it. He forbade blacks to be called "niggers" and registered surprise if they referred to themselves that way. He observed how hard his men worked. "How absurd is the impression about these Southern blacks, growing out of a state of slavery, that they are sluggish or inefficient in labor," he noted.

"At first glance, in a black regiment," he would reminisce, "the men usually looked to a newly arrived officer just alike, but it proved after a little experience that they varied as much in face as any soldiers. It was the same as to character." He tried to learn as much about them as he could: the Wilson brothers told him about their grandmother, the mother of twenty-two, and how she organized a second escape from her plantation after her first one failed; Corporal Simon Crier said that he was going to Liberia after the war because he knew Johnny Reb would never be civilized in his lifetime. Another corporal, Robert Sutton, a meditative, intelligent, and loquacious man with an iron memory, spun out ingenious theories and asked questions well into the night until Higginson, exhausted, dropped off to sleep. "His comprehension of the whole problem of slavery was more thorough and far-reaching than that of any Abolitionist, so far as its social and military aspects went," Higginson reflected. "In that direction I could teach him nothing, and he taught me much."

"It is the fashion with philanthropists who come down here to be impressed with the degradation & stupidity of these people," he observed with contempt. "I often have to tell them that I have not a stupid man in the regiment. Stupid as a man may seem if you try to make him take a thing in your way, he is commonly sharp enough if you will have patience to take him in his own." Believing that discipline endowed them with the self-respect denied them as slaves, he worked hard, he said, "to impress on them that they do not obey officers because they are white, but because they are officers." And as an officer himself he was sensitive to his position. When a new squad of recruits arrived—lame, frightened, wrapped in rags—and he had to assign them various captains, he said he felt like a slave driver, and he hated it. But to Charlotte Forten, a young black woman from the North come to teach the freed slaves, Higginson was an ideal officer whom his soldiers liked and admired. "And he evidently feels towards them all as if they were his children," she said, intending a compliment.

He also tried to figure out why they had not rebelled: "it always seemed to me that, had I been a slave, my life would have been one long scheme of insurrection." Answering his own question, he marveled at his men's patient religious temperament—and their sense of futility: "What was the use of insurrection, where everything was against them?" Diligently he logged their remarks in his journal and devotedly collected their songs, scribbling verses in the darkness as the men sang. And when he wrote publicly of them, which he did in letters to newspapers, politicians, and *The Atlantic Monthly,* he praised them in terms that preserved their dignity and yet did not offend his bigoted readers; he would overcome prejudice, in other words, in increments. In a sense he would in later years use the same strategy of caution when publishing the poems of Emily Dickinson.

On New Year's, 1863, Saxton planned a great celebration of the Emancipation Proclamation, which was to take effect that day. In a grove of live oaks near the camp, black and white congregated together among the wide trees, people arriving on foot, in carriages, on horse- or muleback: cavalry officers, black women wearing brightly colored head scarves, teachers, superintendents, and the band of the Eighth Maine. Higginson, standing on a wooden platform with the other designated speakers, introduced William Henry Brisbane, a

South Carolinian planter who had earlier freed his slaves, and Brisbane read from the Proclamation: "On the first day of January, in the year of our Lord one thousand eight hundred and sixty-three, all persons held as slaves within any State or designated part of a State, the people whereof shall then be in rebellion against the United States, shall be then, thenceforward, and forever free." The crowd roared, men tossed their hats into the air, women hugged one another. "This spontaneous outburst of love and loyalty to a country that has heretofore so terribly wronged these blacks," noted the regiment's physician, Seth Rogers, "was the birth of a new hope."

The Reverend Mansfield French presented Higginson with a silk regimental flag mounted on an ebony and silver staff and embroidered with the motto "The Year of Jubilee has come!" Unbidden, an elderly man and two women, former slaves, burst into song, belting out "My Country 'Tis of Thee." Higginson stood silent, eyes damp. "It made all other words cheap," he wrote that evening; "it seemed the choked voice of a race, at last unloosed."

After the ceremony the men and the officers, black and white, well-wishers and uncertain onlookers, clustered around huge square tables for a feast of ten oxen roasted whole over huge pits and, when crisp, cut with axes. Not as good as at home, recollected a young black woman, but Higginson, who loved it all—the food, the speeches, the salty-sweet taste of freedom under the trailing moss—refused to dine with other white officers and the dignitaries, preferring instead to sit with his own men. He had come south as a believer, and now all around him was something to believe in.

But clad in the bright red trousers he loathed—he could not wait to get his troops into standard army issue—when they marched into Beaufort, muskets bright, boots blackened, they were heckled from the side of the road, and there were fistfights along with the catcalls and slurs. Yet Higginson had heard praise from formerly disdainful white officers, who admitted that no other regiment in the Department outshone his.

Later that month came his first battle. General Hunter, back in Hilton Head as commander of the Department of the South, wanted to enlist fifty thousand more blacks; that was his directive, not the winning of territory or the blocking of lines, so Higginson was ordered to scout the area for recruits among the abandoned forts and plantations. For bait, Higginson carried the regimental flag and copies of the Emancipation Proclamation.

Aboard a small gunboat, the *Ben de Ford,* and flanked by two other vessels, Higginson and his men headed south to a Union post in Fernandina, Florida. From there they would ascend the narrow St. Mary's River. But when he and a detachment of his men scrambled ashore at midnight near Township Landing, the air thick with the sticky scent of pine, they walked into the maw of a rebel cavalry unit. "A man fell at my elbow," Higginson later wrote. "I felt it no more than if a tree had fallen,—I was so busy watching my own men and the enemy, and planning what to do next." Corporal Sutton was wounded, and Higginson himself had a close call when a Confederate officer took direct aim at him—but was shot by three of Higginson's men before he could pull the trigger.

The breathlessness of the fight, the courage of his soldiers, the smell of victory: the small skirmish became, to him, a significant event. "Nobody knows anything about these men who has not seen them in battle," Higginson informed General Saxton. "I find that I myself knew nothing. There is a fiery energy about them beyond anything of which I have ever read."

He and his men continued their reconnoiter up the St. Mary's to a landing near Alberti's Mill in Georgia, the plantation where Corporal Robert Sutton had been a slave. Finding only Mrs. Alberti on the premises, Higginson introduced himself and then presented Corporal Sutton, saying he believed the two of them had already been acquainted. The woman's smile froze. "Ah," she replied, measuring her words. "We called him Bob."

Soldier and slave: "You may make a soldier out of a slave, very readily," Higginson commented, "but you can no more make a slave out of a soldier than you can replace a bird in the egg." Sutton walked Higginson over to the slave prison, a small outbuilding equipped with a huge rusty chain for tying down its victims. The stocks came in two sizes, one with smaller holes for women and children. Higginson conveyed three sets of these stocks, as well as shackles, chains, and keys, back to his supply ship, "good illustrations," he informed General Saxton, "of the infernal barbarism against which we contend."

Higginson banned looting, aware nonetheless how hard it was for the men to resist the luxuries purchased for their former masters by their own sweat. But since cotton, foodstuff, and animals were considered supplies of war, not booty, they confiscated provisions— resin, forty bushels of rice, cordage, and sheep—and loaded them onto the boats. Gun crews then stood ready. Higginson had learned that Confederates lay in wait above the river, and he indeed heard a wave of shouting sweep down from Reed's Bluff just after he and his men had assumed they were out of danger. Bullets slammed into the side of the boat. The ship's captain fell dead, struck in the head by a minié ball. Higginson dashed up to the gun deck from below and, dragging the captain's body out of the line of fire, ordered his men to the hold, where the soldiers tried to shoot through the portholes while they sailed into safe waters.

It had been a small mission, a little affair, which Higginson later admitted he inflated because it was the regiment's first battle. But it had offered him and his men a chance to test each other: "our abstract surmises were changed into positive knowledge. . . . No officer in this regiment now doubts that the key to the successful prosecution of this war lies in the unlimited employment of black troops," he reported to General Saxton. "Their superiority lies simply in the fact that they know the country, while white troops do not, and, moreover, that they have peculiarities of temperament, position, and motive which belong to them alone. Instead of leaving their homes and families to fight, they are fighting for their homes and families, and they show the resolution and the sagacity which a personal purpose gives."

Recounting Higginson's report with condescending disbelief, the *Springfield Republican* conceded that it might silence the enemies of the Negro "who are bent on making him incapable of anything better than labor under a lash." Stuffier, *The New York Times* scolded Higginson for putting his case so strongly "and in rather exalted language, as well as in such a way as to convince the public that the negroes will fight." He was taking on Northern prejudice as well as rebel fire.

Two more expeditions would follow, each more unsuccessful, more demanding, more deadly than the last—except in the symbolic terms dear to Colonel Higginson.

HIGGINSON AND HIS MEN went south to Jacksonville. Union troops had abandoned the city the year before, when Hunter had decided he could not spare the five thousand necessary to hold it, but he now decided that the First South Carolina Regiment, a brigade of less than a thousand men, should use the city as a recruiting station for black soldiers. With Jacksonville secure and more soldiers in the army, the Union might take the entire state of Florida.

Sailing up the glassy St. John's River in early March, Higginson's troops rounded the point below the city in shining daylight. All was calm. The peach trees were in full bloom, and his men, listening in the silent heat, heard no shells or rifle shots from nearby Confederates, whom they had apparently surprised. Evidently the rebels would not bother to defend the town vigorously. A large number of the city's three thousand residents had fled some time ago, and only five hundred, mostly poor, remained. So Jacksonville was again a federal post.

Higginson's men were joined by the Second South Carolina Colored Volunteers, a black regiment under the leadership of Colonel James Montgomery. Formerly known in Kansas as a Jayhawker for his quick-striking raids against Missouri slave owners, and the man with whom Higginson had conspired to free John Brown's cohorts, Montgomery was tall, thin, and brutal, with slightly stooped shoulders and a hard-bitten face. As one commentator observed, "Higginson, the romantic, had raised money to send Sharps rifles to Kansas in the fifties. Montgomery, the realist, had used them."

At the end of March, two more infantry regiments arrived, the Sixth Connecticut and the Eighth Maine, both white. "It was the first time in the war (so far as I know)," observed Higginson, "that white and black soldiers had served together on regular duty." He tried to mitigate friction between them by using his own troops for expeditions upstream while keeping the white troops in town on patrol: separate but equal. Yet when he stationed men outside town to reinforce the perimeter and contain rebel shelling, four black and six white companies worked side by side without demonstrable incident.

Then came the peremptory order to evacuate the city and return to Beaufort. It was a complete and demoralizing shock. Even newspaper reports of the evacuation expressed bewilderment. "A more fatal order for the place, the interests of the people, and the Government, could not have been made," said one. "Every body was taken by surprise, and every body was exasperated, save perhaps a few who feared the negro soldiers would achieve a reputation."

Worse, one of the regiments—a white one—set fire to the beautiful old city before leaving it. "Jacksonville is in ruins," lamented the *New York Tribune*. A south wind blew the flames through mansions, houses, small cottages, churches, warehouses. Deep-rooted oaks, orange groves, tall sycamores—all were scorched and charred. Soldiers, white and black, hollered in approval. Close to tears, Higginson groped his way in the thick blue smoke to pluck one last rosebud from the sooty garden of his former headquarters.

MEN LIKE THE BLACK ACTIVIST Lewis Hayden, who, with Higginson, had tried to batter down the Boston Court House door, and the white activist George Stearns, one of the Secret Six, were recruiting free blacks for the Fifty-fourth Regiment of Massachusetts Volunteer Infantry. They labored night and day, as did Gerrit Smith, another member of the Secret Six, and the eloquent Frederick Douglass, who called "Men of Color, to Arms." Douglass's two sons, Charles and Lewis, enlisted. "In a struggle for freedom the race most directly interested in the achievement of freedom should be permitted to take a hand," said Garth Wilkinson (Wilky) James, ill-fated brother of Henry, Alice, and William—and at seventeen himself a soldier in the Fifty-fourth. The time for a black regiment had finally come in Massachusetts.

Governor Andrew appointed two young abolitionists to head the "Bostons," as the Fifty-fourth was nicknamed. Robert Gould Shaw, the fair-haired son of wealthy philanthropic Yankees and formerly a captain in the Second Massachusetts Infantry, was a veteran of Cedar Mountain and a survivor of Antietam. (That Shaw was also considered handsome—"lean as / a compass-needle," Robert Lowell later wrote—never hurt him or his propaganda value, either in life or in death, as Higginson would shrewdly observe.) Second in command was the Philadelphia Quaker Norwood Penrose Hallowell. Hallowell would eventually lead the Massachusetts Fifty-fifth, the regiment formed after recruitment efforts overflowed the ranks of the Fifty-fourth.

The Fifty-fourth was stationed at Camp Meigs in Readville, Massachusetts, a short distance southwest of Boston, until May 18, 1863, when the men received orders to report to General Hunter in Hilton Head. On May 28, as they paraded through Boston, one thousand men strong, three thousand men and women gathered to hail the troops. It was a day quite different from the abject one in 1854 when Anthony Burns was marched to the wharves under federal guard. And though copperheads (as Southern sympathizers were called) threw stones and scuffled with the police near Battery Wharf, Governor Andrew, William Lloyd Garrison, Wendell Phillips, and Frederick Douglass reviewed the columns of young men along with Shaw's abolitionist parents and his recent bride, who waved from the second-floor balcony of the Sturgis house on Beacon Street. Later it was said that Shaw, riding at the front of the regiment, looked up, saw them, and kissed his sword with a flourish. It was at that moment his sister Ellen knew she would never see him again.

Since the numbers of white enlistments had dropped, black regiments had become more acceptable to their detractors—and necessary to the Northern war effort. And though the much-hated federal draft, instituted in March of 1863, had set off murderous, racist riots the following summer, particularly in New York City—let black men fight for their own freedom, draftees viciously protested—the black regiments were earning respect. The capture of Port Hudson, Louisiana, by troops that included the First and Third Louisiana Native Guards and the First Louisiana Engineers inspired a backhanded compliment from one Union officer: "Our negro troops are splendid," said he. "Who would not be a Niggadier General?"

All this meant Higginson could relax a little. "Any disaster or failure on our part would now do little harm," he wrote to his mother, "whereas at first it might have defeated the whole thing." Asked to make a speech before a (white) Pennsylvania regiment during the Fourth of July celebration, he said with deadpan earnestness that the First South bore this regiment no ill will, for it liked white people—as long as they behaved.

In the spring of 1863, after the Fifty-fourth arrived in South Carolina, Colonel Montgomery ordered Shaw and his men to sail to the mouth of the Altamaha River and shell plantations along the way, regardless of who might still be living there, and once they arrived in the undefended town of Darien, Georgia, he insisted that Shaw's men load all portable goods onto their boats and burn the place to the ground. Montgomery wanted to make southerners feel "that this was a real war," as he said, "and that they were to be swept away by the hand of God, like the Jews of old." He put a match to the last buildings himself. "It was as abominable a job as I ever had a share in," said Shaw.

To Higginson, Montgomery's scorched-earth policy undermined the reputation of the black troops, undoing all the good he had done, and pleased to learn that Colonel Shaw, after Darien, was as disillusioned with Montgomery as he, Higginson reminded Charles Sumner, senator from Massachusetts, that "the colored troops as such are not responsible for the brigand habits of Montgomery. This indiscriminate burning & pillaging is savage warfare in itself— demoralizes the soldiers—& must produce reaction against arming the negroes."

After Shaw formally protested Montgomery's tactics, the Fifty-fourth was removed from Montgomery's command, and General Hunter, who supported Montgomery, was temporarily relieved of his position. Furious, Hunter regarded this as public censure, but President Lincoln, who liked Hunter, suavely assured him otherwise.

Montgomery persisted. Hating slavery but caring little for the slave, as Higginson said, Montgomery had asked a black man in his regiment whom he presumed a deserter if he had anything to say in his own defense. The soldier answered "Nothing," and Montgomery, with nonchalance, replied, "Then you die at half past nine." "I accordingly shot and buried him at that hour," he told Brigadier General George Crockett Strong. When Strong reported the incident to General Benjamin Butler, he concluded, "We need cool things of that kind in this climate."

More than thirty years later, Higginson was still seething. "Montgomery had two soldiers shot for deserting after their payment had been cut down—without court martial," he recalled. "If he had done it to white soldiers, he would have been court martialled himself."

If Montgomery was a hooligan, the army was filled with them, pro- and antislavery men alike. "Do not think this rapid organization of colored regiments is to be an unmixed good to the negroes," Higginson confided to Charles Norton in the early summer of 1863. "There will be much & terrible tyranny under military forms, for it is no easy thing to make their officers deal justly by them."

Take the example of Francis Jackson Merriam, grandson of the famous Boston abolitionist Francis Jackson and formerly one of John Brown's Harpers Ferry raiders, who fled before he was arrested. A hotheaded abolitionist with no regard for the rights of others, he bent the ear of General Hunter, "as fanatics sometimes did," Higginson noted with disgust. Merriam requisitioned several of Higginson's non-commissioned officers, including Corporal Sutton, for a small scouting party along the coast of Georgia. Sutton and the men knew the local terrain well, which Merriam did not; no matter.

Colonel Thomas
Wentworth Higginson,
First South Carolina
Volunteers, 38 years
old, 1862.

He ordered them to row to rebel-held territory on St. Simon's Island. They did, against their better judgment, and they were almost killed. But the next night, when Merriam barked his orders, they recoiled. Not to be countermanded by black men, Merriam and another officer promptly shot two of them "without mercy," Higginson acidly noted, "lest they should interfere with the elevation of the race!"

So much for antislavery men. "The worst acts of tyranny I have known in colored regiments proceeded from those who came there as abolitionists," Higginson declared.

Merriam wasn't finished. He blamed Sutton for the incident— Sutton had refused to seize the guns of the miscreants—and insisted Sutton be court-martialed. Sutton was later cleared of all charges, and Merriam was promoted to captain in the Third South Carolina Colored Volunteers.

HUNTER'S REPLACEMENT WAS Brigadier General Quincy Adams Gillmore, the army engineer whose bombardment of the

Georgia coast had caused the surrender of Fort Pulaski. At first he struck Higginson as fair and approachable; later Higginson would say "he is not a man of the sentiments, & if a large 'Parrott' [cannon] exploded & swept away every member of his staff, he would only take out his pencil & make a note of the angle of fracture."

Gillmore wanted Charleston and intended to take it by degrees: destroy the smaller forts around Fort Sumter safeguarding the city, then seize Sumter, then the city itself.

The first of these steps involved Higginson and his regiment. Gillmore's plan was to cut off supplies to Charleston and its surrounding forts, weakening them, and so Higginson's regiment was to destroy the Jacksonboro railroad bridge on the Edisto River.

On July 9 he and three hundred men set sail aboard the *John Adams* and two smaller boats, the *Enoch Dean* and a gunboat, the *Governor Milton,* the latter two dispatched to navigate the shallow waters beyond Wiltown Bluff. The first stage went well. The vessels pulled into Wiltown in a thick fog around four the next morning and surprised the Confederates, who hastily retreated. As the sun rose, Higginson, on board ship, watched in amazement as two hundred slaves, men, women, and children dressed in bright tatters rushed toward the marshy bank of the river, their worldly possessions wrapped in bundles and balanced on their heads. Refugees: they were the reason he had come south.

Heavy artillery fire drove the *Dean* and the *Milton* downstream, and by the time they tried to move again, they had lost the tide and the *Milton* had been crippled, its engines burst, the engineer killed. Though the *Dean* managed to continue downstream once the tide changed, in the incessant shelling two men were fatally hit, another soldier's head shot off, and Higginson himself felt a sudden hard whack at his side. He staggered back, and though he saw neither blood nor a ripped uniform, the pain was terrible, and he fell.

When the shooting finally stopped, the *Dean* slid back into Wiltown Bluff and reconnoitered with the *John Adams.* The *Milton* had been scuttled—needlessly, thought Higginson.

The railway bridge had not been touched. The mission had failed.

FORTUNATELY HIGGINSON'S WOUND was superficial, and the colonel recovered quickly in the Beaufort hospital, almost proud of the purple bruise, large as two hands, that stretched along his side above the hip.

But his regiment was poorly treated, and he was angry. Decimated by pleurisy and pneumonia, black troops did not receive sufficient medical attention, and Dr. Rogers and Higginson were left to prevent scurvy without vegetables, make bread without yeast, amputate limbs without knives. The troops still suffered from the scorn of many officers, both regular and volunteer, and were begrudgingly equipped with weapons. Higginson's and Montgomery's regiments were told, at one point, that their firearms would be replaced with pikes.

In spite of this, and whatever the success or failure of their various expeditions, his soldiers had worked hard, behaved well, fought fearlessly. Yet they had not been paid since February. Moreover, they would not receive the promised wage of thirteen dollars; their salary had been cut to ten dollars a month. Higginson barraged the *New York Tribune, The New York Times,* the head of the Senate Finance Committee, the War Department, and Charles Sumner with letters: "We presume too much on the supposed ignorance of those men," he fumed. "I have never yet found a man in my regiment so stupid as not to know when he was cheated."

He was also furious when, later, he learned that retroactive pay would be given only to "*free* colored regiments"—a tacit reference to outfits like the Massachusetts Fifty-fourth—not those made up of fugitive slaves who had been "earlier in the field," namely, his First South Carolina. The Fifty-fourth received much more publicity, causing many people to assume it was the country's very first black regiment—they still do—and in later years Higginson would painstakingly explain that five such regiments had already existed by the year 1862.

In actual fact, Higginson's was the first.

But the youthful, rich, and war-scarred Shaw got far more attention than Higginson. This was all the more galling since Higginson would not have minded an appointment to the Fifty-fourth. Shortly after its formation he had written Governor Andrew (in a letter subsequently published in *The Liberator*) bragging about the high rate of enlistment of African Americans in the First South Carolina (350 men in seven weeks). It was a great triumph, he said; so if there was difficulty raising the required number of black soldiers in the

Northeast—which initially there was—he was the man for the job. The governor wasn't interested. Shaw's parents had donated generously to the regiment, and Hallowell, second in command, came from a similarly distinguished philanthropic family. By comparison, Higginson was inexperienced, poor, and much too radical.

A political, not a military, appointee, Higginson also knew he lacked experience. This was an issue—or was made into one, since many appointments remained political. When Shaw petitioned Governor Andrew to remove the Fifty-fourth from Montgomery's command, he replied to the obvious question—why not advance Higginson to that position—by reminding the governor that Higginson had not been tested in battle. Andrew took Shaw's request, almost verbatim, to Secretary of War Stanton, noting that "Higginson, the senior colonel of the brigade, although a brave and chivalrous gentleman of high culture, has never seen much service, and never any in their field until he went to South Carolina."

That is, Higginson had proved only that black men were good enough for skirmishes; Shaw was eager to try the mettle of his black soldiers in active combat. But he would hedge his bets. "It would always be possible to put another line of [white] soldiers behind a black regiment," Shaw allegedly said, "so as to present equal danger in either direction." Higginson was stunned.

Though no abolitionist, Shaw was no friend to slavery, and fully grasping the symbolic importance of the Fifty-fourth, he took his position as its commander quite seriously. He also understood the hurdles the black soldier faced; every commander of a black regiment did: to each was entrusted a chance for undoing the racial prejudices that permitted slavery in the first place. But Shaw cared little about the black man, at least initially, whom he punished in order to teach. Norwood Hallowell remembered him as disciplining the unruly members of the Fifty-fourth by standing them on barrels, "bucked, gagged and, if need be, shot." By contrast, Higginson's training methods were based on sympathy. "In a slave regiment the harsher forms of punishment were, or ought to have been, unknown, so that every suggestion of slavery might be avoided," Hallowell noted. "This was Colonel T.W. Higginson's enlightened method."

The men met in person only once, when Higginson rode over to Beaufort to visit the newly arrived troops. Afterward Shaw told his mother that "I never saw any one who put his whole soul into his work as he does. I was very much impressed with his open-heartedness & purity of character." But as the weeks passed, Shaw himself was hardening. He even cast a more respectful eye on Montgomery.

Montgomery, Strong, Hunter, Gillmore: these were the tough, uncompromising men that war demanded, that soldiering demanded, that Shaw respected. And Higginson? He was kind. War is not kind.

Doubtless Higginson knew he was different from the rest and, like Saxton, considered too sensitive for an important command. He immovably believed that despite huge obstacles, the service of black soldiers was a stepping-stone to liberty, dignity, and full enfranchisement. While this was no doubt true, this was not soldiering.

REASSIGNED TO GENERAL STRONG'S BRIGADE, on July 16 Shaw and his men stubbornly repelled a Confederate attack on James Island, where they were encamped, and saved a white regiment's skin, proving beyond the shadow of a doubt that a black man was a good soldier. After the battle the Fifty-fourth was sent to Cole Island, marching all night through mud and sticky swamp, and then slowly transported in groups of thirty in a small leaky boat to Folly Island.

"Folly Island gives a fair chance at Morris Island; to have Morris Island is to have Fort Sumter, & that is to have Charleston," Higginson remarked, repeating Gillmore's plan. On Morris Island stood the formidable Fort Wagner, a heavily armed earthwork situated near the island's north end and just across the water from Sumter itself. (A previous attempt on Fort Wagner had ended in a rout.) Drenched from thunderstorms, thirsty, and hungry—unlike the officers, they had not eaten in two days—on the morning of July 18, Shaw's exhausted men finally set foot on Morris Island and then marched two more bone-tiring hours.

"Well I guess we will let Strong put those d——d negroes from Massachusetts in the advance, we may as well get rid of them, one time as another," Brigadier General Truman Seymour, who commanded Strong's division, allegedly told Gillmore. According to Higginson, Seymour, a misanthropic man with a careless tongue, had opposed the enlistment of black troops, and Strong was a Democrat indifferent to emancipation.

On the evening of July 18 on Morris Island, Shaw reported to

Robert Gould Shaw, leader of the famed Fifty-fourth Massachusetts, a regiment mistakenly considered the first company of African American troops, 1863. Higginson's First
South Carolina Volunteers was formed the year before.

General Strong. Presumably Strong told Shaw that though the men
of the Fifty-fourth were worn out, they could lead the column
against Fort Wagner, should Shaw choose. He did.

Shaw and his men talked about the decision, and the men held
hands, trying to comfort one another. They exchanged letters and
pictures. Shaw gave some of his papers to his friend Edward Pierce, a
journalist, and rallied the troops, telling them if the color-bearer
fell, he would take the flag. Noisily the men shouted approval.
Shaw's face twitched, and he tossed aside his cigar. Thirty minutes
later he cried, "Forward."

Prepared for hand-to-hand combat, the men stole on foot across a
narrow bar of sand until they were within range of the daunting
earthwork fort, about one hundred yards. The hour was late, about
seven forty-five, and the skies were streaked with purple rays from a
fading sun. Just as the Fifty-fourth was about to rush across the ditch
surrounding the fort, a sheet of fire from small arms lit the darken-
ing night. Men lurched across the ditch, staggered, and fell. Wilky

James, serving as Shaw's adjutant, was hit in the side. Reeling, he was hit again. The column ran past him. Shaw scaled the ramparts, urging his men forward, and was shot through the heart. Undeterred, his men followed. Hand grenades flung from the parapet burst over them as they scaled the face of the fort, and for a fleeting moment one of them, Sergeant R. J. Simmons, planted their flag at its top.

Other officers tumbled to the ground, dead or mortally wounded. Higginson's young nephew Frank guided the retreat of the battered regiment, but the path was so packed with the dead, so crammed with wounded men screaming in pain, that the soldiers could hardly move. A second regiment rushed futilely forward. There were more than fifteen hundred Union casualties.

Shaw's body, which had fallen inside the fort, was subsequently stripped naked and placed on display before being thrown into the bottom of a large pit, the corpses of his vanquished troops tossed on top of his. "Buried with his niggers," a victorious General Hagood presumably said, but another Confederate officer, Lieutenant Iredell Jones, said the Negroes had fought valiantly and were led by as brave an officer as ever lived. Shaw's father instructed General Gillmore not to remove his son's body; it should remain with his men.

Shaw and the entire Fifty-fourth Massachusetts became unassailable martyrs and heroes.

Yet it had been a slaughter. And for what? For a plan, according to Higginson, that was futile, poorly executed, ill conceived, perhaps even racist and cruel?

Thin, weak, and downcast, Higginson decided to return to Worcester on furlough. That might hasten his recuperation, for he wasn't entirely sure what ailed him.

HIGGINSON WENT BACK to Beaufort at the end of August, when the temperature bubbled to ninety-seven degrees. But the tropical heat wasn't the only reason his step had lost its spring. Nothing much had changed. He presided over interminable court-martials. Evenings he still liked to hear the songs of those he again, and unfortunately, called "the dear blundering dusky darlings." But he had no taste for food, he could not sit or stand for long periods, he could not read, and at night he soaked his bedclothes in perspiration. Was this a delayed reaction to the deaths, gory, inexplicably heartless, on every side? Or was it a gnawing suspicion that those waging war in Washington were "vacillating and half proslavery"? Did he wonder whether emancipation meant the kind of enfranchisement he envisioned? Or had Montgomery's audacity and Shaw's martyrdom eclipsed the painstaking, committed, and compassionate abolitionism that he strenuously practiced?

He lay in the officers' hospital early in October. Dr. Rogers guessed malaria. Mary had planned to come south, but he put her off. He suspected that he might leave the army and return north— he wanted to leave—but ambivalence kept him where he was, drilling his regiment, inhaling perfumed air, supervising pickets in the tangled cypress swamps. Charlotte Forten thought he looked thin and drawn. His eyes were hooded.

He remained in limbo, neither sick nor well. It was not that his duties had become perfunctory but rather that his faith in the military as a great equalizer was waning. "This makes me hate all arbitrary power more than ever, this military life, because I see at what a price of possible injustice its efficiency is bought." General Gillmore devalued Saxton. Montgomery and others continued to jockey for promotions not slated for him. Dr. Rogers, himself ill, returned home, and Higginson's regiment, plagued by smallpox, was not sent back to Jacksonville, where the Union suffered another disastrous defeat at the Battle of Olustee, again under General Seymour's dubious command. Nor had his troops been adequately compensated, despite facile assurances from the War Department. "At a time when it required large bounties to fill the Northern regiments with their nine months men," Higginson complained to Charles Sumner, "these men enlisted for three years without bounty, without even State aid to families relying solely on the monthly pay. For five months they received it . . . and then Government suddenly repudiated it and cut them down to $10." Now they were paid seven dollars, not even the ten dollars promised. Two-thirds of the men refused to accept the pittance.

And his men seemed to need him less. "They are growing more like white men; less naïve & less grotesque," he observed, meaning that as proven soldiers they were more independent, disciplined, sure of themselves. Perhaps his time, too, had come. He had turned forty years old.

"I feel that I hv. done my duty entirely," he wrote Mary, but "as to these people, I feel much more clinging yet, & it will be hard to leave them & the work I feel I am doing for them—hard to leave South Carolina & [not] feel that I desert them."

Eighteen months after taking command of the first authorized regiment of black troops in the United States, Colonel Thomas Wentworth Higginson resigned from the army and on the fourteenth of May headed north to he knew not what.

EIGHT

Agony Is Frugal

I found you were gone, by accident," Dickinson wrote to Wentworth Higginson in the winter of 1863, "as I find Systems are, or Seasons of the year, and obtain no cause—but suppose it is a treason of Progress—that dissolves as it goes." Even though they had been corresponding just over a year, she missed him and had hoped to meet him in person. "I should have liked to see you, before you became improbable," she lamented. "War feels to me an oblique place— Should there be other Summers, would you perhaps come?"

If there were other summers, yes; for now she must content herself with his description of the South Carolina Sea Islands—cold comfort. "I too, have an 'Island'—," she retorted, "whose 'Rose and Magnolia' are in the Egg, and it's 'Black Berry' but a spicy prospective, yet as you say, 'fascination' is absolute of Clime."

She was referring to his essay "Procession of the Flowers," which she had condensed in her own inimitable way. "The fascination of summer lies not in any details," he had written, "however perfect, but in the sense of total wealth which summer gives." Fascination is absolute of clime.

She then signed her letter "Your Gnome."

The signature may refer to a comment of his, now lost, about the gnomic quality of her verse. For she liked to quote him back to himself, lobbing phrases at him in her slightly coquettish way. The technique had become part of their conversation, much as their talk of flowers was, for a tender bond had sprung up between them, these two seemingly different individuals, divided by place, temperament, and talent and linked by her first unabashed letter to him, a stranger. But he may have taken her remark about war amiss: war could not be an oblique place for a soldier, never mind the man who considered this war a first step toward the restoration, for all, of human and civil rights. She apologized straightaway. He had been so generous to her, she said, that she wanted only his forgiveness.

Besides, "to doubt my High Behavior, is a new pain," she unhappily remarked.

Though death was too close, too real, too coldly indiscriminate for her to mock, at times she did or seemed to scorn the war: "Color—Caste—Denomination— / These—are Time's Affair— / Death's diviner Classifying / Does not know they are—." And she told truths about death few of us admit: "'Tis so appalling—it exhilirates—." She could transform death, too, into a gentleman caller, a supple suitor, an insect, a fly. Imagination runs free; language is taut. "Agony is frugal—," as she would write, in poems direct, spare, pitiless. Yet this might sound callous to the unpracticed ear. "I shall have no winter this year—on account of the soldiers—," she remarked to Mary Bowles. "Since I cannot weave Blankets, or Boots—I thought it best to omit the season."

Directing her irony against socialites concerned only with the "season" during, of all times, war and also against the sanctimonious organizers of charity fairs, church drives, and sewing circles, she spurned both. ("What Soft—Cherubic Creatures— / These Gentle-women are— / . . . Such Dimity Convictions—.") Instead she measured every grief she met "With narrow, probing, eyes— / I wonder if It weighs like Mine— / Or has an Easier size—." Grief is private; there are no easy sizes. Sometimes soldiers bore her wrath too. "A Soldier called, a Morning ago, and asked for a Nosegay, to take to Battle," she tartly noted. "I suppose he thought we kept an Aquarium." Nosegays for battle? How could one prettify battle?

"Perhaps Death, gave me Awe for friends, striking sharp and early," as she explained to Higginson, "for I held them since, in a brittle love, of more alarm, than peace."

"It feels a shame to be Alive—," as she elaborated in a poem dating from this period:

> It feels a shame to be Alive —
> When Men so brave — are dead —
> One envies the Distinguished Dust —
> Permitted — such a Head —
>
> The Stone — that tells defending Whom
> This Spartan put away
> What little of Him we — possessed
> In Pawn for Liberty —

The price is great —Sublimely paid —
Do we deserve — a Thing —
That lives — like Dollars — must be piled
Before we may obtain?

Are we that wait — sufficient worth —
That such Enormous Pearl
As life — dissolved be — for Us —
In Battle's — horrid Bowl?

It may be — a Renown to live —
I think the Men who die —
Those unsustained —Saviors —
Present Divinity —

Juxtaposing life and death—"dead," "lives," "life," "live," "die"—
Dickinson here salutes the soldier ("Those unsustained—Saviors—
/ Present Divinity—"), who is but a "Pawn," his life exchanged for
abstractions like "Liberty," his existence pulverized "In Battle's—
horrid Bowl": dust to dust, for a botched civilization.

Though to Higginson the soldiers fought for the very concrete
goal of ending slavery, in Amherst, even among antislavery enthusiasts, the war was also a political drama. Edward Dickinson, for one,
had been a congressman opposing the extension of slavery, not its
elimination, and when he declined the Republican nomination for
lieutenant governor in 1861, he denounced "as subversive of all constitutional guarantees, if we expect to reconstruct or restore the
Union, the heretical dogma that immediate and universal emancipation of slaves should be proclaimed by the government, as the means
of putting an end to the war"—though he did say he hoped "that, in
the good providence of God, emancipation may be one of the blessed
results of the war." (The *Springfield Republican,* printing Dickinson's
statement, subsequently ran a rejoinder that declared him a bigot, a
partisan, and a mouse.) As the war dragged on, he updated his position on slavery, or so he said. "He is against slavery as the cause of the
war & to be destroyed," an acquaintance waggishly commented in
1864, "yet, he has always been in action a conservative or a pro slavery man as I think, but he has now forgotten it."

The war affected every family, and Emily Dickinson's was no
exception: quite the reverse, given Edward Dickinson's penchant for

public office. But Dickinson's feelings are unclear. "I like Truth—it is a free Democracy," she said. Likely she approved Austin's paying a substitute to fight in his place—he had been drafted—for five hundred dollars; life, his life, any life, particularly Austin's life, should be spared. Yet she had chosen to befriend Higginson—an activist, a women's rights champion, an ultra-abolitionist—who, even if he could have afforded it, would never have dreamed of buying a substitute to fight for him. But Edward and Austin Dickinson, wealthy men, guiltily insisted that the town of Amherst pay an additional award of one hundred dollars to local enlistees in addition to what was paid by the state and federal government: they weighed life in economic terms. "Do we deserve—a Thing— / That lives—like Dollars—must be piled / Before we may obtain?"

That Dickinson seldom mentioned the war directly inspired literary critics for many years to assume she inhabited only a supernal realm of poetry, far removed from the miserable squabbles of petty men. That can hardly be the case. And she knew that while Higginson claimed that he preferred to live in nature, unscathed by the alarms of war, the man who composed lyrical essays about April days and snowflakes had also depicted slave insurrections with equanimity, if not outright advocacy. And though skeptical about the intentions, hesitations, and prevarications of his government, once Higginson signed on, he unwaveringly committed himself. Dickinson tacitly approved. "Though not reared to prayer—," she wrote him tenderly, "when service is had in Church, for Our Arms, I include yourself."

Of course, then, the war touched her. And she may have tried in her own way to assist the cause. For despite her avowed refusal to publish her poems, several of them appeared during the war: three in *Drum Beat,* for instance, the official paper of the Brooklyn and Long Island Sanitary Fair, which had been organized to raise money for medical supplies for Union soldiers. Edited by Richard Salter Storrs, an Amherst College graduate and friend of Austin and Sue's, the short-lived *Drum Beat* enjoyed a wide circulation, and its roster of contributors included literary luminaries like Oliver Wendell Holmes and William Cullen Bryant. It also spread Dickinson's work, albeit without her name attached. (Poets frequently published anonymously.) After the poem "Blazing in Gold and quenching in Purple" (later mailed to Higginson) ran in its February 29, 1864, issue, under the title "Sunset," it was reprinted in the *Springfield*

Daily Republican and the *Springfield Weekly Republican;* after the March 2 issue carried "Flowers—well, if anybody" (titled "Flowers"), that poem cropped up in the *Springfield Republican* and *The Boston Post.*

Another poem, "These are the days when Birds come back—" (titled "October"), appeared in *Drum Beat's* pages and recollects the final paragraphs in Higginson's essay "The Life of Birds." But whereas Higginson ends his essay with his typical cheer about seasonal rebirth, Dickinson's autumnal poem about birds' taking a backward look in fall ends with a plea that, in this context, we may read as addressing him: "Oh sacrament of summer days, / Oh Last Communion in the Haze— / Permit a child to join— / Thy sacred emblems to partake— / Thy consecrated bread to take / And thine immortal wine!"

Perhaps she idly wondered if Higginson would come across her poem. Nor were these the only poems he might recognize as hers. "Some keep the Sabbath going to Church" appeared in *Round Table,* another newly established paper in New York edited by another Amherst graduate, the Dickinson cousin Charles Sweetser, and "Success—is counted sweetest" turned up in April in *The Brooklyn Daily Eagle.* These two poems had also been given to Higginson; likely he praised them, and clearly she thought they represented her well.

The timing of their appearance is suggestive particularly since Dickinson rarely published before the war or after it. "If fame belonged to me, I could not escape her—," we recall her telling Higginson; "if she did not, the longest day would pass me on the chase—and the approbation of my Dog, would forsake me—then—My Barefoot-Rank is better—." Fame, ersatz celebrity, immortality, and the hollow heart of laurels—the renunciation of worldly prizes—and their allure—ricochet through her poems: "Fame is a fickle food / Upon a shifting plate," she impishly wrote, or in another fragment, "Fame is a bee. / It has a song— / It has a sting— / Ah, too, it has a wing," or yet again, "Fame's Boys and Girls, who never die / And are too seldom born—." Or, during the war, "Some—Work for Immortality— / ," she noted, "The Chiefer part, for Time— / He—Compensates—immediately— / The former—Checks—on Fame— / Slow Gold—but Everlasting—." She chose the slow gold, but it was a choice, and choices imply attractive alternatives, or we would not have to bother choosing.

Perhaps, then, war relaxed her ambivalence toward publication; a public cause is easier to rationalize than a private one, and publication, in this instance, is philanthropy as much as self-aggrandizement. She would not seek fame or shirk it, she had said, concealing her motives not from Higginson as much as from herself. It was what he did too, refusing to jockey for a promotion, pretending it did not matter.

But her published war poetry was not like Whitman's or Whittier's or Herman Melville's. Not intensely personal, specifically topical, or formidably obscure, it revealed her talent without unveiling her soul. In the privacy of her room, however, she spoke more openly of the war. "When I was small, a Woman died— / ," she wrote around 1863, "Today—her Only Boy / Went up from the Potomac— / His face all Victory." The apparition of these faces, of woman and of boy, passes "back and forth, before my Brain." Who is not harassed by war? Similarly, in "Bereavement in their death to feel / ," she writes of "Whom We have never seen— / A Vital Kinsmanship import / Our Soul and their's between—." And war stands for battle within: "The Battle fought between the Soul / And No Man—is the One / Of all the Battles prevalent— / By far the Greater One—." Yet war remains itself, grim with a death and dying so appalling that it exhilarates: "It sets the Fright at liberty— / And Terror's free— / Gay, Ghastly, Holiday!" Fascination is absolute of clime.

What of slavery? of abolition? She does not really say. Or if she confronts the subject head-on, the result is far more conventional than her usual verse: "No Rack can torture me— / My Soul—at Liberty—." Possibly she refers to emancipated slaves when she wonders,

> *Can the Lark resume the Shell —*
> *Easier — for the Sky —*
> *Would'nt Bonds hurt more*
> *Than Yesterday?*
>
> *Would'nt Dungeons sorer grate*
> *On the Man — free —*
> *Just long enough to taste —*
> *Then — doomed new —*

> *God of the Manacle*
> *As of the Free —*
> *Take not my Liberty*
> *Away from Me —*

(This poem reflects Higginson's remark that "you may make a soldier out of a slave, very readily; but you can no more make a slave out of a soldier than you can replace a bird in the egg.") And when she envisions soldiers marching in the distance, she may well be picturing Higginson's regiment in the bright red trousers he loathed:

> *A Slash of Blue! A sweep of Gray!*
> *Some scarlet patches — on the way —*
> *Compose an evening sky —*
>
> *A little Purple — slipped between —*
> *Some Ruby Trowsers — hurried on —*
> *A Wave of Gold — a Bank of Day —*
> *This just makes out the morning sky!*

Working best when pushing metaphor into new places, she insists again that "Publication—is the Auction / Of the Mind of Man—," though in this case she may be associating the merchandising of consciousness with the horrific trade in human beings: "In the Parcel—Be the Merchant / Of the Heavenly Grace— / But reduce no Human Spirit / To Disgrace of Price—." One's self was not for sale. "I do not let go it," she told Higginson, "because it is mine." Likely she referred to her poetry.

And of the young soldier, eager to die, and enamored of fame in the form of victory, she thus compassionately if somberly notes:

> *He fought like those Who've nought to lose —*
> . . . .
>
> *But Death was Coy of Him*
> *As Other Men, were Coy of Death.*
> *To Him — to live — was Doom —*
>
> *His Comrades, shifted like the Flakes*
> *When Gusts reverse the Snow —*

But He — was left alive Because
Of Greediness to die —

So many men, so much death. Romanticized by the green and the young, vainglorious death is yet the subject of another poem:

My Portion is Defeat — today —
A paler luck than Victory —
Less Paeans — fewer Bells —
The Drums dont follow Me — with tunes —
Defeat — a somewhat slower — means —
More Arduous than Balls —

'Tis populous with Bone and stain —
And Men too straight to stoop again —
And Piles of solid Moan —
And Chips of Blank — in Boyish Eyes —
And scraps of Prayer —
And Death's surprise,
Stamped visible — in stone —

There's somewhat prouder, Over there —
The Trumpets tell it to the Air —
How different Victory
To Him who has it — and the One
Who to have had it, would have been
Contenteder — to die —

The poet, whose "Portion is Defeat," pretends to envy those who march off to war, trumpets blaring, drums banging, bells ringing with praise. And yet the poem is funereal, particularly in the second stanza, where the repeating "And" creates an implacable rhythm of accumulating brutal images: "Chips of Blank—in Boyish Eyes—," "Piles of solid Moan—," "Stamped visible—in stone—" (on a headstone). These images drive the poem toward its paradoxical conclusion: the trumpets broadcast victory that no one hears, for only to the victor does victory have meaning, one that lies, ironically, in death. As for the rest of us, we live among unheralded defeats, which are, of course, their own kind of victory: life.

"COULD YOU, WITH HONOR, AVOID DEATH," Dickinson entreated Colonel Higginson, her new friend, capitalizing "Death" and not "honor." To her there was no honor in death, and yet she knew, as she also told him—enfolding a two-line poem within the context of her letter—that we measure gain by loss, just as we measure success by failure:

> Best Gains — must have the Losses' test —
> To constitute them — Gains.

She would miss him, in other words, but she respected his decision to fight and included in another letter a poem—replete with martial images—about dedication, loyalty, individual autonomy, and courage:

> The Soul unto itself
> Is an imperial friend
> Or the most agonizing Spy
> An Enemy could send
>
> Secure against it's own
> No treason it can fear
> Itself it's Sovereign of itself
> The Soul should be in Awe

We need courage because we are self-divided, and thus the single indomitable soul is its own worst enemy ("agonizing Spy"). But when "Secure against it's own," nothing can harm it. A farewell to Higginson of astonishing insight, it is as if she knew of his vacillations, his indecision, his conflicts. She folded the poem into her letter and bade him much more than well.

In camp, when the mail arrived, he sought out her handwriting.

IN JUNE 1863, the month before Higginson was wounded, James Fields published a book of the colonel's *Atlantic* essays— omitting those about slave rebellions, presumably slated for a different collection, which struck Fields as seditious. No matter: Higginson proudly showed off *Out-Door Papers* to all his junior officers and crowed over the good reviews. The *Springfield Republican* went so far as to compare Higginson's euphonious style with Hawthorne's.

Dickinson herself never forgot the day she first opened Higginson's book. "It is still as distinct as Paradise—," she would tell him years hence. "It was Mansions—Nations—Kinsmen—too—to me—." Refined and sharpened, his images seeped into her imagination, and she used his writing, as she did that of the Bible and Shakespeare, in her own, ingesting its metaphors or rhythm and trimming his fat. Take his description of rowing on Lake Quinsigamond just before dawn so he can see the water lilies at first light: "Precisely at half past three, a song-sparrow above our heads gave one liquid trill, so inexpressibly sudden and delicious, that it seemed to set to music every atom of freshness and fragrance that Nature held; then the spell was broken, and the whole shore and lake were vocal with song." Dickinson rewrites it this way:

> *The Birds begun at Four o'clock —*
> *Their period for Dawn —*
> *A Music numerous as space —*
> *But neighboring as Noon —*
>
> *. . . . .*
>
> *The Witnesses were not —*
> *Except Occasional Man —*
> *In homely industry arrayed —*
> *To overtake the Morn —*

Or in another poem, composed later, she again borrows from Higginson:

> *At Half past Three*
> *A Single Bird*
> *Unto a silent sky*
> *Propounded but a single term*
> *Of cautious Melody.*
>
> *At Half past Four*
> *Experiment had subjugated test*

And lo, her silver principle
Supplanted all the rest.

At Half past Seven
Element nor implement be seen
And Place was where the Presence was
Circumference between

A dense poem, it traces the appearance and disappearance of the solitary bird, which after propounding its single note of melody, will disappear—as Dickinson, fugitive poet, does. But the bird and its song echo in the memory of the implied listener, which may be the definition, for her, of circumference: the liminal border between presence and absence. Or as Higginson explains in his essay "Water-Lilies," "that which is remembered is often more vivid than that which is seen. The eye paints better in the presence, the heart in the absence, of the object most dear." Our imagination, like memory, nourishes us long after his beloved water lily disappears: "only in losing her do we gain the power to describe her," he concludes, "and we are introduced to Art, as we are to Eternity, by the dropping away of our companions."

Written before the war, when printed in *Out-Door Papers,* "Water-Lilies" takes on a special elegiac tone, as if forecasting Higginson's future. "Absence is the very air of passion, and all the best description is *in memoriam,*" Higginson writes. "As with our human beloved, when the graceful presence is with us, we cannot analyze or describe, but merely possess, and only after its departure can it be portrayed by our yearning desires; so is it with Nature." Soon he would embark on the memorial series about Harvard men slain during the Civil War, and much of his writing would acquire a retrospective, subdued quality, an amethyst's remembrance, as Dickinson would say. But his notion of the lost being recovered through imagination was no nostalgic romanticism. Rather, for him imagination was intimately connected to an imperturbable nature, immanent and benign. "No man can measure what a single hour with Nature may have contributed to the moulding of his mind," Higginson wrote. "The influence is self-renewing, and if for a long time it baffles expression by reason of its fineness, so much the better in the end." This Emersonian notion was his form of worship—and in certain hours, Dickinson's too. "I was thinking, today—as I noticed, that the 'Supernatural,' was only the Natural, disclosed—," she told him.

Yet unlike Higginson, Dickinson teetered between belief and unbelief. For her, souls seldom touch their objects, as Emerson had written in "Experience," and defy our meager attempt to make sense of them. ("Perception of an Object costs / ," she writes, "Precise the Object's loss—.") But disappointment does not deter her. Rather, she seizes the ephemeral in nature—in human nature—through art, tracing what she called "The Myrrhs, and Mochas, of the Mind." That is, while Higginson staked his life on a meaning latent in the world, Dickinson created that meaning. To her, perception was a matter of probing, whatever the cost, into what Melville had called the very axis of reality, the Pit; as she said, "Heaven over it— / And Heaven beside, and Heaven abroad; / And yet a Pit—." Poetry recorded what, if anything, she found there: "The Zeros taught Us—Phosphorus."

But Higginson had faith, at bottom, in inalienable human rights, and it spurred him to fight for equality, justice, a heaven on earth; whether he would be successful was another matter. And of the two of them, Higginson and Dickinson, he would suffer more disillusionment, although paradoxically it made him a meliorist, his faith firmly placed in the future. But with an imagination at once more alienated and more free, Dickinson stayed angry, witty, agnostic, pantheistic, madcap—although committed, as he was, to the salutary power of art. In an early letter to Higginson, sent in July 1863, when she enclosed the poem "Some keep the Sabbath going to Church—," she suggested we seek what is with us always:

> *So instead of getting to Heaven, at last —*
> *I'm going, all along.*

DICKINSON HAD NOT KNOWN that Colonel Higginson had been wounded in the summer, as she explained, because she had taken ill that September and then went to Boston the following spring to consult with the eminent ophthalmologist Henry Willard Williams of Arlington Street. Something was wrong with her eyes. She could not bear light. "The snow-light offends them," she told her cousin, "and the house is bright." Reading was difficult, if not impossible. "What I see not, I better see— / Through Faith—," she reassured herself, "My Hazel Eye / Has periods of shutting— / But, No lid has Memory—."

The diagnosis for her condition seems to have been rheumatic iritis (anterior uveitis), a disease that comes and goes and whose prognosis is good. An irritation in the iris, possibly congenital, that causes pain, soreness, light sensitivity, and blurred vision, the condition is often associated with diabetes; in Dickinson's case, its onset and causes are unknown.

During the course of her treatment, she stayed with Norcross cousins Louise and Frances in a boardinghouse at 86 Austin Street in Cambridgeport. She answered Higginson's note, forwarded to her there, saying her doctor would not let her go back to Amherst, "yet I work in my Prison, and make Guests for myself—." But the restless bustle of urban life—and her anxiety, her inactivity, her ailment—depressed her. Perhaps she could manage to write her poetry, though the physician had advised against sewing and reading. "I wish to see you more than before I failed—," she lamented to Higginson, her language drastic and similar to that of the poem "I heard a Fly buzz—when I died—," possibly composed around this time:

> *And then the Windows failed — and then*
> *I could not see to see —*

Unaware that he had been injured, she also did not know much about his recovery, she said, but word of it would "excel" her own. That was overstatement. Her eye trouble, Higginson's wound, even Hawthorne's sudden death (which she mentioned to Higginson) spelled the end of an era. She was cut off. "The only News I know / ," she told him with bleak humor, "Is Bulletins all day / From Immortality."

Not until the end of November could she go home, long after the apples had ripened and wild geese, heading south, had darkened the sky. And yet with her eyes not fully healed, she had to return to Boston in the spring and summer of 1865, just at the time the savage war finally ended. Years later she remembered her own private ordeal as "a Calamity," which no doubt it was. Writing to Joseph Lyman, she recalled that "I had a woe, the only one that ever made me tremble. It was a shutting out of all the dearest ones of time, the strongest friends of the soul—BOOKS. The medical man said avaunt ye books tormentors, he also said 'down, thoughts, & plunge into her soul.' He might as well have said, 'Eyes be blind', 'heart be still'. So I had eight weary months of Siberia."

And yet with all this—the treatments, the fear of blindness, the war, the displacement—Dickinson continued to sing from those charnel steps. For in spite of everything, she, like Higginson, discovered self-renewal in natural recurrence, which was not revelation, resurrection, or religious cant. It was a pensive faith, calm and courageous, and a gift to Higginson in a lovely poem about the crickets of late summer:

> *Further in Summer than the Birds*
> *Pathetic from the Grass*
> *A minor Nation celebrates*
> *It's unobtrusive Mass.*
>
> *No Ordinance be seen*
> *So gradual the Grace*
> *A pensive Custom it becomes*
> *Enlarging Loneliness.*
>
> *Antiquest felt at Noon*
> *When August burning low*
> *Arise this spectral Canticle*
> *Repose to typify*
>
> *Remit as yet no Grace*
> *No Furrow on the Glow*
> *Yet a Druidic Difference*
> *Enhances Nature now*

The crickets' chirping—an "unobtrusive Mass," both in the literal sense of being small and in the more figurative religious sense—initially strikes us as pathetic: the crickets are such an inconsequential nation, unlike, say, mighty America. But in them we can hear "August burning low," and though we realize we face death alone and unprotected, the almost primitive sound of these small creatures—a "spectral Canticle"—offers us the solace of "a

Druidic Difference": rituals of birth and death, beginnings and ends, in song.

Likely written just after the war, the poem was mailed to Higginson along with a brief message; Carlo, her dog, had died, she told him, and then she asked needlessly, "Would you instruct me now?"

NINE

No Other Way

*A man of any feeling must feed his imagination;
there must be a woman of whom he can dream.*

Thomas Wentworth Higginson, Malbone

Tuesday, August 16. The heat wave over, fresh rural breezes
rustled the treetops when shortly after two o'clock Colonel
Higginson sauntered over to Main Street from the Amherst
Inn. He had never been to Amherst before. It struck him as a small,
sweet, typical New England town framed by those lovely, lilting
Pelham Hills—and deadly dull on a summer's afternoon.

Slender, long legged, and in the bloom of middle age at forty-six,
his hair black and without a glint of silver, Higginson, with his
ramrod posture and positive step, kept his lapses of confidence to
himself—that "inward darkness," as he once called it. His public
persona demanded the mask, and besides it wasn't entirely false: he
was a preternaturally hopeful man, tediously good-natured, polite,
fastidious, gallant, and benign.

He had been hoping to make this visit for a while. Eight years
had passed since he first opened Dickinson's small envelope with its
fantastic enclosures, but the war had intervened, and right afterward
he had been busy rounding up contributors for the *Harvard Memorial Biographies.* He had written thirteen of the entries himself. And
there were the speaking engagements he did not turn down and
those essays he wrote almost compulsively, as if addicted to the
immediate gratification of seeing his name in print. He wrote
swiftly, easily; he would have liked to dig deeper into his imagination, but there was never time.

He also translated Petrarch's sonnets and the discourses of Epictetus, the Stoic moralist born a slave, whose opening sentence in the

Encheiridion reads, as Higginson put it, "There are things which are within our power, and there are things which are beyond our power." We must let go the things beyond our power. But this seems to protect the status quo, Henry James pointed out in his review of the translation, though James also admitted that Epictetus was "a man among men, an untiring observer, and a good deal of a satirist"—rather like Higginson, as a matter of fact. "When you do anything from a clear judgment that it ought to be done, never shrink from being seen to do it, even though the world should misunderstand it," Higginson had translated from book 35 of the *Encheiridion.* "For if you are not acting rightly, shun the action itself; if you are, why fear those who wrongly censure you?"

While Higginson's Epictetus defined integrity for him, his translation of Petrarch's sonnets revealed passions of a different stripe. "I seem to find her now, and now perceive / How far away she is; now rise, now fall." To him, Laura was the incarnation of art and beauty, though these postwar days, he complained dolefully, "nobody comprehends Petrarch. Philosophers and sensualists all refuse to believe that his dream of Laura went on, even when he had a mistress and a child. Why not? Every one must have something to which his dreams can cling, amid the degradations of actual life, and this tie is more real than the degradation; and if he holds to the tie, it will one day save." He dwelled in possibility.

Emily Dickinson may or may not have been Higginson's Laura, but at home there was poor unhappy Mary, whose suffering he could hardly bear. Virtually paralyzed, her fingers so stiff she turned the pages of a book with a wand, she sat in her chair day after day, forgivably querulous and upset. His home had become a hospital, he confided to his diary, and Mary, crying for the pain he was powerless to relieve, begged him over and over not to leave her, and yet she chided him so mercilessly and so often his friends marveled he did not ship her off to a real hospital. "On the whole I think him an astonishing success under difficulties!—," observed one. "What would become of *you,* for instance, or me, to sleep where he sleeps—embrace what he embraces!"

But that he and Dickinson had not yet met face-to-face, despite Higginson's schedule and his obligations, was not entirely his fault. She had been difficult. Cajole as he might, she would not budge from Amherst. He had proposed that she come to Boston: "All ladies do," he said. Doubtless he said just the wrong thing. "I had promised to visit my Physician for a few days in May," she cordially replied to him in 1866, "but Father objects because he is in the habit of me." He tried to reassure her, inviting her to one of the Radical Club meetings, perfectly respectable, taking place every third Monday of the month at the Sargents' on Beacon Hill. Men—and women—presented papers on religion and science. Emerson was reading one. If that seemed too intimate or not to her liking, there was also the Woman's Club on Tremont Street, which would be celebrating Margaret Fuller's life and work. He himself would read a paper on the Greek goddesses, he added with some pride, although on that particular day, he reflected, he would not be able to pay as much attention to her as he'd like.

Dickinson politely rebuffed him. "I must omit Boston. Father prefers so," she explained. "He likes me to travel with him but objects that I visit." Her refusal didn't deter him from asking again; she had to be more blunt: "I do not cross my Father's ground," she flatly stated, "to any House or town." The incredulous Higginson would understand more, or think he did, when he met her father. "Thin dry & speechless," he remarked with a tad of aversion.

In the summer of 1870, the death of his elder brother Stephen, who had been staying near Amherst, gave Higginson an opportunity to meet at last the strange poet who'd dropped into his world so abruptly, who seemed alternately fragile and sturdy, who bewildered him with an intelligence and a wryness and a will unlike that of anyone he had ever encountered. As far as he could tell, she confounded everyone. In Worcester he had spoken to one of her uncles, who shed no light at all, and though he would soon chat with the current president of Amherst College, he learned little more than he had already divined in their eight-year correspondence—that "there is always one thing to be grateful for—," as she would tell Higginson, "that one is one's self & not somebody else." She was definitely her own self.

She cowed him. "Sometimes I take out your letters & verses, dear friend, and when I feel their strange power, it is not strange that I find it hard to write & that long months pass," he admitted to her in one of the letters of his that do survive. "I have the greatest desire to see you, always feeling that if I could once take you by the hand I might be something to you; but till then you only enshroud yourself in this fiery mist & I cannot reach you, but only rejoice in the rare sparkles of light."

What did he want to be to her? He hardly knew. "I am always the same toward you, & never relax my interest in what you send to me," he told her. "I should like to hear from you very often, but feel always timid lest what I *write* should be badly aimed & miss that fine edge of thought which you bear. It would be so easy, I fear, to miss you." He knew his limits.

If only he could see her, touch her hand, assure himself that she was real. Otherwise, she would remain a fantasy, even an obsession. How was it that she had such an unaccountable way of saying things? Perhaps because she lived with and for herself and her poetry? But to live so alone, so cut off from the rest of the world? "Of 'shunning Men and Women'—," she answered in an early letter, "they talk of Hallowed things, aloud—and embarrass my Dog—He and I dont object to them, if they'll exist their side." Higginson came to see she was not really isolated—it was as if he was thinking out loud: "It isolates one anywhere to think beyond a certain point or have such luminous flashes as come to you—so perhaps the place does not make much difference."

It did not. Remarkable.

He now stood at the door of the frowning Homestead, brown brick, with its gracious side garden and its tall, unwelcoming trees—a country lawyer's place, he noticed with uncharacteristic condescension. Dickinson said she would be waiting. "I will be at Home," she had written him, "and glad."

He pulled the bell. A servant opened the heavy door. Offering his card, he was shown to a dark, stiff parlor cluttered with books and decorated with the predictably dim engravings. The piano lid was raised, but what caught his attention was the table where someone had conspicuously placed his *Out-Door Papers* and his recently published novel, *Malbone.* He had been welcomed.

In a few minutes he heard what sounded to him, as he later said, like a child's step rushing in the hall. Then an airy, slim form appeared: Emily Dickinson, her dress white, her shawl blue, her hair Titian red, parted in the middle and pulled back. She carried two daylilies in her hand, which she placed in his. "These are my introduction," she whispered. "How long will you stay?"

FIVE YEARS HAD PASSED since the end of the war. She had continued to write poetry, but at a far slower rate. In his fine variorum edition of her work, Ralph Franklin, her most recent editor, estimates 229 poems in 1865 but not many more than 12 per year until 1870, when he counts 28. Of course, no one really knows: many poems may be lost or unrecovered or contained in letters themselves lost or unrecovered. One thing seems sure: after the flurry of poems published in 1864, "The Snake" ("A narrow Fellow in the Grass") was the only other one ever to appear in print in her lifetime.

It first surfaced on February 14, 1866, on the front page of the Springfield *Daily Republican.* An implied rejoinder to Whittier's more sentimental "Barefoot Boy," the poem is a carefree account of a boy's "transport / Of Cordiality" with "Nature's People." But nature also eludes him (this is a theme in Dickinson's work), for when the boy stoops to pick up a snake that Whittier's boy never even sees, "It wrinkled And was gone—." And, as the speaker concludes, he

> *. . . never met this Fellow*
> *Attended or alone*
> *Without a tighter Breathing*
> *And Zero at the Bone.*

In that ravishing final image, "Zero at the Bone," Dickinson manages in an instant to link the boy, chilled to the marrow, to the creature of backbone: our fears, ourselves. It's a quick, condensed performance of Dickinson at her bristling best.

Again insisting to Higginson that she "did not print," as she phrased it, she nonetheless enclosed a newspaper clipping of the poem when she wrote him, "lest you meet my Snake," she explained, "and suppose I deceive it was robbed of me." (She may have already given him a holograph copy of the poem and now worried lest he stumble across it in the paper.) But her scruple was a cover, for she seemed just as intent on demonstrating that the poem was worth publishing in the first place.

And like any professional writer, she objected to editorial glad-handing: "defeated too of the third line by the punctuation," she complained to Higginson. "The third and fourth were one—." In the *Republican*'s version of the poem, the first four lines read:

> *A narrow fellow in the grass*
> *Occasionally rides;*

You may have met him — did you not?
His notice instant is,

The question mark ending line 3 does in fact defeat the enjambment of lines 3 and 4 that exists in one of her manuscripts, as follows:

You may have met Him — did you not
His notice instant is —

But whether Samuel Bowles or his literary editor, Dr. Holland, another Dickinson family friend, mangled the poem, neither man robbed her of it. Josiah Holland, though more conservative than Bowles, was himself a writer of popular poems and essays, under the pseudonym Timothy Titcomb, and he, like Bowles, appreciated Dickinson's privacy too much to betray it.

Yet to Higginson she pretended otherwise. The poem had been stolen, she had insisted, and of course she had no other mentor than he, certainly not Bowles or Holland, whose friendship with her she did not mention. "If I still entreat you to teach me, are you much displeased?" she asked, seemingly without guile. And if he was satisfied with her explanation, they could continue on the same footing as before, she said; she would be patient, constant, a good little girl welcoming his criticism ("your knife").

As if to reiterate her willingness to undergo his scalpel, she enclosed another poem:

A Death blow is a Life blow to Some
Who till they died, did not alive become —
Who had they lived — had died but when
They died, Vitality begun —

Written by no little girl, the poem is about people who don't know how to live, and she does, she suggests—through poetry, which released her, energized her, refreshed her, and relieved, as she had said, that awful palsy.

What did he answer? What could he? Unfortunately, Higginson did not want us to know, for though he saved and catalogued a huge inventory of correspondence, diaries, journals, and jottings, he evidently destroyed those personal papers he deemed too intimate for public consumption. But in a fragment of a letter to Dickinson that luckily survives, he sounds less like a colonel, a literary critic, or a buttoned-up editor than a beseeching lover, diffident before the individual he prized above all others. "Still, you see, I try," he told her. He wanted to know her. "I think if I could once see you & know that you are real, I might fare better."

"I would like to be what you deem me," she humbly answered, inviting him to be her guest at the local inn.

"It is hard [for me] to understand how you can live so alone," he said again, "with thoughts of such a quality coming up in you."

These were honest letters; they spoke of heartache and pain, nature and art, and the consolations one may or may not find there. "To undertake is to achieve," Dickinson reminded him in one of the poems she sent him. They spoke of what troubled them: loss, friendship; and more discreetly, far less directly, they spoke of their feelings. He must have opened himself to her. "You mention Immortality," she noted. "That is the Flood subject. I was told that the Bank was the safest place for a Finless mind."

Was Higginson's mind finless? Did he dare tell her of the doubts or ambitions he generally kept to himself? of his desire for immortality? "The 'infinite Beauty'—of which you speak comes too near to seek," she replied.

"To escape enchantment," she added, "one must always flee. Paradise is of the option."

Though infinite Beauty was said to be Paradise, or so she had been taught, she was not so certain. Even if death is seductive—that promise of an eternal Paradise—one must nevertheless live. "Time is a test of trouble," she wrote, including verse in the body of a letter to Higginson in the spring of 1866,

> *But not a remedy —*
> *If such it prove, it prove too*
> *There was no malady.*

She sent him more poems: as well as "To undertake is to achieve," there was "Blazing in Gold and quenching in Purple" (published in *Drum Beat*), "Ample make this Bed—," and the tender lyric "As imperceptibly as Grief."

> *As imperceptibly as Grief*
> *The Summer lapsed away —*

Too imperceptible at last
To feel like Perfidy —

A Quietness distilled
As Twilight long begun
Or Nature spending with herself
Sequestered Afternoon.

The Dusk drew earlier in
The Morning foreign shone
A Courteous yet harrowing grace
As Guest that would be gone

And thus without a Wing
Or service of a keel
Our Summer made her light escape
Into the Beautiful.

Her description of the summer may be her description of him: the guest that would disappear, if he ever came, and her idea of him never quite fulfilled by his presence. And he could assume that the diaphanous summer, making its light escape, is like Dickinson herself, a guest come for a moment to stay but a moment, her grace courteous yet unaccountably exacting, her life sequestered and yet not soundless—never that—but provocative and beautiful. Higginson could recognize her in the summer, and if he came to Amherst in the summer, he certainly would.

"Is it more far to Amherst?"

IN THE SUMMER OF 1867, she dashed off a few lines: "Bringing still my 'plea for culture,' would it teach me now?" she asked, referring this time to his recent *Atlantic* article, "A Plea for Culture." Again she included another poem sure to flatter him:

The Luxury to apprehend
The Luxury 'twould be
To look at thee a single time
An Epicure of me
In whatsoever presence makes

Till for a further food
I scarcely recollect to starve
So first am I supplied.

The Luxury to meditate
The Luxury it was
To banquet on thy Countenance
A sumptuousness supplies
To plainer Days whose Table, far
As Certainty can see
Is laden with a single Crumb —
The Consciousness of thee —

He didn't answer right away; wanting his reply to be perfect, he procrastinated. Then he begged, apologetic, for her to "write & tell me something in prose or verse, & I will be less fastidious in future & willing to write clumsy things, rather than none."

She held firm. She wanted him to visit. "I would like to thank you for your great kindness," she wrote stiffly, "but never try to lift the words which I cannot hold. Should you come to Amherst, I might then succeed, though Gratitude is the timid wealth of those who have nothing." At the letter's close, she returned, more emotionally, to her appeal. He had saved her life, she reminded him. "To thank you in person has been since then one of my few requests. The child that asks my flower 'Will you,' he says—'Will you' and so to ask for what I want I know no other way."

Her request was direct and unequivocal. And she possessed a fine sense of drama.

THOUGH INTRIGUED, perhaps half in love (or so he may have fancied), and doubtless moved by this strange woman, he would not stand at the threshold of the Homestead for yet another year. He would never antagonize Mary with a special trip to see the poetess his wife regarded as crazy.

"Why do the insane cling to you so?" Mary had crossly asked. To Higginson that was a compliment. "The great reason why the real apostles of truth don't make any more impression is this—," he had explained to her many years before, "the moment any person among us begins to broach any 'new views' and intimate that all things aren't exactly right, the conservatives lose no time in holding up their fingers and branding him as an unsafe person—fanatic, vision-ary, insane."

He had not changed. "If every man who is accused of having a crack in his brain is to be silenced, which of us is safe?" he asked. Half-crack'd visionaries: they remained, always, his ideal.

And when he told Dickinson that he had to put off his trip to Amherst because of work, he had spoken the truth. To make ends meet, he clambered aboard trains to lecture in out-of-the-way places, for his writing could not pay all the bills even though Fields in 1866 had offered him one thousand dollars for ten *Atlantic* articles. But when Fields renewed the offer the following year, Higginson turned it down. He hated choosing subjects near at hand, he said, referring to his accounts of army life, which he reluctantly began publishing in 1864 and detested writing.

"I feel this strangely in turning over my army papers, they seem to belong to some one twinborn with me, but who led a wholly dif-ferent life from me," he had written his family. "It is hard to link ourselves to this something which was ourselves but is no longer & never will be again." Although he missed the camaraderie of the men and the daily sense that he was doing good and that he was respected, even loved, for it, Higginson did not idealize the days of grisly war. To write of them—of himself during them—was diffi-cult. "That I was in it [the war] myself seems the dreamiest thing of all," he said.

> I cannot put my hand upon it in the least, and if some one convinced me, in five minutes, some morning, that I never was there at all, it seems as if it wd. all drop quietly out of my life, & I shld read my own letters & think they were some one else's. This is one thing that makes it hard for me to work on them, or write anything about those days.

But he forced himself because he had a mission: to educate the public about the heroism of the black troops. "Until it is done," he knew, "the way will not seem clear for other things."

Still, he was unhappy. He looked haggard. He had been slow to adjust to his new home in Newport, Rhode Island, the temperate seaside perch where Mary and her several cats had moved while her husband skirmished in South Carolina. Though she hoped the salty sea breeze would reinvigorate her, she had come for more than climate: paternal seat of the Channings, with its picturesque coastline, gambrel-roofed houses, and puffed sense of its history, Newport was, as Henry James would say, the "one right residence in all our great country." For centuries it was also a hospitable spot for Quakers, antinomians, Jews, Unitarians, and other freethinking heretics, although the Irish philosopher Bishop George Berkeley, shortly after stepping ashore, took up the local custom and purchased himself two slaves. More recently artists and eccentrics and plutocrats included the James family, the architect Richard Morris Hunt, his brother the painter William Morris Hunt, the matchless John La Farge (one of Higginson's favorites), and Longfellow's witty brother-in-law, Tom Appleton, the man who reputedly said "Good Americans, when they die, go to Paris." (Oscar Wilde later borrowed the remark—and credit for it; Higginson borrowed it too.) Writers also flocked to Newport: Julia Ward Howe, who with Higginson formed a Town and Country Club, the poet Kate Field, Mary Mapes Dodge (author of *Hans Brinker*), and the perky widow Helen Hunt, who, mourning her husband and son, had rented two dainty rooms in the place where the Higginsons boarded.

Higginson preferred the physical beauty of the place to the people and so stretched his long legs along the crooked streets near the shaggy warehouses or poked about the old hulks and fancy yachts in the cluttered mast yards. Ambling over the sturdy unpainted wharves, among rusty anchors and old barrels, he called this part of town Oldport to distinguish it from the more affluent section of the city, with its grand liveries and well-dressed hotels. Year-round residents like the Higginsons paid scant attention to the rich summer people, he wrote in *The Atlantic,* with their gowns and gossip. Instead he lived for the pale, hazy light that in winter played on the water when the sun narrowed and the sky turned the color of charcoal. He sat on the cliffs near the beach and watched red and green sailboats flash before him; he collected driftwood from sandy coves and repeated the names of the rock formations for the sound of them: Hanging Rock, Spouting Rock, Paradise Rocks. It wasn't Massachusetts but would have to serve.

The Higginsons were staying at Mrs. Hannah Dame's boardinghouse on Broad Street, a wide, leafy thoroughfare fronted by great elms and commodious eighteenth-century houses. Seated in a wide chair with its arms rigged as pear-shaped tables, Mary amused her

Thomas Wentworth Higginson at 46,
in Rhode Island, 1870.

guests with her crusty maxims and her innumerable barbs about
people and books. Good-hearted Helen Hunt tried to entertain her,
decorating Mrs. Dame's back parlor with baskets of flowers for a
musical evening of Mendelssohn, Haydn, and Beethoven, arranged
both for Mary's benefit and for Wentworth's, so he could repay the
courtesies of his neighbors without excluding his wife. Otherwise,
he occasionally stepped out to this or that soiree with the vivacious
Mrs. Hunt on his chaste arm.

But he had no political traction. His appointment to the Newport School Committee was vetoed because one of its members
assumed that, as a soldier in the First South Carolina Regiment of
Volunteers of African Descent, he had to be black. Elected regardless
(the mistake was discovered), in sweet retaliation Higginson abol-

ished segregated schools in Newport. For his efforts, he lost the next election.

Proudly calling himself a Black Republican, Higginson viewed Reconstruction as the opportunity to eliminate discriminatory practices and laws; Reconstruction, to him, first meant the redistribution of the land of the former plantations to the freed slaves, for he was not eager to appease former Confederates and, less so, former slaveholders. He also launched a verbal campaign to end segregation in the North as well as the South, on the streetcars of Philadelphia, in the schools of New York, or in the special galleries reserved for black people in Boston theaters. "When the freedmen are lost in the mass of freemen, then the work will be absolutely complete," he wrote. And he advocated full and immediate enfranchisement, which he termed simply fair play. The best preparation for freedom is freedom: "Fail in this result, and the future holds endless disorders," he warned his readers, "with civil war reappearing at the end."

Though he often spoke in public on behalf of the Freedmen's Aid Society (his sister Anna was secretary of the Brattleboro, Vermont, bureau), he declined to join the New England branch as one of its officers. "I do not want to give any more years of my life exclusively to those people now, as much as I am attached to them," he told his sisters. Also, he was dubious about the project: though intending to make good on General Sherman's promise to give every family of former slaves forty acres and a mule, General Saxton, now assistant commissioner of the Freedmen's Bureau in Florida, Georgia, and South Carolina, was blocked at every turn by white farmers who wanted to keep the black population from owning land. Precipitously mustered out of service in 1866, Saxton was replaced by the unscrupulous (Higginson's word) Brigadier General John M. Brannan, a former military head of the Department of the South. "If it had been left to him," Higginson complained, "the freedmen would not have had a house, nor a school, nor a musket, nor a friend; the colored women would have had no liberty, except to be the concubines of the United States officers; nor the men, but to be their servants."

Confiscated land was soon handed back to its former white owners, ex-Confederates were reseated in Congress, and men like Nathan Bedford Forrest, after presiding over the capture—or the massacre—of black troops at Fort Pillow, went on to lead the newly founded Ku Klux Klan. Affairs in the president's office weren't much better. Andrew Johnson failed to carry out the mandate of the Radical Republicans, and Higginson wrote scornfully that "what most men mean to-day by the 'president's plan of reconstruction' is the pardon of every rebel for the crime of rebellion, and the utter refusal to pardon a single black loyalist for the crime of being black." In the North the situation was almost as bad. The expectations heaped on the freed slave were so unrealistic—a racism in reverse—that Higginson cried, "Do you suppose that black men are born into the world such natural saints that none of the vices of the white men are found among them?"

His outcries lost to the ephemera of journalism, Higginson's lasting contributions to Reconstruction were his *Atlantic* essays on the war, collected in 1869 as *Army Life in a Black Regiment.* Including material copied directly from his journals as well as a narrative of his three expeditions, his ruminations on the valor of the black soldier—and his outrage that black soldiers had been underpaid when paid at all—*Army Life* is a minor masterpiece. Today considered gently racist, if not condescending, it nonetheless remains a striking, unusual, and empathetic social document; its account of daily activity in the army during wartime is riveting in its detail, compassion, and humor. Higginson's very real affection for his regiment is evident on every page, as is his pride in what he and his soldiers were able to do, and his transcriptions of the spirituals sung by his men is itself a remarkable—and groundbreaking—contribution to African American folk culture.

At the heart of the book is the voluptuous Sea Islands, a tropical forest of Arden in a world of violence: "Galloping through green lanes, miles of triumphal arches of wild roses,—roses pale and large and fragrant, mingled with great boughs of the white cornel, fantastic masses, snowy surprises,—such were our rides, ranging from eight to fifteen and even twenty miles," he wrote. "Back to a later dinner with our various experiences, and perhaps specimens to match,—a thunder-snake, eight feet long; an armful of great white, scentless pond-lilies. After dinner, to the tangled garden for rosebuds or early magnolias, whose cloying fragrance will always bring back to me the full zest of those summer days."

Edmund Wilson, calling *Army Life* limpid and unaffected, likened it to the memoirs of General Grant, and praising Higginson's lush description, Howard Mumford Jones, a twentieth-century literary critic, called *Army Life* a study in enchantment. But it is also an expression of disenchantment: frustration with stereotypes and pat assumptions, with empty promises and vainglorious men, and surprise at the revelation that you might not be the person you thought you were. It is therefore a book of lights gleaming in the dark, of Southern marshes and Northern confusion, of tangled vegetation and of fearsomeness and fragile hope.

Nowhere is this clearer than in "A Night in the Water," a stunning, almost existential essay composed in Higginson's most straightforward, pellucid style. Again his metaphor is of swimming into unknown territory, and this time he recounts a nighttime excursion when, swimming naked, he is suddenly clutched by fear:

> Doubts trembled in my mind like the weltering water, and that awful sensation of having one's feet unsupported, which benumbs the spent swimmer's heart, seemed to clutch at mine, though not yet to enter it. I was more absorbed in that singular sensation of nightmare, such as one may feel equally when lost by land or by water, as if one's own position were all right, but the place looked for had somehow been preternaturally abolished out of the universe. At best, might not a man in the water lose all his power of direction, and so move in an endless circle until he sank exhausted? It required a deliberate and conscious effort to keep my brain quite cool. I have not the reputation of being of an excitable temperament, but the contrary; yet I could at that moment see my way to a condition in which one might become insane in an instant. It was as if a fissure opened somewhere, and I saw my way into a mad-house; then it closed, and everything went on as before.

Like Dickinson, he too could find poetry in these deep, dark states of mind. They must have known this about each other. But for Higginson the vision of blankness passes. Everything goes on as before. He is a daylight man.

Yet there was more to him than sunshine and reform, and perceptive readers, like Dickinson, could sense it.

In 1869, William Dean Howells, preferring the book's soldiering to its poetry, favorably reviewed it in *The Atlantic,* which he, not Higginson, would soon take over, and observed, rather ruefully, that the nation had grown tired of racial issues.

· · ·

IN NEWPORT, HIGGINSON CHOPPED WOOD early in the morning for exercise. It staved off depression. In the afternoon he swung from parallel bars and taught calisthenics at the gymnasium he had helped found. At dusk he sauntered about town. He also sat at his desk for four hours each day, pen in hand. In addition to the promised articles for Fields, he reviewed books like Thoreau's *Cape Cod*—he had hoped to edit Thoreau's journals—and he continued to contribute a steady stream of articles to *The Independent, The Radical, The Nation,* and the *New York Tribune,* in which he called for the education and enfranchisement of the freed slaves.

And at the same time aching to do something completely different, he inched his way toward a novel.

But aside from the astonishing "Night in the Water," Higginson's finest work remained his political writing. Packing his outrage into sentences of force, grace, and civility that made his anger all the more pointed, he said exactly what he meant. He did not gussy up his prose with scholarly comment or learned allusions. "All Southern white men cannot be instantaneously convinced that their late slave is a man and a brother," he declared in 1865, "nor is it necessary that they should be. It will be enough, for the present, to convince them that he must be treated like one." He declaimed in strong, ringing terms fueled by ethical self-certainty, as when he excoriated northerners and liberals in Congress.

> It is we who are permitting black loyalists to be disarmed, and white rebels to be armed again, under the name of "militia." It is we who are permitting open proclamation of the re-establishment of slavery under the name of "apprenticeship." It is we who consent to the exclusion from the courts and the ballot-box of those who have fought to reopen the ballet-box and re-establish the power of the courts. It is we who are reviving the old assumption that "the people" of the South means the white population, rebel or otherwise; and that the black loyalists are something less than "the people."

Yet he devalued his political writing as unliterary. "It is not that politics are so unworthy, but that no one man can do everything," he wrote in *The Atlantic* essay "A Plea for Culture," which had prompted a note of approval from Dickinson. "There are a thousand rough-hewn brains which can well perform the plain work which American statesmanship now demands, without calling on the artist to cut blocks with his razor. His shrinking is not cowardice," he continued; "this relief from glaring publicity is the natural condition under which works of art mature. . . . A book is the only immortality."

A book—not journalism, not politics, not the transient affairs of the everyday. This is what Emily Dickinson dreamed of. Perhaps he was thinking of her. ("A precious—mouldering pleasure—'tis— / To meet an Antique Book—.")

"In these later years, the arduous reforms into which the life-blood of Puritanism has passed have all helped to train us for art," Higginson observed, "because they have trained us in earnestness, even while they seemed to run counter to that spirit of joy in which art has its being." Higginson caught the drift of what had happened to his—and Dickinson's—Puritan heritage: that cleft between action and art, or what he called earnestness and joy. But he was also rationalizing his steady removal from the cause that had shaped his life, that had brought him to the church and thrust him out of it. Nurtured on the New, steeped in the exuberance of a just reform, Higginson had entered the war half-skeptical, half-hopeful: he saw his country sundered, its ideals politicized, its racism pervasive, and he understood, as if for the first time, how intractable institutions are, how difficult it is to change them. In Newport his political efficacy was nil. "I don't believe there is a man here whom it cost more to come here than it did me," he would reflect in his journal. "I don't believe there has been a blacker Republican than I. I know for one that I have tried to find a sufficient sphere of duty inside the Republican party, and it has been nothing more or less than hard knocks and blows that drove me out of it." His specific references are unclear, but the corruption and meretricious razzle-dazzle of post-war America—the era soon known as the Gilded Age—and the material excess so palpable in Newport disgusted him. "Nobody has any weight in America who is not in Congress," he bleakly observed, "and nobody gets into Congress without the necessity of bribing or button-holing men whom he despises."

Disillusioned by the military, by the government, by the intransigence of the South, he justified his withdrawal into art, claiming—incredibly—that "except to secure the ballot for woman, a contest which is thus far advancing very peaceably, there seems nothing left which need be absolutely fought for; no great influence to keep us from a commonplace and perhaps debasing success." More and more he preferred a different, more creative writing. "My nature seems to be rather that of an artist than that of a thinker," he had confided in Emerson, wishing it were so.

Restless, he also befriended Hawthorne's eldest daughter, the lovely and star-crossed Una, who was briefly engaged to his favorite nephew, Storrow. Calling on Hawthorne's widow and daughters at the Wayside, itself a vestige of former times, Higginson sat in their plain, chilly parlor—perhaps in the very chair where Hawthorne had sat—and thumbed through the great man's notebooks. This was what he wanted: Hawthorne's rectitude, his devotion to his art, his single-mindedness. If he had to ignore Hawthorne's despair or his odd friendship with Franklin Pierce, so be it; all that paled next to the man's achievement. The only immortality is a book.

If his commitment to social change prevented Higginson's devoting himself to art, it also protected him from the fear that, without it, he might lose his sense of direction, as he suggested in "A Night in the Water." But now his mother, recently deceased, was unable to censure him, and the war—and its disappointing aftermath—momentarily scraped his conscience clean, so he rolled up his sleeves and wrote three sketches of "Oldport," the setting for his novel *Malbone,* and two short stories, "The Haunted Window" and "An Artist's Dream." These tales assuaged his guilt about writing *Malbone* because, in them, he punishes the protagonists for doing what he himself wished to do.

Flavored with atmospheric Gothic effects, "The Haunted Window" is interesting less for its contrived plot and moral pabulum than for the fact that the apparition's name is Emilia, a name that Higginson will use again in his novel. Emilia is art, the tempting seductress who drives men mad. And in the other story, pseudo-Hawthorne even to the title ("An Artist's Dream"), Higginson's narrator visits a happily married artist and his beautiful wife, Laura—the Petrarchan reference meant to be self-evident—and realizes that while the couple are passionate about each other, they mostly ignore their child. "Is it," asks Laura, referring to her marriage, "a great consecration, or a great crime." This answer is conventionally obvious, and when she dies, her bereaved husband discovers that it is their child and not his art that can relieve his awful suffering: "the artist had attained his dream," Higginson concludes his fable.

The apex of all this was *Malbone,* the Hawthornean romance he announced to his sisters not long after his second trip to the Wayside, jubilantly reporting that Fields would be printing it serially in *The Atlantic* during the first six months of 1869. This was the book, published later that year, that Dickinson had planted on the table at the Homestead when he came to call.

Malbone is the story of Higginson's doppelgänger, the indolent and fickle Philip Malbone, whose good looks turn the heads of both sexes. Higginson admitted that he had modeled Malbone in part on William Hurlburt, but he is also based on Higginson's nephew Storrow, whose unpardonable sin—a dalliance with another woman?—caused Una Hawthorne suddenly to break their engagement. But Malbone mostly sounds like Higginson himself, recast as the artist who falls in love with his fiancée's untamed half sister, Emilia, often referred to as Emily.

When he wrote *Malbone,* Higginson had not yet met Emily Dickinson in person, so he freely imagined her as lovely but intangible, with "a certain wild, entangled look . . . , as of some untamed outdoor thing, and [with] a kind of pathetic lost sweetness in her voice, which made her at once and forever a heroine of romance." And it is this Emily/Emilia that is his Laura, his ideal, his symbol of the unadulterated, untrammeled pursuit of art. For, as Malbone says, "Every one must have something to which his dreams can cling, amid the degradations of actual life, and this tie is more real than the degradation; and if he holds to the tie, it will one day save him."

But, also like Higginson, Malbone cannot attain his dream lover: he cannot lose himself in his pursuit of the ideal, and thus the affair between Malbone and Emilia ends tragically, when late one night, Emilia drowns in a stormy, featureless sea.

Emilia gone, Higginson thus restores the order of things, as convention prescribes. But convention had nothing to say about the nooks and crannies of an unusual friendship.

THE LONG-ANTICIPATED MEETING: in the Homestead parlor after eight years of correspondence and tantalizing bafflement, Emily Dickinson and Colonel Thomas Wentworth Higginson stood together in the same room. "Forgive me if I am frightened," she apologized. "I never see strangers & hardly know what I say—." Nervous, she talked without stopping. Occasionally she paused to ask him to speak and then started all over again. "Manner between Angie Tilton & Mr. Alcott," he noted, referring to the two gabbiest people he knew, "but thoroughly ingenuous & simple which they are not & saying many things which you would have thought foolish & I wise."

He listed a few of her pungent observations:

"I find ecstasy in living — the mere sense of living is joy enough."

"How do most people live without any thoughts."

"Is it oblivion or absorption when things pass from our minds?"

"Truth is such a *rare* thing it is delightful to tell it."

She told him more about her family. Her father read only on Sunday, "*lonely & rigorous* books," she added for emphasis. She made bread for her father because he liked only hers, Higginson noted, "& says, 'people must have puddings' this *very* dreamily, as if they were comets — so she makes them." Doubtless she was ironic. And hyperbolic. She claimed she had not known how to read a clock until she was fifteen. "My father thought he had taught me but I did not understand & I was afraid to say I did not & afraid to ask any one else lest he should know." Her mother was weak. "I never had a mother," she said. "I suppose a mother is one to whom you hurry when you are troubled." Dickinson endured alone.

They discussed literature. She said that she and her brother had hidden Longfellow's novel *Kavanagh* under the piano cover to outfox their strict father, who forbade it. A friend concealed other books in a bush by the door. To read was to defy with pleasure.

They discussed poetry. Suggestively. Here was another form of transgression and transformation, erotic and inflammatory. "If I read a book," she declared, "[and] it makes my whole body so cold no fire ever can warm me I know *that* is poetry. If I feel physically as if the top of my head were taken off, I know *that* is poetry. These are the only way I know it. Is there any other way."

Poetry, again, as explosive force: he must have felt the pull, the energy, her sexuality. He left exhausted but in the evening walked back to the house. Afterward, hinting at the sexual tension — and release — of the whole experience, he admitted he had never met anyone "who drained my nerve power so much. Without touching her, she drew from me."

"I am glad not to live near her," he concluded.

The remarkable encounter, far exceeding his expectations, was too much for him.

He had flirted with the writer Helen Hunt, he had flirted with others, but he had always chosen the straight and narrow. Emily

Dickinson demanded nothing short of a full commitment. Irreducibly herself, without compromise, she took everything, drained the cup, was irresistible. And to Higginson, far too dangerous.

WHEN HE TOOK HIS HAT for the last time that day, he promised the poet he would come again sometime. "Say in a long time," she mischievously answered, "that will be nearer. Some time is nothing."

As usual she was right.

Her Deathless Syllable

Something indescribable had passed between them, something encapsulated in his remark that she "drew" from him and in her similar observation, sent to him after the visit, that "the Vein cannot thank the Artery." But on the surface, Higginson's coming to Amherst had changed nothing. After he left, he saw his family in Brattleboro before riding back to Newport, which he liked less and less, and to Mary, who suffered more and more. He attended meetings of the Radical Club, delivered his speeches, wrote his journalism, chugged along the railroad to Boston and New York. And he composed an essay defending Sappho, "the most eminent poetess in the world," against prurient hecklers made anxious, he believed, precisely because she was a woman.

Did he recognize the similarities between Dickinson and the Mytilene poet? It seems not; yet while he ranked Sappho "unapproached among women, even to the present day," the timing of the essay suggests Dickinson tugged at the back of his mind, her lapidary lyric reminding him of what he admired in the ancient author. And so, though she had drained him, Higginson could not, would not close the door. He understood now she would never come to Boston to sit in the high-toned drawing rooms of the ladies. He would have to go to her.

Impossible. Instead, both of them savored the safe, satisfying distance of their subtle intimacy.

And she wanted more. When he mentioned the possibility of coming back to lecture at the college, she asked, almost wistfully, "Could you not come without the Lecture if the project failed?" She sent more verse. "When I hoped I feared— / Since I hoped I dared," she wrote, obliquely confiding how much she had anticipated his visit, and in "Remembrance has a Rear and Front" she alluded to her feelings when it was over:

> *Remembrance has a Rear and Front.*
> *'Tis something like a House —*
> *It has a Garret also*
> *For Refuse and the Mouse —*
>
> *Besides the deepest Cellar*
> *That ever Mason laid —*
> *Look to it by it's Fathoms*
> *Ourselves be not pursued —*

She remembered him; she would long remember him. (Does her image of "Rear and Front" refer to the military?) But in the poem's perplexing last lines, Dickinson suggested that in remembrance lay unspeakable, haunting loneliness.

"I remember your coming as serious sweetness placed now with the Unreal—," she commented in September, adding two lines of poetry to the body of her letter, as was her custom:

> *Trust adjusts her "Peradventure" —*
> *Phantoms entered "and not you."*

She then barraged him with questions: Where could she find the poems of Maria White Lowell he mentioned? "You told me Mrs Lowell was Mr Lowell's 'inspiration' What is inspiration?" she cagily asked. As for an article of Wentworth's in *The Woman's Journal,* "perhaps the only one you wrote that I never knew," would he send it? She apologized for the request with dramatic flourish, "Shortness to live has made me bold"; no wonder her brother, Austin, accused her of being theatrical and years later, after her death, said she had posed in her letters to Higginson. But doubtless she posed to Austin, too, concealing from him the turbulence of her feelings and frequently speaking in parables he likely did not comprehend.

She penciled yet another poem for Higginson. This one also may refer to their meeting:

> *The Riddle that we guess*
> *We speedily despise —*
> *Not anything is stale so long*
> *As Yesterday's Surprise.*

Had she been a disappointment? Did she fear she was a riddle gone stale? "You ask great questions accidentally," she remarked. "To answer them would be events."

She drafted more poems to him, evidently unsent. "Too happy Time dissolves itself / And leaves no remnant by— / 'Tis Anguish not a Feather hath / Or too much weight to fly—." Perhaps she did not want him to know, though, how fleeting—how happy—their time together had been. "I was refreshed by your strong Letter," she thanked him in another note, also apparently unmailed. She jotted out her replies to him in rough drafts, making certain that she put herself forward with much the same vigilant care that she lavished on her verse, which, it seems, he now considered extraordinary. "Thank you for Greatness—I will have deserved it in a longer time!" she exclaimed, the future perfect tense wittily revealing her intentions.

She wrote to Higginson as if he grasped her meaning, though he was, as he admitted, often befuddled. But he understood enough to please her, that was clear. And she coached him, coaxed him, comprehended him. "You place the truth in opposite—," she reminded him after his visit, "because the fear is mine, dear friend, and the power your's—." He did not know his own strength; her backbone made of steel, she pretended fragility. Here, in a poem ostensibly describing a grave, she asks Higginson to "Step lightly on this narrow Spot—":

> Step lightly on this narrow Spot —
> The Broadest Land that grows
> Is not so ample as the Breast
> These Emerald Seams enclose —
>
> Step lofty for this name be told
> As far as cannon dwell,
> Or Flag subsist, or Fame export
> Her deathless Syllable

Eight years earlier, she had told him that she could not escape fame if it belonged to her, but since it did not, and probably would not, "My Barefoot-Rank is better." Though real, diffidence was part of her performance. She rejected, fancied, courted, renounced, and intended to collar fame on her own terms, as the last four lines of the poem suggest. A book is the only immortality, Higginson had said. She stood ready, a loaded gun.

Perhaps that is why she sewed her poems together in packets with thread, making them open and close like a folio. Perhaps those packets were intended as books that might sit, with their kinsmen, on a shelf. ("I thank these Kinsmen of the Shelf—," she wrote in "Unto my Books—so good to turn—.") And perhaps she surmised her subtle poems, bestowed on only a few, would disappear in the common light of conventional day—but would persist, as indeed they did, if she chose her readers wisely.

As for other poets, she did not read Joaquin Miller, as she told Higginson, who'd inquired, and she complimented the poems of Helen Hunt, which he'd recently reviewed in *The Atlantic:* "Stronger than any written by Women since Mrs — Browning, with the exception of Mrs. Lewes." Emily duplicated Wentworth's language before pausing and then adding, equivocally, "—but truth like Ancestor's Brocades can stand alone."

It was Higginson's writing she complimented most often, and he in turn wanted to know what she thought of it. When she failed to comment on his *Atlantic* piece "A Shadow," he prodded her, or so we can gather from her somewhat noncommittal reply: "I thought I spoke to you of the shadow—It affects me." Yet his new collection, *Atlantic Essays,* which included "A Letter to a Young Contributor," prompted Emily to ask him again to guide her. Even if he could offer her nothing but encouragement and, those few grammatical touch-ups certain only to tickle her, she desired his opinion, perhaps more than ever.

That opinion was far higher than his critics have guessed. Frequently he praised her poems to friends in Newport, and when he happened on the volume published by another Amherst native, Emily Fowler Ford, he cried, "Amherst must be a *nest* of poetesses." As one friend reported, he boasted that he had "letters from Emily Dickinson containing the loveliest little delicate bits of poetry imaginable—he said they always reminded him of skeleton leaves so pretty," but when asked why they weren't widely available, he answered, "They were *too delicate*—not strong enough to publish." Perhaps he believed this, but perhaps he was protecting Dickinson, who was ambivalent about publishing—at least then. Perhaps both are true.

Higginson did promote the poems of another Amherst native, Helen Hunt, who remembered the Dickinsons from childhood: the pompous father, the invalid wife, the fat and rusticated sister. But Hunt had hated Amherst. "I do think Amherst girls turn out (excuse me—) horridly!" she once declared. That was a lifetime ago. In 1852 she had married Edward Bissell Hunt, an army engineer whom Emily herself remembered as once saying, after a visit, that he'd come back in a year; "if I say a shorter time it will be longer," he'd added. (The memory inspired an early Dickinson sleuth to propose Major Hunt as Dickinson's Master, although the evidence is pretty thin.) But Emily doubtless shared the anecdote with Higginson to tease him about his own vague promise of return.

Inventor of a one-person submarine, Major Hunt was killed when his vessel accidentally exploded, and in 1866, after the Hunts' only surviving son had died of diphtheria, Helen Hunt resettled in Newport, where she and her husband had briefly lived. There the resilient widow met Colonel Higginson, with whom, or so several scholars have speculated, she fell in love.

Maybe so. Hunt did find support in this overburdened husband, and Higginson responded warmly to her, entranced by her zeal for poetry and people. "Her friendships with men had the frankness and openness that most women show only to one another," Higginson later noted, "and her friendships with women had the romance and ideal atmosphere that her sex usually reserves for men." But loyal to Mary and propriety, he checked himself. And to judge by her novel *Mercy Philbrick's Choice,* he disappointed her, for there the Higginson-like character is pitifully harnessed to an invalid relative, "the one great duty of his life." To a friend, Hunt was more explicit: he steps too softly, Hunt said of Higginson, "knocks like a baby at the door, & then opens it a quarter of the way & comes in edgewise!"

Yet he launched her career, advising her to establish herself by writing reviews and then urging her poems, which he considered intensely passionate, on a reluctant Fields, who published them, as it happened, to wide success. Higginson read almost everything she wrote, editing much of her work with his blue pencil. "I shall never write a sentence, so long as I live," Hunt would thank him, "without studying it from the standpoint of whether you would think it could be bettered." He praised her novels, like *Ramona,* which called attention to the plight of Mission Indians and which he otherwise would have considered didactic, but since she never wholly lost her sense of form, far more important to him than any moral mission, he placed Hunt's work above that of any American woman—except, as he later admitted, Emily Dickinson.

Attraction to his fellow boarder was not the only reason Higginson served as Hunt's literary cicerone. He consistently boosted women writers, offering editorial advice as well as entrée into the literary world. In addition to Hunt and Harriet Prescott Spofford, there were Celia Thaxter, Rose Terry Cooke, Kate Field, Lucy Larcom, and Emma Lazarus, to name just a few of the authors whose craft he praised, whose work he edited, whose essays and verse he forwarded to editors like Fields, Theodore Tilton, and, later, Richard Watson Gilder. Quality knew no gender, he insisted, just hard work, commitment, sacrifice. His eulogy of Charlotte Hawes, a friend from his Worcester days, contained his mantra about achieving "perfection in every sentence"—rewriting, if need be, until each word glimmered.

After the war he redoubled his commitment to equal pay for women, equal education, and equal rights under the law, as well as his commitment to their receiving from an early age the kind of material, economic, and emotional support generally denied them. "In almost any town in New England the obstacle in the studious girl is not want of time," he declared, "but want of teaching and encouragement." He wrote hundreds of articles on the subject, the cause of women replacing abolition as his social passion. But war had siphoned off most of the energy of the women's movement, and the movement itself suffered an internal rupture when Elizabeth Cady Stanton and Susan B. Anthony campaigned against the Fourteenth and Fifteenth Amendments. Everyone walks through the door or no one does, insisted Stanton and Anthony, who opposed any amendment giving the vote only to men. More moderate feminists and former abolitionists disagreed, arguing this was the "Negro's hour." The ladies' turn would come. Higginson sided with the moderates. The enfranchisement of black men is what he had fought for, and much as he supported women's rights, he could not support any demand that threatened to protract his thirty-year battle against slavery.

In 1869, Stanton and Anthony founded the all-female National Woman Suffrage Association. (Frederick Douglass had called Stanton and Anthony racist for putting woman suffrage ahead of the gubernatorial candidacy of a black man.) That same year Higginson, along with Lucy Stone, Henry Blackwell, and Julia Ward Howe, formed the American Woman Suffrage Association: "Without deprecating the value of Associations already existing, it is yet deemed . . . an organization at once more comprehensive and more widely representative." They were reformers, not revolutionaries.

The man who had run guns to Kansas, a bowie knife stuck in his boot, had not renounced radicalism as much as he had toned it down, subordinating it to a pragmatism born of experience and disappointment: John Brown had been hanged; and the war waged to free the slaves had lasted four miserable years, cost over six hundred thousand lives, and left in its wake a racist infrastructure in the South and "colorphobia" in the North. "There are things which are within our power, and there are things which are beyond our power," Epictetus had written; change the things we can change.

He tried to explain his position to Stanton, who patiently shook her head. "No! my dear friend we are right in our present position," she replied. "We demand suffrage for all the citizens of the republic in Reconstruction. I might not talk of negroes or women, but citizens." Higginson reverted to the hopeful notion he had once rejected: through suasion, law, and justice, women would gain the vote and the rights they deserved. No longer could he believe, as he once had, in disunion. "The world has always more respect for those who are unwisely zealous than for those who are fastidiously inactive," he admitted to Harriet Beecher Stowe. These days, though, he occupied a middle ground, which he considered the better side of wisdom.

One of his biographers quipped of Higginson that "before the war he never missed a good fight; after it he never joined one." This is not quite fair. Distancing himself without acrimony from Stanton and Anthony's all-or-nothing position on woman suffrage, Higginson did not entirely disagree with it. "If the conservatives think that because it [our organization] is called the Woman Suffrage Association it has no further object, they are greatly mistaken," he declared. "Its purpose and aim are to equalize the sexes in all the relations of life; to reduce the inequities that now exist in matters of education, in social life and in the professions — to make them equal in all respects before the law, society, and the world."

He addressed the first convention of the American Woman Suffrage Association in November 1869 — before he visited Amherst — and he planned to write an "Intellectual History of Women" — "my *magnum opus,* if I can really ever get to it." He praised women's colleges, women's athletics, and a woman's right to choose not to marry or bear children. He nominated women for membership in various bastions of male privilege, such as the National Institute of Arts, Science and Letters, which admitted Julia Ward Howe as a result. By 1873, he was president of the American Woman Suffrage Association, and in his weekly editorials to *The Woman's Journal,* its organ, he wrote sleek essays putting forward its case: "If there is only one woman in the nation who claims the right to vote, she ought to have it." Wondering how and why so many women seemed to oppose suffrage, he continued, "I do not see how any woman can help a thrill of indignation, when she first opens her eyes to the fact that it is really contempt, not reverence, that has so long kept her sex from an equal share of legal, political, and educational rights."

Literary rights, too: "The yearning for a literary career is just now greater among women than among men," he observed. "Perhaps it is because of some literary successes lately achieved by women. Perhaps it is because they have fewer outlets for their energies." Both were true. Women writers had entered the exclusive precincts of the literary marketplace, which, though restricted, was more welcoming than other professional venues. Higginson said he liked ambitious women who strove to achieve something against all odds, and he remarked that their letters to him—Dickinson's included?—"reveal such intellectual ardor and imagination, such modesty, and such patience under difficulties, as to do good to the reader, whatever they may do to the writer." Paternalistic, he nonetheless told them to heed their internal compass and, as if echoing Dickinson, to determine— as he must—how they define success. Success is counted sweetest, she had said, by those who never succeed.

And Higginson, who yearned for literary fame and likewise condemned it, could understand the conflict in others: to publish or not to publish, to advance oneself or not. Though driven, he who castigated his own need for recognition could easily identify with women reluctant to assert themselves. Nudging open literary doors for Helen Hunt, he could have done the same for Emily Dickinson. One suspects he would have, were she tractable, which she was not. Her own ambivalence about publishing her work, her own tensile strength, and her choice of an alternative route of publication— circulating her poems among friends, nurturing her reputation by piquing curiosity—rendered moot what Higginson could offer in the way of conventional channels. And Dickinson would know she did not write for—nor would be appreciated by—humdrum editors and standard readers.

Accused by the cadres of scholars who wish she had contacted a more prescient correspondent, like one of them, Higginson was a vigorous, liberal advocate of women writing, women voting, women educated and free, self-respecting and strong. Of this Dickinson had been amply aware for a very long time. She took what she needed and discarded the rest.

IN THE SPRING OF 1872, Higginson went to Europe, which he had long wanted to do. Depressed by Mary's deteriorated condition, frightened by the sudden death of his brother Francis, disgusted by Newport's empty sparkle, flummoxed by Susan B. Anthony's arrest, and annoyed by the editorial change at *The Atlantic,* where a callow William Dean Howells had replaced Fields as editor, Higginson accepted an offer to sail with his brother Waldo to England for a two-month visit. His sister Anna stayed with Mary; Mrs. Hunt went to California: time, all around, for a change of air.

"I am happy you have the Travel you so long desire," Emily coolly noted on his return, "and chastened—that my Master met neither accident nor Death." Most of all, though, she wanted him to travel to her. "Could you come again that would be far better—," she observed, "though the finest wish is the futile one."

Resuming her role as Scholar, she again sent him poems. "To disappear enhances—The Man that runs away / Is tinctured for an instant with Immortality," one of them begins, her use of "runs away" rather than "goes away" suggesting that she knew how much she had drained his nerve power. She also included the pointed "He preached opon 'Breadth' till it argued him narrow—," about the churchly self-righteous, sure to please him. And then there were the riddles of "The Sea said 'Come' to the Brook."

> *The Sea said "Come" to the Brook —*
> *The Brook said "Let me grow" —*
> *The Sea said "then you will be a Sea —*
> *I want a Brook —Come now"!*
>
> *The Sea said "Go" to the Sea —*
> *The Sea said "I am he*

> *You cherished" — "Learned Waters —*
> *Wisdom is stale — to Me" —*

Is Dickinson the Brook, telling Higginson she wants to grow into a sea by herself? But the Sea wants to keep the Brook as she is, for in the second stanza, once she has swelled to a sea, the Sea turns away, disappointed: " 'Learned Waters— / Wisdom is stale—to Me'—." It was an impasse.

Yet Dickinson coquettishly continued to ask for the advice he proffered, as was their ritual, and she continued to show him what she was writing. "Thank you for the 'Lesson,' " she customarily responded, probably in late 1872. "I will study it though hitherto." And when she mailed him poems or wrote to him, if he did not answer soon, she plaintively tried again. "Could you teach me now?" or "Will you instruct me then no more?"

Likely he recognized how little she needed from him, even technically. Her imagination was voracious, her images disquieting, her vision idiosyncratic, her language alive and gleaming. Yet she wanted to keep him close by and involved. "Longing is like the Seed / ," she wrote him in another poem, "That wrestles in the Ground, / Believing if it intercede / It shall at length be found."

Around this same time she also enclosed a leaf or a flower along with the poem "Dominion lasts until obtained—." It was a gift, an offering, mystical, seductive, brazen: "These are the Brides of permanence— / Supplanting me and you." She also sent one of her most accessible poems, "The Wind begun to rock the Grass," its description keen, about the coming of a summer squall. As usual, she had revised the poem—an earlier version uses the verb "knead" instead of "rock" in the first line ("The Wind begun to knead the Grass— / As Women do a Dough—")—but here is the copy she wanted Higginson to have:

> *The Wind begun to rock the Grass*
> *With threatening tunes and low —*
> *He flung a Menace at the Earth —*
> *A Menace at the Sky —*
>
> *The Leaves unhooked themselves from trees*
> *And started all abroad,*

The Dust did scoop itself like Hands
And throw away the Road.

The Wagons quickened on the Streets —
The Thunder hurried slow —
The Lightning showed a Yellow Beak,
And then a livid Claw —

The Birds put up the Bars to Nests
The Cattle fled to Barns —
Then came one Drop of Giant Rain
And then as if the Hands

That held the Dams had parted hold
The Water Wrecked the Sky
But overlooked my Father's House,
Just quartering a tree.

Strong, unpredictable verbs—wind rocking the grass, leaves unhooking themselves, dust scooping itself "like Hands"—combine to create the steady, inescapable onset of the storm—there is nothing we can do to forestall or prevent it—until the last stanza, when the "Water Wrecked the Sky": relief; then in an instant, horror.

She had asked if he could teach her now. "Your poem about the storm is fine," Higginson answered. "It gives the sudden transitions."

The sudden transitions: one can assume she was satisfied.

MOST OF ALL SHE WISHED he would come back to Amherst. And he did.

He arrived in the sleepy town on December 3, 1873. Though wintry, the air was mild and melting, the village calm, the trees bare, the sky starched, the undergraduates polite and numerous and, as Higginson noticed, obliged to exercise (unlike Harvard boys) and to listen to him lecture on woman suffrage, for which he was paid one hundred dollars.

He also inspected their gymnasium, fidgeted through a rhetoric class, chatted with President Stearns, and managed, as he had promised, to call on Miss Dickinson. Unfortunately for us, there is no transcript. If Higginson scribbled out his impressions for Mary, neither his notes nor the letters survive. Or, sensitive to the fact that Mary envied his freedom and distrusted his penchant for female companionship, particularly for women whose poetry he savored, he may have simply not recorded the visit.

Mary was ill disposed to his taste—she deplored Barrett Browning's *Aurora Leigh*—and surveyed his female friends with misgiving. "I don't dare die and leave the Colonel," she once snapped; "there are so many women waiting for him!" Nor was she particularly fond of Miss Dickinson, who had intrigued her husband with that aside of hers—"there is always one thing to be grateful for—that one is one's self & not somebody else"—which Mary thought "particularly absurd in E. D.'s case."

There is, though, a brief account of his visit in a letter to his sisters: "I saw my eccentric poetess Miss Emily Dickinson who *never* goes outside her father's ground & sees only me & a few others," he reported. Promising to read Dickinson's poetry to them when they came to Newport, he told how she had greeted him, holding a flower, this time a Daphne odora. Again she had clad her diminutive frame in fresh white. But as if distancing himself, for the sake of his sisters or because, once again, Emily had exhausted him, he concluded, "I'm afraid Mary's other remark, 'Oh why do the insane so cling to you?' still holds."

"How long are you going to stay," Dickinson had immediately asked, her voice barely audible. He couldn't stay long but did provide other assurances, promising he would not forget her, and four weeks later he sent New Year's greetings to tell her that he well remembered his recent trip to Amherst "& especially the time spent with you. It seemed to give you some happiness, and I hope it did;—certainly I enjoyed being with you."

These are not the words of the condescending cavalier come to gape at the "eccentric poetess." "Each time we seem to come together as old & tried friends," he reminded her, "and I certainly feel that I have known you long & well, through the beautiful thoughts and words you have sent me. I hope you will not cease to trust me and turn to me; and I will try to speak the truth to you, and with love."

"THANK YOU, DEAR FRIEND, for my 'New Year'; but did you not confer it?" Emily wrote Wentworth in early 1874, just a few weeks after he left. "Had your scholar permission to fashion your's, it were perhaps too fair. I always ran Home to Awe when a child, if anything befell me.

"He was an awful Mother," she continued, making the mother, "Awe," masculine, "but I liked him better than none. There remained this shelter after you left me the other Day."

Grateful for his recent visit, she continued, "Of your flitting Coming it is fair to think. Like the Bee's Coupe—vanishing in Music. Would you with the Bee return, what a firm of Noon!"

She was delighted to receive his recent letter, in which she still "heard him." "We hear after we see."

She then told him a story that reads like an allegory. "Meeting a Bird this Morning," she said, "I begun to flee. He saw it and sung." Did the Bird symbolize Wentworth, who, appreciating her shyness, sang to her—wrote to her—and offered his reassurance?

Both she and Higginson considered writing another form of nature, a second nature, as Emerson had said of art, grown out of the first, as a leaf out of a tree; but less pastoral than the transcendentalist guru, they saw nature as also a haunted house, as Dickinson had said, art a house that tries to be haunted. "When the paths that we have personally traversed are exhausted," Higginson noted in one of the essays Dickinson liked best, "memory holds almost as clearly those which the poets have trodden for us, those innumerable by-ways of Shakespeare, each more real than any high-road in England; or Chaucer's 'Little path I found / Of mintes full and fennell greene.' "

Writing as memory—indeed, memory itself—had become his implicit subject, and seasoning his essays with a characteristic pinch of nostalgia—recall "all the best description is *in memoriam*" from "Water-Lilies"—Higginson sidestepped the sudden transitions. "I have fineness," he said, evaluating himself candidly, "but some want of copiousness and fertility. . . . I wish I could, without sacrificing polish, write with that exuberance and hearty zeal." Grace and decency were his forte. "My gentility is chronic," he observed a little sadly shortly after his visit to Emily, recommending to her—to himself—cultivation of what he called the "ruddy hues of life."

"I wish you could see some field lilies, yellow & scarlet, painted in water colors that are just sent to us for Christmas," Wentworth wistfully wrote to her, knowing what she liked and what she didn't. "These are not your favorite colors, & perhaps I love the azure & gold myself." Then he added an afterthought directed at himself as well as her: "But perhaps we should learn to love & cultivate these ruddy hues."

He deferred to her. Though timorous, she was decisive. She spoke in aphorisms, her poetry and letters demanding that the reader meet her on her terms or not at all. She replied to Higginson by sending an atypically long poem (ten quatrains), carefully prepared, copied in ink, revised, and then recopied, as if to make it precise.

> *Because that you are going*
> *And never coming back*
> *And I, however absolute*
> *May overlook your Track —*
>
> *Because that Death is final,*
> *However first it be*
> *This instant be suspended*
> *Above Mortality.*
>
> *Significance that each has lived*
> *The other to detect*
> *Discovery not God himself*
> *Could now annihilate*
>
> *Eternity, Presumption*
> *The instant I perceive*
> *That you, who were Existence*
> *Yourself forgot to live —*
>
> *The "Life that is" will then have been*
> *A Thing I never knew —*
> *As Paradise fictitious*
> *Until the Realm of you —*
>
> *The "Life that is to be," to me,*
> *A Residence too plain*
> *Unless in my Redeemer's Face*
> *I recognize your own.*
>
> *Of Immortality who doubts*
> *He may exchange with me*

Curtailed by your obscuring Face
Of Everything but He —

Of Heaven and Hell I also yield
The Right to reprehend
To whoso would commute this Face
For his less priceless Friend.

If "God is Love" as he admits
We think that he must be
Because he is a "jealous God"
He tells us certainly

If "All is possible with" him
As he besides concedes
He will refund us finally
Our confiscated Gods —

Entrancing but opaque, the poem hinges on love and loss; the speaker acknowledges the departure of someone, perhaps her beloved, certainly her friend, and the departure gives rise to an extended farewell—a requiem of sorts. *Because* he is going: this provides the reason for the poem; *that* he is going: the speaker acknowledges, without sentimentality, the departure about to take place. But despite distance, or death, the speaker suggests that a real intimacy cannot be destroyed, even by God.

She is also aware that the beloved or friend "who were Existence / Yourself forgot to live—." To inhibit oneself is to forgo life's ruddy colors. This might have been what she detected in his hesitations: he, too, loved the azure and the gold but would have preferred something else. Yet the poem is also one of assurance, for a "refund" awaits both the "I" and the "you" (speaker and listener): their friendship is a pearl of great price.

As if she trusted him to eke out what meaning he could, she mailed the poem to Higginson, who saved it, but when he edited her poems for publication, he excluded it from both volumes. Maybe he didn't think it good—it sustains too many referents, too many ideas, too much abstraction—or maybe he thought it much too personal to share.

ELEVEN

The Realm of You

The transition to civilian life had been difficult. Writing again for the *Atlantic,* Higginson had immediately knocked heads with the pudgy wunderkind Howells, who had the gall to edit his work, and though Higginson kept quiet for a while, in 1871, when Howells apathetically remarked that he liked one of Higginson's articles " 'well enough,' " the insulted Colonel marched the piece over to the newly established *Scribner's Monthly* (edited by, of all people, the Dickinson friend Dr. Josiah Holland). "I hate to write in anything but the Atlantic," he explained the change to his sisters, "but don't quite like the look of things under the new regime & prefer to have two strings to my bow." He wouldn't publish in that magazine for another six years.

It was also the end of an era. Boston was no longer the self-proclaimed literary hub of the universe (Howells himself would eventually relocate to New York). Its Radical Club folded without a trace, detractors laughing in print over its anachronistic self-importance. Younger writers like Bret Harte (whom Higginson initially admired), Howells himself (whom Higginson eventually admired), and Henry James (whom Higginson mistrusted) had been nudging aside the fusty transcendentalists of yesteryear, mocked by a sardonic Henry Adams as poorly dressed hypocrites who gazed out of windows and declared, I am raining. Thoreau and Fuller were dead, Emerson would suffer from aphasia, Whitman remained unspeakable. Dickinson was unknown. Melville was in eclipse, and only the French cared about Poe. Everything was changing. In literature, realism, not romance, was the order of the day.

Spearheaded in America by Howells, realism meant, as Howells said, an accurate representation, not an idealization of reality: real people, their speech, their attitudes, their habits, their everyday business. Though he temperamentally agreed, Higginson had modeled his *Malbone* after a Hawthornean romance, just the kind of writing currently out of fashion. But to Higginson, style, not school, was the sine qua non of literature. Circumventing the debate over realism, he declared French prose writers to be unrivaled (he was thinking of Flaubert), and if their subject matter seemed a bit dour for Americans, who, as Howells famously said, wanted their tragedies to have happy endings, Higginson explained in 1867 that "they rely for success upon perfection of style and the most subtile analysis of human character; and therefore they are often painful,—just as Thackeray is painful,—because they look at artificial society, and paint what they see." Valuing simplicity, structure, freshness, and a catholicity of subject matter, he would embrace Turgenev, Tolstoy, and Stephen Crane.

The world had also been changing physically. Fire had demolished a large chunk of downtown Boston, which, like so many other cities, teemed with immigrants. Fortunes amassed in real estate, banking, railroads, and coal ushered in an era of voluptuous consumption—and building—nowhere better seen than in Newport, where the wealthy erected "cottages" as large as railroad terminals. Though he remained unremittingly optimistic—his reformer's zeal depended on an unshakable faith in a brighter, better future—he despaired, too, that in America "everything which does not tend to money is thought to be wasted."

And at home he was miserable. He dabbled in poetry, puzzling over what he had sacrificed to his marriage—and his chronic gentility—and in 1870 anonymously published a poem, "The Things I Miss":

> For all young Fancy's early gleams,
> The dreamed-of joys that still are dreams,
> Hopes unfulfilled, and pleasures known
> Through others' fortunes, not my own,
> And blessings seen that are not given,
> And never will be, this side heaven.
>
> Had I too shared the joys I see,
> Would there have been a heaven for me?
> Could I have felt Thy presence near,
> Had I possessed what I held dear?
> My deepest fortune, highest bliss,
> Have grown perchance from things I miss.

But except in his journal, he dared not speak aloud the "dreamed-of joys" denied him: the children he never had. Instead he channeled his sorrow into writing of and for them, whether in his popular *Young Folks' History of the United States* or his *Atlantic* essay "A Shadow" or one of his Oldport sketches, "Madam Delia's Expectations," where his identification with them is touchingly clear. A twelve-year-old orphan who works in a traveling tent show is adopted by two maiden ladies and yet so loathes the round of "well-behaved mediocrity"—as did Higginson—that she hustles back to the circus. But with the war over, Mary ill, Boston passé, Newport confining, what could Higginson do? Helen Hunt, in Newport less and less, had married William Sharpless Jackson, a railroad tycoon, and settled in Colorado; his sister Louisa had died; the circus was gone.

Though paid one thousand dollars in advance for his *Young Folks' History,* which would eventually sell far better than any of his other books, he worked round the clock to keep his pockets full. Lee and Shepard, publishers of the *History,* declared bankruptcy. Higginson felt faint, complained of weakness, feared the stroke that had paralyzed his brother Waldo and killed his brother Stephen. "In spite of my fine physique this life of confinement & anxiety is telling on me," he fretted. Mary was worse. "The walls seem only to draw closer around me year by year," he groaned. He did not know how to escape or where to go. His trip to England had boosted his morale— he had met Browning and Trollope, Darwin, and Carlyle—but that had lasted only two months. He wondered if he was a failure after all.

"My life indeed has disappointed me in the tenderest places and I have not had what I needed most—children and freedom. But how few lives succeed!" he tried to console himself. He went back to his writing. "The truth is," he wrote in "Childhood's Fancies," an essay for *Scribner's,* "that the child does not trouble himself to discriminate between the real and ideal worlds at all, but simply goes his way, accepts as valid whatever appeals to his imagination, and meanwhile lives out the day and makes sure of his dinner." It was an enviable life. "The easy faith of children," he concluded, "strengthens our own."

So, too, did faith in friendship.

THE SUDDEN TRANSITIONS came in blows for Emily Dickinson, starting with the death of her father.

A pillar of village affairs, as predictable as the church spire and utterly plainspoken—even his auburn hair shot bolt upright—over the years Edward Dickinson had remained a mirthless man, currying neither favor nor friendship. Without fail he walked the short distance between his home and his office and worked late into the night, when passersby could see the sole flicker of his lamp from the dark street. Conscientious and civic-minded and intending to put his beloved town on the Boston–Albany rail line and, having resigned his position as treasurer of Amherst College—Austin would replace him—in 1873 the seventy-year-old country lawyer decided to run again for a seat in the Massachusetts House. Never a Republican, he offered himself as an Independent in order to separate himself from the issues that he deplored and Republicans seemed to support, like woman suffrage (those women fist-shakers, he fumed, perennially in search of a weak legislature). One suspects he also detested Black Republicans, like Higginson, with their brash insistence on equality and enfranchisement.

Dickinson won the seat, and in January 1874, as representative of the Fourth District of Hampshire County, he rode to Boston, took a room in the Tremont House, and joined his fellow representatives at the domed State House, where he was appointed to the Special Committee of the Senate and House on the Hoosac Tunnel Line of Railroads. The costly tunnel, essential to the success of the railroad project, had been underwritten by the Commonwealth and needed more appropriations. But democracy moves slowly, and the legislative sessions dragged on until June. The thermometer inched up, nothing was settled, and the State House glistened in the white sun of an early heat wave.

On Tuesday morning, June 16, Dickinson rose to his feet to argue on behalf of appropriations for the Troy and Greenfield Railroad. His head felt light, but he managed to finish the speech and at one o'clock walked back to the Tremont House to eat dinner before packing his bag for home. He still felt ill. The physician he called diagnosed apoplexy and, according to Austin, idiotically administered opium or morphine, drugs that "had always been poison to him. Of course it killed him." Edward Dickinson was dead by six o'clock.

Emily, Lavinia, and their mother had been seated in the spacious dining room at the Homestead when Austin entered, a telegram clutched in his fist. "We were all lost, though I didn't know how,"

Emily recalled. Their father was very sick, said Austin, and he and Vinnie must go to Boston right away. The last train had already left. They would take the carriage. But before the harnesses were slung over the horses, another telegram carried word of Edward's death. Alone in a hotel room: it was too horrible.

Austin was particularly distraught. His tie to his father had not been warm, but it was deep, and when Edward's body lay in the Homestead parlor, Austin bent down over the open coffin and kissed his cold face, murmuring, "There, father, I never dared do that while you were living." This was a family that expressed itself in gesture: every morning Lavinia brushed her father's white beaver hat, and Emily, as we know, stood long hours in the hot kitchen kneading dough for the brown bread her father preferred. Dickinson remembered her father's last afternoon at home as special because when she sat with him, the two of them alone—Vinnie was asleep, Mother busy—"he seemed peculiarly pleased, as I oftenest stayed with myself," she informed Higginson, and actually "he 'would like it to not end.' " But the words had made her feel uncomfortable. She told her father he ought to go out and walk with Austin.

The funeral took place on Friday. "Mr. Bowles was with us— With that exception I saw none," she told Higginson. The shops of Amherst had closed, business was suspended, and neighbors and friends, spilling out from the large rooms of the Homestead, settled themselves on chairs dragged from College Hall to the Dickinson lawn. At the Homestead, Austin and Sue's daughter, Mattie, scattered pale white flowers near where Edward Dickinson lay. Gazing down at him, Sam Bowles commented that he "seemed as self-reliant and unsubdued as in life." Emily was nowhere to be seen; she stayed upstairs and wept and, according to her niece, for many weeks afterward wandered about the house, asking in a hollow voice where her father had gone.

"Miss Vinnie told me that she and Emily *feared* their father as long as he lived," reminisced a friend, "and loved him after his death."

The Reverend Jonathan Jenkins conducted the simple service, and then several college professors and businessmen from the town bore the coffin—no hearse—to the graveyard. They were followed by the officers of the college, Amherst's leading citizens, and a delegation of Dickinson's colleagues in the legislature. At the grave site

202 · WHITE HEAT

the Reverend Jenkins read the Lord's Prayer. "His Heart was pure and terrible," Emily afterward wrote to Wentworth, "and I think no other like it exists."

"Though it is many nights," she explained to her Norcross cousins later that summer, "my mind never comes home." She dreamed of her father—never the same dream—and in daylight wondered where he had gone, "without any body, I keep thinking." His absence was deafening. Austin stayed at the Homestead while Sue and the children visited Sue's relatives, but that did not dispel his father's ghost. "Home is so far from Home," she wrote to Higginson, "since my Father died."

"I have wished for you, since my Father died," she again turned to him, "and had you an Hour unengrossed, it would be almost priceless." She wanted him to come to Amherst; he could not now but, naturally, offered condolences to her and the family—"thank you for each kindness," she replied—but as far as she was concerned, she continued, he had actually given her something more precious. He had once written a poem that she recalled. "Your beautiful Hymn," she reminded him, "was it not prophetic?" In the spring of 1873, Wentworth had mailed Emily "Decoration," the poem that he'd just read at the Decoration Day ceremonies in Newport.

It opens with a drowsy conceit: its speaker stands "mid the flower-wreath'd tombs" of fallen Northern soldiers, bearing lilies in his hand. "Comrades!" he cries,

> . . . in what soldier-grave
> Sleeps the bravest of the brave?
>
> Is it he who sank to rest
> With his colors round his breast?
> Friendship makes his tomb a shrine;
> Garlands veil it; ask not mine.

As if struck by the banality of his questions, the speaker then turns in a different direction:

> One low grave, yon trees beneath,
> Bears no roses, wears no wreath;
> Yet no heart more high and warm
> Ever dared the battle-storm.

The ungarlanded grave is that of a woman, herself an unknown soldier, and the protofeminist speaker, now "Kneeling where a woman lies," strews "lilies on the grave / Of the bravest of the brave."

At first, Dickinson's response to the poem was mixed. "I thought that being a Poem one's self precluded the writing of Poems," she had teased, "but perceive the Mistake." The Master, as she called Higginson more and more, had entered her realm unbidden. Yet she obviously appreciated his salute to the nameless woman whose work is unsung, whose battles are unheralded, and whose life unfolds in private spaces.

And when "Decoration" appeared in *Scribner's Monthly* the same month her father died, Dickinson's hesitation about it vanished. "It has assisted that Pause of Space," she told Higginson, "which I call 'Father.' " The poem comforted her; that her "Master" wrote it comforted her; and the notion that someone could see what most people ignored—someone, like her father, alone, intrepid, isolated—that, too, comforted her. Perhaps she even imagined the poem to be about herself; why not? "The broadest words are so narrow we can easily cross them,—but there is water deeper than those which has no Bridge," she wrote to Higginson after rereading it.

Wanting to thank him but not knowing exactly how, she would give him the books, one of poetry, one about action, that her father, before his death, had brought her: George Eliot's *Legend of Jubal, and Other Poems* and Octavius Frothingham's *Theodore Parker,* in which "kind-hearted Higginson," as Parker had dubbed him, was mentioned no fewer than eighteen times. She would send these, she said, if he wanted them—and because her father "had twice seen you." Dickinson, too, expressed herself in gesture.

"MOTHER WAS PARALYZED TUESDAY," Emily penciled a quick note on dark paper to Wentworth in the summer of 1875. "A year from the evening father died. I thought perhaps you would care."

In Mrs. Dickinson's bedroom the shades were half-drawn, and the place smelled of camphor and roses. Over and over she kept asking for Edward, wondering why he did not come. "I am glad of what grieves ourself so much—," Emily wrote Wentworth, "can no more grieve him."

Though feeble, Mrs. Dickinson was alert enough to draw up her will. Her husband had died intestate, and she wanted to make sure her estate went to her daughters. Emily, too, decided to do the same thing, bequeathing everything to Lavinia. Austin could take care of himself and his family, she reasoned. "Knowing that his fraternal love towards me is undiminished, I am sure that his judgment concurs with mine in the disposition of my estate; and my beloved and honored mother also will feel that such disposal, while it is less onerous to her, will be as beneficial, as if I had given all to her." Emily named Vinnie her executrix.

In the meantime, Austin's control of their father's estate left the Dickinson women dependent, for the moment, on the residents of the Evergreens. Vinnie's resentment of this situation, long smoldering, would ultimately result both in the publication and the eventual suppression of her sister's poems.

IN BOSTON IN THE FALL OF 1875, Higginson recited several poems Dickinson had sent him, along with his sister Louisa's, to the assembled ladies of the Boston Woman's Club as they sat expectantly in a large parlor, their feet crossed over Aubusson carpets, their silence rising to the high ceilings. Loyal, he would not divulge Dickinson's identity even though, as he acknowledged, her poems' "weird & strange power excited much interest."

He had also recited Dickinson's poems in Newport, his literary friends arranged expectantly on the couches at Mrs. Dame's, shaded gas lamps warming the room with spectral brightness. Enthusiastic, bighearted, brisk, and a little pushy, Helen Hunt Jackson was thrilled. "I have a little manuscript volume with a few of your verses in it—and I read them very often—," she wrote to her old playmate. "You are a great poet—and it is a wrong to deny to the day you live in, that you will not sing aloud. When you are what men call dead, you will be sorry you were so stingy."

But Dickinson was not stingy with Higginson. (She had been called stingy before, as she had told Higginson in 1862, when editors "asked me for my Mind—and when I asked them 'Why,' they said I was penurious—and they, would use it for the World—." She did not want her mind used for the World.) Likely she granted Higginson permission to read the poems she kept sending him; one doubts he would have done so without it. And again she had drawn

closer to him. Their intimacy sustained by distance and a vague reassurance, often repeated, of another visit at some unspecified time,
she invited him to Amherst again and again. "My Brother and Sisters
would love to see you. Twice you have gone—Master—Would you
but once come—." She then mailed him as many as thirteen poems,
much as she had when they first began corresponding. Five were sent
in January: "The last of Summer is Delight—," "The Heart is the
Capital of the Mind," "The Mind lives on the Heart," "The Rat is the
concisest Tenant," and " 'Faithful to the end' amended."

Though she was no longer sewing groups of poems into packets—
the forty booklets of earlier years—she occasionally gathered several
together, intending no doubt to put them in a booklet at a later time.
This is the case with three of the poems she recently mailed to Higginson. Part of a larger set, they speak to one another as they speak to
him: the last days of summer are a delight, though during them we
look back, she suggests in another poem, because the heart is capital
of the mind. But the mind also feeds on the heart "Like any Para-
site—," hungry, needy, in search of nourishment, and "if the Heart
omit"—or, in an earlier version, "be lean"—it will "Emaciate the
Wit—." And the rat, who is the "concisest Tenant": "Balking our
Wit," it shows that our conscious selves—our minds, our wisdom—
have limits.

Central to these poems is the image of the heart, and it's even part
of " 'Faithful to the end' amended," where Dickinson replies to
Christ's injunction in Revelation, "Be thou faithful unto death, and
I will give thee a crown of life."

> *"Faithful to the end" amended*
> *From the Heavenly clause —*
> *Constancy with a Proviso*
> *Constancy abhors —*
>
> *"Crowns of Life" are servile Prizes*
> *To the stately Heart,*
> *Given for the Giving, solely,*
> *No Emolument.*

Faith, constancy, loyalty, poetry—all ends in themselves, given
freely without recompense or the slightest expectation of it. "The
stately Heart"—capital of the mind—loves what or whom it

pleases. Sovereign, independent, brave—it is in its own way immortal: it exists in poetry.

The poem was also one of gratitude. Dickinson recognized that Higginson generously gave what he had to give, and she appreciated his constancy, his commitment, his articulation, at least, of the values she held dear. Particularly vis-à-vis her chosen vocation: "the writer, when he adopts a high aim, must be a law to himself, bide his time, and take the risk of discovering, at last, that his life has been a failure," he had said.

They were writing each other frequently. "I often go Home in thought to you," she admitted. She wanted to send him a copy of George Eliot's new novel, *Daniel Deronda*. "It makes me happy to send you the Book," she told him; he promised not to read it beforehand in its serialized version. "To abstain from 'Daniel Deronda' is hard—you are very kind to be willing," she replied. And they discussed her poems. The one they called "Immortality" (" 'Faithful to the end' amended"?) had pleased him, he told her. "I believed it would," she answered. She also asked to see some of his verse. "You once told me of 'printing but a few Poems.' I hoped it implied you possessed more—Would you show me—one?" He mentioned he would come to Amherst—the constant theme—but could not just yet. "I was lonely there was an 'Or' in that beautiful 'I would go to Amherst,' though grieved for it's cause," she answered. Mary was ill.

She showered him with compliments. She reread his work.

> *I sued the News — yet feared — the News*
> *That such a Realm could be —*
> *"The House not made with Hands" it was —*
> *Thrown open wide — to me —*

What better praise?

Yet Higginson did not come. She wrote again. It was the spring of 1876.

> *The things we thought that we should do*
> *We other things have done*
> *But those peculiar industries*
> *Have never been begun.*

Mary was sicker than ever, he explained. "I wish your friend had my strength for I don't care for roving—," Dickinson answered. "She perhaps might, though to remain with you is Journey." Though she now frequently asked after Mary's health, she calmly referred to her as Higginson's "friend," not his wife.

As if she worried that his friendship depended in part on Mary's approval, Dickinson reached out to this "friend," dispatching notes and rosebuds and an occasional poem. Softening, Mary responded to the poet's attentions with her own gift. "May I cherish it twice, for itself, and for you?" Dickinson replied, and to the Colonel she said, "I am glad to have been of joy to your friend, even incidentally." At Christmas, Emily reciprocated, sending Emerson's *Representative Men,* "a little Granite Book you can lean upon," as she aptly called it—Emerson tried-and-true—and when Mary's father died, in August, she tenderly commiserated. Wentworth thanked her. "I am glad if I did not disturb her," Emily answered him. "Loneliness for my own Father made me think of her."

Totemic assumptions about Emily Dickinson and Thomas Higginson do not for a moment let us suppose that she, proffering flowers and poems, and he, the courtly feminist, very much married, were testing the waters of romance. But about their correspondence is its faint hint or, if not of that, then of a flirtation buoyed by compassion, consideration, and affection. Surely neither of them expected or wanted their dalliance—if that is the word—to lead anywhere specific. Yet each of her notes bursts with innuendo, attachment, warmth, flattery. She startled him—made him self-conscious—and that startled her in return. "Your letters always surprise me," she had told him. "My life has been too simple and stern to embarrass any," she declared, dismissing with obvious pleasure, his shyness. He recommended Turgenev to her; she still wanted to read Higginson's poetry. "I hoped you might show me something of your's—one of the 'few Verses'—the 'scarcely any,' you called them. Could you be willing now?" she asked in 1877.

She said she consumed everything he wrote: if true, it was no small feat. "Thank you for having written the 'Atlantic Essays,' " she once told him. "They are a fine Joy—though to possess the ingredient for Congratulation renders congratulation superfluous." She beguiled him. She took *Oldport Days* off the shelf. "I was re-reading 'Oldport,' " she said. She liked the final chapter, "Footpaths," best.

"Largest last, like Nature." Then she added a poem, signing it "Your Scholar—."

> *A Wind that woke a lone Delight*
> *Like Separation's Swell —*
> *Restored in Arctic confidence*
> *To the Invisible.*

The tributes did not stop. "Though inaudible to you, I have long thanked you." She admired his gravitas. "Your thought is so serious and captivating, that it leaves one stronger and weaker too, the Fine of Delight." She admired his probity. "That it is true, Master," she wrote him in January 1876, "is the Power of all you write." And wittily she admired his candor. "Candor—my Preceptor—is the only wile," she reminded him. "Did you not teach me that yourself, in the 'Prelude' to 'Malbone'?"

She again broached the possibility of his visiting Amherst. "I almost inferred from your accent you might come to Amherst," she exclaimed. "I would like to make no mistake in a presumption so precious—but a Pen has so many inflections and a Voice but one, will you think it obtuse, if I ask if I quite understood you?" She had not understood; he did not come, and likely that was better for both of them. Imagination kept them strong and constant and truthful, after Dickinson's fashion. They spoke to each other without bounds, or at least that's what they aimed for; letters drew them together as solid flesh could not.

And she trusted him, or she counted on him enough to use him as a ruse when Helen Hunt Jackson requested that she contribute a poem to the "No Name" volume of contemporary writing soon to be published by Roberts Brothers of Boston. The contributors would be anonymous, Jackson reminded her, and if Dickinson wished, she would write out Dickinson's poetry in her own hand. "Surely, in the shelter of such *double* anonymousness as that will be, you need not shrink." Dickinson was silent. Visiting Amherst, Jackson again importuned the poet, this time in person; Emily must submit her poems. "I felt [li]ke a [gr]eat ox [tal]king to a wh[ite] moth," Jackson afterward apologized, "and beg[ging] it to come and [eat] grass with me [to] see if it could not turn itself into beef! How stupid." Dickinson didn't budge. Jackson lobbied harder. "Let somebody somewhere whom you do not know have the same pleasure in reading yours," she begged.

Not wanting to offend the well-meaning and effusive Mrs. Jackson, Emily asked Wentworth for his help. "I told her I was unwilling," she wrote him,

> and she asked me why?—I said I was incapable and she seemed not to believe me and asked me not to decide for a few Days—meantime, she would write me—She was so sweetly noble, I would regret to estrange her, and if you would be willing to give me a note saying you disapproved it, and thought me unfit, she would believe you— I am sorry to flee so often to my safest friend, but hope he permits me—.

Dickinson was telling the truth when she told Jackson she was incapable of publishing her poems. Like her, they would not cross her father's ground.

If Jackson did not grasp Dickinson's position, Emily could count on Wentworth to act as paternal gatekeeper. He could declare her poetry—and herself—unsuitable for public consumption. This was a ploy, of course, for she had published, she could publish, and she did not wish to publish except in the ways she chose, when she chose. But Higginson collaborated with her in her reticence, their unspoken pact sealed by their commitment not to each other but to art. Quoting from "Letter to a Young Contributor," the essay that, fifteen years earlier, had brought her to him in the first place, she reminded him of what it had meant to her: "Often, when troubled by entreaty, that paragraph of your's has saved me—'Such being the Majesty of the Art you presume to practice, you can at least take time before dishonoring it.' "

Misunderstanding her request, Higginson had assumed she had been asked to contribute a story, not a poem, to the No Name Series, possibly because its first publication happened to be Jackson's own novel, *Mercy Philbrick's Choice.* Under the circumstances, he tried to be as supportive as possible. "My dear friend," he tactfully responded. "It is always hard to judge for another of the bent of inclination or range of talent; but I should not have thought of advising you to write stories, as it would not seem to me to be in your line." The mistake discovered, he again encouraged Emily, as if he couldn't

Helen Hunt Jackson, 1875.

help himself, to seek a wider audience—and the fame it would surely bring.

She replied with typical savvy. "I thought your approbation Fame," she gently said, "and it's withdrawal Infamy."

He did not press her further. That, too, was part of the pact. But the unstoppable "H. H." rushed in where diplomatic, well-bred Brahmin men dared not tread. Calling on Dickinson in the fall of 1878, she saw the poet at the Homestead for a second time, although Dickinson typically hid from everyone except children and Higginson. Friends of Vinnie's who came to the house might glimpse a pale-robed Emily in the garden with her blossoms, much as if she were Rappaccini's daughter, but as soon as she heard the gate bang, she vanished like smoke, and when Vinnie asked a group of youngsters to sing for Emily, the weird sisters sat on the second floor, invisible, while the concert took place on the first. Yet Emily had agreed to admit Helen Jackson to the Homestead and talk with her. Perhaps she considered Jackson Higginson's emissary and did not wish to offend him, or perhaps she admired Jackson's fierce tenacity and her even fiercer advocacy.

After the meeting, Jackson again begged for a poem or two—she lowered the number—for the No Name Series. What about "Success—is counted sweetest," already published? Dickinson finally relented, and her poem appeared in 1878 in *A Masque of Poets,* entitled "Success." It occupies a "special place" in the book, said Jackson, "being chosen to end the first part of the volume."

After the book appeared, in its wisdom the literary public assumed the poem was Emerson's.

ON THE THIRD ANNIVERSARY of her father's death, Dickinson hoped the Colonel might come to comfort her. "Though we know that the mind of the Heart must live if it's clerical part do not," she wrote to Higginson. "Would you explain it to me?"

"I was told you were once a Clergyman," she continued. "It comforts an instinct if another have felt it too. I was rereading your 'Decoration.' You may have forgotten it." She wrote out her own version of his poem:

> *Lay this Laurel on the One*
> *Too intrinsic for Renown —*
> *Laurel — vail your deathless Tree —*
> *Him you chasten, that is He!*

Higginson later said that Dickinson's short poem distilled the essence of his, and when he first read it, he replied quickly, asking if she was still writing verse. "I have no other Playmate," she responded, enclosing four samples and naming each of them: "a Gale, and an Epitaph, and a Word to a Friend, and a Blue Bird, for Mrs. Higginson." The "Gale" begins "It sounded as if the streets were running"; the "Epitaph" opens with "She laid her docile Crescent down"; the "Word to a Friend" starts with "I have no Life but this—"; and "After all Birds have been investigated and laid aside—" is the "Blue Bird," sent for Mrs. Higginson.

The first of them, "It sounded as if the streets were running / And then—the streets stood still—," represents Dickinson at her most puckish—and her most attentive—as she meticulously re-creates the slightest atmospheric change, inner and outer, both before the onset of storm and after it subsides ("Nature was in an Opal Apron / Mixing fresher Air.") The poem "She laid her docile Crescent down" is indeed an epitaph: "this confiding Stone / Still states to Dates that have forgot / The News that she is gone." And the "Blue Bird" (the poem for Mary), which paid tribute to Mary's strength, implicitly affirmed her own:

> *After all Birds have been investigated and laid aside —*
> *Nature imparts the little Blue Bird — assured*
> *Her conscientious Voice will soar unmoved*
> *Above ostensible Vicissitude.*
>
> *First at the March — competing with the Wind —*
> *Her panting note exalts us — like a friend —*
> *Last to adhere when Summer cleaves away —*
> *Elegy of Integrity.*

The poem she called "Word to a Friend" is clearly and lovingly addressed to Higginson, though it's not exactly a love poem. When copying it to give to him, for instance, she substituted "the Realm of you" for two earlier versions of the line, which read "the loving you" and "the love of you."

But if not of love, she was nonetheless speaking of something as expansive, precious, and vital.

> *I have no Life but this —*
> *To lead it here —*
> *Nor any Death — but lest*
> *Dispelled from there —*
>
> *Nor tie to Earths to come —*
> *Nor Action new —*
> *Except through this Extent —*
> *The Realm of you —*

. . .

THE SUDDEN TRANSITIONS: It was Higginson's turn. In the late summer of 1877, after long years of painful invalidism, Mary Channing Higginson died.

"The Wilderness is new—to you": Dickinson wrote him at once. Now it was she who could stretch out a hand.

"Master, let me lead you."

TWELVE

Moments of Preface

"Your Face is more joyful, when you speak." Emily Dickinson looked at the photograph Higginson had mailed her, comparing it with the face she herself had seen twice. "I miss an almost arrogant look that at times haunts you—but with that exception, it is so real I could think it you."

His arrogant look evaporated with Mary's death. Accustomed to her presence—and her dependence—he found himself agitated, helpless, unmoored. "How little there seems left to be done," he muttered, "how strange and almost unwelcome the freedom." He might lecture in the West, which he had long wished to do, for he could not stay alone in their rented rooms in Newport. He might go back to Europe. He might even go to Amherst.

> *With sorrow*
> *That the*
> *Joy is*
> *past, to*
> *make you*
> *happy first,*
> *distrustful,*
> *of its*
> *duplicate*
> *in a*
> *hastening*
> *world.*
> *Your scholar*

Dickinson scribbled her note on graph paper, then quickly sent another:

> *Perhaps she does not go so far*
> *As you who stay — suppose —*

Thomas Wentworth
Higginson, in
photograph sent to
Emily Dickinson,
1876.

Perhaps comes closer, for the lapse
Of her Corporeal Clothes —

"If I could help you?" she asked.

MORE PRACTICED THAN HE in the stages of bereavement,
she counseled him kindly and by degrees. "Danger is not at first, for
then we are unconscious, but in the after—slower—Days. Do not
try to be saved—but let Redemption find you—as it certainly
will—Love is it's own rescue, for we—at our supremest, are but it's
trembling Emblems."

Redemption will find him; his love for Mary will console him;
perhaps he will love again. "To be human is more than to be divine,"
Dickinson wisely reminded him, "for when Christ was divine, he was
uncontented til he had been human."

At least one Dickinson biographer has suggested that Vinnie
hoped Higginson, with his wife dead, would marry her sister. Dickinson herself did not explicitly express any such wish beyond her

relentless entreaty that Higginson return to Amherst. "I remember nothing so strong as to see you," she wrote him. "I hope you may come."

And when Samuel Bowles—nervous, ill, unable to sleep—died in early January 1878 ("Dear Mr Bowles found out too late," Dickinson grieved, "that Vitality costs itself"), again she turned to the Colonel. "I felt it shelter to speak with you," she told him the day Bowles was buried. "When you have lost a friend, Master you remember you could not begin again, because there was no World. I have thought of you often since the Darkness—though we cannot assist another's Night—." One wonders in vain how Higginson responded: tenderly, no doubt, and hinting that he might come to Amherst after all.

Instead he went south. A military Rip Van Winkle (or so he saw himself) bent on revisiting Jacksonville and Beaufort after more than a dozen years—it had been that long—Higginson in 1878 sought out a place he and Mary had not shared, and a moment in history, his moment, forever gone. Fifty-four years old and sporting what Edmund Wilson later called his "inalienable muttonchop whiskers," Higginson, a private citizen not a soldier, landed in Jacksonville, which at one time he could have burned to the ground with just a nod of his head. "I began to feel fearfully bewildered," he remarked, "as if I had lived a multitude of lives." In South Carolina he trotted on horseback over the new shell road linking Beaufort to Port Royal. The old fortifications had disappeared, and Higginsonville, the freedmen's village named for him, had blown away in a tornado. In its place stretched a large, flat national cemetery. "An individual seems so insignificant in the presence of the changes of time," Higginson remarked; "he is nothing, even if his traces are mingled with fire & blood."

But he happened upon the wife of one of his soldiers, hoeing the field she'd hoed fifteen years earlier. "The same sky was above her, the same soil beneath her feet," he commented, "but the war was over, slavery was gone. The soil that had been her master's was now her own by purchase." Rarely did he find ex-soldiers who likewise did not own their house and at least a patch of land. He shook hands with black teachers, preachers, and a black constabulary. "What more could be expected of any race, after fifteen years of freedom?" he asked. To us, he may sound supercilious, but he had run his fingers over the cold iron manacles worn by these same people, whose freedom, fifteen years before, was not at all assured.

And though there was poverty, there were no grievances, or none he cared to report. In Beaufort the houses had been repainted a cottony white, and even though the black population had few opportunities beyond menial employment, Higginson managed to find former soldiers from his regiment doing well. Corporal Sutton was a traveling minister; Sergeant Thomas Hodges, a master carpenter; and Sergeant Shemeltella, gun in hand, was patrolling the woods he had once picketed near Port Royal Ferry.

No one mentioned any "conspicuous" outrages, as he prudently noted in the July *Atlantic,* where he stated that he disbelieved rumors about the white population's plotting to reenslave the black. "I hold it utterly ungenerous, to declare that the white people of the South have learned nothing by experience, and are incapable of change." Although he said he could not of course form an opinion on the status of black women—they, unlike black men, were denied the vote—he had decided to see the glass half-full. Yet not two years earlier, six black men had been murdered, five in cold blood, and one white man killed in Hamburg, South Carolina, in an attempt to intimidate black voters and restore white supremacy. Incensed, Higginson had denounced the craven northern Democrats who, he believed, had made the massacre possible; two years later, in 1878, he was claiming that, if anything, black men and women suffered more indignity in the North—the Connecticut legislature had refused to authorize a black military company, and Rhode Island forbade interracial marriage—and as for the savageries (though unexaggerated, he said) of the Ku Klux Klan and the carpetbaggers, they had for the moment ceased.

Higginson looked for progress and found it, and yet he wasn't utterly impervious to the simmering hatreds roiling the South. He admitted that the Republican party desperately, desperately needed to strengthen its grassroots organization, though he reiterated, almost nonchalantly, that each state should work out its own salvation. Federal intervention was a thing of the past. Reconstruction was over.

The sun having set on what remained of Higginson's militant radicalism, he would no longer storm this barricade, his sense of injustice clear, clean, absolute. Nor did he shoulder regret.

· · ·

"THE HOPE OF SEEING YOU was so sweet and serious—that seeing this—by the Papers, I fear it has failed," Emily wrote him, attaching a clipping from the *Springfield Republican.* Since he was still a celebrity of sorts, his comings and goings of interest to the general public, she had unfortunately learned of his trip south from a newspaper squib. He had not gone back to Amherst. Nor did he intend to go now. Instead he headed off to Europe again, promising to visit her in the fall. "Is this the Hope that opens and shuts," she skeptically replied, "like the eye of the Wax Doll?"

Despite her disappointment, she knew he needed to be away from anything that might remind him of Mary. She provided another poem.

> *How brittle are the Piers*
> *On which our Faith doth tread —*
> *No Bridge below doth totter so —*
> *Yet none hath such a Crowd.*
>
> *It is as old as God —*
> *Indeed — 'twas built by him —*
> *He sent his Son to test the Plank —*
> *And he pronounced it firm.*

It was difficult to keep faith; no one knew this better than she. And that was never truer than the spring before Higginson sailed, when her frail mother fell and broke her hip, when for months Austin shook with fever, and when the first seizures of epilepsy racked her nephew Ned. "I have felt like a troubled Top," Emily told Elizabeth Holland, "that spun without reprieve."

Still Wentworth did not come. This time armed with introductions and anecdotes—he had studied with Longfellow, he had dined with Mark Twain—in London and Paris he played the public intellectual sprung from the land of buffalo and savages. In Paris he attended meetings on prison reform, about which he knew nothing; he heard Victor Hugo at the Voltaire centenary; he met with the aging revolutionaries of 1848; he tried and failed to have women admitted to the Association littéraire internationale; he met Turgenev, whose work he adored. He traveled through Normandy and then to Germany, stopping in Cologne and Bingen and Frankfurt, rereading Goethe, and in Nuremberg he saw Dürer's house.

In London he spoke at a woman suffrage meeting and at the Freemasons' Tavern in support of keeping picture galleries open on Sundays; he scoffed at the smooth-faced boys guarding the queen as poor specimens compared with his black regiment; and he cringed when he learned Whitman was the American poet du jour, not Lowell or Whittier. He again visited with two of his heroes, Darwin and Carlyle. Darwin looked older and frailer than last time. Carlyle, steeped in solitude, called himself a man left behind, waiting for death.

The comment so rattled Higginson that as soon as he arrived back in Newport, he collected his things and within two weeks had settled himself at 17 Kirkland Street in Cambridge, near boyhood haunts. Intending to remarry, build his own home, and raise the children he longed for, the very next month he announced his engagement to Mary (Minnie) Potter Thacher of Newton, Massachusetts, a gray-eyed woman with a peachy complexion, twenty-two years younger than he.

No one had suspected the romance, least of all Emily, who wrote him soon after his return stateside to say how "joyful" she was. "There is no one so happy her Master is happy as his grateful Pupil," she politely wrote him. "The most noble congratulation it ever befell me to offer—," she cryptically added, "is that you are yourself." This was one of her highest compliments.

But extemporizing lamely, she apologized for not having spotted his essay on Hawthorne in the recent *Literary World.* She had "known little of Literature," she explained, "since my Father died—that and the passing of Mr Bowles, and Mother's hopeless illness, overwhelmed my Moments, though your Pages and Shakespeare's, like Ophir—remain." His writing, staunch as the biblical city, might persist, but after the announcement of his impending marriage, it seems she considered him less accessible—even less dependable—than before. Certainly the frequency of her letters to him dropped precipitously, as if she no longer looked toward her Master Preceptor with the same confidence and hope, whatever hope there may have been, that he would stay true to her.

Yet she did not want to lose him entirely. When he mailed her a presentation copy of *Short Studies of American Authors,* she responded with typical humor, disingenuousness, and perspicacity: she knew too little of Poe's work to judge Higginson's assessment and noted that Mrs. Jackson "soars . . . lawfully," the "lawfully" qualifying her praise. Circumspect about Howells and James, she observed, "one hesitates," for she rightly inferred qualms about these two writers: "Your relentless Music dooms as it redeems."

And if he delayed answering her, she still accosted him directly. "Must I lose the Friend that saved my Life, without inquiring why?" she asked with bite. "Affection gropes through Drifts of Awe—for his Tropic Door."

But as far as we know she did not tell him that her affections had groped—and found—a different tropic door: she had fallen in love with her father's best friend.

Such coincident occasions: as if she, forsaken by Higginson, had found Judge Otis Phillips Lord, whose wife had died shortly after Mary. Such symmetry: Higginson marries a much younger woman, very different from himself and from Dickinson; Dickinson, almost fifty, falls in love with a much older man, as if, in her case, she preferred her new Preceptor (she trotted out the word for Lord, too) more like her father in age and outlook than like Higginson. It is curious, suggestive, a mystery.

But Otis Lord himself is not mysterious. Born in 1812 in Ipswich and a graduate of Amherst College, class of 1832, Lord was a mainstay in college affairs and by the 1860s a frequent guest of its treasurer, Edward Dickinson. Earlier he had studied law in Springfield; attended Harvard Law School; served six terms in the Massachusetts General Court, five in the House of Representatives, and one in the Senate; currently he sat on the Massachusetts Supreme Judicial Court. From 1844 he resided in Salem with his wife, Elizabeth Farley Lord, whom he married the year before. They had no living children.

An accomplished orator, Lord was also a crusty conservative who did not exercise his eloquence, as had Wendell Phillips, on behalf of the slaves but treated their champions to his blistering scorn. Sue Dickinson vividly remembered how

> Judge Lord never seemed to coalesce with these men, although he was often here with them. . . . But his individuality was so bristling, his conviction that he alone was the embodiment of the law, as given on Sinai so entire, his suspicion of all but himself, so deeply founded in the rock bed of old conservative Whig tenacities, not to say obsti-

Judge Otis Lord.
"Calvary and May
wrestled in his
Nature."

nacies, that he was rather so anxious an element to his hostess in a
group of progressive and mellow although staunch men and women.

Like his friend Edward Dickinson, he had scoffed at both the
Free-Soil and the Know-Nothing parties and supported the antislavery Whigs insofar as their positions did not interfere with the
Constitution or property rights. His opinions, tenaciously held,
likely ended his political career, for as much as he was admired, he
was also known as hotheaded, gruff, and arrogant—and, besides,
old-time Whigs had virtually disappeared. After his death he was
eulogized as "strong in his intellect, strong in his emotions, strong
in his friendships, strong in his dislikes and prejudices, strong in
thought, and strong in language, and, above all, strong in his
integrity." This, too, resembles Edward Dickinson. "Calvary and
May wrestled in his Nature," Dickinson would acutely characterize
Lord, but she could have been speaking of her father.

Though formidable in the courtroom and ruthless at the bar, Lord
reputedly was a decent, intelligent man with a taste for Shakespeare;
after the death of his wife, he presented Emily with a concordance to
the plays. And he and she exchanged vows of love, or so we imagine

from the drafts and fragments of letters to Lord discovered among Dickinson's papers.

Like the Master letters (which also exist only in drafts), these rock with passion, subtlety, and wit, and yet they, too, like the Master letters, tease the reader rather than illuminate the relationship between Dickinson and a man eighteen years her senior, or what she called "the trespass of my rustic Love upon your Realms of Ermine." For again there is much we do not know: which of the drafted letters, never mind the scribbles on the insides of envelopes or on the back of pharmacy paper, ever reached Judge Lord in a final form; whether Dickinson seriously considered leaving the village of Amherst for the smokier city of Salem; or even when a family friendship warmed to passion, whether right after Mrs. Lord's death or after Higginson's marriage. "Yet Tenderness has not a Date—," Dickinson reminds us, "it comes—and overwhelms—The time before it was—was naught, so why establish it? And all the time to come it is, which abrogates the time—." In 1876 she had mentioned to Higginson that the judge had been with her a week in October— Mrs. Lord had been a witness to Dickinson's will—and the following year she remarked, again to Higginson, that "Judge Lord was with us a few days since—and told me the Joy we most revere—we profane in taking." That discloses little.

Nor do the drafts and scraps of love letters reveal whether Lord and Dickinson spoke of marriage, though it seems they did. On one note, penciled to him, she wrote, "Sweetest Name, but I know a sweeter—Emily Jumbo Lord—Have I your approval?" On another, she affectionately remarked, "You said with loved timidity in asking me to your dear Home, you would 'try not to make it unpleasant'— So delicate a diffidence, how beautiful to see!"

That was in 1882, and by then they had composed their own lexicon of love, replete with various characters of innuendo: "That was a big—sweet Story—," Dickinson teased, "the number of times that 'Little Phil' read his Letter, and the not so many, that Papa read his, but I am prepared for falsehood, on subjects of which we know nothing, or should I say Beings—is 'Phil' a 'Being' or a 'Theme,' we both believe and disbelieve a hundred times an Hour, which keeps Believing nimble—. 'Phil' have one opinion and Papa another— I thought the Rascals were inseparable."

Yet someone—Austin or Lavinia?—took scissors to the love letters, snipping out sections but preserving enough for us to take notice of Dickinson's ardor, ingenuity, and consummate style. "My lovely Salem smiles at me"—a picture he had given her?—"I seek his Face so often—but I have done with guises," she writes. Was she saying she preferred his countenance in the flesh or that she no longer wished to hide her love of him from others? Or both: "I confess that I love him—I rejoice that I love him—I thank the maker of Heaven and Earth—that gave him to me to love—the exultation floods me. I cannot find my channel—the Creek turns sea—at thought of thee." Unlike her poem to Higginson, in this case the Brook did come to the Sea.

In another draft of a letter, she recounts her nephew Ned asking if Judge Lord belonged to any church; she had said no, not technically. Ned replied, " 'Why, I thought he was one of those Boston Fellers who thought it the respectable thing to do.' 'I think he does nothing ostensible,' " she answered serenely. In that same letter, quoting the book of Revelation—and playing on the word "will" (Judge Lord had likely helped draw up her will): "Don't you know you have taken my will away and I 'know not where' you 'have laid' it? Should I have curbed you sooner? 'Spare the "Nay" and spoil the child'?"

She played with poetry in her letters to Higginson, but with Lord she juggled legal terms—bankruptcy, penalty, warrant—with erotic zing. "To lie so near your longing—to touch it as I passed, for I am but a restive sleeper and often should journey from your Arms through the happy night," she wrote, "but you will lift me back, wont you, for only there I ask to be." Then again she would remind him, "Dont you know you are happiest while I withhold and not confer—dont you know that 'No' is the wildest word we consign to Language?" What had she refused him?

His letters arrived Mondays. "Tuesday is a deeply depressed Day—," she scribbled on a scrap of paper; "it is not far enough from your dear note for the embryo of another to form . . . but when the Sun begins to turn the corner Thursday night—everything refreshes—the soft uplifting grows till by the time it is Sunday night, all my Life [cheek] is Fever with nearness to your blissful words [rippling words]." He came to visit, and when he left, she mused, "Were Departure Separation there would be neither Nature nor Art, for there would be no world."

These tatters of passion reach us through Austin, who may have rescued them from Vinnie's fire. Years later, when Mabel Loomis Todd was preparing a book of Dickinson's letters, he presumably handed her an old brown envelope and with typical understatement said the contents were curious. Todd read the letters, stuffed them back into the envelope, and though she decided not to publish them, she did not give them back. Instead, she placed them under lock and key in a camphorwood chest containing other treasured Dickinson papers, and not until her daughter, Millicent Todd Bingham, published the slim blue-covered *Emily Dickinson: A Revelation* in 1954, a portrait of Lord as the frontispiece, were the contents of the envelope divulged.

Among the secrets never divulged are whether Judge Lord read or admired Dickinson's poetry and whether she even showed it to him. Surely he was aware that her reputation had traveled beyond the Pelham Hills. In the summer of 1878, the *Springfield Republican* alleged that the undisclosed author of the popular stories by Saxe Holm was not, as supposed, Helen Hunt Jackson but an Amherst recluse with a connection to literature and flowers who, clad in white like Hawthorne's Hilda, devoted her life to a single idea. Clearly the author of those stories saw into the heart of small spaces, and a subtle writer, which Jackson definitely was not, shunted not the world but its pain. Another paper, the *Springfield Union,* jumped on the speculating bandwagon and declared that the anonymous author had to be a Dickinson.

With brusque discourtesy, the *Republican* then denied its own allegation. "We can only say that we happen to know that no person by the name of Dickinson is in any way responsible for the Saxe Holm stories," barked the editor, his voice sounding very much like Austin's.

THE ELDEST OF FIVE SISTERS, Minnie Thacher was the niece of the first Mrs. Henry Wadsworth Longfellow and, as Higginson observed, "an old-fashioned girl." Shy and modest, she never wore a low-necked dress in her life, nor, thank goodness, had she bored holes in her ears to dangle rings from; rather, she was "exquisitely refined & dainty in all her ways," Higginson bragged as if he had never cared a fig for women's rights or their independence.

His family was speechless. Having assumed that if he remarried, he would naturally choose his bride from the ranks of the woman suffrage movement, they never imagined he might pluck her out of a bouquet of pastel Newport damsels. His friends were flabbergasted. To their uneasy inquiries, Higginson explained that he had no choice: home and family were his "only safety," he had emphatically said. "I'm adrift in the universe without it." Coming from the freedom fighter of yore, the admission was peculiar, but the man who feared drowning in a river of his own fancy needed to cling to a raft, pretty and predictable. Brittle are the piers.

The couple had met two years earlier in Newport, where Minnie had evidently stayed for a few days with the Higginsons, and Higginson courteously admired her prose sketches, *Seashore and Prairie,* mentioning them in *The Woman's Journal* as exhibiting the "clear good-sense and . . . modest faithfulness" of their author. He divulged little else about the hasty courtship. Instead he circulated the compliments of friends polite enough to congratulate the couple: Celia Thaxter compared Minnie to Pallas Athene, and Louise Moulton said she was mayflowers and moonlight. Higginson shared the metaphors with Dickinson, who responded with a satiric laugh: "I shall pick 'May flowers' more furtively," she said, "and feel new awe of 'Moonlight.'"

A small wedding took place on the first of February, 1879, at the home of Minnie's parents in West Newton. Samuel Longfellow, Higginson's longtime friend from divinity school, presided, and the Harvard poet himself also joined the small group. Fit and dapper, Higginson stood next to his charming bride as if nothing had happened: not his dismissal from Newburyport almost thirty years earlier, not Thomas Sims or the Anthony Burns debacle, not Kansas, the war, South Carolina, emancipation: none of it.

Perhaps, then, it was to lay his past to rest that the newlyweds trekked south to Harpers Ferry for their honeymoon. Supposedly they went to meet Minnie's relatives, but the real reason, at least for Higginson, was to walk among sites connected to bygone days: the small firehouse in the armory yard from which John Brown had shot at federal troops, the courthouse where he was tried, the jail yard where he was confined: ghostlike, all of it.

In Cambridge, though, he leaped into life. If rejected as an outsider in Newport, as he had believed, in Cambridge he was the Colonel, a local hero, popular and sought after. "I shall no doubt do something or other to dispel it before a great while," he joked to a friend. Elected president of the Young Men's Republican Club and appointed the governor's chief of staff, he declined to run for mayor of Cambridge but did serve two years in the Massachusetts legislature, where he opposed compulsory Bible reading in public schools and supported abolishing the poll tax qualification to vote. He campaigned for woman suffrage and backed the establishment of Harvard Annex (later Radcliffe) so that young women could receive an education comparable to that of Harvard men. Maybe they'd enter Harvard itself someday. He hoped his daughter would.

That daughter, named Louisa for his mother and sister, was born in January 1880 and seven weeks later died of cerebral meningitis. The instant she heard, Dickinson contacted the bereaved father.

> The Face in Evanescence lain
> Is more distinct than our's —
> And our's surrendered for it's sake
> As Capsules are for Flower's —

Higginson answered her right away, and she wrote again. "Most of our Moments are Moments of Preface," she instructed this Master with gentle pith. We begin; that is all. Signing her note "Your Scholar," she did not tease him this time; his description of the infant Louisa had touched a chord, and just a few months later she was telling him about an Indian woman at her kitchen door, carrying baskets and a "dazzling Baby" that reminded her of the little girl she never met. If a gulf had opened between them, Higginson's daughter temporarily bridged it.

And when another daughter, Margaret, was born to the Higginsons the following year, Dickinson congratulated the Colonel with unalloyed pleasure. "I know but little of Little Ones, but love them very softly —," she said, welcoming this little one with a verse:

> "Go traveling with us"!
> Her Travels daily be
> By routes of ecstasy
> To Evening's Sea —

And Higginson was ecstatic. Wheeling the baby carriage beneath the wide elms flanking his beloved Cambridge streets, he nabbed passersby to show off his achievement before trundling back home to the Queen Anne–style house, dark brown and all the rage, that he had built on Buckingham Street, between Mount Auburn Cemetery and Harvard College. It was the first house the Colonel ever owned,

Higginson home, Buckingham Street, Cambridge, Massachusetts, 1880.

and as soon as it was finished, he placed an old brass knocker on the front door above the brass plate with "S. Higginson" engraved on it; both items were from the old house on Kirkland Street. But in the front hallway he hung something of his own: the sword decorated in the colors of his regiment that the freedmen of South Carolina had presented to him, with gratitude, before he left Beaufort.

"It is such inexpressible happiness to have at last a permanent home," he told his sister, echoing Emily, though in his case it was the return of the native, settled, after all these bleeding and peripatetic years.

IN AMHERST, DICKINSON herself had settled into a routine of passion and solicitude, sketching out love letters to her judge while tending her mother night and day, tirelessly soothing her, reading to her, fanning her in the heat, and lying to her in all weather about her condition. "The responsibility of Pathos is almost more than the responsibility of Care," Emily told Elizabeth Holland. One day slid into another. "I hardly have said, 'Good Morning, Mother,' when I hear myself saying 'Mother,—Good Night—.'"

If Dickinson seemed happier, her romance with Lord was the

likely reason—that and her having assumed a new authority at the Homestead. Relieved of her father's stony frown, no matter how she loved it, and Mrs. Dickinson's moralizing, Emily no longer had to fight for independence; now she just assumed it and wore it well. If she and Austin dared talk about the extension of consciousness after death, a subject their mother considered "very improper," Dickinson airily quipped that her mother "forgets we are past 'Correction in Righteousness.' " The children were adults, as if for the first time.

There were other indications of change, small but subtle: when asked, Dickinson offered to contribute three poems to a charity raising money for indigent children. Again she turned to Higginson. "I have promised three Hymns to a charity, but without your approval could not give them," she said. This time she was not asking whether she should submit them or if he would reject the appeal on her behalf. She had already agreed to furnish the poems and wanted only to know if he thought them appropriate.

Happy to read her work and no doubt pleased, he replied quickly. "The thoughtfulness I may not accept is among my Balms—," she thanked him, "Grateful for the kindness, I enclose those you allow, adding a fourth, lest one of them you might think profane—They are Christ's Birthday—Cupid's Sermon—A Humming-Bird—and My Country's Wardrobe—Reprove them as your own."

The most concise and visually fanciful poem of the lot, the hummingbird ("A Route of Evanescence") proceeds from an absent center, around which Dickinson puts color in motion to mimic the fluttering of the tiny bird:

> A Route of Evanescence
> With a revolving Wheel —
> A Resonance of Emerald,
> A Rush of Cochineal

"My Country's Wardrobe," intended as an amusement, cheekily decks the nation in patriotic garb: "Her triple suit as sweet / As when 'twas cut at Lexington," but "Christ's Birthday" ("The Savior must have been") tilts in a slightly different direction and is likely the poem she thought "profane," with its conceit that the Savior is a "docile Gentleman" come far on a cold day—his birthday—to save his "little Fellow men." (This poem was presumably sent to the Evergreens as accompaniment to an iced cake for Christmas.)

These light, droll, and charming poems differ sharply from "Mine Enemy is growing old" ("Cupid's Sermon"). The most conspicuously personal of the lot, it mixes regret with advice, acceptance with rue, and neither mentions Cupid nor furnishes a sermon, at least not directly:

> *Mine Enemy is growing old —*
> *I have at last Revenge —*
> *The Palate of the Hate departs —*
> *If any would avenge*
>
> *Let him be quick —*
> *the Viand flits —*
> *It is a faded Meat —*
> *Anger as soon as fed is dead —*
> *'Tis Starving makes it fat —*

Is "growing old" her enemy, or is her enemy growing old? As is often the case, Dickinson avoids a specific context; she will not staple her meaning down. The poem opens wide and burrows deep, touching the quick of our anger while distancing itself from the emotion it names. Its homiletic is an irony, and yet the poem is not ironic. And like much of her verse, it affords us the frisson of emotion before we are sure of what we experience. It speaks intimately, blasphemously, sensually even when we can't quite parse her grammar.

As Higginson knew, her poetry is also a seduction: it dances before the reader, enticing the reader before darting away; it is dangerous, daring, dubious; it flaunts its independence from the habits of predictable reading. And it insists on itself—one is always glad one is oneself—with panache, concealing what it creates, creating what it conceals, both at the same time. The experience is explosively nonverbal.

In her room, on the backs of envelopes or on snippets of brown writing paper—the odds and ends of literary genius—Dickinson composed, a poseur deeply sincere, a consummate flirt, a sorceress, a prestidigitator in words soaring beyond the law. Candor is the only wile. Said the poet Allen Tate, Cotton Mather would have burned her as a witch.

THIRTEEN

Things That Never Can Come Back

Imperturbable among the sturdy trees that Austin had planted—magnolia and ginkgo and of course evergreen—the Evergreens was an eleven-room Victorian poem, ambitious and impersonal but whimsically indifferent, at least on the surface, to the staid Homestead next door. Painted in a serene buttery color, its trim finished in cranberry, its windows festooned with striped green awnings, and all this topped by a large square tower, the place was in its calm way quite self-assured, announcing itself these last twenty-five years as the home of Susan and Austin Dickinson.

Their elder son, Ned, had grown into a stylish man of twenty years, intense, romantic, and devoted to the distinguished Dickinson name. On Sundays one could glimpse him, cane in hand, his mouth severe and brooding, his head held high, as he walked to church and took his place in the Dickinson pew, proudly wearing his shiny beaver coat. At night, though, grand mal seizures tore through his dreams. Hearing him scream, Austin would sit up in bed and then leap over the footboard to run upstairs and lie atop the convulsing boy. Next morning Ned remembered nothing, and his family, with Dickinson reticence, told him as little as possible about why his tongue was sore where he had bitten it.

Yet Ned had to have known he would not walk in his father's or his grandfather's shoes. Partly because of his epilepsy, he took classes at Amherst College in 1880 as a special student who neither received grades nor matriculated. But measuring success with her iconoclastic stick, his aunt Emily could not have cared less. " 'Aunt Emily, speaking of someone who was a good scholar but not interesting,' " Ned carefully remembered her words, " ' "She has the facts but not the phosphorescence of learning." ' " He talked to her about Dickens and George Eliot and the news of politics and foreign affairs

Edward (Ned) Dickinson,
20 years old, 1881.

Martha (Mattie)
Dickinson.

that she liked—he supplied her with illustrated reviews when her eyes were bothering her—and he entertained her with his satiric impersonations. He also reminded her of Austin, Ned's sister later recalled, as if Austin "had gone back and become a young brother again."

Ned's sister, Martha, or Mattie, as she was commonly called, turned fifteen in 1881. Like her brother, she was strong willed and feisty, and she, too, worshipped her eccentric aunt. If her brother and Aunt Lavinia, wrapped in warm woolen blankets, were sleigh riding on a cold afternoon, Mattie was just as happy to run over to the Homestead and Aunt Emily's room, where little pots of hyacinth bulbs lined the four windowsills, waiting for spring. They talked about Mattie's future, her beaux, books. It was a privilege almost as good as those gingery treats Aunt Emily slipped into her niece's pockets when Mattie was a girl.

Ned and Mattie's younger brother, a flaxen-haired boy named after Sue's father, was born relatively late in the Dickinson marriage. Adored by his family and fussed over by the entire village, Gib, as he was known, pedaled about town on his iron velocipede with a huge, golden smile. "He gathered Hearts," noted Emily, "not Flowers." She petted and teased him. "Your Urchin is more antique in wiles than the Egyptian Sphinx," Emily said in recounting one of his clever retorts to Gib's mother: " 'Were'nt you chasing Pussy,' said Vinnie to Gilbert? 'No—she was chasing herself.' "

Gib also happened to be one of the few joys in his father's pinched life. Having matured into a difficult man, Austin Dickinson never suffered fools, and to him most people were foolish. Frequently cold and acerbic, particularly in social situations, which bored him, he kept largely to himself, though he did like to be noticed. He raced his buggy down Main Street, and arriving at the Evergreens, swerved the vehicle hard onto one wheel before skidding to a stop in front of his carriage house. A yellow wide-brimmed planter's hat atop his coppery hair, he spurned drab clothes, and while he often wore a light driving ulster in the carriage, at town meetings he reputedly donned lavender pants and a Prince Albert coat. His kid shoes had a strange, square cut, and he seldom smiled. He also loved art. He bought painting after painting, indistinguishable, stiff genre landscapes of the latter-day Hudson River school and notable English, French, and Dutch artists of high academic style. Foraging through picture galleries, his tired, hungry children in tow, he bid for pictures with a recklessness that pushed him way beyond his means. It was another form of fast driving.

A model citizen, respected and wealthy and in command of significant local projects, like the new building for the First Congregational Church, Austin hankered for the destiny he peevishly regarded as his due, for he believed himself underappreciated, just as his father and grandfather each had felt. But he wanted to ditch all of it, his patrimony, Amherst, those binding expectations, and yet he stayed near the college his grandfather had founded, took on his father's practice, and lived in the house his father built, never free of its obligations. In this, he was unlike Emily, who, bending family expectations to her will, became more of who she was.

But like her, Austin disliked change in his immediate environment. He avoided confrontation. He hated going to court. And in time he blamed his wife for his aimless sense of failure, carping at her frills and furbelows and the empty life she and the children were leading. Ironically, his petulant eccentricities were themselves extravagant and expensive. He could not see the hypocrisy; instead he believed himself misunderstood. His one true solace was Gib.

Less conflicted in her attraction to rank and style, Sue gadded about town in the Dickinsons' fine double carriage, snug in the comforting folds of her sealskin coat. Consorting with the elect, she snubbed the rest. At the sumptuous Evergreens, she entertained such eminent guests as Henry Ward Beecher, Wendell Phillips, the sculptor Daniel Chester French, and Frederick Law Olmsted, whom Austin consulted on town beautification. Ralph Waldo Emerson once sat in her armchair. It was like "meeting God face to face," she later reminisced. (Emily evidently declined the privilege.)

Sue's high-handedness earned her a reputation as "socially ambitious"—"perhaps a little too aggressive, a little too sharp in wit and repartee," one Amherst chronicler observed. To a New England villager, this was a cardinal sin. "Sue saw no one as a child or a young woman," sniped a rival; "she always longed for good society but was too obscure and too poor to have any. All this explains her wild craze for people and celebrities." Regardless, her teas and musicales and receptions were locally famous, and invitations were greedily sought. One was invited for half past six, supper was usually served just after seven, and if the guests were few—only eight or so—they sat in the walnut-paneled dining room under a delicately carved ceiling. Sue scattered yellow flowers on the sideboard and in wintertime set fresh roses in vases throughout the parlor, where the party assembled if the number was large. Divided into groups of three and four, they pulled up to little tables while servants carried the oysters and coffee aloft on small trays.

Or she engineered bashes that lasted past eleven o'clock. These were remembered long afterward by friends as "rare hours, full of merriment, brilliant wit, and inexhaustible laughter, Emily with her dog, & lantern! Often at the piano playing weird and beautiful melodies, all from her own inspiration," Catherine Anthon told Mattie. "Your dear Mother also—so witty and intellectual, & uncommon in *every way*—." Amherst undergraduates similarly glowed over the memory of Mrs. Dickinson, "a really brilliant and highly cultivated woman of great taste and refinement." And though she drew inward in later life, disappointed and aggrieved, in her eighties she was eager to learn about Einstein's theories.

Emily Dickinson's strong tie with Sue survived Sue's marriage, the birth of Sue's children, and Sue's ascension on a social ladder that Emily herself disdained. If the *salonnière* sought the approval of the many and the eremitic poet preferred her privacy, so be it. Envious neighbors later speculated that, with little flourishes of Jamesian cruelty, Sue deeply hurt Emily, but as usual the evidence is scant, and it seems, rather, that Sue continued to appreciate her sister-in-law—she always had—for despite their physical proximity, Emily consistently showered her with notes and letters that, gathered together, tell of friendship, empathy, forgiveness, and sheer delight.

According to Sue's daughter, both women were busy with household tasks and saw each other when they could, arranging private conferences in the back hall of the Homestead. Writing forged a lifelong connection between them. "The tie between us is very fine," Dickinson said toward the end of her life, "but a Hair never dissolves." And of all the extant poems Dickinson heaped on friends, she addressed more to Sue than to anyone else.

> *Dear Sue —*
> *With the*
> *Exception of*
> *Shakespeare, you*
> *have told me of*
> *more knowledge*
> *than any one living —*

> *To say that sincerely*
> *is strange praise —*

What knowledge did Sue supply? Did it include the sexual? Dickinson's early notes and letters to Sue, churning with unmistakable passion, ripened in later years but were not less affectionate, admiring, or pointed; Sue was, as Dickinson characterized her, the sister a hedge away:

> *One Sister have I in our house —*
> *And one, a hedge away.*
> *There's only one recorded,*
> *But both belong to me.*
>
> . . . .
>
> *I spilt the dew —*
> *But took the morn;*
> *I chose this single star*
> *From out the wide night's numbers —*
> *Sue — forevermore!*

Doubtless there were the frustrations, mishaps, miscommunications—pundits can be right—that exist in all families. "But Susan is a stranger yet— / ," Dickinson wrote Sue some time in the 1870s.

> *The ones who cite her most*
> *Have never scaled her Haunted House*
> *Nor compromised her Ghost —*
>
> *To pity those who know her not*
> *Is helped by the regret*
> *That those who know her know her less*
> *The nearer her they get —*

THE HOMESTEAD, THE EVERGREENS, the dirt path in between; summers and winters and the yeasty-sweet fragrance of baking bread; Mrs. Dickinson's helplessness and infirmity, Vinnie's care and Emily's kindnesses; the circus that came to town ("I feel the

David Todd and
Mabel Loomis,
engagement
photograph,
1877.

red in my mind") and those flying, febrile visits from Judge Lord—
externally, life in the gentle hamlet ran in a reliable groove, except,
that is, for the occasional civic misfortune, like the fire that razed the
wooden buildings downtown in a single night as if a hellion, raging
after freedom, had broken the rules of village decorum.

"THE THINGS THAT NEVER can come back, are several— / ,"
Emily Dickinson sent her poem to Elizabeth Holland, recently wid-
owed: "Childhood—some forms of Hope—the Dead—."

She might have added the dependable surface of everyday routine.

It was in the fall of 1881 that a good-looking young couple from
Washington, D.C., swooped down on bucolic Amherst. David Peck
Todd was the new professor of astronomy, come to teach at the college and run the observatory, and with him was his adorable wife of
two years, Mabel Loomis Todd, whose ample social skills were an

undeniable asset. A good pianist always willing to perform in public, Mabel was also a trained soprano (she had studied at Boston's New England Conservatory) and a budding artist who dabbled in water-colors and oils and exhibited her works with a burning urgency that bordered on the desperate. "I think everyone will exclaim over it," large-eyed Mabel once confided to her diary on finishing a painted panel of poppies. "I do feel so much power & genius in myself, strug-gling for utterance in any way, of which these little pictures are hardly the loophole for it to peep out."

This was a woman thirsty for attention. In Amherst she would find it.

That her father was a clerk at the United States Nautical Almanac Office in Washington did not stop her from claiming that he had rubbed shoulders with Alcott and Thoreau and Whitman or that her mother was descended from Priscilla Alden. But Mabel herself had not yet collected her literary giants; that would come. And even though her mother had preferred a more illustrious match for a daughter with such genius, in 1879 Mabel married David Peck Todd, whom she said she loved. Sober, smart, steady, and to Mabel sexy, he appreciated his new wife's multiplying talents, and as Mabel also noted, was a direct descendant of Jonathan Edwards.

An assistant at the Nautical Almanac Office and Observatory in Washington, David Todd expected to rise toward his well-scrutinized stars, and with Amherst College offering what appeared to be a good opportunity—with the potential for an observatory in the offing—the couple placed their young daughter with Mabel's parents and set out for Massachusetts. Meant for finer things, Mabel hated housekeeping and drudgery, and despite her considerable attraction for her lover-husband, as she called him—her journal brims with accounts of their lovemaking—she had been discon-certed by her pregnancy. "My little one will, I feel, be always second-ary to my husband in my life," she admitted with a touch of prescience.

Primed for adventure, the convivial twenty-five-year-old—born the same year Austin and Sue were married—leaped into the center of the town's social life, the Evergreens, where she could play whist or perform Scarlatti, sing Schubert, and chat brightly with the crème de la crème. Having been "taken in" at once by the marvelous Dick-insons, Mabel was particularly smitten with the darkly beautiful Sue, gloriously arrayed in a scarlet shawl, who "stimulates me intellectually more than any other woman I ever knew," Mabel rhapsodized. Sue was the hub around which all things orbited, and Mabel wanted to be everything Sue was, to have everything she had.

And Sue, appreciating Mabel in the ways that Mabel needed appreciation, placed her new friend at the center of the Dickinson picnics and lawn teas, their games on the grass and their noisy outings to Shutesbury or Sunderland Park during the dog days of summer. Or she invited Mabel to the Evergreens, and the grateful younger woman was soon passing part of every day there, either teaching Mattie to play the piano or merrily letting the love-besotted Ned, only five years her junior, waltz her about the dance floor.

Without much thought to the possible consequences, Mabel received Ned's tokens of admiration with schoolgirlish pleasure: his bouquets of garden roses, his peremptory calls, his companionship on those languorous horseback rides through the countryside. She consented when he asked her to wear his father's enameled fraternity pin; after all, she reasoned, more status was attached to the pin of one's father than to one's own. Sue, who considered Mrs. Todd an excellent escort for her untried, untutored son, suspected nothing, or so Mabel gathered. "She thinks it is such a fine thing for her young son to have a 'brilliant & accomplished married lady for his friend,' & likes to have him pay me attention." But Mabel was fully aware that Ned, a serious chap declaring himself to be forever devoted, vowed he would never marry if he could not have Mabel, which he could not. "I could twist him around my little finger," she gaily said; "he would go off and kill somebody if I bade him."

When the disconsolate Ned died of a heart attack fifteen years later, he was in fact unmarried. And townsfolk gossiped that he never recovered from his infatuation with Mabel Todd, who, rapidly tiring of him, suddenly broke off what she called "their little affair" as soon as she could replace him. In pain and anger, Ned dashed to his mother to confess everything, which by that time included more than Mrs. Todd's dalliance with him. The irrepressible Mrs. Todd had set her cap for Austin, and Austin had succumbed.

It had happened during those heated summer days when the regal Austin Dickinson, his bearing somber and aristocratic, his ice-blue eyes fixed on Mabel, stole away with her from the group picnicking at Sunderland Park. They leaned on the old rail fence, gazing out at the far-reaching view, aware of the smell of new-mown grass and each other close by. Ned suddenly seemed unfledged and virginal (Mabel's word), and besides, as Mabel confidently declared in her diary, "dear" Mr. Austin Dickinson "is so very fond of me." She was right, and on an indolent September evening they fell into each other's arms—or crossed the Rubicon, as Austin martially called their declaration of love. (Consummation came later.) Mabel blazed with self-congratulatory pleasure: "to think that out of all the splendid & noble women he has known, he would *pick me* out—only half his age—as the mostly truly congenial friend he ever had!" Soon the couple were stealing away, wildly exhilarated (yet another of Mabel's phrases) by those dreamy walks back to the Todds' boardinghouse or out on the river road above South Deerfield in the Dickinson carriage.

When apart, they resorted to pen and paper. "It nearly broke my heart to go through the day yesterday with only that passing sight of you," Austin wrote Mabel on one occasion; on another: "I love you, I admire you, I idolize you. I am exalted by your love for me." On still another: "The sun cannot shine without you, the birds can make no melody. The flowers have no other beauty nor perfume—all is a meaningless waste. I love you darling, with my love, & my love is timeless & sleepless—cannot be divided—insatiable."

As for Mabel, over and over she claimed she trusted Austin as she trusted God. "The way in which you love me is a consecration—it is the holy of holies," she cried, elevating their longing for each other far above the commonplace or customary. No longer would she be fickle or flirtatious; no longer would she need to be: "The greatest proof I have *ever* had that I am different from ninety-nine others, & that my girlish hope—that I had something rare in me—was well-founded, lies in the great, the tremendous fact that I own the entire love of the rarest man who ever lived." Professing her feelings without guilt, she seemed without the slightest concern that her infatuation might interfere with or otherwise compromise her relationship with her husband, to whom she remained naively staunch. Sue would soon accuse her of taking the best of two men.

That same torrid fall, 1882, David Todd had left Amherst for three months on an astronomical expedition to the Lick Observatory in California, and though Mabel was initially to accompany him, at the last moment David went alone. He should never have gone so far for so long, he reputedly admitted years later. Mabel had missed him for a while. "Ned has been very devoted—more so than ever," she wrote in her journal. "But my only real joy in staying is because Mr. Dickinson is here, & looks out for me & has me on his mind." By the time David returned, Austin Dickinson, though not yet Mabel's physical lover, was portraying himself to the impressionable Mabel as the victim of a loveless misbegotten marriage with a woman who frequently refused him sexual intercourse and who so profoundly dreaded childbearing that she had aborted four pregnancies before Ned was born; and having tried to abort Ned, too, he morosely continued, she had caused the boy's epilepsy. Austin could by his own lights then reasonably ask, "Where is the wrong in preferring sunshine to shadow! Does not the unconscious plant lean toward light?"

It would take another year of intense verbal foreplay before Mabel and Austin consummated their affair, and when they did, they chose the dining room, windows shut, blinds closed, of the ancestral Homestead.

WHAT DID EMILY KNOW? "Emily always respected real emotion," Mabel Todd's daughter recalled, adding that Emily was glad that her brother found some comfort in his abject life. But that's a self-serving answer. Vinnie, on the other hand, knew a great deal. Captivated by Mrs. Todd and perpetually distrustful of Sue, Vinnie had been enlisted early in the clandestine romance. Mabel folded her love letters to Austin in envelopes addressed to Vinnie, which Austin surreptitiously picked up at the post office when fetching his sister's mail. After reading them and destroying the originals, he tucked copies of the letters into a large envelope that he handed to Vinnie. "If anything happens to me," he instructed her, "Burn this package at once—without opening."

Emily kept her distance, much to Mabel's frustration. During her first months in Amherst, Mabel had heard delicious stories about Austin's batty sister, the one called the Myth by locals. "She has not been outside of her own house in fifteen years, except once to see a new church, when she crept out at night, & viewed it by moonlight," Mabel breathlessly informed her parents. "She dresses wholly in white, & her mind is said to be perfectly wonderful. She writes finely, but no one *ever* sees her. . . . Isn't that like a book? So interesting." Sue read Mabel some of Emily's strange, powerful poems. "All the literary men are after her to have her writings published," Mabel bragged with a touch of envy.

But Sue had warned Mabel about the Dickinson sisters. "'You will not allow your husband to go there, I hope!'" Sue reportedly counseled. "'Because they have not, either of them, any idea of morality. . . . I went in there one day, and in the drawing room I found Emily reclining in the arms of a man. What can you say to that?'"

Sue's cautionary tale probably had less to do with Emily and Judge Lord, the apparent target of Sue's disapprobation, than with her unformed suspicions about the ubiquitous Mabel, but in any event Mabel did not enter the sacred precincts of the Homestead until the fall of 1882. Before Austin would cross another Rubicon, Mabel would have to cross this one.

Vinnie finally invited Mabel to the Homestead, where Mabel enthusiastically played the old Dickinson piano and sang in her warbly soprano for the strange creatures who listened from afar. The enfeebled Mrs. Dickinson heard the music from her room; Emily was of course invisible. "It was odd to think, as my voice rang out through the big silent house that Miss Emily in her weird white dress was outside in the shadow hearing every word, & the mother, bed-ridden for years was listening up stairs," Mabel puzzled in her journal. "When I stopped Emily sent me in a glass of rich sherry & a poem written as I sang. I know I shall see her," Mabel concluded with the blinkered brightness of youth.

Shortly after her musical introduction at the Homestead, Mabel painted Emily a picture of the flower commonly known as the Indian pipe, or ghost plant. A sturdy growth that, lacking chlorophyll, never turns green, the all-white Indian pipe was an inspired choice and doubtless a tribute to the legendary sister of her soon-to-be lover. Emily was touched. In thanks she slipped a copy of her "Humming Bird" poem ("A Route of Evanescence") into the folds of her thank-you note. "That without suspecting it you should send me the preferred flower of life, seems almost supernatural," she told a rapturous Mabel. "I have just had a most lovely note from my—I may call her—dear friend Miss Emily Dickinson," Mabel wrote in her journal, flushed with what she considered unmitigated success. "It fairly thrilled me—," she added, "which shows that my susceptibility to magnetic friendships is not entirely confined to men,—as I have occasionally thought of myself."

Mabel Todd would never lay eyes on Emily Dickinson, not even at Mrs. Dickinson's funeral a month later.

. . .

EMILY NORCROSS DICKINSON'S DEATH, at seventy-eight, was a shock to her two daughters even though, since her stroke, they had long expected it. No one was more surprised at her own grief than Emily. She had lost a compass she had not known she needed. And their years together had changed their relationship. She no longer resented or mocked her mother, as she had when she first contacted Higginson. "The great mission of pain had been ratified — cultivated to tenderness by persistent sorrow, so that a larger mother died than had she died before," she explained to her Norcross cousins. But she herself had become a larger daughter. To Elizabeth Holland she elaborated: "We were never intimate Mother and Children while she was our Mother—but Mines in the same Ground meet by tunneling and when she became our Child, the Affection came—."

The day of the funeral, November 16, 1882, Mabel Todd sat quietly with the mourners. Vinnie had placed a small bouquet of violets in her mother's hand, but Emily, as was to be expected, did not leave her room. A cousin recalled that when she said good-bye, Emily opened the door a crack and, pale and worn, thanked her for coming so far.

Afterward the Homestead was strangely empty for the first time. Besides the two servants they continued to employ, it was just Vinnie and Emily—and, queerly, Austin. "My Brother is with us so often each Day, we almost forget that he ever passed to a wedded Home," Dickinson noted, doubtless with a raised eyebrow.

"BLOW HAS FOLLOWED BLOW, till the wondering terror of the Mind clutches what is left, helpless of an accent." It had been a season of loss. Ralph Waldo Emerson's death the previous April had marked the end of an era. Colonel Higginson was one of the hundreds of mourners who boarded a special funeral train bound for Concord, where throngs of fans walked up and down the streets before crowding into the church to hear the service that Higginson dismissed as lacking the "coals of fire" only Emerson could supply.

Though Emily was saddened by Emerson's death, the passing of her friend Charles Wadsworth cut more closely. She and the Reverend Wadsworth had stayed in touch—"a intimacy of many years,"

Gilbert (Gib) Dickinson.

she called it—and having returned to Philadelphia from the Pacific coast, he had visited her just two years before. "He rang one summer evening to my glad surprise—," she told a friend of his. " 'Why did you not tell me you were coming, so I could have it to hope for,' I said—'Because I did not know it myself. I stepped from my Pulpit to the Train,' was his quiet reply. He once remarked in talking 'I am liable at any time to die,' " she added, "but I thought it no omen."

For comfort this time there was Otis Lord, not Wentworth Higginson. "Your Sorrow was in Winter—," she wrote the Judge, referring to his wife's death, "one of our's in June and the other, November, and my Clergyman passed from earth in spring, but sorrow brings it's own chill. Seasons do not warm it."

Nor would sorrow cease, even during the warm months that Austin and his sisters loved. August was Austin's favorite, when he could listen to the crickets—subject of Emily's poem "Further in Summer than the Birds"—and the month when Gib was born. And Gib, who warmed all seasons, turned eight that summer of 1883. His little friends celebrated with cocked hats and banging drums, and when they marched over to the Homestead and around Emily's garden, she stood by and smiled.

Just a month later, in late September, he was taken ill after playing with a friend in a nearby mudhole. It was typhoid fever. He died the afternoon of October 5.

The night before had been terrible. Emily had noiselessly gone over to the Evergreens—certain neighbors gossiped that she had not been inside the place for fifteen years—and, according to Vinnie, received a nervous shock when she saw Gib's flaming cheeks. It was the odor from the disinfectants, neighbors speculated, that caused her to blanch and faint. It may have been the boy's heart-piercing delirium. " 'Open the Door, open the Door, they are waiting for me,' " Emily recorded the boy's deathbed words.

"Emily was devoted to Gilbert," Vinnie sighed.

During the funeral, Emily lay in bed. Sue, too, missed the service—she could not bear to go—and for months saw no one. When she finally emerged from the Evergreens, she was wrapped in the black crepe of bereavement she wore forever after. Bereft and abandoned by her husband, she was never the same, and neither was Emily, who would herself die just three years later.

But she reached out to Sue, offering comfort where there was none. "I see him in the Star, and meet his sweet velocity in everything that flies—," she told the sister beyond the hedge. "His Life was like the Bugle, which winds itself always, his Elegy an echo— his Requiem ecstasy." Whatever she knew about her brother, whatever she felt about Mabel, she would not fail Sue.

And Austin? "Gilbert was his idol and the only thing in his house which truly loved him, or in which he took any pleasure," Mabel lamented.

Within two months of Gib's death, she and Austin were lovers at last. "I kept him alive through the dreadful period of Gilbert's sickness and death," Mabel justified herself. "He could not bear the atmosphere of his own house, & used to go to his sisters', & then he or Lavinia would send for me—& it was on those oases from the prevailing gloom in life that he caught his breath & gathered strength to go on."

They met as often as possible: Austin bundled Mabel into his carriage for long rides through the tall pines, or they rendezvoused mornings or afternoons, or both, at the Homestead. In the evening,

Austin would stop by the Todds', especially when David worked late at the college. Austin kept up appearances at the Evergreens, and for many years Mabel continued to have a physical relationship with her husband, who remains a cipher. When Mabel confessed everything to him, he seems not to have offered any objections. Perhaps he feared losing her, or maybe he feared Austin, a powerhouse in this small town and the éminence grise of the college who raised David's salary when or if he saw fit. Years later his daughter herself wondered how "he, the youthful serious young scientist—how could he have accepted the situation—an old aristocrat twice his age, who looked down upon him as a plebeian, and preempted his wife as by the divine right of his august preference?" But likely David had affairs of his own. "I do not think David is what might be called a monogamous animal," Mabel would later confide to her journal. "While I know that he loves me to the full of his nature, he is not at all incapable of falling immensely in love with somebody else, & having a very piquant time of it."

And David was himself half in love with the hapless, arrogant Austin. Austin told Mabel that he and David confided in each other "beyond anything I have known among men." After the two men built a Queen Anne–style cottage for the Todds in the Dickinson meadow, Mabel and Austin seem to have occasionally made love with a "witness"—David?—in the room. By the turn of the century, David Peck Todd was said to be acting strangely; in 1917 he retired from Amherst College, and in 1922, declared insane, he was permanently institutionalized. Adultery, he told his daughter in 1933, had ruined his life.

Not surprisingly, Mabel's outraged parents were far less forgiving when they learned of Mabel's affair. More baffling is the fact that Mabel's reputation was unblemished for a fairly long time. She figured the reason was that Austin could consort with whatever ladies he liked because the town considered him beyond reproach. Besides, as she convinced herself somewhat contradictorily, "every one knows that he has been wretchedly disappointed in his domestic life, and all universally pity & respect him." (Mabel thought nothing, years later, of circulating rumors about Sue: that her father's alcoholism had killed him, for instance, and that a dalliance with Samuel Bowles had destroyed the Dickinson marriage.) As for herself, she refused to submit to base convention, with its primitive view of divorce—and, anyway, "the law of God is to me far higher than calf skin & parchment," she declared, improvising on the transcendentalism of an earlier day.

Many awestruck undergraduates jostled one another to sign Mabel's dance card at their various balls, and years later the story of her amorous adventure charmed the scholarly raconteur of Victorian sexual culture Peter Gay, who discovered that the thoroughly modern Mabel meticulously documented the frequency of her sexual intercourse and her orgasms with a set of symbols in her diary far easier to interpret than many of Emily Dickinson's poems.

Mabel and Austin's romance lasted for the remaining twelve years of Austin's life. The couple tried to stay impervious to Sue and Mabel's disapproving families and the cloaked gaze of their Amherst neighbors. This was easier for Austin than Mabel. "Our life together is as white and unspotted as the fresh driven snow," Austin would reassure her. "This we know—whatever vulgar minded people, who see nothing beyond the body—may think—or suspect. . . . We were born for each other—and we will stay with each other."

But the inhabitants of the Evergreens felt, as Ned later said, that they'd been sliced with a sword. And yet after his father's death, Ned snuck Mabel into the Evergreens so she could view Austin's body one last time. The family sat in the dining room while Mabel leaned over Austin's casket and kissed his cheek. "The whole town weeps for him," she grieved. "Yet I am the only mourner."

FOURTEEN

Monarch of Dreams

F rancis Ayrault is himself in mourning, for whom we don't know, and now alone in the world except for a five-year-old stepsister, he retires to an old family farmhouse, off the beaten track, where he will lose himself, literally, to his dreams.

Completed the summer after Emily Dickinson died, *The Monarch of Dreams* is a throwback to the kind of romance Higginson had not written in twenty years. It is also his tribute to the intrepid woman who committed her life to her art, who insisted on writing her own way, on publishing as she saw fit when and only when she chose to do so, who remained faithful to her vision of the elasticity, luxuriance, and magic of language, who questioned everything and did not for a moment alter her path for anyone. In a sense she was the poet, the monarch of dreams, he could never be. And in the end, to justify his own failure, he had to condemn what he valued most and believed he could not have.

This is the story: In the spring of 1861, just after the firing on Fort Sumter, the careworn Ayrault, descended "from a race of day-dreamers with a taste for ideal and metaphysical pursuits," decides to experiment in controlling his own dreams.

The bedroom door locked, the farmhouse quiet, Frank, as his sister calls him, falls asleep, his dreams soon blotting out everything, all his daylight interests and every person he knows, including his sister. Night after night silent hordes mill about him, unfeeling, resembling himself, siphoning off his individuality and his will. " 'Does all dreaming without action,' he wonders, 'thus leave a man lost within the crowd of himself?' " He does not control his dreams; they control him.

War inches nearer, regiments are recruited, and men rally to the cause, rousing Frank from his torpor. He enlists and "felt himself a changed being," writes Higginson, reverting to his pet metaphor for his own army days: "he was as if floating in air and ready to take wing for some new planet." But though Higginson in 1862 may have been moved to action, his pale alter ego stays pinioned to his dreams. The night before his regiment is scheduled to head to the front, Frank falls asleep and dreams that a colossal mob of figures—all himself—pins his arms and blocks his path while from afar he hears drums beating and the crackle of fireworks. A whistle shrieks, and the local train, jam-packed with flesh-and-blood soldiers, chugs out of the station, carrying "the lost opportunity of his life away—away—away."

Higginson's sister thought he must be having a breakdown. "It is a warning not a glorification," he wearily replied. But she was more perceptive than he knew. For what he intended as admonishment was at the same time a celebration: the romantic artist dwells in realms of possibility, and though punished, Frank conducted the very experiment that had long tempted Higginson, attracted since boyhood to poetry, literature, even the fantasy of a perfect woman, his Laura, whoever she might be. But he had never been able to lose himself in his fantasies, throwing caution and duty to the wind.

For though he might aspire to the lofty realm of beauty, Higginson owed allegiance to the world of action, and because his intellectual precocity was channeled early into both scholarship and civic duty, he could not therefore break free, as John Brown or Dickinson had, and light out for a territory of one. "To live and die only to transfuse external nature into human words, like Thoreau; to chase dreams for a lifetime, like Hawthorne; to labor tranquilly and see a nation imbued with one's thoughts, like Emerson,—this it is to pursue literature as an art": this is what he wanted, what he most admired, and what he had to censure in himself.

Fortunately, though, in his early years the salutary influence of Theodore Parker, Margaret Fuller, and Emerson more or less bridged the gap between public service and private longing. Build your own world, Emerson had said. That was not so easy; better to build your own character, which linked one to the world. Higginson copied a sentence from Emerson's essay "Man the Reformer" onto the flyleaf of one of his journals, remarking that no other sentence had ever influenced him more: "Better that the book should not be quite so good, & the bookmaker abler & better, & not himself often a ludicrous contrast to all that he has written." Then he added, this "has made me willing to vary my life & work for personal development, rather than to concentrate it & sacrifice myself to a specific result."

This was partly true. "The trouble with me is too great a range of tastes and interests," Higginson once acknowledged. "I love to do everything, to study everything, to contemplate and to write. I never was happier than when in the army entirely absorbed in action duties; yet I love literature next, indeed almost better." He could not choose. He thus never completely surrendered himself to poetry or to action, whether in politics, in the army, or after the war, in an unerring commitment to one of his causes.

And after the war it just wasn't possible for him to be both an imaginative writer and a public citizen. So he shuttled back and forth, unlike Dickinson, who, replying to Keats's "Ode on a Grecian Urn" and Elizabeth Barrett Browning's *Vision of Poets,* brought beauty and truth together in poetry.

> *I died for Beauty — but was scarce*
> *Adjusted in the Tomb*
> *When One who died for Truth, was lain*
> *In an adjoining Room —*
>
> *He questioned softly "Why I failed"?*
> *"For Beauty", I replied —*
> *"And I — for Truth — Themself are One —*
> *We Brethren are", He said —*
>
> *And so, as Kinsmen, met a Night —*
> *We talked between the Rooms —*
> *Until the Moss had reached our lips —*
> *And covered up — Our names —*

Beauty and truth are "Kinsmen," united in words, not deeds, and even though death covers up "names," achieved no doubt in the pursuit of beauty and truth, the poet speaks after death, keeping beauty and truth linked and alive.

Years later Higginson singled out "I died for Beauty—" as one of the poems that took his breath away, and doubtless he saw in it the reconciliation, through poetry, of a conflict he never quite resolved. But there was another, unspoken issue for Higginson. The dilemma of Frank Ayrault, isolated by his self-absorption and yielding to his dreams "as a swimmer yields his body to a strong current," suggests Higginson worried that, alas, at bottom he had nothing, neither beauty nor truth, to dream about. This anxiety also lies at the heart of "A Night in the Water," when, as Higginson submerges himself in the river, the world as he knows it dissolves: "I began to doubt everything, to distrust the stars, the line of low bushes for which I was wearily striving, the very land on which they grew, if such visionary things could be rooted anywhere," Higginson wrote. "I had no well-defined anxiety, felt no fear, was moved to no prayer, did not give a thought to home and friends." But without the shore he was nowhere, he was nothing. And yet if he was unable to dive into the dark waters of his own imagination or fully into the world of action, here, in this tour de force, he swam out much farther than he had planned.

Then he stepped back. Unlike Dickinson, he always stepped back. Most of his short stories are set pieces wagging fingers at moony young men for their addiction to art or beauty. More successful than these efforts are his polemical writings and some of his nature essays. (Few of his accomplishments—and none of his disappointments— ever meant more to him than Thoreau's admiration of "Snow.") When he joined the ranks of the literary professional, he wrote with restraint, wit, and unpretentious ease, but when no longer an impassioned advocate, he did not produce documents quite as powerful as his essays about slave uprisings and women's rights—and about army life in the South with the black troops he adored.

It would be interesting to know if he mailed Dickinson an early version of *Monarch of Dreams* and, if he had, how she responded. He had started the story in 1877, just after Mary's death. But he could not complete it. He didn't know how it should end. And then when he decided to remarry, he put the tale away. Marriage supplied the regularity he needed; as he had told his friends, "I'm adrift in the universe without it." He, too, hugged the shore.

In 1886, right after Dickinson died—her death likely motivating him to finish it at last—he picked up the story again. For he was now justifying the road he, not she, had taken: safe and solid and wide awake. Pleased with the result even though *The Atlantic* rejected it, he published *Monarch of Dreams* at his own expense when no other editor stepped into the breach. "My favorite child," he called the slim, leather-covered book. And yet he really didn't accept the story's pat lesson: that a life of reverie concentrates the self too much, making solipsists of us all. After all, Higginson was himself a dreamer. His active pursuit of abolition and social justice had itself come by way of the dream of a better world.

THE END OF HIGGINSON'S TERM in the Massachusetts legislature had not stopped him from battling institutional xenophobia or discrimination against Irish, German, and Jewish immigrants. "The Pilgrims landed," he reminded nativists; "that is the essential point. They were not the indigenous race." He continued to advocate equal rights for women even though he had parted company with his allies at *The Woman's Journal* when they endorsed Benjamin Butler, presumably a woman suffrage candidate, for governor. In 1884 he alienated himself further when he refused to censure Grover Cleveland in the presidential race, as Lucy Stone had done, because of the man's peccadilloes. (Cleveland had sired a child out of wedlock.) A "mugwump," Higginson had lost patience with the Republicans and defected to the new youth movement, casting his vote as an independent and believing that a new age—and a new political party—loomed on the horizon. But much to the chagrin of his friends, he naively advised women to put off equal rights until political corruption no longer existed.

Regardless, and without a trace of irony, Higginson would call the nineteenth century the woman's century. Women may not have secured the vote—men still wouldn't give up their dinners—but change was afoot, he claimed, and as if to prove it, when he left *The Woman's Journal,* he wrote a weekly column for *Harper's Bazaar* about American social life. Yet this was no suffrage forum. Mary Booth, *Bazaar*'s editor, had warned Higginson early on that it was "inexpedient," as she put it, "to advocate women's suffrage therein, either explicitly or implicitly." The magazine abstained from questions of religion and politics, she told him, "while maintaining a firm and progressive attitude. . . . In a word, it has always sought to carry out the Emersonian doctrine of always affirming and never denying." (Why not affirm suffrage? He seems not to have asked.)

Taking the job and toeing the line, Higginson wrote pieces that were decidedly progressive, humorous, firm, and on occasion as dry as those he had written thirty years earlier. "The Mendelssohn family had not the slightest objection to their gifted Fanny's composing

Higginson and daughter, Margaret, on tricycle, Cambridge, 1885.

as much music as she pleased," he noted, "provided it appeared under the name of her brother Felix." Collected in 1887 in the book *Women and Men,* these short essays, neither fusty nor unsympathetic, chattily—and encouragingly—discuss women's education, economics, and illness (arguing, in the last instance, that men are more prone to nervousness), but they don't sizzle.

He also published a rugged and quite good biography of Margaret Fuller, "in a literary way," he boasted with good reason, "almost the best thing I did." Countering the lily-livered Fuller memoir compiled by his cousin William Henry Channing, Emerson, and James Freeman Clarke, Higginson set out to convert the tragedy of her life into an intrepid triumph over inertia and the status quo. (Returning from Rome in 1850 with her son and husband, Fuller had drowned in a shipwreck just four hundred yards off Fire Island, New York. Assuming that she had brought along her manuscript about the revolutions of 1848, a distraught Emerson dispatched Thoreau to Fire Island to determine whether any of its pages had washed up on the beach, and when none were found, the saga of Fuller as incomplete genius was born.) But as Higginson saw it, Fuller's commitment to the activist life had been as rich and rewarding as his own—indeed, it had inspired him—and he never forgot what she had said the country needed: "no thin idealist, no coarse realist, but a man whose eye reads the heavens, while his feet step firmly on the ground, and his hands are strong and dexterous for the use of human implements."

With writing still his only source of income, he was as prolific as ever, contributing to a bevy of journals, including *The Atlantic, The Century, The Nation, The Literary World, The Critic, The Forum, Scribner's, Harper's,* and *The Independent,* but he frequently declined engagements, blaming an unnamed nervous ailment that clouded his vision, or he excused himself on behalf of his wife, Minnie, who had taken to her bed for months at a time with an unexplained illness. His face lined, his hair silvery, he still brimmed with optimism, campaigning, as ever, for an American literature and for democracy, the two intimately related: "I affirm that democratic society, the society of the future, enriches and does not impoverish human life, and gives more, not less, material for literary art," he had declared in 1870. Two decades later he still insisted that the root of all living language, its snap and pop, comes from "actual life—the life of every day," which is to say from the people: "You must go to the men around the anvil, the shoemakers on their benches, and the gossips in the village shops. They make the words, they make them strongly."

Higginson spoke out against privileges accruing to a single class, caste, race, or gender, and as for the new "aristocracy of the dollar," who converted dreams of justice into dreams of gold, he believed that "the aristocracy of the millionaires is only a prelude to the aristocracy of the millions." (Andrew Carnegie loved Higginson's lecture on the subject.) An evolutionary gradualist, he would loosely ally himself with Edward Bellamy's utopian Nationalist clubs but called himself a progressive cooperationist, not a nationalist. The nationalization of industry seemed to him undemocratic; this position was in keeping with his faith in a free market democracy, although he admitted government ownership of energy and railroads not a bad idea. Nor were workingmen's compensation, compulsory education, and profit sharing. "Sow a victim, and you reap a socialist," he observed with sympathy for the worker. Yet he apparently said nothing when seven hundred strikes occurred in Massachusetts in 1887 and, unlike Howells, did not protest the execution of the Haymarket anarchists. These were battles for a new generation. He had fought his.

FIFTEEN

Pugilist and Poet

Death claimed her far too early, he later recalled, but she would persist.

Though himself frequently ill, Higginson kept up their correspondence as best he could. Still, there were long lapses between his letters to Emily. And hers to him, though when she could, she wrapped small gifts for his daughter—a Valentine, a poem, a book, a turquoise brooch in a square wooden box with roses painted on the lid—that have disappeared from public view. But since her nephew Gib's death, in 1883, an unexplained illness had stalked her, and in the summer of 1884 she took a turn for the worse. She blacked out, fell, and when she woke, a physician was glooming over her. "The doctor calls it 'revenge of the nerves,' " she quipped, "but who but Death had wronged them?" For several days she seemed delirious, or at least not quite rational. More herself by the following February, she sent John Cross's *George Eliot's Life* to Higginson, now piquantly observing that "Biography first convinces us of the fleeing of the Biographied—."

She had begun to flee.

And she added to her letter the four lines of poetry originally written for Sue after the death of Gilbert:

> *Pass to thy Rendezvous of Light,*
> *Pangless except for us —*
> *Who slowly ford the Mystery*
> *Which thou hast leaped across!*

Not yet would she say good-bye, but this was a prelude.

"I WORK TO DRIVE the awe away, yet awe impels the work," Dickinson had written her cousins the previous spring. Otis Lord had died in March; it was a severe blow, and it may be that she never quite recovered. "How *can* the sun shine, Vinnie?" Emily reportedly asked on hearing the news. "I have not been strong for the last year," she then told a friend. "The Dyings have been too deep for me, and before I could raise my Heart from one, another has come."

"The Crisis of the sorrow of so many years is all that tires me," she explained to Elizabeth Holland, referring to the passing of her father, her mother, Charles Wadsworth, her darling nephew. "All this and more, though *is* there more? More than Love and Death? Then tell me it's name!"

Working to drive the awe away, awe impelling the work: the remark echoes the one she had made to Higginson back in 1862, that "I sing, as the Boy does by the Burying Ground—because I am afraid." Writing calmed anxiety and answered questions by posing them, particularly about love and death and what she had told Higginson was "the Flood subject," or immortality. And immortality implied not just everlasting life in religious terms but poetry, "Exterior—to Time—."

Awe impels the work. "Circumference, thou bride / of awe,— possessing, thou / Shalt be possessed by / Every hallowed Knight / That dares to covet thee": these perplexing, evocative lines she sent Daniel Chester French, the architect and Amherst native, on the unveiling of his statute of John Harvard in Cambridge. "Success is dust, but an aim forever touched with dew," she added, as if to remind him that the moment shall pass, fresh as it seems. And frequently she returned to those twinned subjects, poetry and immortality, in these last years. "My Business is Circumference," she had informed Higginson so many years before, and that was still true. Circumference, the reaching of limits and beyond them, was its own form of immortality, which relieved both the joy and pain of living. For when undergoing some sort of crisis just before and during the war, as we recall, she had written an astonishing number of poems, many of her greatest, but afterward the quantity declined to as few as ten in a year. And before her last illness she had been writing again at a steady rate, twenty poems annually and, by the editor Ralph Franklin's count, as many as forty-two in 1884, the year Lord died.

She had not been sending Higginson as many poems as previously: the year of Mary's death she sent eight but only two in 1878, the year after, and one in 1879, when Higginson remarried. But she mailed six in 1880, two in 1881, and four in 1882. (These last include "How happy is the little Stone," "Come show thy Durham Breast to her who loves thee best," "Obtaining but our own extent," and possibly "The Moon upon her fluent route.") The next year, 1883, she sent "No Brigadier throughout the Year."

> *No Brigadier throughout the Year*
> *So civic as the Jay —*
> *A Neighbor and a Warrior too*
> *With shrill felicity*
> *Pursuing Winds that censure us*
> *A February Day,*
> *The Brother of the Universe*
> *Was never blown away —*
> *The Snow and he are intimate —*
> *I've often seen them play*
> *When Heaven looked upon us all*
> *With such severity*
> *I felt apology were due*
> *To an insulted sky*
> *Whose pompous frown was Nutriment*
> *To their temerity —*
> *The Pillow of this daring Head*
> *Is pungent Evergreens —*
> *His Larder — terse and Militant —*
> *Unknown — refreshing things —*
> *His Character — a Tonic —*
> *His Future — a Dispute —*
> *Unfair an Immortality*
> *That leaves this Neighbor out —*

Though the subject of this poem is the blue jay — she had attached a clipping about birds to her manuscript — it is tempting to read it, once offered to Higginson, as a lighthearted homage to him, a brigadier in his own right as civic as the jay; a neighbor, a warrior, a "Brother of the Universe" intimate with "Snow" (Higginson's essay) and with nature ("pungent Evergreens"), his character a tonic deserving, without doubt, of a certain immortality. He admired the poem enormously, but when he included it in *Poems*, Second Series, he placed it under the rubric of "Nature," not "Life." He was a shy, self-effacing man.

Had she changed her mind about publishing in these later years? Chiding Dickinson for her intractability, Helen Hunt Jackson flatly stated that "it is a cruel wrong to your 'day & generation' " not to publish and asked to serve as Dickinson's literary executor should Jackson outlive her. "Surely, after you are what is called 'dead,' " Jackson pushed, "you will be willing that the poor ghosts you have left behind, should be cheered and pleased by your verses, will you not?"

Jackson had recommended Dickinson's work to Thomas Niles, the editor at Roberts Brothers who had published the No Name Series. "The kind but incredible opinion of 'H. H.' and yourself, I would like to deserve—," Dickinson wrote Niles in response to his inquiry, mailing him "How happy is the little Stone," which she'd recently given Higginson: "How happy is the little Stone / ," it begins in mock innocence, "That rambles in the Road alone, / And does'nt care about Careers / And Exigencies never fears—."

A year passed. In the spring of 1883, as if to reopen the discussion, she mailed Niles "Further in Summer than the Birds" and "It sifts from leaden sieves," poems Higginson had received in 1866 and 1871; perhaps his enthusiasm had encouraged her to try them out on Niles. She also sent him one of her favorite books, a volume of poems by the Brontë sisters: she was as serious as they.

Niles was nonplussed. "I would not for the world rob you of this very rare book," he burbled. "If I may presume to say so, I will instead take a M.S. collection of your poems, that is," he diffidently added, "if you want to give them to the world through the medium of a publisher." Apparently she did not, although it's not quite clear what she did want, for she kept mailing poems, sending "No Brigadier throughout the Year," and when he said that "the Bird seemed true," dispatching three more: "a Thunderstorm—a Humming Bird, and a Country Burial," she called them, as if poems with titles—she did not ordinarily use them—might be more suitable for a benighted public.

Higginson had also read these—"The Wind begun to rock the Grass," "A Route of Evanescence," and "Ample make this Bed,"— and it seems he had praised them. No doubt she hoped Niles would too. "Ample make this Bed— / Make this Bed with Awe— / In it wait till Judgment break / Excellent and Fair," she wrote. When mailed to Niles, the poem can be read as a covert bid for his good opinion. Yet it's impossible to know if she would have consented, after all, to a book had Niles been keener. When he subsequently thanked her for the "specimens," he noncommittally asked if he might hang on to them; possibly his polite apathy confirmed Dickinson's dim view of publishers: insensitive and meretricious.

Higginson was different. For though she masqueraded as his student, both of them had acceded to the ruse, he admitting after her death that he knew he could teach her nothing. At the same time it does not seem as though she mentioned Niles to him. She kept her secrets well.

Writing Wentworth during that same spring of 1883 — and calling herself his "Pupil" out of well-worn, reassuring habit — Emily revived their dwindling correspondence. "Emblem is immeasurable—," she told him, "that is why it is better than Fulfillment, which can be drained." Her prose more nimble than his, her poetry more audacious and trenchant, she continued to flatter and upstage him, dipping into his work and rewriting it for her own use, for as she noted, he said great things inadvertently. Listen to his long-winded comment on the line "And yet I live!" in Petrarch's Sonnet 251, which he compares with Shakespeare: "What immeasurable distances of time and thought are implied in the self-recovery of those words. Shakespeare might have taken from them his 'Since Cleopatra died,'— the only passage in literature which has in it the same wide spaces of emotion." As was her habit, Emily briskly rephrased Higginson. "Antony's remark to a friend, 'since Cleopatra died' is said to be the saddest ever lain in Language—," she wrote to Otis Lord. "That engulfing 'Since'—."

In the spring of 1884, after Otis Lord had suffered his lethal stroke, she wrote to her cousins, "I hardly dare to know that I have lost another friend. Till the first friend dies, we think ecstasy impersonal, but then discover that he was the cup from which we drank it, itself as yet unknown." Yet in spite of her own illness and the wearing horror of so many deaths, there was something indomitable about Emily Dickinson, who could still with scrupulous care watch the bobolinks in the meadow and reiterate that blossoms and books were the solace of sorrow. They were. " 'Supernatural,' was only the Natural, disclosed—," she had said to Higginson in one of her first, tantalizing letters:

> *Not "Revelation"—'tis — that waits,*
> *But our unfurnished eyes —*

Her robust passion for nature unimpaired almost twenty years later, she committed herself to joy in the very act of living, even if that commitment required necessary delusions that, as she and Higginson would both suggest, keep human behavior ethical. They had not abdicated belief; they redefined it. As Dickinson wrote in a late poem,

> *Those — dying then,*
> *Knew where they went —*
> *They went to God's Right Hand —*
> *That Hand is amputated now*
> *And God cannot be found —*
> *The abdication of Belief*
> *Makes the Behavior small —*
> *Better an ignis fatuus*
> *Than no illume at all —*

"FAITH IS *DOUBT*," Emily told Sue. Perhaps in a bleak moment or when he wrote to her in the letters that do not survive, Wentworth had agreed with her. Mostly he did not. "What channel needs our faith except the eyes?" he had asked in an early poem, and in 1891 he said that "next to the yearnings of human affections, the most irresistible suggestion of immortality comes from looking up at the unattainable mystery of the stars." Emily was more specific, more poignant. "I hear robins a great way off," she lyrically wrote to her cousins, "and wagons a great way off, and rivers a great way off, and all appear to be hurrying somewhere undisclosed to me. Remoteness is the founder of sweetness; could we see all we hope, or hear the whole we fear told tranquil, like another tale, there would be madness near. Each of us gives or takes heaven in corporeal person, for each of us has the skill of life."

And some, she might have added, possess the skill of poetry. She did include this ebullient poem about singing:

> *The most triumphant bird*
> *I ever knew or met,*
> *Embarked upon a twig today,*
> *And till Dominion set,*
> *I perish to behold*

A photograph marked "Emily Dickinson,
died Dec. 1886," from daguerreotype taken ca. 1853,
authenticity not established.

So competent a sight,
And sang for nothing scrutable,
But impudent delight —
Retired, and resumed
his transitive estate,
To what delicious accident
does finest glory fit!

One sings for nothing scrutable. Remoteness is the founder of sweet song.

THE UNBELIEVABLE RUMOR of Helen Hunt Jackson's fatal illness prompted Emily to write Wentworth immediately. "Please say it is not so," she begged him in the summer of 1885, afraid of what he might answer. The news was bad. Jackson died on August 12. Higginson published a memorial sonnet in *The Century,* which he sent in manuscript to Dickinson, who replied with her own farewell:

> *Not knowing when Herself may come*
> *I open every Door,*
> *Or has she Feathers, like a Bird,*
> *or Billows, like a Shore —*

Shortly afterward she contacted Wentworth again, enclosing an elegiac poem that quietly lauds him.

> *Of Glory not a Beam is left*
> *But her Eternal House —*
> *The Asterisk is for the Dead,*
> *The Living, for the Stars —*

For years he had been her living friend. And she thanked him.

EMILY RELAPSED IN THE FALL of 1885. Canceling a Boston trip, Austin sat at his sister's bedside. By December she seemed to improve for a time but soon sank lower. She was breathing with difficulty. There were convulsions. Otis Bigelow, her physician, prescribed olive oil and chloroform. On Thursday, May 13, he stayed by her side all day, but as Austin scribbled in his diary, "Emily seemed to go off into a stark unconscious state toward ten—and at this writing 6 PM has not come out of it." She never regained consciousness.

Bigelow diagnosed Bright's disease, a kidney disorder, but it was not necessarily the cause of her death, for the symptoms that began shortly after Gib's death—those terrible headaches, the vomiting—

and the ensuing stretches of good health may be consistent with severe primary hypertension, leading to cardiac failure or stroke. Or with cancer. In 1886 there were no medical interventions that might have saved her.

"IT WAS SETTLED BEFORE MORNING BROKE that Emily would not wake again this side," Austin noted on Saturday, May 15. "The day was awful. She ceased to breathe that terrible breathing just before the whistles sounded for six. . . . I was near by."

"AUDACITY OF BLISS, said Jacob to the Angel 'I will not let thee go except I bless thee'—Pugilist and Poet, Jacob was correct—," Dickinson reconceived Genesis at the very end of her life, posting a final note to Wentworth Higginson, some of the last lines she was ever to write, tribute to a subtle friendship.

And though Higginson may have been the angel who saved her life, as she had often reminded him, when she retold the story of Jacob and the angel, it was she, both poet and pugilist—and a monarch of dreams—who would, could, will bless him, and who never let go these many, many years.

SIXTEEN

Rendezvous of Light

Those two sisters living alone, their bond insoluble, their rebuff of conventions rock hard: to Higginson, who stepped inside the Homestead once again — it had been nearly thirteen years — the place was a living House of Usher, updated and New Englandly. The day was lustrous, calm, and gemlike. The morning haze had burned off, leaving the sky blue and hopeful, and the village was dressed for spring in bright green, violet, and wild geranium. But at the Homestead the long shades were drawn, and in the library sat a small white casket.

Inhaling, Higginson peered down at Emily Dickinson's beautiful unfurrowed brow. He did not hesitate at calling her beautiful now. And as he sadly noticed, she was youthful too, without a gray hair or a wrinkle.

"How large a portion of the people who have interested me have passed away," he mourned.

Higginson's unusual friend had died just days before. He had received the sad news, likely by telegram, on the seventeenth. So many deaths: Helen Hunt Jackson not a year earlier, when Dickinson herself, upset, had contacted him to say Jackson had written she could not walk "but not," Dickinson cried, "that she would die." Now Emily herself was gone. He knew she had been ill, for earlier that spring she had told him she had been sick since November, "bereft of Book and Thought," she had said, "by Doctor's reproof." But he had not thought, as Emily had said of Jackson, that she would die.

Of course he would go to the funeral. Emily herself had probably requested that her family invite him. She had stipulated everything: the simple service, the men who would carry her casket, perhaps even the soft white flannel robe in which Sue tenderly wrapped her. Vinnie scattered pansies and lilies of the valley on the piano and placed a sprig of violets at Emily's neck, as she had done with their

mother, along with a pink flower called *Cypripedium,* or lady's slip-
per. She also set two heliotropes by her hand "to take to Judge Lord,"
Higginson heard her say.

The funeral took place on Wednesday the nineteenth. The Reverend Jonathan Jenkins, who came from Pittsfield to offer a short
prayer, and the Reverend Mr. Dickerman, pastor of the First Congregational Church, read from 1 Corinthians 15: "For this corrupt-
ible must put on incorruption, and this mortal must put on
immortality."

Higginson then pulled himself to his feet, announcing he would
recite a poem, the one Emily had often read to her sister: Emily
Brontë's "Last Lines." It was "a favorite with our friend," he added,
"who has now put on that Immortality which she never seemed to
have laid off."

> *No coward soul is mine,*
> *No trembler in the world's storm-troubled sphere:*
> *I see Heaven's glories shine,*
> *And faith shines equal, arming me from fear.*

The poem seems a valediction to each of the mourners gathered
there in the Homestead parlor:

> *Though earth and man were gone,*
> *And suns and universes cease to be,*
> *And Thou were left alone,*
> *Every existence would exist in Thee.*

THE HONORARY PALLBEARERS, including the president of
Amherst College, bore the small coffin from the library into the hall
and then out the back door, but per Emily's express instructions, the
men who worked for the Dickinsons over the years—Stephen Sulli-
van, Pat Ward, Tom Kelley, Dennis Scannell, Dennis Cashman, Dan
Moynihan—conveyed the casket, high on its wooden bier, through
the Dickinson meadow to the cemetery. It was the path through the
meadow, thick with daisies and buttercups, that Miss Emily herself
must often have taken to visit her parents' graves.

Convulsed in grief and draped in black, a hollow-eyed Mabel
Todd accompanied the small group to the cemetery, walking behind

the family cortege. The air was iridescent, the white sun streaming on the mourners, who gathered around the open grave, which Sue had lined with a spate of flowers and green branches. "It was a never to be forgotten burial," commented a family friend, "and seemed singularly fitting to the departed one."

As the casket was lowered down and farther down, Mabel Todd took one last look. Emily Dickinson, she said, had gone back "into a little deeper mystery than that she has always lived in."

SUE DICKINSON COMPOSED AN OBITUARY for the *Springfield Republican.* Printed on May 18, the day before the funeral, it addressed all the rumors flying around her sister-in-law; the rumors had flown around her sister-in-law for years. There was a great deal public about this private person, and Sue wanted to set the record straight. "Not disappointed with the world," she wrote, "not an invalid until within the past two years, not from any lack of sympathy, not because she was insufficient for any mental work or social career—her endowments being so exceptional—, but the 'mesh of her soul,' as Browning calls the body, was too rare, and the sacred quiet of her own home proved the fit atmosphere for her worth and work."

Emily's writing and conversation were incomparable, she went on to say. "Like a magician she caught the shadowy apparitions of her brain and tossed them in startlingly picturesqueness to her friends, who, charmed with their simplicity and homeliness as well as profundity, fretted that she had so easily made palpable the tantalizing fancies forever eluding their bungling, fettered grasp."

And in the end Emily eluded everyone. "Now and then some enthusiastic literary friend would turn love into larceny, and cause a few verses surreptitiously obtained to be printed," Sue admitted. "Thus, and through other natural ways, many saw and admired her verses, and in consequence frequently notable persons paid her visits, hoping to overcome the protest of her own nature and gain a promise of occasional contributions, at least, to various magazines."

One such was Wentworth Higginson.

THEIR FRIENDSHIP HAD BEEN BASED on absence, geographic distance, and the written word. They had exchanged letters in which they invented themselves and each other, performing for each other in the words that filled, maintained, and created the space between them. "What a Hazard a Letter is!" Emily had exclaimed to him. "When I think of the Hearts it has scuttled and sunk, I almost fear to lift my Hand to so much as a Superscription." Yet she hazarded them for a lifetime and to Wentworth for almost twenty-five years.

He knew what she meant, albeit in his own way. "It is true of all of us that the letter represents the man, odd or even," he observed. "It is, indeed, more absolutely the man, in one sense, than he himself is, for the man himself is inevitably changing, beyond his own control, from moment to moment, from birth to death." What a hazard a letter is: quicksilver and irrevocable and frequently misunderstood. Yet somehow these two people, who lived in the intimacies and distances and secrets of words — somehow these two people created out of words a nearness we today do not entirely grasp.

Dickinson's letters, all of them, blaze with a passion for sight and smell and sound and the enduring pleasure, whatever its cost, of friendship. The soul has bandaged moments, true, difficult to express, but there are points of contact, vehement, aflame, effulgent beyond words, that compel our entire being. That was her gamble. These are my letters to the World, she so famously said.

"Through the solitary prowess / Of a Silent Life —."

And Higginson? For her he represented the dappled world. And he gave it what he had, glad to give and still shy of what he might have found had he dwelled, as she did, uncompromisingly inward. But there was much he had understood.

"Are you too deeply occupied to say if my Verse is alive?" she had once asked this kindhearted man. "Should you think it breathed — and had you the leisure to tell me, I should feel quick gratitude —."

Two weeks before she died, still trusting that he, with his gift of sympathy, would understand, she in effect returned to the same question.

"Deity — does He live now?" she asked him. "My friend — does he breathe?"

Part Three

Beyond the Dip of Bell

SEVENTEEN

Poetry of the Portfolio

The wheels of Austin Dickinson's gleaming carriage screeched to a halt in front of the main gate of the Evergreens, and hearing the racket, Harriet Jameson bounded from her desk to the window. "I have no doubt he had a delightful drive with charming company," she caustically remarked, settling herself back down and continuing her letter. "The gossips say the intimacy existing between him and Mrs. Todd is as great as ever." To think that Mrs. Todd, utterly unrelated to the poet, had stood at poor Emily's grave shedding copious tears. "Many people are leaving Mrs. T 'alone'—," Mrs. Jameson delivered the town's verdict with smug satisfaction. For this was unimpeachable New England, where emotional displays were insupportable and, if ventured by an outsider, outrageous.

Ignorant of the village scuttlebutt, Wentworth Higginson returned to Amherst a few months after Dickinson's funeral as the guest of Sue and Austin. Austin ushered the Colonel about town: two men of the world, or so Austin liked to believe, riding through the bucolic scenery in which Austin took almost boyish pride. Wicker baskets on back porches were filled with ripe apples, and the nearby hills decked in crimson and gold. Chatting away, Austin likely did not speak of Mabel except in a most general way, and one assumes that instead of town tattle the men talked of Emily's poetry, which Lavinia was determined to see published.

Lavinia: alone in the now cavernous Homestead, surrounded by her cats, she was fretful and thin, the flesh having dropped from her bones in those last agonizing months before Emily died. And why had she been robbed of her one companion on earth, she indignantly wondered, until, that is, she discovered her sister's poetry. She had known, of course, that her sister wrote poetry, but she was unprepared for the hundreds and hundreds of poems in Emily's room, in the small bureau, some sewn together in booklets, others scribbled on the backs of envelopes, and she decided there and then that these poems would be published, preserved, respected. She would have her sister back.

It would not be an easy job. Vinnie knew that. Not only had Emily often written in a crabbed hand—as Higginson reminisced, it seemed she took her "first lessons by studying the famous fossil bird-tracks in the museum of that college town"—but the poems themselves looked to be in a state of confusion. Though Emily had collected some of them in small packets (Mrs. Todd called them fascicles, and the technical term has stuck) and grouped others in sets, many poems seemed incomplete. But literature was improvisation, much like Emily's concoctions at the piano, remembered by all who heard them, and her poems were always in progress, meant to be revised, reevaluated, and reconceived, especially when dispatched to different readers, as her editors would soon discover. (As the poet Richard Howard has pointed out, finishing poems may not have interested her: "her true Flaubert was Penelope, to invert a famous allusion, forever unraveling what she had figured on the loom the day before.") She kept variants and appears not to have chosen among them, sometimes toying with as many as eight possibilities for words, line arrangement, rhyme, enjambment; nor did she choose among alternative endings. And frequently she composed on scraps of paper—newspaper clippings, brown paper sacks—or around the edges of thin sheets, the writing almost illegible. Or she incorporated parts of poems into the letters, which themselves were acts of poetry.

Nor had she left instructions about how she might want her poems to appear in print, or whether they should appear in print at all. Nor did she tell us if the physical and visual properties of her manuscripts were as semantically important to her as contemporary critics contend.

From an editorial point of view, the situation was a mess.

Sue would have been the person most capable of sorting through Emily's manuscripts, readying them for publication, but Vinnie mistrusted her. ("I was to have compiled the poems—," Sue stretched the truth a bit, writing to the editor of *The Independent* in 1891, "but as I moved slowly, dreading publicity for us all, she [Vinnie] was angry and a year ago took them from me.") Months passed, and though Sue had a boxful, she did nothing with them, or so Vinnie decided even though Sue had mailed a few poems, much as she had in the past, to men well situated in the literary world. To *The Century*'s editor, Richard Watson Gilder, she mailed, perhaps at Higginson's request, a poem she titled "Wind" ("The Wind begun to rock the Grass"), noting that "Col. Higginson, Dr. Holland, 'H.H.' and many other of her literary friends have long urged her {Emily} to allow her poems to be printed, but she was never willing to face the world." Gilder turned her down flat. The result from other magazines was equally discouraging.

Mabel Todd knew all of this. Austin told her everything: of Sue's failures—a source of pleasure for Mabel—and of Vinnie's manic determination. And Mabel had already decided that she alone was Emily's special companion—though one the poet had refused to see—for even if no one else did, Mabel believed in the sincerity of her own feelings. And gripped by Emily's spectral reputation, she identified with this wisp of a woman, who, though an Amherst insider by birthright, had quietly rejected its mores and earned admiration from the well-known likes, as Sue put it, of Josiah Holland, Helen Hunt Jackson, and Colonel Higginson. There was a lesson here.

If Mabel's neighbors these days deemed her an adulteress less sympathetic than Hester Prynne, she resolved to be just as famous. "I know I have the gift of expression," she reasoned. "But if I were to become sufficiently well-known, to be asked for articles and stories, that sort of stimulus would be very sweet to me. I do long for a little real, tangible success. . . . It is so beautiful to be appreciated! . . . after six years of being pressed down, & sat upon, & throttled!" She published reviews in *The Nation,* just as Higginson had once advised Helen Hunt Jackson to do—since 1877 he himself had been writing its "Recent Poetry" column—and Austin presented her with a hand-carved oak writing desk. He also sent one of her stories to George William Curtis at *Harper's,* who rejected it. But the ever-buoyant Mabel did not quit or wait; with energy to burn, she wrote up her recent trip to Japan, where her husband, David, had been appointed the chief of the United States Eclipse Expedition. "Ten Weeks in Japan" soon appeared in *St. Nicholas* magazine, and over the next five years, as Mabel noted in her diary, her reviews and articles flooded the *Illustrated Christian Weekly,* the New York *Evening Post, St. Nicholas,* and *The Nation.* Eventually there was, as she crowed, "a notice of me in *Woman's Journal*" and, far better, an invitation from the Boston literary doyenne Annie Fields, asking Mabel to

Mabel Loomis Todd in 1885, at 29, Austin Dickinson's lover
and soon to be Emily Dickinson's champion and co-editor,
with Thomas Wentworth Higginson, of the first three
volumes of Dickinson's poetry.

tea at her famous Charles Street home on the bank of the river. Writing was the best revenge.

Emboldened by success, she wanted to publish her and Austin's love letters, anonymously of course, their names discreetly omitted. Doubtless Austin scuttled the project. Yet he remained her secular religion, their love sacred, its grandeur her moral shield against guilt or infamy—or Sue, whom she transformed into a monster of cruelty and sloth. Mabel would rise above them all, she knew, as the advocate of the sublime, and if she could not articulate the sublime in a book of her lover's letters, then why not in a book of poetry? By associating herself with the mythic Emily, Mabel could infuriate Sue and trump the entire town.

The timing was right. Mabel knew that Vinnie wanted above all else to see her sister's poems in print, and Vinnie, exasperated by Sue and aware of Mabel's Dickinson fixation, craftily showed her several of the poems. To be published, they would have to be copied, of course, the originals kept safe. Soon Mabel was transcribing them. Years later Vinnie would insist Mabel had begged for the privilege in order to enhance her own reputation, not Emily's, and Mabel would claim Vinnie had solicited her unpaid and loyal assistance, which she freely gave.

Vinnie also enlisted Higginson when he again stayed at the Evergreens during the summer of 1888, while attending a meeting of the American Philological Society. Agreeing that a private printing of Emily's poems would not circulate her work widely enough, he pledged his assistance—editing the poems, finding a publisher— even though he had recently been ill. And he promised to write a preface to the volume; his imprimatur would help get it noticed.

With Higginson on board and Vinnie an unrelenting overseer, Mabel worked harder and harder. Transcribing poems first by hand and then on her new Hammond typewriter, by the winter of 1889 Mabel was copying two or three a day out of the "wilderness" of them all: "they are almost endless in number," she moaned. By her own admission she was also altering a large number of the poems as she copied, substituting words where she thought fit or choosing among the alternates Dickinson had written in the margins. "I felt their genius and I knew the book would succeed," she said. "At the same time, their carelessness of form exasperated me. I could always find the gist & meaning, and I admired her strange words and ways of using them, but the simplest laws of verse-making she ignored, and what she called rhymes grated on me." So she improved them.

And she continued to bang out her own compositions, articles for *The Youth's Companion, Frank Leslie's Popular Monthly, The Century,* and the *Christian Union* (mostly nonfiction), until, exhausted, she hired an assistant, Harriet Graves, to help her with the hundreds of poems still left. When Miss Graves proved a disappointment, Mabel copied more poems herself on her brand-new World typewriting machine before switching back to copying them by hand; it actually took less time and helped her commit the poems to memory, which she liked to do. Devoting three or four hours a day to the poems, she later remembered their mesmerizing effect. "They seemed to open the door into a wider universe than the little sphere surrounding me which so often hurt and compressed me," she said, "and they helped me nobly through a very trying time."

Temporarily finished, in the fall of 1889 Mabel finally met Colonel Higginson. In Boston with her daughter (David was on another eclipse expedition, this time in Angola), the ardent Mrs. Todd greeted the courtly Colonel on November 6, 1889, at her cousin's Beacon Street home—far plusher than her own sparse rooms—and the unlikely collaboration commenced. Together they sifted through the huge stash of poems Mabel had brought: 634 by Mabel's count, 600 copied personally by her.

"He staid an hour or more," Mabel recorded in her diary, "and we examined the poems and discussed the best way of editing them." Already writing for posterity in mythopoeic journal entries—these were distinct from her jottings in a daily diary—Mabel enhanced her role as Dickinson's perspicacious sponsor. According to her, Higginson fretted that the poems, despite their fine ideas, were rough, mystical, and far too difficult to elucidate. "But I read him nearly a dozen from my favorites," she claimed, "and he was greatly astonished."

Of course he had been astonished for more than twenty years, and he had already promised his support, which he never withdrew even after Vinnie and Mabel, jealous of each other, publicly vied for center stage, disputing who loved the poems better, who grasped them more, who flagged and who never faltered or whose motives were clear and clean—and why Mabel had copied them in the first place. Through all of this, Higginson said little. Steadfast and unflappable, this booster of women writers and envoi of the literary establishment (an epithet that made him grimace), despite all—despite aesthetic orthodoxies and the peculiar stock he placed in them—despite this, he believed, as he always had, in Emily Dickinson.

IN THE FALL OF 1889, Thomas Wentworth Higginson was sixty-five years old. Though his hair grew thinner still, and whiter, and his health was dicey, he had run for United States Congress the year before and had been defeated, he said, without regret. The equanimity was feigned. His platform of civil service reform may have seemed irrelevant to many voters—that much was understandable—

but a substantial number in the black community, as it turned out, were against him, and his conciliatory attitude toward the South inflamed Frederick Douglass, who accused Higginson and all the mugwumps of disloyalty "not only to that political organization [the Republican party], but to the cause of liberty itself."

He did not ignore the criticism and, in his next collection of essays, *Travellers and Outlaws: Episodes in American History,* issued an implicit rejoinder to his detractors, for though the book included an antiquarian article on Salem sea captains, it also featured Higginson's essays on Denmark Vesey, Nat Turner, the Maroons of Jamaica, and the insurgent slave Gabriel, all reprinted as if to remind readers two decades after the Civil War that relations between black and white were as vexed, contradictory, and racked by prejudice as they'd been in 1831, when Turner's rebellion unleashed a white Reign of Terror (Higginson's term). The book didn't sell and received few reviews.

As ever, though, his writing about politics reflected but one side of him. In the same year, 1889, that *Travellers and Outlaws* appeared, Higginson fulfilled a private dream, publishing his very first book of verse, *The Afternoon Landscape: Poems and Translations,* which he dedicated to his old schoolmate the poet James Russell Lowell. Before the Civil War and after, Higginson never stopped writing poetry, and while he recognized the boundaries of his talent, he nonetheless sought a form in which he could express "internal difference— / ," as Dickinson had put it, "Where the Meanings, are." Such were the twin poles of his commitment to the life of the mind and the life of the activist, each tugging at the other. "No Man can be a Poet & a Book-Keeper at the same time," Nathaniel Hawthorne had cried while just a boy. This was not just the plaint of an adolescent fed on the Romantic poets; this had become the unwritten law of American culture.

Since Higginson's poetry was inhibited by its own kind of book-keeping, particularly in its predictable prosody, it is hard to imagine him delighted by the heap of Dickinson verse delivered by Mrs. Todd. But he was. "There are many new to me which take my breath away," he exulted, "& which also have *form* beyond most of those I have seen before." Form: its conventions were his nemesis, for in his own work he could not heed his Emerson and remember that poetry is not meters but a meter-making argument.

Reviewers, generally as orthodox as he, found his work congenial.

And much of it is; take the sonnet "The Snowing of the Pines," for example:

> Softer than silence, stiller than still air,
>> Float down from high pine-boughs the slender leaves.
>> The forest floor its annual boon receives
>> That comes like snowfall, tireless, tranquil, fair.
> Gently they glide, gently they clothe the bare
>> Old rocks with grace. Their fall a mantle weaves
>> Of paler yellow than autumnal sheaves
>> Or those strange blossoms the witch-hazels wear.
> Athwart long aisles the sunbeams pierce their way;
>> High up, the crows are gathering for the night;
>> The delicate needles fill the air; the jay
> Takes through their golden mist his radiant flight;
>> They fall and fall, till at November's close
>> The snow-flakes drop as lightly — snows on snows.

Despite archaisms ("athwart") and the awkward inversions ("The forest floor its annual boon receives"), the poem's final sestet vividly recreates the coming stillness (the descending alliteration of "fill," "flight," "fall, "fall," and "flakes"), and its last line recalls one of the very first poems Dickinson showed him, "Safe in their Alabaster Chambers—," with its striking "Soundless as Dots, / On a Disc of Snow."

But the comparison ends there. For if we put Higginson's poetry next to Dickinson's, we automatically traduce it and overlook the lyric poignancy of a poem like his "Sea-Gulls at Fresh Pond," which strikingly anticipates Yeats's far grander "Wild Swans at Coole":

> O lake of boyish dreams! I linger round
>> Thy calm, clear waters and thine altered shores
>> Till thought brings back the plash of childhood's oars, —
>> Long hid in memory's depths, a vanished sound.
> Alone unchanged, the sea-birds yet are found
>> Far floating on thy wave by threes and fours,
>> Or grouped in hundreds, while a white gull soars,
>> Safe, beyond gunshot of the hostile ground.
> I am no nearer to those joyous birds
>> Than when, long since, I watched them as a child;
>> Nor am I nearer to that flock more wild,

> *Most shy and vague of all elusive things,*
> *My unattainable thoughts, unreached by words.*
> *I see the flight, but never touch the wings.*

To see the flight, but never touch the wings: Higginson could be writing of Dickinson, for he had in fact said almost that same thing to her when he admitted, as he said, that it would be so easy to miss her. "I cannot reach you," he had cried, "but only rejoice in the rare sparkles of light." And Dickinson hovers over his poems "The Dying House" and "Astra Castra," the latter dedicated to free spirit ironically held in check by the sonnet form itself—that is, by the conventional versifier, Colonel Higginson. Yet the nascent poet in him recognizes, without envy, that this spirit dwells "beyond all worlds, all space, all thought, / . . . transformed."

> *Could we but reach and touch that wayward will*
> *On earth so hard to touch, would she be found*
> *Controlled or yet impetuous, free or bound,*
> *Tameless as ocean, or serene and still?*
> *If in her heart one eager impulse stirs,*
> *Could heaven itself calm that wild mood of hers?*

A man of limits, to be sure, Higginson was gifted enough to sense what lay beyond him.

The volume was handsome, its tan covers decorated with gilt lettering. Overall, though, the book spoke of resignation even in its title, *The Afternoon Landscape,* for the fresh morning of transcendentalism and abolition had yielded at last to that "certain Slant of light, / ," as Dickinson had written, of "Winter Afternoons—."

BUSY WITH HIS VARIOUS PROJECTS and stricken by a stomach ailment of unknown origin, Higginson initially could not devote much time to the Dickinson poems. But he had promised Vinnie that once the poems were divided into three categories (A, B, and C), he would carefully look them over. Likely that task had fallen to Vinnie as well as Mrs. Todd, but Mabel remembered only her own work: "A contained those of most original thought expressed in as nearly good form as ED ever used," she explained. "B those of striking ideas, but showing too much of her peculiarities of construction to be used unaltered for the public; & C those impossible for such use, however brilliant & suggestive."

It was hard work. "My brain fairly reels," she cried to Austin. But on November 18, not two weeks after meeting with Higginson, she dispatched the poems, all labeled, to the Colonel, who scrawled "Emily Dickinson's poems" in his diary in uncharacteristically bold letters. In less than a week he contacted Mrs. Todd. "My confidence in their *availability* is greatly increased. It is fortunate there are so many because it is obviously impossible to print all & this leaves the way open for careful selection."

Reading through half of Mabel's A list, Higginson grouped the poems thematically under headings such as "Life," "Nature," and "Time / Death / Eternity." "Perhaps you can suggest more subdivisions," he proposed. "The plates will cost rather less than $1 per page and there can often be two poems on a page—rarely more than one; say $230 for 250 pp including 300 poems." Three weeks later he again reported that "I am at work with many interruptions on the poems; have gone through 'B' and transferred about twenty to 'A' (we *must* have that burglar—the most nearly objective thing she wrote.) 'C' I have not touched."

With Higginson so fully committed, Vinnie grew impatient with Mabel, who was heading for Chicago. Why hadn't she contacted Higginson again? "You are acting for me & *not* yourself," Vinnie scolded. "I can't believe he has gotten any word from *you*. I wrote him you would call upon him & maybe he expects you whenever you are ready to do so. It is a great disappointment & surprise that this *delay* must be. I *now* regret the poems are in his hands." Mrs. Todd must see the Colonel immediately, Vinnie commanded, to urge him forward, and when Mabel did not comply, Vinnie picked up a pen and wrote him herself. He answered with good news: he had "selected and arranged" about two hundred of Dickinson's poems "to begin with. Then, if you wish, others may follow:

Life	44
Love	23
Nature	60
Time & Eternity	72

Vinnie liked the headings, and when Higginson recommended someone write an article about the poems to prepare the public—he seems to have forgotten that he had volunteered—Vinnie asked him to do it. Miffed, Mabel said nothing.

Aware of the exceptional character of Dickinson's genius, Higginson also suspected that readers and publishers might dismiss the poetry out of hand. Gingerly, he contacted acquaintances in the business. Houghton Mifflin thought he had lost his mind, and at Roberts Brothers, Thomas Niles stiffly reminded the Colonel that he always thought it "unwise to perpetuate Miss Dickinson's poems," which, as he pompously concluded, he regarded as notable chiefly for their defects.

Out of respect for Higginson, however, Niles took a slight risk. If Lavinia Dickinson would pay for the plates of a small edition— "which shall be exempt from copyright, all future issues to be subject to 15% copyright on the retail price of all sold"—he would print a limited run of the poems.

Vinnie accepted with pleasure.

NILES HANDED THE DICKINSON manuscript over to the writer Arlo Bates, his outside reader, and though Bates admitted that the author of this rude verse "came very near to that indefinable quality which we call genius," he recommended publishing only half the poems, and those rigorously edited. Some of the ones Bates omitted—and we cannot be entirely sure which they were— Higginson regarded as Dickinson's finest, but Mabel began editing the selections, crossing out Dickinson's dashes, correcting her punctuation and spelling, omitting capitals, and regularizing rhyme at will.

Forever after, Higginson would be remembered as the graceless editor who shamelessly cut Dickinson down to Victorian size. But which editor, Todd or Higginson, changed what? Who was the more obtuse? Even Ralph Franklin, in an excellent study of extant Dickinson manuscripts and their copies, cannot definitively say whether Higginson or Mabel Todd bore the chief responsibility for tailoring Dickinson to fit prevailing norms. Mrs. Todd, who cropped poems when first transcribing them, herself later conceded, "I changed words here and there in the two hundred to make them smoother— he changed a very few." But Higginson went along.

Enamored of Dickinson's poetry but convinced it contained faults, Mabel had decided to prepare the poet to meet the public in as respectable a garb as possible; her torrid affair with the poet's brother did not imply that she would throw all convention to the wind, far from it. Higginson, on the other hand, considered the poems a rarity but knew he had to spoon-feed a palatable version to that selfsame and ponderous public he had upbraided and cajoled and fought against for many years. He thus occasionally objected to Mabel's interference. "I find with dismay that the beautiful 'I shall know why, when time is over' has been left out," he protested in July of 1890, after he saw the completed manuscript and restored the poem from memory. And when Mrs. Todd wanted to correct Dickinson's grammar in the poem "I died for Beauty—," substituting "laid" for the ungrammatical "lain" ("When One who died for Truth was lain"), he protested and won.

During the summer, Higginson and Mrs. Todd corresponded, making the final alterations for which they have been blamed ever after—as if any of us, had we lived over one hundred years ago, might not have floundered in similar ways. For language like this had never been seen before; nothing like it, really, ever appeared again. Still, both editors erred on the side of what they thought was caution. In the poem "These are the days when Birds come back—," Mabel wished to change the fourth line, "These are the days when skies resume," to the more prosaic, unlyrical "These are the days when skies put on." Higginson again went along. And over Mabel's own protest, he himself demanded that the last line of "The Grass so little has to do" be changed from "I wish I were a Hay—" to "I wish I were the hay." "It cannot go in so," he presumably said, "everybody would say that *hay* is a collective noun requiring the definite article. Nobody can call it *a* hay!" As a result the last lines were printed "And then to dwell in sovereign barns / And dream the days away,—/ The grass so little has to do, / I wish I were the hay!" Strict grammar here makes no sense.

Then there was the matter of titles. Dickinson did not use them. On occasion when writing to a correspondent, she might identify her poems with something like them; for instance, she had labeled the poems "Further in Summer than the Birds" and "It sifts from Leaden Sieves—" "My Cricket and the Snow" when writing to

Thomas Niles. And when printed in newspapers, her poems were titled, but whether by her or an editor, we don't know. That's it. But Higginson wanted titles, and Mrs. Todd agreed, even though, as she said, she did "not believe, myself, in naming them; and although I admire Mr. Higginson very much, I do not think many of his titles good." In later years she again claimed Higginson had been more addicted to titles than she, or, as she defended herself, she "was exceedingly loath to assign titles to any of them which might not be unmistakably indicated in the poem itself."

Yet when editing *Poems,* Third Series, without Higginson, Mabel encumbered the poems with as many titles as she and Higginson together used previously. Both of them, then, were guilty of saddling Dickinson's complex, subtle, and tricky work with unwieldy headings that read like monosyllabic penny dreadfuls: "Almost!" "The Secret," "Dawn," "Real," "Setting Sail," "Too Late," "Why?" and "In Vain." Regardless, the editors left more than a quarter of the poems untitled, affording the room for interpretation that a Dickinson poem demands: "Presentiment—is that long shadow—on the Lawn—," "A *wounded* deer leaps highest," "The Brain within its groove," "I've seen a Dying Eye," and "I reason, earth is short."

And sometimes they omitted whole stanzas, as is the case with "Because I could not stop for Death—," where they left out the lines "Or rather—He passed Us— / The Dews drew quivering and Chill— / For only Gossamer, my Gown— / My Tippet—only Tulle—." Other times they removed punctuation and in so doing cut terror from the heart of a poem. Compare, for instance, these two versions of "Two swimmers wrestled on the spar." The following is Dickinson's original:

> *Two swimmers wrestled on the spar —*
> *Until the morning sun —*
> *When One — turned smiling to the land —*
> *Oh God! the Other One!*
>
> *The stray ships — passing —*
> *Spied a face —*
> *Opon the waters borne —*
> *With eyes in death — still begging raised —*
> *And hands — beseeching — thrown!*

This is the handiwork of Higginson and Todd:

> *Two swimmers wrestled on the spar*
> *Until the morning sun,*
> *When one turned smiling to the land.*
> *O God, the other one!*
>
> *The stray ships passing spied a face*
> *Upon the waters borne,*
> *With eyes in death still begging raised,*
> *And hands beseeching thrown.*

In each version the words are the same, but by omitting dashes and smoothing line breaks, the editors blunted the poem's edge with a quiet if disconsolate picture of prayer.

Despite the editorial heavy-footedness and in some instances outright butchery, Dickinson's poems remarkably retain their meaning, their power to reach beyond what can be seen, heard, or felt. Consider the poem ineptly titled "Death and Life." The dashes have been removed, the punctuation regularized, and yet the images of amputation, beheading, and assassination concoct a world—or a God—cruel in its murderous indifference to life:

> *Apparently with no surprise*
> *To any happy flower,*
> *The frost beheads it at its play*
> *In accidental power.*
> *The blond assassin passes on,*
> *The sun proceeds unmoved*
> *To measure off another day*
> *For an approving God.*

If the strategies of Todd and Higginson differed slightly, the result was the same, and both editors were eventually pilloried for bowdlerizing the poet's work. But they did not suppress or occlude it; rather, they presented it to an audience like them that, after many years of saccharine poetasting and propaganda, hungrily devoured the fresh, intricate, and dramatically novel verse.

. . .

LAVINIA DID NOT WISH Mabel to receive any credit for the Dickinson book. None. "I dare say you are aware our 'co-worker' is to be 'sub rosa,'" Vinnie wrote to Higginson, "for reasons you may understand." Not only was he confused, but he was barely able to read Vinnie's swerving cursive, which he naively asked Mabel to decipher. "I have her letter to Mr. Higginson," Mabel seethed in her diary, "& I am trying not to be furious."

Mabel assumed Vinnie wanted to avoid a fight with Sue, who, as it happened, by having submitted Emily's poems to magazines, made copyright a problem. Though Lavinia insisted the poems belonged entirely to her—that Emily had left them solely to her—Todd and Higginson now needed permission to use "There came a Day—at Summer's full" because Sue had sold it to *Scribner's Magazine* three months before the book was scheduled to appear. Higginson thought Sue could be enlisted as part of the forthcoming volume; surely her tender obituary of Emily in the *Springfield Republican* would beautifully introduce the book. Lavinia—and Mabel of course—recoiled. Higginson's essay would preface the volume, as promised; discussion over.

And there was, too, the issue of Mrs. Todd's name on the book's title page. "Your name should appear somewhere": Higginson ignored Vinnie's objection, suggesting that the title page contain both their names, if that did not seem too awkward for so small a book. When Mabel expressed delight, he placed hers prominently: "It is proper that yr name shld come first as you did the hardest part of the work."

By then he had finished a long essay on Dickinson, introducing her and her strange verse to the public. Published in the *Christian Union* in September 1890—slated for the *Century,* it would appear there too late—the essay is the longer, more relaxed form of what would become Higginson's preface to the poems. Far less defensive than the brief preface, the essay begins in Higginson's conversational style:

> Emerson said, many years since, in the "Dial," that the most interesting department of poetry would hereafter be found in what might be called "The Poetry of the Portfolio," the work, that is, of persons who wrote for the relief of their own minds, and without thought of publication. Such poetry, when accumulated for years, will have at least the merit of perfect freedom; accompanied, of course, by whatever

drawback follows from the habitual absence of criticism. Thought will have its full strength and uplifting, but without the proper control and chastening of literary expression; there will be wonderful strokes and felicities, and yet an incomplete and unsatisfactory whole. If we believe, with Ruskin, that "no beauty of execution can outweigh one grain or fragment of thought," then we may often gain by the seclusion of the portfolio, which rests content with a first stroke and does not over-refine and prune away afterwards.

With the metaphor of "Poetry of the Portfolio," Higginson intended to nip in the bud any criticism of Dickinson's unusual form, for the Higginson who had been Dickinson's ally—sometime muse, sometime guardian, sometime epistolary inamorato—had always insisted that form serves thought, and Dickinson's poems wonderfully "delineate, by a few touches, the very crises of physical or mental struggle."

He went on to praise enthusiastically such poems as "Glee—The great storm is over," "I never saw a moor," and "Soul, wilt thou toss again?":

> Soul, wilt thou toss again?
> By just such a hazard
> Hundreds have lost, indeed,
> But tens have won an all.
>
> Angels' breathless ballot
> Lingers to record thee;
> Imps in eager caucus
> Raffle for my soul!

"Was ever the concentrated contest of a lifetime, the very issue between good and evil, put into few words?" he marveled. And when reproducing "I died for beauty," he compared it for weirdness—a good quality—with the work of William Blake, and no one, he cagily added, would dare criticize Blake for defects in draftsmanship. "When a thought takes one's breath away, who cares to count the syllables?" With a courage that shrank from nothing, Dickinson looked straight into the heart of darkness, he concluded, again recalling the unforgettable stanzas of "Safe in their Alabaster Chambers—" sent him so many years ago, those daringly condensed lines that, he said, struck a note much too fine to be lost or excised:

> *Grand go the years in the crescent above them;*
> *Worlds scoop their arcs, and firmaments row,*
> *Diadems drop and Doges surrender,*
> *Soundless as dots on a disk of snow.*

THE BOOK WAS DONE. Bound in white, framed in gold and stamped in the same color, it was slim, handsome, understated. On the front was a picture of silver Indian pipes. Its title was simply *Poems.*

"I am *astounded,*" Higginson cried, holding the book in his hands. "How could we ever have doubted about these?"

How could he have doubted anything? He suddenly realized, in dismay, that Dickinson's letters to him had contained poems as good as the ones just printed: "No Brigadier throughout the Year," for instance, and "A Route of Evanescence" and "Dare you see a Soul at the 'White Heat'?" and "The nearest Dream recedes—unrealized—" and "When I hoped I feared—" and "Before I got my eye put out—" and "It sifts from Leaden Sieves" and "A Bird, came down the Walk"—so many of the poems she had sent to him over the years.

Your riches taught me poverty.

"This shows we *must* have another volume by and by," he cried, "& this must include prose from her letters, often quite as marvellous as her poetry."

The floodgates were open. Higginson turned in relief to the cunning and unsinkable Mrs. Todd, "the only person who can feel as I do about this extraordinary thing we have done in recording this rare genius."

"I feel," he burst out, "as if we had climbed to a cloud, pulled it away, and revealed a new star behind it."

EIGHTEEN

Me—Come! My Dazzled Face

The first edition of *Poems* by Emily Dickinson sold out, the second edition was snapped up by Christmas, and Niles released a third and then a fourth in January. In all, the book would go through eleven printings in 1891 and sell almost eleven thousand copies. Higginson was astounded.

The poems humbled critics, even those who carped about faulty rhymes or poor poetic technique (vide Arlo Bates), and it delighted readers. Fed for years on Tennyson, Patmore, and Longfellow or, more recently, on the folksy verse of James Whitcomb Riley and the jingles of Rudyard Kipling, to say nothing of the verse of Thomas Bailey Aldrich, they were evidently tired of the didacticism and overrefinement of poetry without heat. Edmund Clarence Stedman, no radical, suggested as much in the introduction to his popular *Poets of America,* published the year before Dickinson died. "A poet, most of all, should not believe in limitations," he wrote, "and so, if poetry has lost its hold, it is in some degree because no brilliant leader compels attention to it, devoting himself to the hazard of arduous and bravely ventured song." Fifteen years later, when he published his *American Anthology,* Stedman included twenty-one selections by Emily Dickinson.

Looking backward, we can say that 1890 ushered in a new period of Newness, to rephrase Higginson. Telephone lines would soon link New York and Chicago; Thomas Edison was about to patent his motion picture camera, the Kinetoscope; and William K. Vanderbilt had already erected a birthday present for his wife at Newport in the form of a marble palace that cost eleven million dollars. In New York Harbor a former munitions dump on Ellis Island would serve as a processing center for as many as eight thousand immigrants a day; in Chicago Jane Addams opened Hull House. The Populist party was about to be formed, and armed Pinkerton guards would soon fire on the striking Homestead steelworkers. More than two hundred Lakota Sioux were massacred at Wounded Knee, and in the 1896 case of *Plessy v. Ferguson,* the Supreme Court would uphold the "separate but equal" doctrine that legitimized Jim Crow. Only Justice Harlan dissented, declaring the Constitution color-blind.

In literature, Jacob Riis exposed the squalid conditions of urban life in *How the Other Half Lives.* William Dean Howells published his novel *A Hazard of New Fortunes,* whose subjects were capitalism, social conscience, and socialism, and George Washington Cable brought out a collection of essays, *The Negro Question,* rejecting the myth of African American inferiority. William James's long-awaited *Principles of Psychology,* soon a standard college text, refreshed the vernacular with phrases like "stream of consciousness" and "bitch-goddess success." But the bitch-goddess continued to possess the soul of a conspicuously consuming America. This and American indifference to art had long been Henry James's theme and was, in part, dominant in the work of a young Edith Wharton, who in 1891 published her first story, "Mrs. Manstey's View," about an elderly woman whose garden view will be blocked by a new high-rise next door. (In 1905, Higginson ranked her novel *The House of Mirth* "at the head of all American fiction, save Hawthorne alone.")

To Higginson—as to James and, later, to Wharton—the scramble for cash, splash, and speed in postwar America had elbowed out any concern for art or style. "Nobody reads Thoreau; only an insignificant fraction read Emerson, or even Hawthorne," he had complained in his diary. But when incorporating this passage into his novel *Malbone,* he then remonstrated with himself by taking up the position of the reformer, not the aesthete: "If you begin with high art, you begin at the wrong end," he admonished. "The first essential for any nation is to put the mass of the people above the reach of want."

That was all well and good, but Higginson also knew the reading public to be recalcitrant and stodgy, far stodgier than he was, even in his most conservative, Whitman-assailing moments. And since he still believed in a democratic art—an art of open arms—Higginson welcomed Dickinson to the public stage; she could touch anyone, as he explained in *The Nation* in 1890, because her thrilling poems, with their "irresistible needle-touch," pierce directly into the heart of things. Each fragment encompasses an emotional whole, self-contained and complete, and its exterior austerity is no harsher than the New England landscape she represents and celebrates. To Hig-

Austin Dickinson, 61 years old, 1890.

ginson, Dickinson pushed back against America's crass materialism, a point William Dean Howells also made, with Higginson's approval, when he reviewed her book of poems in *Harper's:* if "nothing else had come out of our life but this strange poetry we should feel that in the work of Emily Dickinson, America, or New England rather, had made a distinctive addition to the literature of the world, and could not be left out of any record of it."

Yet the book's wild success had not altered Mabel's personal situation, for Austin had not broken with Sue. "I have hoped and hoped and expected, and I have nothing more to say," she declared, not meaning what she said. Apprised of some internecine warfare—it's not clear if he knew the cause—Higginson grumbled that it was hard to steer among Dickinsons. Sue had not replied to his letter asking how she liked the volume and, worried that he had unwittingly offended her, he confided his concern to Mabel, who swore Sue had no reason to be angry. But Higginson suspected otherwise. As for Lavinia, even though Sue and Mattie refused to talk to her, she cared only about the success of her sister's poems—and she wanted another volume of them published as soon as possible.

Mabel was by now Dickinson obsessed. She kept a scrapbook of reviews, she composed an article on Dickinson's poetry (rejected by several magazines), she peddled her father's essay on Dickinson (also rejected), she wrote an encyclopedia entry on Dickinson, and in Springfield she lectured on the poet's life and work, which she would continue to do at various literary events, charging ten dollars per talk, plus expenses. She virtually performed Emily, effortlessly assuming center stage as the poet's shepherd and spokesperson. And to her great satisfaction, she was much more successful than Sue at selling Emily's poems to magazines and newspapers; *The Independent* bought three in the first month of 1891.

Higginson, too, participated in the Dickinson boomlet, which he helped to create by inviting Boston literati—Howells, Samuel Longfellow, the historian William Roscoe Thayer, and a young Harvard philosophy instructor, George Santayana, who could not attend—to his comfortable parlor. Just a few feet away from the regimental sword hanging in a hallway crowded with family portraits, Higginson recited a selection of his Dickinson letters. "I think there is in literary history no more interesting self-revelation," he afterward told the drama critic Brander Matthews. Higginson then called Dickinson a genius—a word he used sparingly—when lecturing to New York's Nineteenth Century Club, and to explain her unusual style, he fell back on his beloved Thoreau, who had said in "The Last Days of John Brown" that "the *art* of composition is as simple as the discharge of a bullet from a rifle." Dickinson seldom missed the mark.

The audience having been adequately prepared, Higginson believed Dickinson could now appear as herself—without editorial mangling—but Mabel continued to rework the *Poems* for the new editions, tweaking rhymes and adjusting grammar. Higginson protested. Such changes must stop. "Let us alter as little as possible, now that the public's ear is opened," he would tell her as they began selecting poems for the second volume. He meant it. Mabel did not listen.

In their cordial way, the editors had grown apart. Giddy with success and convinced of her own wisdom, Todd still wished to regularize Dickinson—"put so in order to have the rhyme perfect," as she told Higginson, so when, for example, she mailed "Whose are the little beds—I asked" to *St. Nicholas* magazine, she took the following lines—

> *Her busy foot she plied —*
> *Humming the quaintest lullaby*
> *That ever rocked a child.*

and replaced them with the nursery-rhymish

> *She rocked and gently smiled*
> *Humming the quaintest lullaby*
> *That ever soothed a child.*

Vehemently objecting, Higginson restored the lines when working on the second volume of poems. Similarly, when Todd wanted to replace the last lines of "Dare you see a Soul at the 'White Heat'?," Higginson put his foot down. Let us alter as little as possible.

And as he continued to read Dickinson, we can watch Higginson overcome his squeamishness. "One poem only I dread a little to print—that wonderful 'Wild Nights,'—lest the malignant read into it more than that virgin recluse ever dreamed of putting there," he wrote to Mrs. Todd. "Has Miss Lavinia any shrinking about it? You will understand & pardon my solicitude. Yet what a loss to omit it! Indeed it is not to be omitted." And it was not.

Regardless, the editors snipped this, sorted that, with Mabel perpetually inclined to alter Dickinson's subjunctives. And they also "corrected" grammar, changing, for instance, "Further in Summer than the Birds—" to "Farther in summer," spoiling the internal rhyme (further / birds) and tampering with the meaning. In "They dropped like Flakes—," they converted the first five-line stanza into a quatrain and changed the poem's last two lines to regularize the rhyme. Yet even when tucked under their reductive titles, the poems were not entirely defanged. Take, for instance, the quietly ferocious (and untitled) "It was not Death, for I stood up." In spite of the editors' substitution of commas for dashes and their lowering

the cases of the nouns, the funereal images—simultaneously concrete and abstract—parse that inchoate feeling that is despair:

> *It was not death, for I stood up,*
> *And all the dead lie down;*
> *It was not night, for all the bells*
> *Put out their tongues, for noon.*
> *It was not frost, for on my flesh*
> *I felt siroccos crawl, —*
> *Nor fire, for just my marble feet*
> *Could keep a chancel cool.*
> *And yet it tasted like them all;*
> *The figures I have seen*
> *Set orderly, for burial,*
> *Reminded me of mine,*
> *As if my life were shaven*
> *And fitted to a frame,*
> *And could not breathe without a key;*
> *And 't was like midnight, some,*
> *When everything that ticked has stopped,*
> *And space stares, all around,*
> *Or grisly frosts, first autumn morns,*
> *Repeal the beating ground.*
> *But most like chaos, — stopless, cool, —*
> *Without a chance or spar,*
> *Or even a report of land*
> *To justify despair.*

Bells put out their tongues, siroccos crawl on the flesh, feet are by
contrast cold and stiff, and yet "It was not night," or "frost" or "fire,"
and "yet it tasted like them all." And what is "it"? Not death, but
something analogous, something that occurs when "everything that
ticked has stopped," and "grisly frosts . . . / Repeal the beating
ground": motion is stilled, the clocks are irrelevant when living
earth accedes to immobile winter, and we exist "Without a chance
or spar" to help us. There's no overrefinement or platitude here.

PERHAPS HIGGINSON ACQUIESCED to Todd's unwar-
ranted liberties or insisted on his awful titles because he never did

quite suppress his ambivalence about some of Dickinson's poems. At once declaring their genius and then, sometimes, deploring their immature form, he handled them as he treated current affairs, with an odd amalgam of conservatism and radicalism. The man who recommended that abolitionists secede from the Union, the man who bore arms against the South in the name of liberty, the man who loved Thoreau and Margaret Fuller and African spirituals and then peddled moderation, conciliation, and the verse of Helen Jackson knew that no one had ever seen poetry like this. And yet despite dedication, appreciation, and loyalty, he suggested she would have wanted to improve her work had she lived to publish it. Schoolmarmish, he reminded Mrs. Todd that "it might do well for you to suggest in your preface [to the second volume] that we never can tell to what rigorous revision these poems might have been subjected, had the author printed them herself. They are to be regarded in many cases as the mere unfinished sketches or first studies of an artist, preserved for their intrinsic value, not presented as being in final form."

In her preface to *Poems,* Second Series, Todd obligingly apologized for the ragged quality of the poems, though she did say, likely also at Higginson's prompting, that "all interference not absolutely inevitable has been avoided. The very roughness of her own rendering is part of herself, and not lightly to be touched; for it seems in many cases that she intentionally avoided the smoother and more usual rhymes." Determined to rebut whatever jibes the first volume had suffered, Todd also squashed rumors about Dickinson as a lovelorn invalid wrapped in seclusion and nursing a broken heart. Austin, for one, would have none of it. "She had tried society and the world, and found them lacking," Mabel wrote with clenched teeth. "She was not an invalid, and she lived in seclusion from no love-disappointment. Her life was the normal blossoming of a nature introspective to a high degree, whose best thought could not exist in pretence."

At Higginson's urging, this time Mabel signed the preface and she placed his name ahead of hers on the flyleaf. In the meantime, he had been busy with his own introductory essay, the delightful "Emily Dickinson's Letters," which publicized the second book of poems by gently narrating the course of his relationship with its author, beginning with the day he encountered her query "Are you too deeply occupied to say if my Verse is alive?"

Today Higginson's essay is often denigrated both by Higginson detractors and Dickinson enthusiasts (usually they are of the same party). Yet it's a trove of firsthand facts and insights about the poet who defied the protocols to which he, as her editor and friend, admitted he often fell prey. "It would seem that at first I tried a little,—a very little—to lead her in the direction of rules and traditions," he observed, not quite remembering, "but I fear it was only perfunctory, and that she interested me more in her—so to speak—unregenerate condition."

Though acquiescing to the charade of preceptor and student, he knew he could teach her little, and humble before her, or so he recollected, "I soon abandoned all attempt to guide in the slightest degree this extraordinary nature, and simply accepted her confidences, giving as much as I could of what might interest her in return."

Writing for the public, he does not tell us what Dickinson gave him; perhaps he never knew himself. But he does recall wanting to see more, do more, know more, and be more to her. "Perhaps in time I could have got beyond that somewhat overstrained relation which not my will, but her needs, had forced upon us," he reminisced as honestly as he could. "Certainly I should have been most glad to bring it down to the level of simple truth and every-day comradeship; but it was not altogether easy."

Dictating the terms of their relationship, Dickinson demanded more than ordinary companionship, if indeed she knew what shape that might take. And she admired the outdoors that Higginson represented and his perpetual defiance of social pieties even while he seemed to uphold them. Hers was an inward life; his outward. But he moved her. She saw beyond the mottled air of Boston, its benignities and reverent causes, and would not come to his Radical Club, knowing that radicalism is not clubbable. Neither is art. But she sensed the art in Higginson.

If his strength lay in action, hers lay in words, which she would never subordinate to rule. Nor did he, though over time he considered compromise necessary for success in a fallen world. And yet he had staked so much of his life on finding the right word to inspire and inflame and liberate, quite literally, those who needed it. So what had happened to him? This blackest of all Black Republicans had become disillusioned. The livid pulpit orator of Worcester witnessed not just the breakdown of racial barriers, long overdue, but the breakdown of linguistic promise. Emancipation when? And for whom? The questions still hung in the air, unanswered and, it seemed, unheard in the scramble for celebrity riches.

Yet if no longer spouting revolution, Higginson stayed a reformer, and in later years the elegance of his prose well served his charming reminiscences not because it emptied the past of meaning but because it firmly and without apology affirmed his earlier radicalism. He had been a champion of the tough-minded, the far-flung, the sovereign, and the crack'd, and of Emily Dickinson, whose words were, all in all, a form of action too.

SWATHED IN WHITE, like its author, *Poems,* Second Series was released on November 9, 1891. It sold posthaste.

Again the emblem on the cover was Dickinson's Indian pipes. Again the editors placed her poems, 166 of them in this volume, into broad categories: "Life," "Love," "Nature," and "Time and Eternity." But this time the editors included poems about poetry ("Essential oils are wrung") and passion ("Wild nights! Wild nights!" and "Going to him! Happy letter!") and doubt ("Their height in heaven comforts not"). Reviewers fidgeted. The more the poetry moved them, it seemed, the more they balked. The New York *World* haughtily asked if the "admirers" of Dickinson's "experimental vagaries" do her any service by printing more of her "crudities," and *The Critic* groused about "too much of the same thing," namely, "jerky and disjointed writing, and occasional faults of grammar." *The Literary World* dubbed the poems "neuralgic darts of feeling." And when Thomas Bailey Aldrich read Howells's review of Dickinson, he cringed. "I honestly think his mind unbalanced," he said. Aldrich, Howells's successor at *The Atlantic Monthly* who ushered it into a period of decline, then trounced Dickinson's poems as well as Higginson himself. "I fail to detect in her work any of that profound thought which her editor professes to discover in it," he concluded his review. "The phenomenal insight, I am inclined to believe, exists only in his partiality; for whenever a woman poet is in question Mr. Higginson always puts on his rose-colored spectacles."

The condescension of Aldrich was nothing compared with the consternation of the British press, which denounced Dickinson's crude American infraction of poetic form. That amused Alice James, the sister of William and Henry. "It is reassuring to hear the English

Lavinia Dickinson, 1880s.

pronouncement that Emily Dickinson is fifth-rate, they have such a capacity for missing quality; the robust evades them equally with the subtle," she snickered. But the book sold, and Mabel, delirious with yet another victory over Sue, busied herself with more Dickinson projects: a yearbook of Dickinson's epigrams and poetic fragments and a set of new lectures throughout New England that would attract as many as two hundred expectant listeners in auditoriums, drawing rooms, churches, and town halls. She had a mission.

And it has proved invaluable. Because she had been systematically collecting and copying Dickinson's letters since 1892, we owe the discovery and preservation of many of them largely to her Herculean effort. But the Dickinson family was hard as ever to navigate, and Higginson, at first part of the letter project, sniffed trouble when Vinnie wrote to ask how it was going. He bowed out. "I had expected to leave the letters entirely to you & at any rate the *work* of them & the profit," he told Mrs. Todd. "I do not now wish to do any of the editing or to read the proofs, but if you should think that my name would help the book or that Miss L. should be indulged, I would do whatever you think about it."

Mabel later explained that Lavinia, upset, had gone to Higginson behind her back because she, Mabel, was also working on a book about eclipses for Roberts Brothers—Mabel knew how to take advantage of an opportunity—and Lavinia thought this other project interfered with Mabel's commitment to Emily. That may have been true. But Lavinia also begrudged Mabel's limelight-grabbing—and lucrative—appropriation of her sister. Sternly she explained to Higginson in an eight-page letter (now lost) that Mrs. Todd should not share in royalties and, moreover, that nothing would ever induce her to "give the copyright of Emily's mind to anyone."

Higginson wisely stepped aside, and half-sorry to hear Mabel had almost finished her collection of Dickinson's letters, he ruefully noted in the summer of 1893 that it "will be the last, I suppose, & will not only yield the final news of E. D. but take from me a living companionship I shall miss."

His affection for Dickinson had splashed onto Mrs. Todd. Over the years he and she remained in touch, the Colonel careful always not to offend Sue when he occasionally went to Amherst, where he stayed at a hotel so as not to show preference. And after Austin's death, Higginson tried to console Mabel. "I wish as I always do, that Massachusetts were not so unreasonably long a state, that you might not live so far from me," he said. It sounds as if he were writing to Emily, with whom Mabel was so closely linked. But it was the ethereal, wonderful poet whom he loved, that "mystic and bizarre Emily," he called her, "born at once between two pages, as Thoreau says summer passes to autumn in an instant."

THE PANIC OF 1893 delayed publication of the letters, and the book would not appear anyway until Vinnie and Mabel, then squabbling, settled their argument over royalties. Vinnie, who kept the copyright, wanted to dole out royalties to Mrs. Todd rather than have the publisher divide the proceeds. "I think she can trust my honor," huffed Vinnie. Austin had by then intervened on Mabel's side, arguing for a legal contract, and Vinnie finally consented to splitting earnings, although, as it turned out, there were none.

Wounded, Mabel avenged herself in the preface by not acknowledging Vinnie's role in collecting the letters and, for that matter, by not even mentioning Vinnie's name.

MABEL WAS ALSO EDITING a third series of Dickinson poems, this time without Colonel Higginson, and on her own at last she did not have to follow Higginson's injunction to alter as little as possible. Consequently, of the three volumes, *Poems,* Third Series (1896), is the most expurgated. Higginson flinched, albeit with diplomacy. "It is noticeable, also, that in a few of the poems," he noted, "there is an unexampled regularity of form, beyond anything to be found in the earlier volumes."

Reviewers were less tactful. "Her vogue has passed," declared one critic. "Now such reputation as she has among minor lyricists is imperiled by the indiscretion of her executors." The poems did not sell.

But a seventy-two-year-old Higginson rode to the rescue. For the next ten years most of his poetry columns in *The Nation* included a mention of Emily Dickinson, whether he was praising the verse of Celia Thaxter or Stephen Crane (whom he called an amplified Dickinson) or Edwin Arlington Robinson's *Captain Craig Poems,* suggesting that Robinson's poetry was "often like that of Emily Dickinson when she piques your curiosity through half a dozen readings and suddenly makes all clear." He compared Hamlin Garland's verse unfavorably to Dickinson's, he heard the poetry of Dickinson in the English lyricist Winifred Lucas, and it was he who prodded Stedman to represent Dickinson amply in his *American Anthology.* When Brander Matthews composed a list of significant American authors, Higginson chided him for excluding someone as unique and talented as she.

AUSTIN DICKINSON HAD DIED in the summer of 1895 from what his doctor diagnosed as a tired heart. Plagued by Mabel's persistent unhappiness, Vinnie's moods, and the cold misery of his own disconsolate family, Austin had been complaining of shortness of breath, exhaustion, and poor appetite for almost a year. The families warred on, and he wore out.

Six months later, on February 7, 1896, Mabel and a lawyer, Timothy Spaulding of Northampton, marched over to the Homestead to put a deed of sale under Vinnie's nose that would transfer to the Todds an additional strip of Dickinson land, fifty-three feet wide, running east of the property that Austin had already given them. Mabel claimed that Austin had promised her this land—worth two thousand dollars—as remuneration for her work on Emily's poems. But Austin's promises were mostly hollow. He had failed to include Mabel in his will—it was "best for now," he lamely consoled her—and instead, to circumvent Sue, bequeathed to Vinnie his share of his father's estate with the verbal proviso that Vinnie pass it on to Mabel. He must have known Vinnie would never convey Dickinson property to anyone, least of all Mabel.

Mabel said she assumed that Vinnie would immediately comply with Austin's wish, a mighty naive assumption for a woman not particularly naive.

Yet Vinnie did sign the deed that cold February night. At Mabel's request it was not filed right away; Mabel wanted to conceal the arrangement from Sue and so planned to be out of the country, in Japan, accompanying her husband on another astronomical junket, when the deed became public knowledge.

The Todds came home to Amherst in the fall of 1896, just after *Poems,* Third Series, appeared, to find Vinnie suing them for fraud. Alleging that Mrs. Todd had duped her into signing the deed, Vinnie said she thought she was merely putting her name to a friendly agreement forbidding construction on the contested site. Aghast, Mabel immediately countersued for slander. That suit was scheduled to be heard first, and when Mabel did not turn up in court (no one knows why)—her attorney may have suspected what her biographer calls "moral quicksand"—the judge, denying a continuance, proceeded with Vinnie's suit.

That trial commenced in March 1898.

It was a tawdry business, since what was really on trial was Mabel Todd's affair with the poet's brother. Naturally this was not directly stated, and fortunately for Mabel the deposition of Vinnie's servant, Maggie Maher, never became public; nor was Maggie called to the stand, where she would have testified that she knew of Mabel and Austin's adultery. But in a significant tactical error, Mabel put the poems at the center of her defense. The land in question, she argued, was her reward for poems that took her the better part of ten years to copy, edit, and arrange for publication. Evidently Mrs. Todd had forgotten that she was considered an opportunistic interloper: how dare she profit financially, legally, or personally from Emily Dickinson's poems?

Amherst buzzed with the scandal, but Sue Dickinson stayed aloof, ensconced at the Evergreens, her absence from the courtroom noticeable and in its silent way eloquent. Yet day after day, Ned and Mattie listened to their aunt and their father's lover trade ugly accusations, each adversary playing her part to the hilt. Head held high, Mabel strode into the courtroom in a modish black and white hat. And in blue flannel dress, long crepe veil, and yellow shoes, Vinnie costumed herself as the self-reliant Yankee spinster, eccentric and familiar, shrewd and helpless, Hepzibah Pyncheon with vinegar.

There was no real contest. Though commentators then and later assumed Vinnie had perjured herself by lying about the deed, on April 15, 1898, Judge John Hopkins decided the case in favor of Lavinia and the New England propriety, primogeniture, and real estate she represented. The deed was rendered void, the Todds ordered to pay Vinnie's legal fees, and when Mabel appealed the decision, Justice Oliver Wendell Holmes, then presiding over the Massachusetts higher court, upheld the verdict.

"I shall die standing up," Mabel fumed. "There will be no weak admission that persecution has keeled me. But I am so tired in my soul!"

Mabel Loomis Todd locked the trunk in which she kept her collection of Dickinson poems and letters, and for the next fifty years their ownership remained a source of legal contention, Dickinson heirs calling Mrs. Todd a whore and a thief. As an adult her daughter, Millicent Todd Bingham, worked hard to rehabilitate Mabel's reputation while ruing the "blight of self-interest and self-glorification [that] had fallen upon her." Maybe it had. But what we do know for sure is that the feud erased the contribution of Thomas Higginson to Emily Dickinson's spectacular debut.

> *Me — Come! My dazzled face*
> *In such a shining place!*
> *Me — hear! My foreign Ear*
> *The sounds of Welcome — there!*

NINETEEN

Because I Could Not Stop

I n the pinkish twilight of a September evening in 1904, after nearly twenty-one years abroad, Henry James was back in America, strolling along the brick streets of Cambridge. The university was no longer a small, leafy affair, he noticed. Knots of motley immigrants jostled long-skirted Radcliffe women on the crowded sidewalks, and further on, walking by Craigie House, he mused how the companionable Longfellow's home was now a watering hole for sightseers. Democracy levels it all: distinction, nuance, individuality.

This was just the sort of hauteur that exasperated the local Cambridge belletrist, Thomas Wentworth Higginson, who considered James a formidable talent deracinated by his refusals — chief among them, his repudiation of America. "American literature is not," Higginson emphatically declared, "and never can be, merely an outlying portion of the literature of England." Though he himself admired Jane Austen, whom he reread every year along with his beloved Thoreau, Higginson also believed American literature sprang — should spring — from that rich, self-renewing idiom in which "the mixture of nationalities is constantly coining and exchanging new felicities of dialect": from the African spirituals he had so scrupulously copied; the twang of Western writers such as Bret Harte and Mark Twain, with whom he'd become friends; the argot of the Italian newcomer and of those who sailed in steerage from beyond the Pale. This was true cosmopolitanism, not the sinuous, self-regarding sentences of Henry James.

And unlike James, Higginson still hoped to heal the rift between art and public life, or what so long ago he had called, more generally, the dreamer and the worker. This had been the aim, as he saw it, of Thoreau, a writer snubbed by James, to whom Higginson constantly returned, again quoting Thoreau's definition of style — "the art of composition is as simple as the discharge of a bullet from a rifle." Thoreau, John Brown, Lincoln, Grant: these men — not James or

Higginson himself, as he knew too well—closed the gap between private and public with the plain, clear speech of eloquent meaning.

Doubtless some of Higginson's irritation with James, not unlike the grudge he bore Whitman, had its origins in the war, which James curiously had managed to avoid. Or had he? Higginson cannily wondered. "Mr. James has no doubt placed himself as far as possible beyond the reach of the Civil War by keeping the Atlantic Ocean between him and the scene where it occurred," Higginson dryly commented. "But when I recall that I myself saw his youngest brother, still almost a boy, lying near to death, as it then seemed, in a hospital at Beaufort, S.C., after the charge on Fort Wagner, I can easily imagine that the Civil War may really have done something for Mr. James's development, after all."

Yet Higginson agreed with James that art was to be evaluated in aesthetic, not moral terms. "Let the picture only be well drawn; and the moral will take care of itself; never fear," Higginson insisted. His preferred modern poets were Elizabeth Barrett Browning and Heinrich Heine, and he said that "in case I were going to prison and could have but one book, I should think it a calamity to have Tennyson offered me instead of Browning." These days he gravitated toward Lanier and Poe and Swinburne, whom he praised for their metrical experimentation, as well as the young William Butler Yeats, whom he had met in England.

Not as square a critic as a subsequent generation of modernists would characterize him—neither as moralistic nor as mediocre—in 1890 Higginson co-edited a collection of *American Sonnets,* noting that "in attempting to enforce . . . [fixed] laws, it is easy to become as pedantic and wearisome as the later Greek grammarians." Regardless, his taste was often inhibited by a finicky reticence, as it was in the case of Whitman, who still rankled him, although a mellower Higginson in old age acknowledged the poet's gifts and said he'd like Whitman's "Joy, Shipmate, Joy!" carved on his tombstone. But in 1870, just a few months before he went to Amherst for the first time, he declared that the "American poet of passion is yet to come." Had he failed to see the genius under his nose? For a while, perhaps. But he eventually understood enough to let others—us—have her.

And though he initially hesitated about publishing Dickinson's verse, once *Poems* appeared and he looked at it, as if for the first time, he never changed his mind about her brilliance. In 1895 he said she possessed an ability to touch depths other poets may only dream of.

The next year, when Mabel Todd brought out the third and last volume of Dickinson poems, he recurred again to Thoreau's aggressive metaphor: "She is to be tested," Higginson declared, "not by her attitude, by her shot. Does she hit the mark? As a rule she does." In 1903, when Higginson turned eighty and it seemed Dickinson's star had set, he was unfazed. "We take for granted the somewhat exaggerated estimates of Margaret Fuller, Helen Hunt Jackson, and Emily Dickinson," griped one critic riled by Higginson's feminism. Higginson shrugged. Poems such as "Vanished" (his title) would never be forgotten, he claimed, and while this isn't one of her best poems, it does reveal his awe in her presence—and his nagging sense of what he had lost and still missed:

> *She died,* —this *was the way she died;*
> *And when her breath was done,*
> *Took up her simple wardrobe*
> *And started for the sun.*
>
> *Her little figure at the gate*
> *The angels must have spied,*
> *Since I could never find her*
> *Upon the mortal side.*

Unable to find her on the mortal side, Higginson invented her: "a strange, solitary, morbidly sensitive, and pitifully childlike poetic genius who could afford, in all simplicity, to fall back upon her own companionship, and the companionship of animals, without caring to grow in wisdom," he wrote with cloying sentimentality. A concoction of his and Mabel Todd's, this image of Dickinson as reclusive-savant served both of them well: Mabel desperately wanted to enlarge her role in Dickinson affairs as the cicerone of a retiring genius, and Wentworth, who likely distrusted his own fondness toward Emily, wanted to keep her at bay. For though he may have been smitten with the crack'd and solitary singer who drained his nerve power, he would never have admitted to or acted on his feelings.

In the end, though, it was Emily who had closed the door, a door never opened to Mabel but unbolted, in part, for him. Their relationship was long-standing, deep, affectionate, real, and her poetry, whether he fully grasped all of it or not—he did grasp a great deal—said what he wished to say but more keenly, directly, daringly, and with more brio. He knew it. Eccentric and unmistakable and naming those uncharted places, her poetry "stands at the opposite remove from the verse of Longfellow," Higginson noted in 1903—and Longfellow's popularity, he hastened to add, was "the last fate" Dickinson would have "wished for." There was nothing really strange about her vaunted seclusion; she merely shunned what she called "an admiring Bog."

In fact, he envied the strength it took to withstand the world, since he, an obliging son of Puritans, could never brook isolation for long; his conscience hurled him, over and over, into the field of action. But the writers he most admired—Hawthorne, Thoreau, even the abolitionist Whittier—were recluses of a sort, as Higginson observed in an essay on the thorny subject of solitude. Even Shakespeare, a writer on the public stage, so skillfully concealed his private life that many doubted he wrote his own plays. "It would be easy to make up a long list of authors of eminence who have deprecated instead of encouraging all personal information," Higginson declared, "and who would have been eminently unfitted to live in an age or land of interviewers."

Desiring the solitude he could not sustain, Higginson thrived in that age of interviewers; Dickinson, not at all. They respected each other the more for it.

"Perhaps the more we are destined to have in common," Higginson concluded, "the more we shall take refuge in what we can preserve of 'retiracy.' " The modern age erased individuals: Higginson agreed with Henry James more than he let on.

"FEW OF US NOW REMAIN who were baptized into the light & hope of the 'Transcendental' movement," Higginson had remarked just days after his seventieth birthday. "To that & to the Anti Slavery movement I always feel that I owe most of what makes life worth living."

Bearing the scar on his chin that he had earned while storming the Boston courthouse, Higginson still framed the war as a contest between freedom and enslavement, with freedom victorious; the simplification, though considered radical in 1893, papered over the inequities and indignities that black Americans, legally free, now endured. In retrospect, then, Higginson sometimes seems a man of denial: the war was over, slavery abolished. Garrison had closed *The Liberator* in 1865, and all was presumably well.

Higginson himself is partly to blame for this perception. The ongoing series of reminiscences he published in his later years had a sedative effect on his readers, distancing them from the derring-do of his more militant and feminist past. In 1896, for instance, his gastric ailment bedeviling him, he sat up in bed, propped with pillows, to write a memoir called "The Recollections of a Radical"—that is, before he jettisoned the title as too combative and unliterary. Borrowing instead from Wordsworth's *Excursion* ("A man he seems of cheerful yesterdays / And confident tomorrows") he renamed his book *Cheerful Yesterdays.*

Though the title sounds a bit smug, *Cheerful Yesterdays* is nonetheless the recollection of a public-spirited, self-proclaimed reformer who refuses to recant the radicalism that, by 1898, seemed quaint—or, worse yet, was dismissed as the very fanaticism that caused the war and after it divided the nation. Higginson took umbrage. A commitment to basic human rights is not fanaticism, and as for Reconstruction, if it ended poorly, as he wrote in *The Nation* in 1899, it was because southerners kept blacks in a condition "just as near slavery as possible; to limit their right of contract, their right of locomotion, and their range of labor." Former slaveholders had driven out northerners come to invest energy, time, and cash; "the typical carpet-bagger," he said, "was simply the man who was left behind to do mischief."

But overall *Cheerful Yesterdays* said little about racial inequality, Jim Crow, or the recent disenfranchisement of black voters in the South. Instead, Higginson devised a narrative of his life in terms of progressive reform conceived in the ravishing innocence of radicalism and matured into hope for the coming century: "To those who were living when the American nation lifted and threw off from its shoulders the vast incubus of human slavery," he asked, "what other task can seem too great to be accomplished?"

YET THE SUBJECT OF PREJUDICE was on his mind. Higginson joined the Anti-Imperialist League, formed in 1898 to protest American foreign policy and especially the brutal effort to annex the Philippines. With William James, Mark Twain, William Dean Howells, Andrew Carnegie, and Samuel Gompers, Higginson thoroughly rejected the so-called White Man's Burden (Kipling would coin the phrase in '99) and condemned jingoistic American politicians, his disgust the inevitable result of a lifelong commitment to justice and liberty. "Freedom is freedom," he cried, "and it is not for a nation born and reared on this theory to ignore it in judging the affairs of others."

That meant he had to reconsider the present condition of American blacks. "These people have a right to the freedom of civilization, the freedom of political rights, the freedom not merely to escape being held as slaves, but to have a position as free men that is worth having," he wrote in the *Boston Evening Transcript,* his oratorical style again strong. In the presidential election of 1900, Higginson threw his support to the anti-imperialist William Jennings Bryan and, aware the black voter would be leery of a Democratic candidate, joined with Garrison's son and George Boutwell, head of the Anti-Imperialist League, to write the "Address to the Colored People of the United States." The black population, Higginson said, "must cut adrift from every organization which wars on darker races, as such, and begins to talk again of 'the natural supremacy of the Anglo-Saxon.' We fought through a four years' war to get rid of that doctrine, and enlisted nearly 200,000 black soldiers for the purpose."

That the African American had no real advocate in government soon became abundantly clear to Higginson, who read with mounting fury Bryan's newspaper, *The Commoner,* in which Bryan stated over and over that he believed black Americans inferior to Anglo-Saxons. Higginson angrily wrote Bryan; the letter is worth quoting at length:

> I have yours of Nov. 23rd, and it perhaps justifies me in writing to you with a frankness which I might not otherwise have regarded as proper. You ask me to assist in finding efficient agents for "The Commoner." Excuse me if I reply that, although I headed your electoral ticket in this state during the last presidential election, I never could have done it had you taken the position assumed in "The Commoner" of Nov. 1st, in regard to what you call the "social equality" question. In this number of the paper you take a position which appears to me utterly retrograde and mediaeval; & wholly inconsistent with your general attitude.
>
> You also show in your way of arguing either ignorance or indifference in respect to American history when you say that no man or

party has advocated social equality between the white man and the black man. The simple fact is that no man concerned in the great anti-slavery movement in its early days ever advocated anything else. In my own case from the first time I had a house of my own in 1847, a fugitive slave always had a refuge there, and was treated as a social equal; and when, in the year 1857, I raised emigrant parties and accompanied them into your state and Kansas, it was always under the same fiat. It is humiliating to me to think that a newspaper, calling itself Democratic in a region thus made free, should take such an attitude as you now assume.

It is in my opinion an essential part of Democracy that social distinctions should be merely individual, not racial. Character is character; and education is education. What social gradations exist should be based on these, and these alone; and even these should be effaced as rapidly as possible. What are you or what am I that we should undertake to advocate any social law that shall place us above men like Frederick Douglass or Booker Washington? No point which "The Commoner" advocates seems to me so important as this, and whatever its other merits, it here seems to me so utterly in the wrong, that I have no wish to subscribe for it myself or to have it sent me and can only wish, if it holds to this attitude, that it may be discontinued.

Similarly, in 1904 Higginson wanted to know what so-called freedoms African Americans actually enjoyed: "a freedom tempered by chain-gangs, lynching, and the lash" he angrily wondered. Loathing the deep vein of racism that underlay violence perpetrated on black Americans, he snapped with antebellum fury, "Was any white man ever lynched, either before or since for insulting the modesty of a colored girl?" As for the fear, northern and southern, of miscegenation, he would have none of it. "As the memories of the slave period fade way, the mere fetich [sic] of colorphobia will cease to control our society," he imagined, "and marriage may come to be founded, not on the color of skin, but upon the common courtesies of life, and upon genuine sympathies of heart and mind."

In 1905 he wrote an introduction to *The Aftermath of Slavery* by Dr. William Sinclair, an ex-slave, in which Sinclair cogently argued that southern whites, wishing to reenslave black Americans, murdered thousands of them while denying them the vote. Though

Higginson took the long view—"I am a man old enough to recall a time when there existed all around us at the North instances of the same kinds of injustice of which we now properly complain when we see it in the South"—he rebuked individuals like the white supremacist Thomas Nelson Page, whose novels Higginson had already censured. The next year he reproached Brander Matthews for not paying much attention to "the fact of colorphobia, still so dangerous & inhuman a feature of our civilization."

While he largely agreed with the Great Accommodator, Booker T. Washington, that education—for Washington, vocational education—was for African Americans the royal road to economic independence, he reminded his readers that "it is important for this race to produce its own physicians, lawyers, preachers, and above all, teachers." And he chided Harvard graduates in a poem published the same year that Henry James rambled the streets of Cambridge:

> *They saved you; charged Fort Wagner; they held out,*
> *Held the road wide that Sherman might pass through.*
> *You built Shaw's statue; can you calmly doubt*
> *That those who marched with him should vote, like you?*

IN 1908, AFTER TWO DAYS of gruesome race riots in Springfield, Illinois, not far from the place where Lincoln lay entombed, Higginson joined with John Dewey, William Dean Howells, and W. E. B. Du Bois to demand suffrage for black Americans, as Du Bois put it, on the same terms as whites. From this challenge came the National Association for the Advancement of Colored People.

Higginson then retreated; revolutions do go backward, as he once said. He talked of conciliation between black and white instead of the demand for equal rights. It's difficult to know exactly why except in the terms he himself offered: political expediency and prudence, the same combination that lay behind his telling Dickinson not to publish her poems right away; the public was not ready for her, nor she for it. A curious mix of caution and courage, Higginson yet showed himself to be, in the end, mordantly skeptical about the capacity for people to change. "No white community will ever consent to the political supremacy of either the black man or the col-

Thomas Wentworth Higginson at 80, in 1903.

ored man or the yellow man," he wrote to the National Negro Conference. "I make this declaration philosophically and as a result of observation and reflection and absolutely without feeling of prejudice, for I have none."

"*CHEERFUL YESTERDAYS* IS INDEED, in spite of its cheer, a book of ghosts, a roll of names, some still vivid but many faded," observed Henry James, "redolent of a New England in general and a Boston in particular that will always be interesting to the moralist."

To James, Higginson was a man of compunction and good deeds, not an artist. He was echoing the minority view of Higginson—today the majority view—first put forward in 1871 by Theodore Tilton, then editor of *The Independent*.

> He is too much of a moralist to lose himself in literature, and so fails of realizing the highest success in that department; and too much of a litterateur to throw himself into reform to sink or swim with some great movement or cause; and so fails to awaken the enthusiasm or quite command the sympathies of the reforming class. In fact, he never quite loses himself in anything, and so never quite finds himself in anything, never touches the high mark of his power, never realizes the ideal set for him by warm-hearted friends.

Higginson pasted Tilton's criticism into his scrapbook.

Yet no one would dispute his magnanimity or fair-mindedness. His seventieth and seventy-fifth and eightieth birthdays prompted testimonial dinners in Boston and Cambridge, with speeches and newspaper articles ritually praising his physique, his energy, and, more keenly, his kind but sad mouth. A portrait painted when he was eighty depicts him seated, his hair white as bone, whiskers white as sugar. He wears a double-breasted wool jacket and large necktie with stripes. He looks forward, almost defiantly, but at the same time seems uncomfortable sitting still. There is a hint of a watch fob and the glitter of a ring, but his hands are thin, and the outlines of his skinny knees poke through folds of cloth. His eye, though heavy lidded, is fixed on the future. "There are so many younger writers to be recognized & encouraged," he said. He liked to summarize Goethe: "The old trees must fall in order to give the younger growth a chance. . . . It is not the 19th century but the twentieth, which now becomes interesting."

More and more he meditated on the meaning of fame, that bugbear of a subject: spurred by ambition since youth, he frequently stood on the Boston Common in front of Augustus Saint-Gaudens's bronze memorial to Robert Gould Shaw and the Massachusetts Fifty-fourth, thinking about what might have been, "but for some inches of space, one trivial turn of Fate's arrow, I had been riding there, foredoomed to Shaw's glory immortal." Did he secretly covet that glory? Of course. But the price was martyrdom, and his paternalism, if that's what it was, had inspired him to save, not sacrifice, the troops in his command.

If Dickinson had dreamed of posthumous fame, Higginson sensed that for him the pendulum would likely swing in the other direction. "All teaches us that fame is, in numberless cases, the most fleeting of all harvests; that it is, indeed, like parched corn, which must be eaten while it is smoking hot or not at all," he wrote. The titles of his essays tell their own story: "Favorites of a Day," "A Contemporaneous Posterity," "Concerning High-Water Marks," "The Literary Pendulum." As for himself, he said he was like a horse that never won a race but "was prized as having gained a second place in more races than any other horse in America."

LESS THAN FIVE MONTHS after Higginson's death, in 1911, George Santayana, the Harvard professor of philosophy who had been a student of William James's and, in his turn, was a teacher of T. S. Eliot, Wallace Stevens, and Walter Lippmann, delivered a lecture in California that, when published, influenced an entire generation of moderns. "The Genteel Tradition in American Philosophy," as it was called, described America as a country with two mentalities. Predictably excoriating the busy Americans "occupied intensely in practical affairs," Santayana also criticized their obverse: those soggy writers who floated in the "backwater" of an abstract, fatuous transcendentalism. Longfellow, James Russell Lowell, Whittier, Bryant, and Holmes (the so-called fireside poets) toppled from the canonical mantel on which they had been enshrined—and Higginson sank with them into the sea of obscurity.

Alice James had in fact thought the Dickinson poems were "sicklied o'er with T. W. Higginson," and the poet Amy Lowell would dismiss Higginson as a bungler too dim for the dauntless poet. "There is not, to my mind, a sadder page in history than the picture of good, well-meaning Mr. Higginson trying to guide Emily's marvelous genius," Lowell wrote to Mrs. Todd. "You will find that all the modern poets and critics rate her as I do, and it is owing to you, who have collected her poems and letters with such care, that we know what she was, and a debt of gratitude do we all owe you." Mabel Todd was content not to share the limelight with Higginson, now deceased, and willing to pass on to him the blame for editorial folderol.

But Dickinson survived her early editors as a modernist first class, her work transcendent yet concrete, knotty and well wrought. Her conscience agonized, her inward look was availing: she had a knack for seeing the unseen—and for the "uncertain certainty" (her phrase) of consciousness. In 1913, after Sue's death, Mattie, now Martha Dickinson Bianchi and herself an aspiring poet, inherited the poems in her mother's possession and, Lavinia having died in 1899, secured the rights to them. In 1914, she renewed the copyright on the collections edited by Higginson and Todd and published 147 poems in a volume called *The Single Hound* to commemorate—and rehabilitate—the relationship between Sue and Emily that Mabel had suppressed. The timing was perfect. Dickinson was hailed as an "unconscious and uncatalogued *Imagiste*," a Puritan with a pagan imagination writing short, concentrated, subtle poems "dug out of her native granite."

Dickinson, it was soon said, had discarded the Calvinism of her forebears while preserving their sense of tragedy and with a hard-won faith had resisted the incursions of religious evangelism and its secular counterpart, pie-eyed transcendentalism. This is the theme of Conrad Aiken's 1924 influential reevaluation of Dickinson (Aiken was a student of Santayana's). As epigrammatic symbolist, Puritan, and freethinker, she fended off the call of the genteel with its requirement that upper-class ladies sew for soldiers, join a Browning club, and recite *Hiawatha*. Instead, the vigorous and self-sufficient Emily Dickinson stood for the life of the impassioned mind, the embodied soul.

Yet for all her gifts, to the literary establishment Dickinson remained a wacky Old Maid. "Once adjust oneself to the spinsterly angularity of the mode," Aiken concluded, sounding far more conservative than Higginson, "its lack of eloquence or rhetorical speed, its naive and often prosaic directness, one discovers felicities of thought and phrase on every page."

And Higginson? Symbolizing prudery, he stayed the emblem of weak-kneed gentility, lacking substance, his mind an old music box (to borrow from Santayana) of worn-out tunes. Dickinson's early biographer, the poet Genevieve Taggard, belittled him as a brave, humane meddler—the "hero of a hundred *Atlantic* paragraphs"—who went to war "in high feather" and by the early 1930s, was lumped with the dull "Cambridge" group of academics. Dickinson was avant-garde, Higginson an heirloom. And since the modernists of the first part of the twentieth century disdained the grubby world of politics and held themselves aloof not just from old-fashioned narrative but from public events and national crimes, they turned their aesthetic back on racism (to say nothing of women's rights and suffrage). Higginson's brave political iconoclasm—which had attracted Dickinson—thus fell by the literary wayside. Few litterateurs read or cared about his pungent writing on Nat Turner, Denmark Vesey, or the slave called Gabriel. As a consequence, and out of context, he became easy to ridicule, as in Adrienne Rich's fine poem "I Am in Danger—Sir—," where Dickinson appears as " 'Halfcracked' to Higginson.' "

Rarely was Higginson evaluated by literary people with the kind of evenhandedness of the Dickinson scholar who in 1968 observed that "one should not demand more acumen of an individual than of the whole tribe of critics of the 1890s." Yet that's not the whole story either. Returning to Cambridge after the war had not been good for Higginson's future; in Newburyport and Worcester, he shone; in Beaufort, he shone; he rallied the troops through oratory and his moral courage. But after the war he slowly adopted the hypnotic equitability that helped brand him Dickinson's half-baked editor. Too bad: he was the women's rights activist who declared in 1852 that "we must choose between the past forms which once embodied the eternal spirit, and the other forms which are to renew and embody it now. . . . The old has the court, the senate, the market; the new has the poets, the people, and posterity."

Yet this radical and, in later years, this apostle of moderation was the man Emily Dickinson trusted, for there was something of the radical and conservative, activist and recluse, in her nature, too. Innovator, maverick, and marvel, anatomist of the heart and mind, she scribbled poems on the backside of recipes for cocoanut cake, and when her father insisted that the neighborhood pastor question her for heresy, she submitted. "It is remarkable," Hawthorne once noted, "that persons who speculate the most boldly often conform with the most perfect quietude to the external regulations of society." Nor did she fuss over sanitary commissions or suffrage. " 'George Washington was the Father of his Country,' " she joked. " 'George Who?' That sums all Politics to me." The world that counted would catch up to her, not her to it.

. . .

LIKE DICKINSON, Higginson never stopped writing. Seated either in his cozy book-lined study, his desk near a window, or in the larger room on the second floor where he installed a typewriter, he flooded newspapers and magazines with essays and reviews. He opposed all proposals to restrict immigration, he advocated religious tolerance—including toleration for atheism—and woman suffrage. (He turned down membership in the National Institute of Arts, Science and Letters until it admitted women.) He produced new books on Whittier and on Longfellow as well as a short biography of his grandfather. And aware that the end was near, he assigned that portion of himself assignable, donating to the Boston Public Library his huge collection on literature by and about women, over one thousand volumes gathered over the years while he was hoping to write their history. He called the massive library his Galatea Collection and included in it his letters from the un-Galatea, Emily Dickinson.

He planned to translate Aristophanes' *The Birds* from the Greek ("very good for elder years," he chortled). And though he spoke at the funerals of almost all his friends, he did not visibly sadden or tire. Or withdraw from the present. He did not condemn technology or mass culture. "I wish we had automobiles when I was a boy," he joked. "The old times were good, but the new times are better."

And he offered what had become his credo: "Best of all, is to lead, even at the very last, a life so full and useful that the thought of death occurs but as a momentary interruption; an incident that may come to us as easily, perhaps, as when a steamer moves from the wharf— so noiselessly that we do not know ourselves to be riding on a new element until we look back on the receding and irrevocable shore."

He had not forgotten his Whitman after all.

> *Joy! shipmate — joy!*
> *(Pleas'd to my Soul at death I cry;)*
> *Our life is closed — our life begins;*
> *The long, long anchorage we leave,*
> *The ship is clear at last — she leaps!*
> *She swiftly courses from the shore;*
> *Joy! shipmate — joy!*

NOR DID HE EVER FORGET EMILY. Within a week of his eighty-fifth birthday, on December 22, 1908, Higginson, along with

Henry James and William Dean Howells, was commissioned by *Harper's Bazaar* to write a short piece on the afterlife. Consenting, Higginson said he had little to add to his essay on immortality, written nearly forty years earlier: "that I am glad we live in a universe large enough, and that humanity is vast enough, to give an hundred souls an hundred different methods of reaching truth." And besides, for him, poetry supplied all the intimations of immortality he ever needed; dare you see a soul at the white heat.

And so when he sat down to write the piece, he bade farewell, albeit indirectly, to her one last time, again quoting from the Brontë poem "Last Lines" that she had asked him to read at her funeral.

> *Though earth and man were gone,*
> *And suns and universe ceased to be,*
> *And Thou were left alone,*
> *Every existence would exist in Thee.*

THE NIGHT WAS GENTLE. Purple crocuses had poked through the damp earth, the forsythia were in yellow bloom, the city smelled of honeysuckle and spring. A slight breeze rippled over gauzy curtains, lamps burned low, and at half past eleven, Thomas Wentworth Higginson died.

The funeral took place two days later, on May 13, 1911, and while unfussy in some respects, it was completely unlike Dickinson's obsequies some twenty-five years earlier. For this was a public event, full of pomp and circumstance, although Higginson had specifically requested there be no eulogy. There was, as ever, a simplicity to his character.

Wrapped in the regimental flag of the First South Carolina, Higginson's casket was borne from Buckingham Street to the First Parish Church, near the Cambridge Common, on the shoulders of African American men, members of Company L, Sixth Regiment, Massachusetts Volunteer Militia (Colored), and accompanied by its color guard, J. Homer Pryor, Captain. The delegation included Sergeant W. E. Carter and Privates Henry Falson, Edward R. Chelmsford, Thomas Brown, Edward A. Brewer, Charles Bassett, Isaac Lassiter, Toland J. Edwards, William H. Wilson Jr., Henry Grouse, and William F. Scott. They entered the vestibule of the old church to the low beating of a drum, and had they glanced around, they could have seen the place packed with luminaries, black and white, past and present, crowding the aisles as the light streamed through the tall windows: Higginsons, Channings, Cabots, Eliots, Putnams, and Storrows, the mayor of Cambridge, the presidents of Harvard, Emerson's children, Charles Francis Adams, Colonel N. P. Hallowell of the Massachusetts Fifty-fifth, councilmen and aldermen, former governor John D. Long, George Mifflin of Houghton Mifflin, members of the Massachusetts Historical Society and representatives of the Cambridge and Boston public libraries, as well as the students, also black and white, he had helped through college, perhaps Virginia Alberta Scott, Radcliffe's first black student, and of course the sons and daughters, all black, of Civil War veterans. From Higginson's antislavery days, only Franklin Sanborn remained, and he was there too, sitting unstooped among the wreaths and banners.

There was a reading from Psalms; one of Higginson's early hymns, "To Thine Eternal Arms, O God"; then a poem, a song, a benediction. The Loyal Legion played taps as the casket was removed from the church.

The body had been cremated, the ashes buried at Mount Auburn Cemetery to the roll of more drums, and the flag of the First South Carolina Regiment was presented to the Loyal Legion post. His headstone did not bear a quotation, just a few lines commemorating Higginson's military rank and his service to the country's first soldiers of African descent.

On a busy roadway, Route 21, in Beaufort, South Carolina, stands a plaque similarly commemorating the regiment and its commander. But the pendulum has indeed swung far from him, and he is hardly remembered.

EXCEPT, OF COURSE, by Dickinson herself: "I will not let thee go," she had told him, "except I bless thee."

> *Because I could not stop for Death —*
> *He kindly stopped for me —*
> *The Carriage held but just Ourselves —*
> *And Immortality*

. . . .

Since then — 'tis Centuries — and yet
Feels shorter than the Day
I first surmised the Horses' Heads
Were toward Eternity —

Acknowledgments

I could not have written this book without relying on the brilliance of the many Emily Dickinson scholars, editors, and enthusiasts who have, for more than a century, illuminated and recited and sung and set to music her work, or without the dedicated historians who have paid scrupulous tribute to Thomas Wentworth Higginson and his varied accomplishments. Their contribution to this book is threaded throughout the notes, but here I'd like to thank by name a few of those people who have graciously come to my aid, in one way or another, during the past six years.

I am greatly obliged to the following collections and individuals for access to archival material: Daria D'Arienzo, curator, and Margaret R. Dakin, assistant to the head of Archives and Special Collections, Amherst College Library; Albert Shirley Small Special Collections Library, University of Virginia Library (Papers and forgeries of Emily Dickinson, MSS 7658, Clifton Waller Barrett Library of American Literature, Special Collections, University of Virginia Library); Earle Havens, acting keeper of Rare Books and Manuscripts, Department of Rare Books & Manuscripts, and Special Collections, Boston Public Library, as well as Sean P. Casey and Barbara Davis; Leilani Dawson, the Brooklyn Historical Society; Michael Ryan and Jennifer B. Lee, Rare Book & Manuscript Library, Columbia University; Leslie A. Morris, curator of Modern Books and Manuscripts, Houghton Library, Harvard University, as well as Mary Haegert, Susan Halpert, Jennie Rathbun, Emily Walhout, and

Thomas Ford, photographic liaison for Houghton Library, and Carmella Napoleone at Imaging Services; Tevis Kimball, curator, and Kate Boyle, Special Collections, Jones Library, Amherst, Massachusetts; Patricia Michaelis, director, Library and Archives Division, Kansas State Historical Society; Mary M. Huth, assistant director, Rare Books & Special Collections, Rush Rhees Library, University of Rochester; Karen V. Kukil, Sophia Smith Collection, Smith College; the Harriet Beecher Stowe House and Library; Christopher Densmore, curator, Friends Historical Library, Swarthmore College Library; Nicolette A. Schneider, Syracuse University Special Collections Research Center; Peter J. Knapp, special collections librarian and college archivist, Watkinson Library, Trinity College; Diane E. Kaplan, head of Public Services, Manuscripts and Archives, Yale University.

I would also like to thank the following collections for the right to reprint material from their collections and to thank the following individuals associated with them: Thomas Knoles and Susan M. Anderson, American Antiquarian Society; Patricia M. Boulos, Boston Athenæum; Earle Havens, acting keeper of Rare Books and Manuscripts, Department of Rare Books & Manuscripts, and Special Collections, Boston Public Library, as well as Sean P. Casey and Barbara Davis; Jessy Randall, curator and archivist, Colorado College Special Collections, Colorado College Special Collections; Patricia Michaelis, director, Library and Archives Division, Kansas State Historical Society; Lia Apodaca, Library of Congress; Natalie Russell, Huntington Library, San Marino, California; Peter Drummey, Massachusetts Historical Society (Annie Adams Fields, diary, 30 January 1868, Annie Field Papers, Massachusetts Historical Society); Itty Mathew, Rights and Reproductions, New-York Historical Society; Thomas Lannon, The New York Public Library (Emily Fowler Ford papers and Genevieve Taggard papers, Manuscripts and Archives Division, The New York Public Library, Astor, Lenox, and Tilden Foundations); William L. Clements Library, University of Michigan; and Edward Gaynor, Papers and forgeries of Emily Dickinson, MSS 7658, Clifton Waller Barrett Library of American Literature, Special Collections, University of Virginia Library. I apologize to anyone whose name I may have inadvertently forgotten or never knew, for so very many librarians and archivists made this project possible.

I am grateful to Ellen Fladger, head of Special Collections, Union

College, for her ongoing generosity and support; ditto the indefatigable Mary Cahill, head of Interlibrary Loan, at Union College. Speaking of generosity: again Kent Bicknell has proven himself munificent, helpful, and always willing to share the marvelous papers and books in his burgeoning treasure trove of American literature. So too I am grateful to Philip Gura, who was willing to let me use his Dickinson daguerreotype reproduced in these pages.

I have been fortunate enough to work with marvelous students, both in my Dickinson seminar at Union College, and at Columbia University, where my nonfiction colleagues Patty O'Toole, Richard Locke, and Lis Harris graciously selected the novelist Thorn Kief Hillsbery as my Hertog Fellow. At Union, I am also indebted to the fine work of Shaun Kirk, and, at Columbia, of Kate Daloz, Abigail Rabinowitz, and Kim Tingley, who happily took on many painstaking bibliographical and other tasks with real panache. And many thanks to Robert Polito, director of the Writing Program at the New School, who has created a superb working environment for writers. I am also grateful to Stephen Motika of Poets House, as well as Lee Briccetti and Margo Viscusi, who invited me to celebrate the republication of Susan Howe's *My Emily Dickinson* and Emily Dickinson in the twenty-first century.

To friends, I owe much more than thanks. For reading the entire manuscript with typical insight, imagination, and discernment, I am indebted to novelist Christopher Bram; to my former editor, the sensitive author Frances Kiernan; and to the indomitable Byron Dobell; so too am I indebted to the special friendship of novelist Binnie Kirshenbaum, who read several chapters of the manuscript with typical sensitivity and clear-eyed candor. And over the years, I've learned from and been sustained by the invaluable companionship, conversation, and charm of David Alexander, Jack Barth, Frederick Brown, Ina Caro, Robert Caro, Jack Diggins, Benita Eisler, Wendy Gimbel, Elizabeth Harlan, Doug Liebhafsky, Richard Lingeman, Molly Haskell, Rochelle Gurstein, Herbert Leibowitz, Robert D. Richardson, Jr., Stacy Schiff, the late, lamented Saul A. Silverman, Susan Yankowitz, and Larzer Ziff. And thanks very specially, too, to my beloved friend, the poet and translator, Richard Howard, who reminds me always "only a hidden life is there / to be looked for, not found."

I am thoroughly indebted to the incomparable Victoria Wilson, my editor, a woman of decisiveness, perspicacity, kindness, and wit.

Again, it has been a privilege to work with her, and I thank her more than I can say for shepherding this book from inception to production with typical intelligence and good sense. I am also grateful to her superb colleagues at Knopf: Carmen Johnson, Vicky Wilson's assistant, whose diligence, meticulousness, and gentle support go beyond the call of duty; Abigail Winograd, who confronted the difficulties of copyediting this manuscript, with all its poems and variants of poems, with courage and smarts; to Caryn Burtt, for her scrupulous attention to permission and legal matters; to Jason Booher and to Victoria Wilson, for the book's jacket design; and to Iris Weinstein, for the text design. I am also grateful to my agent, Lynn Nesbit, for her bracing honesty, integrity, and humor, and to everyone I've had the pleasure of working with at her agency; a special thanks, too, to Tina Simms and the wonderful and encouraging Richard Morris.

For their love and their extraordinary and tenacious courage, I salute my parents, Helen and Irving Wineapple.

For his love, his breadth, his brilliance, and for the depths of his music, inner and outer, I thank my husband, Michael Dellaira, an intimate part of every word in this book and the best part of anything I do. With characteristic open-heartedness and insight, he suggested I dedicate it to the sustaining friend I recently lost—the amazing writer that the world lost—for we shall not see her like again. To Michael and to Sybille, then, forever astonishing.

Notes

For frequently cited names, the following abbreviations are used:

DICKINSONS
ED	Emily Dickinson
EdD	Edward Dickinson (father)
END	Emily Norcross Dickinson (mother)
LD	Lavinia Dickinson (sister)
MDB	Martha Dickinson Bianchi (niece)
SGD	Susan Gilbert Dickinson (sister-in-law)
WAD	(William) Austin Dickinson (brother)

HIGGINSONS
AH	Anna Higginson (sister)
LH	Louisa Higginson (sister)
LSH	Louisa Storrow Higginson (mother)
MCH	Mary Channing Higginson
MTH	Mary (Minnie) Thacher Higginson
TWH	Thomas Wentworth Higginson

OTHERS
HHJ	Helen Hunt Jackson
MLT	Mabel Loomis Todd
MTB	Millicent Todd Bingham

For frequently cited books, the following abbreviations are used:

AB	MTB, *Ancestors' Brocades*
Austin and Mabel	Longsworth, *Austin and Mabel*
Dear Preceptor	Wells, *Dear Preceptor*

Fr	ED, *The Poems of Emily Dickinson,* variorum ed. or *Reading Edition* (see note below)
Home	MTB, *Emily Dickinson's Home*
Letters	ED, *The Letters of Emily Dickinson*
LL	Sewall, *The Lyman Letters*
Poems, First Series	ED, *Poems,* ed. MLT and TWH, 1890
Poems, Second Series	ED, *Poems,* ed. TWH and MLT, 1891
Revelation	MTB, *Emily Dickinson: A Revelation*
Sewall	Sewall, *The Life of Emily Dickinson*
Strange Enthusiasm	Edelstein, *Strange Enthusiasm*
TWH	MTH, *Thomas Wentworth Higginson*
Werner	Werner, *Emily Dickinson's Open Folios*
YH	Leyda, *The Years and Hours of Emily Dickinson*

For frequently cited writings by TWH, the following abbreviations are used:

Afternoon Landscape	*The Afternoon Landscape*
Army Life	*Army Life in a Black Regiment*
Book and Heart	*Book and Heart: Essays on Literature and Life*
Civil War Journal	*The Complete Civil War Journal and Selected Letters*
Contemp.	*Contemporaries*
CY	*Cheerful Yesterdays*
L&J	*Letters and Journals*
Magnificent Activist	*The Magnificent Activist*
Malbone	*Malbone: An Oldport Romance*
Monarch	*The Monarch of Dreams*
New World	*The New World and the New Book*
Part	*Part of a Man's Life*
Thalatta	Longfellow and TWH, *Thalatta: A Book for the Seaside*
Wishes	*Woman and Her Wishes*
W&M	*Women and Men*

For frequently cited libraries and manuscript depositories, the following abbreviations are used. (Note that in quoting primary materials, including poems, I have retained the writer's original spelling and punctuation so that the reader may better hear the author's voice.)

AAS	American Antiquarian Society, Worcester, Mass.
Amherst	Amherst College Archives and Special Collections, Amherst College Library, Amherst, Mass.
BPL	Rare Books and and Manuscript Department and Special Collections, Boston Public Library
Butler	Special Collections, Nicholas Murray Butler Library, Columbia University Libraries, New York
Colorado	Special Collections, Tutt Library, Colorado College, Colorado Springs, Colo.
Houghton	Houghton Library, Harvard University, Cambridge, Mass.

Huntington	Huntington Library, Art Collections, and Botanical Gardens, San Marino, Calif.
Kansas	Kansas State Historical Society, Topeka, Kans.
LC	Library of Congress, Washington, D.C.
MHS	Massachusetts Historical Society, Boston
NYPL	Manuscripts and Archives Division, New York Public Library
Smith	Sophia Smith Collection, Smith College, Northampton, Mass.
Stowe Center	Harriet Beecher Stowe Center, Hartford, Conn.
UVA	Clifton Waller Barrett Library of American Literature, Albert and Shirley Small Special Collections Library, University of Virginia Library, Charlottesville
Yale	Manuscripts and Archives Department, Sterling Memorial Library, Yale University Library, New Haven, Conn.

THE FRANKLIN NUMBERS

Because most of Emily Dickinson's poems were unpublished in her lifetime, we do not know which version of them, if any, she considered "final," and prior to 1955, the variants were not available to the public. Rather, most of her editors, like Thomas Wentworth Higginson and Mabel Todd, chose—have to choose—which version of the poem they would print and/or how they would print it. But in 1955, Thomas H. Johnson, with the assistance of Theodora Ward, published a three-volume edition of Dickinson's poems "including variant readings critically compared with all known manuscripts." This groundbreaking edition of poems also established the numbering system (instead of titles, which Dickinson herself rarely used) commonly employed in Dickinson studies.

Subsequently, the most recent compilation of Dickinson's work and its variants is the R. W. Franklin three-volume variorum edition, published in 1998. Franklin, who published the *Manuscript Books of Emily Dickinson* in 1981, includes more and recently discovered Dickinson poems and renumbers them. Though not complete—and inevitably contested—the Franklin version is, to date, the best we have. I have used its numbering system, which supersedes Johnson's, but since few readers have access to the three-volume edition, in quoting from Dickinson's poetry I drew on the single version of the poem that Franklin chose to include in his one-volume, readily available *Reading Edition.*

Still, there are exceptions. If a poem Dickinson sent to Thomas Wentworth Higginson, for instance, is not the version included in the *Reading Edition,* I quoted from the version of the poem printed in the variorum edition. It is identified by number and with the alphabetical designation (A, B, C, or D) employed by Franklin. And, in several cases, I quoted from the variorum edition and used its alphabetical designation when referring to a particular version of a poem sent to a particular recipient.

CHAPTER ONE: THE LETTER

3 "This is my letter to the World": Fr 519.

3 "Are you too deeply occupied to say if my Verse is alive?": ED to TWH, April 15, 1862, *Letters,* 2:403.

4 after reading from a statement: See Lucy Stone, "Protest against the Laws of Marriage," Protest Read at Wedding Ceremony, May 1, 1855, reprinted in Dorothy Emerson, *Standing Before Us,* p. 57.

4 "I enjoy danger": TWH, Kansas notebook, Houghton.

5 "Could I make you and Austin—proud—": ED to SGD, [summer 1861. Many of Johnson's dates are speculative, and so unless I can be sure of the date or an approximation of it, I have put it in brackets.], *Letters,* 2:380.

5 "Should you think it breathed—": ED to TWH, April 15, 1862, *Letters,* 2:403.

5 "the most curious thing about the letter was the total absence of a signature": TWH, "Emily Dickinson's Letters," p. 444.

5 "I'll tell you how the Sun rose—": Fr 204.

5 "The nearest Dream recedes—unrealized—": Fr 304.

5 "the impression of a wholly new and original poetic genius": TWH, "Emily Dickinson's Letters," p. 445.

5 "I read your Chapters": ED to TWH, April 25, 1862, *Letters,* 2:405.

6 "Safe in their Alabaster Chambers—": Fr 124.

6 "There may be years" . . . "Charge your style with life": TWH, "Letter to a Young Contributor," pp. 403, 404.

7 "I foresee that 'Young Contributors' will send me worse things": TWH to James T. Fields, Houghton, quoted in *YH,* 2:55.

7 "Two such specimens": TWH to James T. Fields, April 17, 1862, Huntington.

7 "Since that Letter to a Young Contributor": TWH to LSH, April 18, 1862, Houghton.

7 "I tried a little": TWH, "Emily Dickinson's Letters," p. 448.

7 "surgery"; "It was not so painful as I supposed": ED to TWH, April 25, 1862, *Letters,* 2:404.

7 "with a naive skill": TWH, "Emily Dickinson's Letters," p. 445.

7 "but in your manner of the phrase"; "they are better than Beings": ED to TWH, April 25, 1862, *Letters,* 2:404–405.

7 "In a Life that stopped guessing": ED to SGD, [1878], *Letters,* 2:632.

7 "does not care for thought"; "begs me not to read them"; "except me—"; "I sing": ED to TWH, April 25, 1862, *Letters,* 2:404.

8 "When far afterward—": ED to TWH, June 7, 1862, *Letters,* 2:408.

8 who "came to my Father's House": ED to TWH, April 25, 1862, *Letters,* 2:405.

8 "I cannot think of a bliss as great": TWH, Field Book, September 20, 1861, Houghton.

9 he unsuccessfully tried to organize a military expedition: See TWH to Sydney Howard Gay, May 5, 1861, Butler.

9 "I have thoroughly made up my mind"; "This war, for which I long": TWH, journal, August 25, 1861, Houghton.

9 "a column of newspaper or a column of attack": TWH, "Letter to a Young Contributor," p. 409.

9 "The General Rose—decay—": Fr 772.

9 "South Winds jostle them—": Fr 98E.

9 "Your letter gave no Drunkenness": ED to TWH, June 7, 1862, *Letters,* 2:408.

10 "You think my gait 'spasmodic'—"; "The 'hand you stretch me in the Dark' ": ED to TWH, June 7, 1862, *Letters,* 2:409.

10 " 'To publish'—"; "if fame belonged to me": ED to TWH, June 7, 1862, *Letters,* 2:408.

10 "We play at Paste—": Fr 282A. She was also slyly alluding, it seems, to his "Gymnastics" essay: "Practise . . . thoroughly and patiently, and you will in time attain evolutions more complicated, and, if you wish, more perilous." See TWH, "Gymnastics," p. 292.

10 "Would you have time to be the 'friend' ": ED to TWH, June 7, 1862, *Letters,* 2:409.

11 "As if I asked a common Alms": Fr 14.

11 "But, will you be my Preceptor": ED to TWH, June 7, 1862, *Letters,* 2:409.

11 "the Dreamer & worker—": TWH, "Dreamer and Worker" notebook, Houghton.

11 "I fancy that in some other realm": TWH, "Letter to a Young Contributor," pp. 410–411.

12 "cross her Father's ground": ED to TWH, June 1869, *Letters,* 2:460.

12 "The Soul selects her own Society—": Fr 409.

12 "The Truth must dazzle gradually—": Fr 1263.

13 "Of our greatest acts": ED to TWH, [June 1869], *Letters,* 2:460.

14 "Thank Heaven!": MLT, diary, March 3, 1891, Yale. Mabel Loomis Todd kept both diaries and journals; the former contain topical remarks written on or close to the date of entry. The journals consist of longer, more reflective passages that, in some cases, are written at some time distant from the dates or events described.

14 "Never gave them to me": See *AB,* p. 152n.

CHAPTER TWO: THOMAS WENTWORTH HIGGINSON:
WITHOUT A LITTLE CRACK SOMEWHERE

17 "Don't you think it rather a pity": TWH, "The Sunny Side of the Transcendental Era," p. 6.

17 "It would seem as strange to another generation": TWH to LSH, July 10, 1859, Houghton.

18 Not surprisingly, in later years: See "Epistle to the Reader," in John Hale, *A Modest Inquiry into the Nature of Witchcraft* (1702), quoted in Burr, *Narratives of New England Witchcraft Cases,* p. 402.

19 "the star that gilds": LSH, quoted in *TWH,* p. 56.

19 "half dead": LSH to TWH, December 27, 1861, Houghton.

19 "I think sometimes he will offer his wife and children": LSH, diary, n.d., Houghton.

19 "his hospitality was inconveniently unbounded": TWH, "The Woman Who Most Influenced Me," p. 8.

19 The deficit mounted: Morison, *Three Centuries of Harvard,* pp. 220–221; see also *Strange Enthusiasm,* p. 13.

20 "In works of Love": *TWH,* p. 2.

20 "Born in the college, bred to it": *CY,* p. 39.

20 "I rarely write": TWH, "How I Was Educated," *Forum,* April 1886, p. 178.

22 "splendid talents but no application": TWH, journal, April 30, 1841, Houghton.

22 "I feel overflowing with mental energies": *TWH,* p. 52.

22 "If I have any genius": TWH to LSH, January 31, 1843, Houghton.

23 "all the argument": Ralph Waldo Emerson, "Circles," in *Essays and Poems,* p. 409.

23 "What I would not give to know": *TWH,* p. 64.

23 "They have truth and earnestness": Emerson, quoted in *Dear Preceptor,* p. 45.

23 "I did not know exactly what I wished to study": *CY,* p. 91.

23 "I cannot live alone": See *TWH,* p. 63.

24 "Whatever be her faults of manner": TWH, quoted in *Dear Preceptor,* p. 41.

24 "Mrs. Higginson is very queer": Quoted in *Strange Enthusiasm,* p. 152.

25 his sister Anna: See *W&M,* p. 88.

25 "I don't care about outside show": TWH to Mary Channing, July 28, [1844], Houghton.

25 "God's fanatic": TWH, quoted in Renehan, *The Secret Six,* p. 4.

25 "I heard that he was 'poison' ": ED to Mary Bowles, [late 1859], *Letters,* 2:358.

25 as one of his biographers observes: *Dear Preceptor,* p. 59.

26 "not infallible but invaluable": TWH, "The Sympathy of Religions" (originally written 1854–1855), *Radical,* February 1871, p. 1.

26 "just and even fellowship, or none": Emerson, "The Transcendentalist," in *Essays and Poems,* p. 200.

26 "The career of man has grown large": TWH, "The Character of Buddha," *Index,* March 16, 1872, p. 83.

26 "Any man with some Yes in him": TWH to LSH, [November 1844], Houghton.

26 "In Cambridge we are in peace": TWH, "Other Days and Ways in Cambridge and Boston," typed ms., February 3, 1911, AAS.

26 "I crave action": *TWH,* p. 69.

26 "Free breath is good": TWH, "The Woman Who Most Influenced Me," p. 8.

27 "I have repented of many things": *TWH,* p. 65.

27 "Times change / and duties with them": TWH, "Tyrtaeus," *Harbinger,* November 1, 1845, p. 332.

27 "a higher element": TWH to MCH, September 4, 1846, Houghton.

27 "The land our fathers left to us": TWH, "National Anti-Slavery Hymn," *Liberator,* July 17, 1846, p. 116.

27 "The idea of poetic genius is now utterly foreign to me," *TWH,* pp. 64–65.

28 "He has abandoned much": TWH, application for readmission to Harvard Divinity School, September 19, 1846, Houghton.

28 "Setting out, as I do": *TWH,* pp. 67–68.

28 "There are times and places": TWH, quoted in *Strange Enthusiasm,* p. 89.

29 "Mr. Higginson was like a great archangel": Harriet Prescott Spofford, quoted in *TWH,* pp. 95–96.

29 "It will hurt my popularity in Newburyport": *TWH,* p. 88.

29 "They are so much more dependent on me": TWH to LSH, September 19, 1848, Houghton.

29 "My position as an Abolitionist": TWH to LSH, September 6, 1849, Houghton.

29 "I think I would have come to the same thing": TWH to Mrs. Southwell, July 21, 1898, AAS.

30 "There are always men": TWH, quoted in *Strange Enthusiasm,* p. 104.

30 "marched like an army without banners": TWH, "Two Antislavery Leaders," p. 143.

31 "on behalf of everything, almost": Henry James, "American Letter," p. 678.

31 "Remember that to us": *TWH,* p. 142.

31 "Assent—and you are sane—": Fr 620.

31 "Without a little crack somewhere": "The Eccentricities of Reformers," in *Contemp.,* p. 328.

32 "I hope, however, that there is less real danger": "might damage the cause": TWH, letter to the *Liberator,* October 10, 1851, p. 163.

32 "If Maria Mitchell can discover comets": *Wishes,* p. 9.

33 A woman "must be a slave or an equal": *Wishes,* p. 25.

33 "I, too, wish to save the dinner": *Wishes,* p. 23.

33 "A woman such as you would make": "Rights and Wrongs of Women," *Harper's New Monthly Magazine,* June 1854, p. 76.

33 "What sort of philosophy is that": TWH, "Ought Women to Learn the Alphabet?" p. 145.

34 "Nothing makes me more indignant": TWH to Isabelle B. Hooker, February 19, 1859, Stowe Center.

CHAPTER THREE: EMILY DICKINSON:
IF I LIVE, I WILL GO TO AMHERST

35 "Biography first convinces us": ED to TWH, February 1885, *Letters,* 2:864.

35 "It passes and we stay—": Fr 962.

35 the "only Kangaroo among the Beauty"; "when I state myself": ED to TWH, July 1862, *Letters,* 2:412.

36 a leading citizen of "unflagging zeal": WAD, "Samuel Fowler Dickinson," 1889, quoted in Sewall, p. 41.

36 a new "priest factory": Le Duc, *Piety and Intellect at Amherst College,* p. 5.

36 "they have compleated the College": Lucretia Dickinson to EdD, December 5, 1820, Houghton.

37 "My life," he sternly warned: EdD to END, June 4, 1826, Houghton.

37 "unobtrusive faculties": ED to WAD, February 18, 1852, *Letters,* 1:180.

37 "There is a vast field": EdD to END, May 15, 1826, quoted in Pollak, *A Poet's Parents,* pp. 15–16.

37 "A man's success": EdD to END, October 22, 1826, quoted in Pollak, *A Poet's Parents,* p. 49.

37 "Your proposals are what I would wish": END to EdD, August 8, 1826, quoted in Pollak, *A Poet's Parents,* p. 37.

39 "That rule was not made for me": EdD, quoted in *YH,* 1:256.

39 "Fathers real life and mine": ED to WAD, December 15, 1851, *Letters,* 1:161.

39 An oft-repeated anecdote: See *Home,* p. 112.

39 "Father was very severe to me": ED to WAD, April 2, 1853, *Letters,* 1:237.

39 "There must have lurked in her expressive face"; Jenkins pronounced her "sound": Jenkins, *Emily Dickinson,* p. 82.

40 "They do not need a severe course": EdD, draft of article published in the *New-England Inquirer,* January 5, 1827, Houghton.

40 "How does it affect us": EdD, draft of article published in the *New-England Inquirer,* February 23, 1827, Houghton.

40 "We are warranted in presuming": EdD to END, August 3, 1826, quoted in Pollak, *A Poet's Parents,* p. 35.

40 "Let them bend all their energies": EdD, draft of article published in the *New-England Inquirer,* April 20, 1827, Houghton.

42 "She dont appear at all as she does at home": Lavinia Norcross, quoted in *YH,* 1:21–22.

42 "They shut me up in Prose—": Fr 445.

42 "Bliss is the sceptre of the child": Fr 1583.

42 "I so love to be a child": ED to Abiah Root, [1850], *Letters,* 1:104.

42 "I wish we were children now": ED to WAD, April 12, 1853, *Letters,* 1:241.

42 "Two things I have lost with Childhood—": ED, n.d., misc. fragments, *Letters,* 3:928.

42 "The Things that never can come back, are several—": Fr 1564.

42 As an adult, she played games: See Jenkins, *Emily Dickinson,* p. 40.

43 "The realization of our vivid fancy": See MDB, preface to *The Single Hound,* by ED, pp. x–xi.

43 "How enviable their fame!"; "What man has done": EdD to END, July 12, 1826, quoted in Pollak, *A Poet's Parents,* p. 29; see also p. 54 of that work. Pollak rightly points out that Edward Dickinson is quoting Edward Young's "Night Thoughts"; Emily will later do so as well.

43 "half a house, & a rod square": EdD, quoted in *YH,* 1:30.

44 "It does seem to me": EdD to END, March 18 [1838], Houghton.

44 Had Mrs. Dickinson been willing to relocate: *AB,* p. 233.

44 "His failing was he did not understand himself": Quoted in *YH,* 2:224.

44 "I think it will do him the very most good": ED to WAD, June 20, 1852, *Letters,* 1:213.

44 proof positive that he was the man: See HHJ to Henry Root, [winter 1855], Colorado.

45 When it passed at the end of May: See Merriam, *The Life and Times of Samuel Bowles,* 1:117.

45 "Our house is crowded daily": ED to WAD, June 19, 1853, *Letters,* 1:257.

45 "of every bird & flower": LD to MLT, April 30, 1883, Yale.

46 "I look around me": WAD to Martha Gilbert, [May 11, 1852], quoted in *Home,* p. 241.

46 "I ask myself, Is it possible": WAD to Martha Gilbert, [May 11, 1852], quoted in *Home,* p. 242.

48 "early, earnest, indissoluble": ED to Charles Clark, [June 16, 1883], *Letters,* 3:779.

48 "I, you must know": Green, "A Reminiscence of Emily Dickinson," p. 291.

48 "Vinnie is full of Wrath": ED to Jonathan L. Jenkins, September 1877, *Letters,* 2:592.

48 "The tie is quite vital": *LL,* p. 70.

48 "A dire person!": quoted in *AB,* p. 146n.

48 Although Thomas Wentworth Higginson's father: For an account of TWH's religious upbringing, see *CY,* pp. 35–36.

49 "Were I a christian, my dear": EdD to END, March 18, 1838, Houghton.

49 "with a militant Accent": ED to Elizabeth Holland, [January 1875], *Letters,* 2:537.

49 "the working of God's spirit among us": EdD, quoted in Wolff, *Emily Dickinson,* p. 126.

49 "Christ is calling everyone here": ED to Jane Humphrey, [April 3, 1850], *Letters,* 1:94.

50 "I feel that I am sailing": ED to Abiah Root, March 28, 1846, *Letters,* 1:31.

50 "I was almost persuaded to be a christian": ED to Abiah Root, January 31, 1846, *Letters,* 1:27.

50 one of the "lingering *bad* ones": ED to Abiah Root, May 7, 17, 1850, *Letters,* 1:98.

50 "The shore is safer, Abiah": ED to Abiah Root, [1850], *Letters,* 1:104.

50 "I was taken to a Funeral": ED to TWH, [June 1877], *Letters,* 2:583.

50 "Sermons on unbelief ever did attract me": ED to SGD, November 27–December 3, 1854, *Letters,* 1:311.

50 " 'We thank thee Oh Father' ": ED to MCH, [late summer 1876], *Letters,* 2:561.

51 "Doubts of all things earthly": Herman Melville, *Moby-Dick, Billy Budd and Other Writings* (New York: Library of America, 2000), p. 423.

51 "Her compositions were strikingly original": Daniel Taggart Fiske to MLT, Yale.

51 "firmly established in the faith": See *Catalogue of Amherst Female Seminary,* (Amherst, Mass.: Adams, 1835).

51 "We have a very fine school"; "I am growing handsome very fast indeed!": ED to Abiah Root, May 7, 1845, *Letters,* 1:13.

51 "small, like the Wren": ED to TWH, July 1862, *Letters,* 2:411.

52 Emily once "put four superfluous kittens": MDB, preface to *The Single Hound,* by ED, p. xiii.

52 "That her thesis is partially true": Bishop, "Unseemly Deductions," p. 20.

54 she was said to confide to a visitor: See Green, "A Reminiscence of Emily Dickinson," p. 291.

54 "Home was always dear to me": ED to WAD, February 17, 1848, *Letters,* 1:62.

54 "There is a great deal of religious interest here": ED to Abiah Root, January 17, 1848, *Letters,* 1:60.

54 "There were real ogres at South Hadley then": *Home,* p. 75.

54 "They thought it queer": ED, quoted in Clara Newman Turner, "My Personal Acquaintance with Emily Dickinson," in Sewall, 1:269.

54 "I have neglected the *one thing needful*": ED to Abiah Root, May 16, 1848, *Letters,* 1:67.

55 "Home," she would write: ED to Perez Cowan, [1870], *Letters,* 2:483.

56 "Sewing Society has commenced again": ED to Jane Humphrey, January 23, 1850, *Letters,* 1:84.

56 "vain imaginations," as she jested: ED to Abiah Root, January 29, 1850, *Letters,* 1:88.

56 "Pain—has an Element of Blank—": Fr 760.

57 "She was full of courage": Quoted in Sewall, 1:222.

57 "far surpassing"; "and that sublimer lesson": ED to Edward Everett Hale, January 13, 1854, *Letters,* 1:282–283.

57 the "friend who taught me Immortality": ED to TWH, April 25, 1862, *Letters,* 2:404.

58 what was "most grand or beautiful in nature": ED to Edward Everett Hale, January 13, 1854, *Letters,* 1:282.

58 "My dying Tutor": ED to TWH, June 7, 1862, *Letters,* 2:408.

58 "My earliest friend": ED to TWH, [spring] 1876, *Letters,* 2:551.

58 "We are the only poets": ED to SGD, October 9, 1851, *Letters,* 1:144.

59 "Oh Susie, I would nestle close to your warm heart": ED to SGD, [February 1852], *Letters,* 1:177.

60 "Is there anything debasing in human love—": WAD to SGD, [spring 1853], Houghton.

60 "It seems strange to me, too": WAD to Martha Gilbert, March 27, 1853, *YH,* 1:266.

60 each an absolute monarch: See *Home,* p. 413.

61 "We're all unlike most everyone": ED to WAD, April 8, 1853, *Letters,* 1:239.

61 "I guess we both love Sue": ED to WAD, March 27, 1853, *Letters,* 1:236.

61 "a dear child to us all": ED to WAD, May 16, 1853, *Letters,* 1:250.

61 "I feel as if love sat upon my heart": *YH,* 1:187. The author of the novel was Jane Porter.

61 "I knew, I knew it *could* not last—": *YH,* 1:161.

61 "Those unions, my dear Susie": ED to SGD, *Letters,* 1:209–210.

62 "Captivity is Consciousness— / So's Liberty—": In "No Rack can torture me—," Fr 649.

CHAPTER FOUR: EMILY DICKINSON:
WRITE! COMRADE, WRITE!

63 confirmed his sister's "opinion": *YH*, 1:213.

63 "As the great world goes on": ED to WAD, [October 25, 1851], *Letters*, 1:151.

63 "And I, and Silence, some strange Race": In "I felt a Funeral, in my Brain," Fr 340.

63 "I'm afraid I'm growing *selfish*": ED to Jane Humphrey, [April 1852], *Letters*, 1:197.

64 "I don't go from home": ED to Abiah Root, [July 25, 1854], *Letters*, 1:298–299.

64 Instead, she stayed at home: See *YH*, 1:301–302.

64 "everybody knows everybody": HHJ to Henry Root, [winter 1855], Colorado.

64 "Oh Sir, may one eat of hell fire": MDB preface to *The Single Hound*, by ED, p. xiv.

64 "I fear I grow incongruous": ED to Elizabeth Holland, March 18, 1855, *Letters*, 2:319.

65 "I am out with lanterns": ED to Elizabeth Holland, [January 26, 1856], *Letters*, 2:324.

66 "To put this World down, like a Bundle—": Fr 404.

66 "In such a porcelain life": ED to Samuel Bowles, [August 1858], *Letters*, 2:338.

66 "I would like more sisters": ED to Mary Haven, February 13, 1859, *Letters*, 2:346.

66 "and finding the life with her books and nature": LD, quoted in Sewall, 1:153.

66 "strange things—bold things": ED to Jane Humphrey, April 3, 1850, *Letters*, 1:95.

67 "The Heart has many Doors—": Fr 1623; "Doom is the House without the Door—": Fr 710.

67 "So we must meet apart—": Fr 706.

67 "We used to think, Joseph": *LL*, p. 78.

67 "what they call a metaphor in our country"; "But the world is sleeping": ED, *Indicator*, February 7, 1850, quoted in *Letters*, 1:92, and *YH*, 1:168.

68 " 'I should expire with mortification' ": ED to WAD, October 21, 1847, *Letters*, 1:49.

68 "*Write! Comrade, write!*": ED to SGD, [March 1853], *Letters*, 1:226.

68 "I've been in the habit *myself* of writing": ED to WAD, March 27, 1853, *Letters*, 1:235.

68 "Some keep the Sabbath going to Church—": Fr 236.

68 "I'm ceded—": Fr 353.

69 "When we stand on the tops of Things—": Fr 343.

69 "If your Nerve, deny you—": Fr 329.

69 "I reckon—When I count at all—": Fr 533.

69 "He fumbles at your Soul": Fr 477A.

70 "Literature is attar of roses": TWH, "Letter to a Young Contributor,"

p. 410. See also "Essential Oils—are wrung— / The Attar from the Rose," Fr 772.

70 "This was a Poet—": Fr 446.

70 "Your praise is good—": ED to SGD, [Summer 1861], *Letters,* 2:380.

71 a "man of God of the old school": Whicher, *This Was a Poet,* p. 110; blank atheism: Wadsworth, "The Gospel Call," p. 77. The fullest treatment of Wadsworth may be found in Paul M. Miller, "The Relevance of the Rev. Charles Wadsworth to the Poet Emily Dickinson," pp. 3–69.

71 "And the Church below": *YH,* 1:353.

71 "But every now and then": Mark Twain, quoted in *YH,* 2:112.

71 "the affliction which has befallen": Charles Wadsworth to ED, [before spring 1862], *Letters,* 2:392. The date is persuasively argued by Habegger, *My Wars Are Laid Away in Books,* pp. 415–420. But that's as far as anyone can responsibly go. In 1924, Dickinson's niece, Martha Dickinson Bianchi, published an uncorroborated story that, if true, would fulfill all requirements of romance: A few days after they met, Wadsworth appeared on the doorstep in Amherst, Vinnie crying, " 'Sue, come! That man is here!—Father and Mother are away, and I am afraid Emily will go away with him!' " Bianchi continues: "But the one word he implored, Emily would not say. Unable to endure his life under the old conditions, after a short time he left his profession and home and silently withdrew with his wife and only child to a remote city, a continent's width remote, where echo at least could not mock him with its vain outcry: dying prematurely, the spell unbroken." MDB, *The Life and Letters of Emily Dickinson,* p. 47.

71 "Black with his Hat": ED to James Clark, October 1882, *Letters,* 3:742.

71 "My Life is full of dark Secrets": ED to James Clark, [November] 1882, *Letters,* 3:744.

72 "several times in love, in her own way": *Home,* pp. 374, 413.

72 "my Aunt had lovers": MDB, preface to *The Single Hound,* by ED, p. xvi.

72 "I've got a cough"; "Open your life wide": ED to unknown recipient, [early 1861], ED, *The Master Letters,* pp. 26, 28.

72 "Master. / If you saw a bullet": ED to unknown recipient, [early 1861], ED, *The Master Letters,* pp. 32–43.

73 "Perhaps you think me *stooping!*": Fr 273A.

74 she continued to alter them: Both Thomas Johnson's three volumes, ED, *The Poems of Emily Dickinson,* and Ralph Franklin's marvelous *Poems of Emily Dickinson* (Fr) show the variation in manuscript copies and insofar as possible provide the complete editorial and textual history of each poem.

74 " 'It is finished' ": ED to Elizabeth Holland, [June 1878], *Letters,* 2:613.

74 "foreign to my thought": ED to TWH, June 7, 1862, *Letters,* 2:408.

74 letter to the World: Fr 519.

74 "It's a great thing to be 'great' ": ED to Louise Norcross, [December 1859], *Letters,* 2:345. Habegger, *My Wars Are Laid Away in Books,* p. 712, corrects the original misdating of the letter.

74 poetry of the portfolio: See TWH, preface to *Poems,* and chapter 14 of this book.

74 "My Splendors, are Menagerie—": Fr 319.

75 "Because I could not stop for Death—": Fr 479.

75 "I heard a Fly buzz—when I died—": Fr 591.

75 "We like March—his Shoes are Purple—": Fr 1194.

75 "An altered look about the hills—": Fr 90.

75 "Power is only Pain—": In Fr 312.

75 "First—Chill—then Stupor—then the letting go—": In Fr 372.

75 "Narcotics cannot still the Tooth": Fr 373.

76 "I had some things that I called mine—": Fr 101.

76 "On subjects of which we know nothing": ED to Otis Lord, n.d., *Letters*, 2:728.

76 "Some things that fly there be—": Fr 68.

76 "When Jesus tells us about his Father": ED to Mrs. Hills, n.d., *Letters*, 3:837.

76 "This World is not conclusion": Fr 373.

76 "I sing . . . as the Boy does": ED to TWH, April 25, 1862, *Letters*, 2:404.

77 "She dealt her pretty words like Blades—": Fr 458.

77 "he appalls, entices": ED to TWH, [December 1879], *Letters*, 2:649.

77 "Title divine—is mine!": Fr 194A.

79 "His growth was by absorption": See Merriam, *The Life and Times of Samuel Bowles*, 1:101.

79 he supported the antislavery Republican John C. Frémont: See Koscher, "The Evolution, Tone, and Milieu of New England's Greatest Newspaper," p. 3.

79 "Mr. Bowles is quite handsome": See Annie Adams Fields, diary, January 30, 1868, MHS.

79 "His nature was Future": ED to SGD, January 1878, *Letters*, 2:600.

80 with his "vivid Face and the besetting Accents": ED to Samuel Bowles, [1875], *Letters*, 2:540.

80 "the Queen Recluse": Samuel Bowles to WAD, Friday, [January 9, 1863], Houghton.

80 "I have been in a savage, turbulent state": Samuel Bowles to WAD, Saturday, [May 1863], Houghton.

80 "I am much ashamed Mr. Bowles": ED to Samuel Bowles, [August 1860], *Letters*, 2:366.

80 "When the Best is gone—": ED to Mary Bowles, [spring 1862], *Letters*, 2:405.

80 her sister was "always watching for the rewarding person": *Home*, p. 413.

80 "I am so far from Land": ED to Samuel Bowles, [January 11, 1862], *Letters*, 2:390.

80 "Nobody knows this little Rose": Fr 11A (titled "To Mrs. ———, with a Rose"); "I taste a liquor never brewed": Fr 207A (titled "The May-Wine"); "Safe in their Alabaster Chambers": Fr 124A (titled "The Sleeping"). Also appearing in *The Republican:* " 'Sic transit gloria mundi' " (Fr 2B) in 1852, "Blazing in gold and quenching in purple" (Fr 321B) on March 30, 1864 (titled "Sunset"), and "A narrow Fellow in the Grass" (Fr 1096A) on February 14, 1866 (titled "The Snake"). See chapter 8.

CHAPTER FIVE: THOMAS WENTWORTH HIGGINSON:
LIBERTY IS AGGRESSIVE

81 "Come strong": Samuel May Jr. to TWH, May 25, 1854, BPL.

81 "It is of no use": Anthony Burns, quoted in Dana, *The Journal*, 2:625.

81 "Give all the notice you can": Samuel May Jr. to TWH, May 25, 1854, BPL.

81 "point the finger of scorn"; "As if Southern slave-catchers were to be combated": *CY*, p. 148.

82 "I am a clergyman and a man of peace": Theodore Parker, quoted in *Massachusetts Spy*, May 31, 1854.

82 the "froth and scum of the meeting": *CY*, p. 152.

83 "You cowards, will you desert us now?": *CY*, p. 71.

83 "That meeting at Faneuil Hall was tremendous": TWH to Mary Curzon, [1854], Houghton.

83 "The law must be executed": "Slave Case in Boston," *National Era*, June 1, 1854, p. 87.

83 Later that night Batchelder died: See William F. Channing to TWH, February 8, 1898, Houghton. When Higginson inquired many years later, Channing replied that his friend Charles T. Jackson, who examined the wound, initially said it was

> that of a pistol ball, but was linear, of a certain length, and made by a cutting instrument sharp at both edges. It was also deep. Yet the astounding fact remains, as will appear later, that the wound was produced by a pistol shot. . . . He said that after the door had been battered down, the marshal's posse inside had charged the attacking party with clubs and cutlasses. He saw their leader, Thomas Wentworth Higginson, penned in a corner of the recessed doorway, wounded by a cutlass in the face, and being hammered by the officers with clubs. "Then," said he, "I fired and one of the officers fell." He said they would have killed Higginson, if he had not fired. I asked him how Batchelder could have been shot when the wound was long like the thrust of a sword, instead of round like a pistol ball. He explained that he had loaded his pistol with a slug which had doubtless struck lengthwise.

83 "We went to bed one night old fashioned": Amos Adams Lawrence, quoted in McPherson, *The Battle Cry of Freedom*, p. 120.

83 "Massachusetts antislavery differs much": George Hillard to Francis Lieber, October 2, 1860, Huntington.

84 "That attack was a great thing for freedom": TWH to LSH, May 29, 1854, BPL.

84 "supposing it to be so arranged": *TWH*, p. 145.

84 "A revolution is begun!": TWH, "Massachusetts in Mourning!" p. 14.

84 "the crime of a gentleman": TWH to Maria Weston Chapman, November 30–December 7, 1854, BPL.

84 "It is the only way": George J. Higginson to TWH, June 10, 1854, BPL.

84 "My penalty cannot be very severe": TWH to LSH, May 29, 1854, BPL;

"it would be best for the 'cause' ": Lucy Stone to TWH, July 15, 1854, BPL.

86 shops closed their doors: See Schama, *Dead Certainties,* p. 312, and Samuel May Jr. to TWH, June 2, [1854], BPL.

86 not to "conceal Fugitives and help them on"; "I am glad to be deceived no longer": TWH, "Massachusetts in Mourning!" p. 14.

86 "Liberty is aggressive": Ralph Waldo Emerson, *Journals,* 14:385, quoted in Von Frank, *The Trials of Anthony Burns,* p. 229.

86 transcendentalist in arms: The term is used by Frederickson regarding Higginson in *The Inner Civil War,* p. 37.

86 "I knew his ardor & courage": Dana, *The Journal,* 2:629.

86 "the only Harvard Phi Beta Kappa": Henry David Thoreau, quoted in Renehan, *The Secret Six,* pp. 64–65.

87 After all, it had been a local Baptist clergyman: After he was returned to Virginia, Burns was confined, treated poorly, and then sold on the auction block. Removed to North Carolina, he was purchased—and freed—with money Leonard Grimes had raised.

87 "Ever since the rendition of Anthony Burns": "A Ride through Kanzas," in *Magnificent Activist,* p. 88.

88 "to kill every God-damned abolitionist": David Rice Atchison, quoted in Drake, "The Law That Ripped America in Two," p. 63.

88 "These are times": Henry Ward Beecher, quoted in Nevins, *Ordeal of the Union,* 2:431.

88 "Never before in my life": *CY,* p. 202.

89 "I almost hoped to hear": *TWH,* p. 167.

89 "Colored men are thrust illegally out of cars in New York": TWH to George Curtis, January 23, 1857, Houghton.

89 "We the Undersigned": Worcester Disunion Circular, Pamphlets, Houghton.

89 "It is written in the laws of nature": TWH to LSH, January 21, 1857, Houghton.

89 It had the salubrious effect: See *CY,* pp. 207–208.

90 "swallows a Missourian whole": TWH, "Anti-slavery Festival," *Liberator,* January 16, 1857, p. 1.

90 "best Disunion champion you can find": Franklin Sanborn to TWH, September 11 or 28, 1857, Kansas.

90 "that religious elevation": *CY,* p. 219.

91 "I long to see you with adequate funds": TWH to John Brown, May 1, 1859, BPL.

91 "The world has always more respect": TWH to Harriet Beecher Stowe, October 11, 1868, Stowe Center.

91 As it began in blood: TWH, *Liberator,* May 28, 1858, quoted in *Strange Enthusiasm,* p. 211. See also Von Frank, "John Brown, James Redpath, and the Idea of Revolution" for a discussion of how Higginson's *Atlantic* essays on slave uprisings may have fueled Brown's fire.

92 "Sanborn, . . . is there no such thing as *honor*": TWH to Franklin Sanborn, November 17, 1859, BPL.

92 "Gerrit Smith's insanity—& your letter": TWH to Samuel Gridley Howe, November 15, 1859, BPL.

92 "I believe John Brown to be the representative man of this century": George Luther Stearns, quoted in Renehan, *The Secret Six,* p. 244.

92 Brown's death . . . "will make the gallows as glorious as the cross": See Robert D. Richardson, *Emerson,* p. 545.

92 "Nobody was ever more justly hanged": Hawthorne, "Chiefly about War-Matters," p. 54.

92 "Under a government which imprisons any unjustly": Thoreau, *Civil Disobedience,* in *Walden, and Civil Disobedience,* p. 245.

92 "John Brown is now beyond our reach": TWH, quoted in *Strange Enthusiasm,* p. 231.

93 "What satirists upon religion are those parents": TWH, "Saints and Their Bodies," p. 584.

94 "These men and women, who have tested their courage": TWH, "Physical Courage," p. 732.

94 "Would you like an article on the Maroons": TWH to James Russell Lowell, October 23, 1859, Houghton.

95 "If it be the normal tendency of bondage": TWH, "The Maroons of Surinam," p. 553.

95 "I began this book on returning": TWH, Field Book, opposite flyleaf, 1885, Houghton.

95 "In these unsettled days it is perilous": TWH, journal, June 8, 1849, Houghton.

95 "On other days": TWH to LSH, June 5, 1850, Houghton.

96 "Thoreau camps down by Walden Pond": TWH, "My Out-Door Study," collected in *Out-Door Papers,* p. 305.

96 "The birds are as real and absorbing": TWH, journal, October 30, 1860; "I will trust this butterfly": TWH, journal, October 1861, both Houghton.

96 "I need ask for nothing else": TWH, Field Book, May 20, 1860, Houghton.

96 "He was the only critic": TWH to LSH, January 29, 1862, Houghton.

96 "I had more [mail] about 'April Days' ": *TWH,* pp. 157–158.

97 "I do not find that my facility grows so fast as my fastidiousness": *TWH,* p. 158.

97 "The more bent any man is upon action": TWH, "My Out-Door Study," p. 303.

97 "We talk": TWH, "My Out-Door Study," p. 304.

98 "My size felt small—": ED to TWH, April 25, 1862, *Letters,* 2:405.

CHAPTER SIX: NATURE IS A HAUNTED HOUSE

101 "I enclose my name—," ED to TWH, April 15, 1862, *Letters,* 2:403.

101 "Is it Intellect that the Patriot means": ED to TWH, [late May 1874], *Letters,* 2:525.

101 even if "you smile at me": ED to TWH, [July 1862], *Letters,* 2:412.

102 "I saw no Way—": Fr 633.

102 "To learn the Transport by the Pain—": Fr 178.

102 "Perhaps you laugh at me!": ED to Elizabeth and Josiah Holland, [summer 1862], *Letters*, 2:413.

102 "I dwell in Possibility—": Fr 466.

102 " 'Hope' is the thing with feathers—": Fr 314; "I'm Nobody! Who are you?": Fr 260; "I like to see it lap the Miles—": Fr 383.

103 "Each Life converges to some Centre—": Fr 724.

103 "He put the Belt around my life—": Fr 330; "The Soul has Bandaged moments—": Fr 360; "The Zeros taught Us—Phosphorus—": Fr 284; "Nature—sometimes sears a Sapling—": Fr 457; "Remorse—is Memory—awake—": Fr 781; "Doom is the House without the Door—": Fr 710; "I had been hungry, all the Years—": Fr 439; "One need not be a Chamber—to be Haunted—": Fr 407; "Crisis is a Hair": Fr 1067.

103 "I reason, Earth is short—": Fr 403.

103 "Inebriate of air—": In Fr 207.

104 "After great pain, a formal feeling comes—": Fr 372; "There's a certain Slant of light": Fr 320; "It was not Death, for I stood up": Fr 355.

104 "God is a distant—stately Lover—": Fr 615.

104 "I've known her—from an ample nation—": Fr 409.

104 "I felt a Cleaving in my Mind—": Fr 867.

104 "Breaking in bright Orthography": In Fr 333.

104 "The Martyr Poets—did not tell—": Fr 665.

104 " 'We take no note of Time' ": ED to Abiah Root, September 8, 1846, *Letters*, 1:37.

104 "I often part with things I fancy I have loved": ED to Susan Gilbert, [1854], *Letters*, 1:305–306.

104 "Of nearness to her sundered Things"; "Bright Knots of Apparitions": Fr 337.

105 "A loss of something ever felt I—": Fr 1072.

105 "A Light exists in Spring": Fr 962.

105 "Dear March—Come in—": Fr 1320.

106 "The nearest Dream recedes—unrealized—": Fr 304.

107 "Sorrow seems more general": ED to Louise and Frances Norcross, [December 1862; misdated in Johnson], *Letters*, 2:436.

107 "They dropped like Flakes—": Fr 545.

107 He had murmured, "My God": ED to Louise and Frances Norcross, [March 1862], *Letters*, 2:397–398.

107 "Nobody here could look on Frazar—": ED to Louise and Frances Norcross, [late March 1862], *Letters*, 2:398.

107 "says—his Brain keeps saying": ED to Samuel Bowles, [March 1862], *Letters*, 2:399.

107 "This is the Hour of Lead—": In Fr 372. This famous poem ("After great pain, a formal feeling comes—") was written around this time (spring–fall 1862).

108 "there is no remoteness of life and thought": Hawthorne, "Chiefly about War-Matters," p. 43.

108 "General Wolfe, on the eve of battle": TWH, "Letter to a Young Contributor," p. 409.

108 "I'm sorry for the Dead—Today—": Fr 582.

108 "If the anguish of others helped with one's own": ED to Louise and Frances Norcross, [December 1862; misdated in Johnson], *Letters,* 2:436.

108 "I noticed that Robert Browning": ED to Louise and Frances Norcross, [December 1862; misdated in Johnson], *Letters,* 2:436.

108 "It dont sound so terrible—quite—as it did—": Fr 384

108 "We—tell a Hurt—to cool it—": In Fr 548.

108 "An actual suffering strengthens": In Fr 861. ED sent the second stanza of this poem to TWH in 1866: "Time is a test of trouble / But not a remedy— / If such it prove—it prove too / There was no malady" (Fr 861B).

108 "Of all the Sounds despatched abroad": Fr 334B.

109 "The bee himself did not evade the schoolboy": TWH, "Emily Dickinson's Letters," p. 445.

109 "A Bird, came down the Walk—": Fr 359.

110 "I could well wish she were a native of Massachusetts": Ralph Waldo Emerson, quoted in Hall, *The Story of "The Battle Hymn of the Republic,"* p. 103.

110 His first volume . . . , went through three printings: See Rochelle Gurstein, "The Importance of Being Earnest," pp. 40–45.

111 "I felt a Funeral, in my Brain": Fr 340.

112 Spofford's short story "Circumstance": See [SGD], "Harriet Prescott's Early Work," p. 19, and St. Armand, *Emily Dickinson and Her Culture,* p. 173.

112 "Now all the swamps are flushed with dower": Harriet Spofford, "Pomegranate-Flowers," p. 575. Spofford's fiction impressed Dickinson, who asked Sue to send her more.

113 "It is no discredit to Walt Whitman": TWH, "Literature as an Art," p. 753.

113 "to my gymnasium-trained eye": *CY,* pp. 230–231.

113 "We all looked to him": TWH, quoted in Nelson and Price, "Debating Manliness," p. 497.

113 Higginson thus resented *Drum-Taps:* See TWH, "Literature as an Art," p. 753.

114 "Could you tell me how to grow—": ED to TWH, April 25, 1862, *Letters,* 2:404.

114 "I had rather wince, than die": ED to TWH, July 1862, *Letters,* 2:412.

114 "I thanked you for your justice": ED to TWH, June 7, 1862, *Letters,* 2:408.

114 "Your Riches, taught me, poverty—": Fr 418B. Higginson recalls receiving this poem in her second letter (postmarked April 25, 1862) although Franklin alleges the poem, along with "Success—is counted sweetest," was enclosed with the letter she sent to him in July 1862.

115 she may have composed in memory of Benjamin Newton: See Whicher, *This Was a Poet,* p. 92.

115 "Success—is counted sweetest": Fr 112D.

116 "You say 'Beyond your knowledge' "; "I think you called me 'Wayward' ": ED to TWH, [August 1862], *Letters,* 2:414–415.

116 "Of Tribulation—these are They": see Fr 328, sent with a letter [of July 1862], *Letters,* 2:411–412.

116 "A Bird, came down the Walk—": Fr 359; "Before I got my eye put out—": Fr 336B; "I cannot dance opon my Toes—": Fr 381A; "Dare you see a Soul at the 'White Heat'?": Fr 401C.

116 "Are these more orderly?": ED to TWH, [August 1862], *Letters,* 2:414.

117 "When I try to organize—my little Force explodes": ED to TWH, [August 1862], *Letters,* 2:414.

117 "You told me in one letter": ED to TWH, [August 1862], *Letters,* 2:415.

117 "A Letter always feels to me like immortality": ED to TWH, [June 1869], *Letters,* 2:460.

118 "Of our greatest acts we are ignorant—": ED to TWH, [June 1869], *Letters,* 2:460.

118 "There's a certain Slant of light": Fr 320.

118 "Sweet hours have perished here": Fr 1785.

119 "an article upon wildflowers": *Springfield Republican,* November 1862.

119 "If, in the simple process of writing": TWH, "Procession of the Flowers," p. 657.

119 "Nature is a Haunted House—": ED to TWH, n.d., *Letters,* 2:554.

119 "I trust the 'Procession of Flowers' was not a premonition": ED to TWH, February 1863, *Letters,* 2:424.

CHAPTER SEVEN: INTENSELY HUMAN

120 "must put the slavery question in a wholly new aspect"; "I have never written any political article there before": TWH to LSH, May 30, 1861, Houghton.

120 "Slavery is the root of the rebellion": TWH, "The Ordeal by Battle," p. 94.

120 "the far greater horrors of its suppression": TWH, "Nat Turner's Insurrection," p. 179.

120 "she was a woman, she was a slave": TWH, "Nat Turner's Insurrection," p. 181.

120 "My Life had stood—a Loaded Gun—": Fr 764; see Howe, *My Emily Dickinson,* p. 129.

120 "but for this reverse we never should have the law of Congress": *L&J,* p. 156.

121 "No prominent anti-slavery man": TWH to LSH, November 1, 1861, Houghton.

121 "Each Life converges to some Centre—": Fr 724.

121 "What I could write I have written": *CY,* pp. 248–249. TWH, Field Book, August 31, 1862, Houghton.

121 "as if one had learned to swim in air": *CY,* pp. 248–249.

121 "In each set . . . there are mingled": TWH to LSH, October 13, 1862, Houghton.

122 a "man of somewhat fluid gender identifications": Nelson and Price, "Debating Manliness," p. 504.

122 "slender & graceful, dark with raven eyes & hair": TWH to LSH, September 20, 1845, Houghton.

122 "All that my natural fastidiousness and cautious reserve": *TWH,* p. 126.

123 "There was a young curate of Worcester": See *CY,* p. 251.

123 "The government sent agents down here": Charles Francis Adams Jr., April 6, 1862, quoted in Ford, *A Cycle of Adams Letters,* p. 128.

124 "overlook means in his zeal for ends": November 27, 1862, *Civil War Journal,* p. 52. All quotations, unless noted, have been checked against Higginson's Civil War journal at Houghton Library and published in TWH, *The Complete Civil War Journal and Selected Letters of Thomas Wentworth Higginson.* The journal often contains the same phrasing as Higginson's letters to his wife and mother.

125 Though Saxton was to report to Hunter: For a fuller discussion of the history of the black soldier in the Union army, see Cornish, *The Sable Arm,* chapters 2 and 5; see also TWH, "The First Black Regiment," p. 521.

125 "from the dull and tedious drudgery": Cabell and Hanna, *The St. Johns,* p. 208.

125 "a mere plantation-guard or a day-school in uniform": TWH, "Scattered Notes re Colored Troops," Houghton.

125 "Intensely human": TWH to LSH, May 6, 1863, Houghton.

125 "I had been an abolitionist too long": *Army Life,* p. 3.

126 "like vexed ghosts of departed slave-lords": December 10, 1862, *Civil War Journal,* p. 251.

126 "The first man who organizes & commands": TWH, journal, November 23, 1862, Houghton.

126 a small book of Shakespeare's sonnets: I am indebted to Kent Bicknell for showing me TWH's copy of Shakespeare, with its notes by TWH.

127 No black soldier in Higginson's regiment: See Grimké, November 27, 1862, *The Journals,* p. 405.

127 "It needs but a few days": November 27, 1862, *Civil War Journal,* pp. 47–48.

127 Emerson, he recalled had squirmed: See TWH to Charles Eliot Norton, March 30, 1892, Houghton.

127 "He will be a marked man": John Greenleaf Whittier to Mary Curzon, December 24, 1862, Houghton.

128 "How absurd is the impression about these Southern blacks": December 1, 1862, *Civil War Journal,* p. 53.

128 "At first glance, in a black regiment": *Part,* p. 131.

128 "His comprehension of the whole problem of slavery": *Army Life,* p. 48.

129 "It is the fashion with philanthropists": November 21, 1863, *Civil War Journal,* p. 175.

129 "to impress on them": January 7, 1863, *Civil War Journal,* p. 79.

129 "And he evidently feels towards them all": Grimké, "Life on the Sea Islands," p. 669.

129 "it always seemed to me"; "What was the use of insurrection": *Army Life,* pp. 192–193.

129 And when he wrote publicly of them: See, for instance, TWH, "Leaves from an Officer's Journal," p. 521; the journal was printed in *Army Life* with some changes.

130 "This spontaneous outburst of love and loyalty": Rogers, "Letters of Dr. Seth Rogers," p. 340.

130 "My Country 'Tis of Thee": See letter from Harriet Ware, January 1,

1863, in Pearson, *Letters from Port Royal*, p. 130; see also "Higginson's Black Brigade," *Springfield Republican*, January 1, 1863, p. 1.

130 Higginson stood silent: see Grimké, January 1, 1863, *The Journals*, p. 430.
130 "It made all other words cheap": January 1, 1863, *Civil War Journal*, p. 77.
130 Not as good as at home: See Taylor, "Memoir of Susie King Taylor" in *Reminiscences of My Life in Camp*, p. 18, and Grimké, January 1, 1863, *The Journals*, p. 430.
131 "A man fell at my elbow": *Army Life*, p. 56.
131 "Nobody knows anything about these men": TWH, "The War in Florida," *New York Times*, February 10, 1863, p. 2.
131 "Ah. . . . We called him Bob": *Army Life*, p. 66.
131 "You may make a soldier out of a slave": TWH, "Safety Matches," p. 4.
131 "good illustrations": Report of Col. T. W. Higginson, First South Carolina Infantry (Union), February 1, 1863, in U.S. War Department, *The War of the Rebellion: A Compilation of the Official Records of the Union and Confederate Armies*, series 1 (Washington, D.C.: U.S. Government Printing Office, 1885): 14:197.
132 "our abstract surmises": Report of Col. T. W. Higginson, in *The War of the Rebellion*, 14:198.
132 "who are bent on making him incapable": "Col. Higginson's Estimation of Black Soldiers," *Springfield Republican*, February 6, 1863, p. 2.
132 "and in rather exalted language": "The Blacks in Battle," *New York Times*, February 10, 1863, p. 4.
133 With Jacksonville secure: See Rufus Saxton to Edwin M. Stanton, March 14, 1863, in Moore, *The Rebellion Record*, document 132.
133 "Higginson, the romantic, had raised money": Cornish, *The Sable Arm*, p. 150.
133 "It was the first time in the war": *Army Life*, p. 89.
133 "A more fatal order for the place": See Moore, *The Rebellion Record*, document 148, p. 638.
133 "Jacksonville is in ruins": *New York Tribune*, March 28, 1863.
134 "In a struggle for freedom": Garth Wilkinson James, "Memoir," p. 11.
134 "lean as / a compass-needle": Robert Lowell, "For the Union Dead," in *Life Studies and For the Union Dead*, p. 71.
135 "Our negro troops are splendid": Quoted in Generals' Reports of Service, in *The War of the Rebellion*, 14:133.
135 "Any disaster or failure on our part": TWH to LSH, May 18, 1863, Houghton.
135 Asked to make a speech: See Grimké, July 4, 1863, *The Journals*, p. 492.
135 "that this was a real war": quoted in Letter from Robert Gould Shaw, June 9, 1863, in *Soldiers' Letters, from Camp, Battlefield and Prison*, ed. Lydia Minturn Post (New York: Bunce & Huntington, 1865), p. 249.
136 "the colored troops as such are not responsible": TWH to Charles Sumner, June 20, 1863, Houghton.
136 After Shaw formally protested Montgomery's tactics: See the Hunter-Lincoln correspondence in U.S. War Department, *The War of the Rebellion*, series 1, 14:469–470.
136 "Then you die at half past nine": George Crockett Strong to Benjamin Franklin Butler, June 29, 1863, in Benjamin F. Butler, *Private and Offi-*

cial Correspondence of Gen. Benjamin F. Butler, during the Period of the Civil War (Norwood, Mass.: Plimpton Press, 1917), 3:94.

136 "Montgomery had two soldiers shot": TWH to Richard Watson Gilder, April 16, 1897, NYPL.

136 "Do not think this rapid organization": TWH to Charles Eliot Norton, June 28, 1863, Houghton.

136 "as fanatics sometimes did": TWH to Richard Hinton, Higginson Papers, Kansas.

137 "without mercy": TWH to Charles Eliot Norton, June 28, 1863, Houghton.

137 "The worst acts of tyranny": TWH to Edna Dow Cheney, September 13, 1865, Smith.

137 Merriam wasn't finished: See Halpine Report, June 2, 1863, Military Order of the Loyal Legion Collection, box 14, Houghton. See also Poole, "Memory and the Abolitionist Heritage," pp. 210–213.

138 "he is not a man of the sentiments": TWH to Colonel W. W. H. Davis, February 19, 1865, UVA.

139 Dr. Rogers and Higginson were left: Rogers, "Letters of Dr. Seth Rogers," p. 346. See also, for instance, TWH, "The First Black Regiment," p. 521.

139 "We presume too much on the supposed ignorance of those men": TWH, letter to the *New York Times,* February 21, 1864, p. 5; see also *Army Life,* appendix D, p. 222.

139 "*free* colored regiments": see TWH to Charles Sumner, June 20, 1864, Houghton.

139 The Fifty-fourth received much more publicity: See, for example, TWH, *Massachusetts in the Army and Navy,* p. 83, and TWH, "The Shaw Memorial," p. 194.

140 "Higginson, the senior colonel of the brigade": John Andrew to Edwin Stanton, June 29, 1863, in U.S. War Department, *The War of the Rebellion: A Compilation of the Official Records of the Union and Confederate Armies,* series 3 (Washington, D.C.: U.S. Government Printing Office, 1899), 3:424; see also Keith Wilson, "In the Shadow of John Brown: The Military Service of Colonels Thomas Higginson, James Montgomery, and Robert Shaw in the Department of the South," in Smith, *Black Soldiers in Blue,* p. 324.

140 "It would always be possible": *CY,* p. 257.

140 "bucked, gagged and, if need be, shot": Hallowell, *The Negro as a Soldier in the War of the Rebellion,* p. 9.

140 "I never saw any one": Shaw, *Blue-Eyed Child of Fortune,* p. 339.

141 "Folly Island gives a fair chance": *Civil War Journal,* pp. 157–158.

141 "Well I guess we will let Strong": Truman Seymour, quoted in Shaw, *Blue-Eyed Child of Fortune,* p. 51.

141 Seymour, a misanthropic man: see TWH to Sydney Howard Gay, May 23, 1864, Butler.

142 Shaw and his men talked: See testimony of Nathaniel Paige, in Berlin, Reidy, and Rowland, *The Black Military Experience,* p. 534.

143 "the dear blundering dusky darlings": September 12, 1863, *Civil War Journal,* p. 167.

144 "vacillating and half proslavery": *Army Life*, p. 95. See also *Civil War Journal*, p. 81.

144 "This makes me hate all arbitrary power": January 29, 1864, *Civil War Journal*, p. 187.

144 "At a time when it required large bounties": TWH to Charles Sumner, November 24, 1863, Houghton.

144 "They are growing more like white men": February 11, 1864, *Civil War Journal*, p. 183.

144 "I feel that I hv. done my duty entirely": TWH to MCH, January 28, 1864, Houghton.

CHAPTER EIGHT: AGONY IS FRUGAL

146 "I found you were gone, by accident"; "I too, have an 'Island'—": ED to TWH, [February 1863?], *Letters*, 2:423.

146 "The fascination of summer": TWH, "Procession of the Flowers," p. 656.

147 "to doubt my High Behavior": ED to TWH, [1863], *Letters*, 2:425.

147 "Color—Caste—Denomination—": Fr 836.

147 "'Tis so appalling—it exhilirates—": Fr 341.

147 "Agony is frugal—": In Fr 1196.

147 "I shall have no winter this year—": ED to Mary Bowles, [c. August 1861], *Letters*, 2:377.

147 "What Soft—Cherubic Creatures—": Fr 675.

147 "With narrow, probing, eyes—": In Fr 550.

147 "A Soldier called, a Morning ago": ED to Samuel Bowles, [August 1862], *Letters*, 2:416.

147 "Perhaps Death, gave me Awe": ED to TWH, [February 1863?], *Letters*, 2:423.

147 "It feels a shame to be Alive—": Fr 524.

148 he denounced "as subversive": See the *Springfield Daily Republican*, October 17, 1861.

148 "He is against slavery as the cause of the war": See *YH*, 2:92.

149 "I like Truth—it is a free Democracy": *LL*, p. 71.

149 Austin's paying a substitute: The going rate was three hundred dollars, about six thousand dollars in today's money.

149 That Dickinson seldom mentioned the war: In recent times there have been a number of scholars attending to Dickinson and the Civil War, beginning with Wolosky's *Dickinson;* see also Berkove, " 'A Slash of Blue!' "; Lee, "Writing through the War"; Marcellin, " 'Singing off the Charnel Steps' "; and Wardrop, "The Poetics of Political Involvement and Non-Involvement." I am indebted to this work.

149 "Though not reared to prayer—": ED to TWH, [February 1863?], *Letters*, 2:423.

149 After the poem "Blazing in Gold and quenching in Purple": See Dandurand's pioneering "New Dickinson Civil War Publications"; "Blazing in Gold and quenching in Purple": Fr 321; "Flowers—well, if anybody": Fr 95A.

150 "These are the days when Birds come back—": Fr 122B. See also TWH, "The Life of Birds," p. 376:

> In autumn, they come timidly from the North, and, pausing on their anxious retreat, lurk within the fading copses and twitter snatches of song as fading. Others fly as openly as ever, but gather in flocks, as the Robins, most piteous of all birds at this season,— thin, faded, ragged, their bold note sunk to a feeble quaver, and their manner a mere caricature of that inexpressible military smartness with which they held up their heads in May.
>
> Yet I cannot really find anything sad even in November. When I think of the thrilling beauty of the season past, the birds that came and went, the insects that took up the choral song as the birds grew silent, the procession of the flowers, the glory of autumn,— and when I think, that, this also ended, a new gallery of wonder is opening, almost more beautiful, in the magnificence of frost and snow, there comes an impression of affluence and liberality in the universe, which seasons of changeless and uneventful verdure would never give. The catkins already formed on the alder, quite prepared to droop into April's beauty,—the white edges of the May-flower's petals, already visible through the bud, show in advance that winter is but a slight and temporary retardation of the life of Nature, and that the barrier which separates November from March is not really more solid than that which parts the sunset from the sunrise.

150 "if she did not, the longest day would pass me": ED to TWH, June 7, 1862, *Letters,* 2:408.

150 "Fame is a fickle food": Fr 1702; "Fame is a bee": Fr 1788; "Fame's Boys and Girls, who never die": Fr 892.

150 "Some—Work for Immortality—": Fr 536.

151 "When I was small, a Woman died—": Fr 518.

151 "Bereavement in their death to feel": Fr 756.

151 "The Battle fought between the Soul": Fr 629.

151 "It sets the Fright at liberty—": In Fr 341.

151 "No Rack can torture me—": Fr 649.

151 "Can the Lark resume the Shell—": In Fr 754.

152 "you may make a soldier out of a slave": TWH, "Safety Matches," p. 4. There is, of course, no telling which came first, the poem or the essay, although it's likely that the poem preceded Higginson's essay; perhaps it is one she sent him that has escaped our notice and he borrowed from. Or Higginson may have used the phrase earlier. (He used it later, in "Some War Scenes Revisited," p. 9.) And, finally, if the phrase was in the public domain, as it may also have been, that both authors linked the bird's resuming its egg to issues of freedom and bondage is mighty suggestive.

152 "A Slash of Blue! A sweep of Gray!": Fr 233.

152 "Publication—is the Auction": Fr 788.

152 "I do not let go it": ED to TWH, [August 1862], *Letters,* 2:415.

152 "He fought like those Who've nought to lose—": Fr 480.

153 "My Portion is Defeat—today—": Fr 704.

154 "Could you, with honor, avoid Death": ED to TWH, February 1863, *Letters,* 2:424.

154 "Best Gains—must have the Losses' test—": Fr 499.

154 "The Soul unto itself": Fr 579A.

154 In June 1863: The collection *Out-Door Papers* includes such nature pieces as "April Days," "My Out-Door Study," "Water-Lilies," "The Life of Birds," "Procession of the Flowers," and "Snow," as well as essays on physical culture, such as "Saints, and Their Bodies," "A Letter to a Dyspeptic," and "The Health of Our Girls."

154 The *Springfield Republican* went so far: *Springfield Republican,* June 6, 1863; June 20, 1863; quoted in *YH,* 2:79.

155 "It is still as distinct as Paradise—": ED to TWH, [spring 1876], *Letters,* 2:552.

155 "Precisely at half past three": TWH, "Water-Lilies," p. 466.

155 "The Birds begun at Four o'clock—": Fr 504B.

155 "At Half past Three": Fr 1099.

156 "that which is remembered": TWH, "Water-Lilies," p. 473.

156 "Absence is the very air of passion": TWH, "Water-Lilies," p. 473.

156 "No man can measure what a single hour with Nature"; "The influence is self-renewing": TWH, "Procession of the Flowers," pp. 656, 657.

156 "I was thinking, today—": ED to TWH, [February 1863], *Letters,* 2:424.

157 "Perception of an Object costs": Fr 1103.

157 "The Myrrhs, and Mochas, of the Mind": In Fr 1608.

157 "Heaven over it—": In Fr 508.

157 "The Zeros taught Us—Phosphorus": Fr 284.

157 "So instead of getting to Heaven, at last—": In Fr 236.

157 "The snow-light offends them": ED to Louise Norcross, [1865], *Letters,* 2:439.

157 "What I see not, I better see—": Fr 869.

158 "yet I work in my Prison": ED to TWH, June 1864, *Letters,* 2:431.

158 "I wish to see you more than before I failed—": ED to TWH, [June 1864], *Letters,* 2:431; "I heard a Fly buzz": Fr 591.

158 word of it would "excel" her own: ED to TWH, June 1864, *Letters,* 2:431.

158 "The only News I know": Fr 820B.

158 "a Calamity"; "I had a woe": *LL,* p. 76.

159 "Further in Summer than the Birds": Fr 895D.

159 But in them we can hear "August burning low": Alfred Habegger interprets the poem similarly. See *My Wars Are Laid Away in Books,* pp. 492–493; see also Charles Anderson's fine reading in *Emily Dickinson's Poetry,* pp. 169–175.

160 "Would you instruct me now?": ED to TWH, [January 1866], *Letters,* 2:449.

CHAPTER NINE: NO OTHER WAY

161 It struck him: TWH, journal, August 16, 1870, Houghton.

161 that "inward darkness": TWH, quoted in *Strange Enthusiasm,* p. 99.

162 "a man among men": See Henry James, "The Works of Epictetus" (origi-

nally published as "Higginson's Works of Epictetus" in the *North American Review*, April 1866, pp. 599–606), review of *The Works of Epictetus*, trans. TWH, in Henry James, *Literary Criticism*, 1:12.

162 "When you do anything from a clear judgment": TWH, trans., *The Works of Epictetus*, p. 392.

162 "I seem to find her now": TWH, "Sunshine and Petrarch," p. 308.

162 "nobody comprehends Petrarch": *Malbone*, p. 150.

162 His home had become a hospital: See TWH, journal, December 23, 1866, Houghton, and *TWH*, pp. 276–277.

162 "On the whole": HHJ to Kate Field, March 7, 1866, BPL.

162 "All ladies do": TWH to ED, [late winter 1869], Houghton.

162 "I had promised to visit my Physician": ED to TWH, [1866], *Letters*, 2:450.

163 "I must omit Boston": ED to TWH, June 9, 1866, *Letters*, 2:453.

163 "I do not cross my Father's ground": ED to TWH, [June 1869], *Letters*, 2:460. Given the date of Higginson's letter, which I can ascertain by reference to his papers and meetings, the Dickinson letters dated by Johnson (in brackets) may be in error: they may have been written two years later. Of course, Johnson may be correct if ED was responding to a series of requests from TWH.

163 "Thin dry & speechless": TWH to MCH, August 16, 1870, Houghton.

163 "there is always one thing to be grateful for": quoted in TWH to AH, December 9, 1873, Houghton.

163 "Sometimes I take out your letters & verses": TWH to ED, *Letters* 2:461.

164 "I am always the same toward you": TWH to ED, [late winter 1869], *Letters*, 2:461–462.

164 "Of 'shunning Men and Women'—": ED to TWH, [August 1862], *Letters*, 2:415.

164 "It isolates one anywhere": TWH to ED, May 11, 1869, Houghton.

164 "I will be at Home": ED to TWH, August 16, 1870, *Letters*, 2:472.

164 "These are my introduction": ED, quoted in TWH to MCH, August 16, 1870, BPL.

165 "A narrow Fellow in the Grass": Fr 1096.

165 It first surfaced: It was subsequently reprinted in *The Weekly Republican*.

165 "lest you meet my Snake": ED to TWH, [1866], *Letters*, 2:450.

165 "defeated too of the third line by the punctuation": ED to TWH, [March 1866], *Letters*, 2:450.

166 "If I still entreat you to teach me": ED to TWH, [March 1866], *Letters*, 2:450.

166 "A Death blow is a Life blow to Some": Fr 966.

167 "Still, you see, I try": TWH to ED, May 11, 1869, Houghton.

167 "I would like to be what you deem me": ED to TWH, [June 9, 1866], *Letters*, 2:453.

167 "It is hard [for me] to understand": TWH to ED, May 11, 1869, Houghton.

167 "To undertake is to achieve": Fr 991.

167 "You mention Immortality"; "The 'infinite Beauty'—"; "To escape enchantment": ED to TWH, June 8, 1866, *Letters*, 2:454.

167 "Time is a test of trouble": ED to TWH, June 8, 1866, *Letters,* 2:454.

167 "Ample make this Bed—,": Fr 804C; "As imperceptibly as Grief": Fr 935D.

168 "Is it more far to Amherst?": ED to TWH, [early 1866], *Letters,* 2:450.

168 "Bringing still my 'plea for culture' ": ED to TWH, [July 1867], *Letters* 2:457.

168 "The Luxury to apprehend": Fr 819.

169 "write & tell me something": TWH to ED, May 11, 1869, Houghton.

169 "I would like to thank you for your great kindness": ED to TWH, [June 1869], *Letters,* 2:460.

169 "Why do the insane cling to you so?": MCH, quoted in TWH to AH, December 9, 1873, Houghton.

169 "The great reason why the real apostles of truth": *TWH,* p. 68.

170 "If every man who is accused": TWH, "Divergent Reformers," *Independent,* March 26, 1868, p. 4.

170 "I feel this strangely": TWH to AH and LH, December 30, 1864, Houghton. However, Higginson published these accounts at regular intervals from September 1864 until August 1867, and they became the basis for *Army Life in a Black Regiment.*

170 "That I was in it [the war] myself": TWH to AH and LH, April 9, 1865, Houghton.

170 "Until it is done": *TWH,* p. 252.

171 the "one right residence": Henry James, *Notes of a Son and Brother,* p. 67.

171 Higginson borrowed it too: See *Malbone,* p. 93: " 'Good Americans when they die go to Paris,' said Philip."

171 he called this part of town Oldport: See "Oldport in Winter," *Atlantic Monthly,* May 1867, pp. 612–618, and "Oldport Wharves," *Atlantic Monthly,* January 1868, pp. 61–68.

173 "When the freedmen are lost in the mass of freemen"; "Fail in this result": TWH, "Fair Play the Best Policy," *Atlantic Monthly,* May 1865, pp. 623, 625.

173 "I do not want to give any more years of my life": TWH to AH and LH, October 8, 1865, Houghton.

173 "If it had been left to him": TWH, "The South Victorious in Georgia," *Independent,* May 24, 1866, p. 4.

174 "what most men mean to-day": TWH, "Too Many Compliments," *Independent,* October 26, 1865, p. 4.

174 "Do you suppose that black men are born": TWH, "Political Notes," *Springfield Republican,* May 9, 1867, p. 1.

174 "Galloping through green lanes": *Army Life,* p. 106.

174 Howard Mumford Jones: See Howard Mumford Jones, introduction to *Army Life in a Black Regiment,* by TWH (Lansing: Michigan State University Press, 1960), pp. vii–xvii.

175 "Doubts trembled in my mind": *Army Life,* pp. 123–124. Contemporary academic critics read Higginson's book and, in particular, this chapter as deflected homoeroticism and cross-racial identity. See Christopher Looby, " 'As Thoroughly Black as the Most Faithful Philanthropist Could Desire': Erotics of Race in Higginson's *Army Life in a Black Regiment,"* in

Stecopoulos and Uebel, *Race and the Subject of Masculinities,* pp. 71–115, and Looby, "Flowers of Manhood."

176 "All Southern white men": TWH, "The Logic of Must," *Independent,* September 7, 1865, p. 4.

176 "It is we who are permitting black loyalists to be disarmed": TWH, "Too Many Compliments," *Independent,* October 26, 1865, p. 4.

176 "It is not that politics are so unworthy": TWH, "A Plea for Culture," pp. 34, 36.

177 "A precious—mouldering pleasure—'tis—": Fr 569.

177 "In these later years, the arduous reforms": TWH, "Literature as an Art," p. 754.

177 "I don't believe there is a man here": TWH, journal, May 16, 1876, Houghton.

177 "Nobody has any weight in America": *Malbone,* p. 99.

177 "except to secure the ballot for woman": TWH, "Literature as an Art," p. 745.

177 "My nature seems to be rather that of an artist": TWH to Ralph Waldo Emerson, July 4, 1864, Houghton.

178 "Is it . . . a great consecration": TWH, "An Artist's Dream," *Atlantic Monthly,* July 1867, p. 103.

178 "the artist had attained his dream": TWH, "An Artist's Dream," p. 108.

179 he had modeled Malbone: The name Malbone also refers to the late-eighteenth-century miniaturist Edward Malbone, born in Newport.

179 "a certain wild, entangled look": *Malbone,* p. 8.

179 "Every one must have something": *Malbone,* p. 150.

179 "Forgive me if I am frightened"; "Manner between Angie Tilton & Mr. Alcott"; and subsequent quotations: TWH to MCH, [August 16, 17, 1870], BPL.

180 anyone "who drained my nerve power"; "I am glad not to live": TWH to MCH, notes, [August 1870], BPL.

181 "Say in a long time": TWH to MCH, notes, [August 1870], BPL.

CHAPTER TEN: HER DEATHLESS SYLLABLE

182 "the Vein cannot thank the Artery": ED to TWH, [c. October 1870], *Letters,* 2:479.

182 "the most eminent poetess in the world": TWH, "Sappho," p. 83.

182 "unapproached among women": TWH, "Sappho," p. 86.

182 "Could you not come without the Lecture": ED to TWH, [October 1870], *Letters,* 2:482. This letter exists in pencil draft only at Amherst; there is no copy among TWH's papers at BPL. We therefore do not know if it was sent to Higginson, though I suspect it was.

182 "When I hoped I feared—": Fr 594; the poem had evidently been composed five years earlier.

182 "Remembrance has a Rear and Front": Fr 1234.

183 "I remember your coming": ED to TWH, September 26, 1870, *Letters,* 2:479–80.

183 "Trust adjusts her 'Peradventure'—": Fr 1177.

183 "You told me Mrs Lowell was Mr Lowell's 'inspiration' ": ED to TWH, [October 1870], *Letters* 2:481.

183 no wonder her brother: MLT, journal, October 18, 1891, Yale.

183 "The Riddle that we guess": Fr 1180A, in ED to TWH, [October 1870], *Letters,* 2:480.

184 "You ask great questions accidentally": ED to TWH, September 26, 1870, *Letters,* 2:479.

184 "Too happy Time dissolves itself": Fr 1182.

184 "I was refreshed by your strong Letter": ED to TWH, [October 1870], *Letters,* 2:481.

184 "Thank you for Greatness": ED to TWH, [October 1870], *Letters,* 2:481.

184 "You place the truth in opposite—": ED to TWH, [October 1870], *Letters,* 2:481.

184 "Step lightly on this narrow Spot—": Fr 1227.

184 if it belonged to her: ED to TWH, June 7, 1862, *Letters,* 2:408.

185 "I thank these Kinsmen of the Shelf—": Fr 512.

185 "Stronger than any written": ED to TWH, November 1871, *Letters,* 2:491.

185 "I thought I spoke to you of the shadow": ED to TWH, [October 1870], *Letters,* 2:481.

185 "Amherst must be a *nest* of poetesses"; "letters from Emily Dickinson": TWH, quoted in Lydia B. Torrey to Emily Fowler Ford, November 16, 1872, NYPL.

186 "I do think Amherst girls turn out (excuse me—) horridly!": HHJ to Henry Root, March 1854, Colorado.

186 "if I say a shorter time it will be longer": TWH, notes, [August 16, 17, 1870], BPL.

186 "Her friendships with men had the frankness": TWH, "Mrs. Helen Jackson (H. H.)," p. 256.

186 "the one great duty": HHJ, *Mercy Philbrick's Choice,* p. 71.

186 "knocks like a baby at the door": HHJ to Kate Field, March 7, 1866, BPL.

186 "I shall never write a sentence": *Contemp.,* p. 156.

186 He praised her novels: See *Contemp.,* p. 163.

187 "perfection in every sentence": TWH, "Charlotte Prince Hawes," *Radical,* January 1867, p. 283.

187 "In almost any town in New England": TWH, "The Higher Education of Woman: A Paper Read before the Social Science Convention, May 1, 1873," in *Journal of Social Science* (1873): 38.

187 Everyone walks through the door: See Gornick, *The Solitude of Self,* for a particularly illuminating analysis of the radical and liberal feminism created at this juncture.

188 "Without deprecating the value": Circular letter signed by Lucy Stone, Caroline M. Severance, Julia Ward Howe, TWH, and George H. Vibbert, August 6, 1869, Stowe Center.

188 "No! my dear friend": Elizabeth Cady Stanton to TWH, June 13, 1868, BPL.

188 "The world has always more respect": TWH to Harriet Beecher Stowe, October 11, 1868, Stowe Center.

188 "before the war he never missed a good fight": *Dear Preceptor,* p. 248.

188 "If the conservatives think": TWH, quoted in Stanton, Anthony, and Gage, *History of Woman Suffrage,* 2:803.

188 an "Intellectual History of Women"—"my *magnum opus*": TWH, p. 284.

189 "If there is only one woman in the nation": TWH, *Common Sense about Women,* pp. 397–398. This volume collects most of Higginson's writings from *The Woman's Journal.*

189 "The yearning for a literary career"; "reveal such intellectual ardor": TWH, *Common Sense about Women,* pp. 259–260.

190 "I am happy you have the Travel"; "Could you come again": ED to TWH, [1872], *Letters,* 2:500.

190 "To disappear enhances—The Man that runs away": Fr 1239C.

190 "He preached opon 'Breadth' till it argued him narrow—": Fr 1266.

190 "The Sea said 'Come' to the Brook—": Fr 1275.

191 "Thank you for the 'Lesson' ": ED to TWH, [late 1872], *Letters,* 2:501.

191 "Could you teach me now?" or "Will you instruct me then no more?": ED to TWH, [1873], *Letters,* 2:511. These are from two different letters.

191 "Longing is like the Seed": Fr 1298A.

191 "Dominion lasts until obtained—": Fr 1299.

191 "The Wind begun to knead the Grass— / As Women do a Dough—": 796A; "The Wind begun to rock the Grass / With threatening tunes and low—": Fr 796D.

192 "Your poem about the storm is fine": TWH to ED, December 31, 1873, Houghton.

193 "I don't dare die": MCH, quoted in Elliott, *This Was My Newport,* p. 84.

193 "particularly absurd in E. D.'s case": MCH quoted in TWH to AH, December 9, 1873, Houghton.

193 "I saw my eccentric poetess"; "How long are you going to stay": TWH to AH, December 9, 1873, Houghton.

193 "& especially the time spent with you": TWH to ED, December 31, 1873, Houghton.

193 "Thank you, dear friend, for my 'New Year' ": ED to TWH, [January 1874], *Letters,* 2:518.

194 "When the paths that we have personally traversed": TWH, *Oldport Days* (Boston: J. R. Osgood, 1873), p. 266.

194 "I have fineness": TWH, journal, February 20, 1869, Houghton.

194 "My gentility is chronic": TWH to unknown recipient, December 26, 1873, Houghton.

194 "I wish you could see some field lilies": TWH to ED, December 31, 1873, Houghton.

195 She replied to Higginson: For an account of the revisions, see Fr, 3:1135–1139.

195 "Because that you are going": Fr 1314.

CHAPTER ELEVEN: THE REALM OF YOU

197 " 'well enough' ": Walter Dean Howells, quoted in TWH to William Dean Howells, September 30, 1871, Houghton.

197 "I hate to write in anything but the Atlantic": TWH to LH and AH, [1871], Houghton. The piece in question is "A Day of Scottish Games," published in the January 1872 issue of *Scribner's Monthly* (pp. 329–336).

197 Henry Adams: See [Adams], "Frothingham's Transcendentalism," p. 470.

198 "they rely for success": TWH, "Literature as an Art," p. 747.

198 "everything which does not tend to money": *Malbone,* p. 98.

198 "For all young Fancy's": See *Afternoon Landscape,* p. 88.

199 "In spite of my fine physique": TWH, journal, April 18, 1873, Houghton.

199 "The walls seem only to draw closer": TWH, journal, September 25, 1875, Houghton.

199 "My life indeed has disappointed me": TWH, journal, December 22, 1876, Houghton.

199 "The truth is . . . that the child does not trouble himself": TWH, "Childhood's Fancies," *Scribner's Monthly,* January 1876, p. 362.

200 Never a Republican: See EdD to WAD, February 18, 1874, quoted in *Home,* p. 451.

200 His head felt light: For the account of Dickinson's death, see MLT to TWH, July 9, 1891, Yale, p. 224.

200 "We were all lost, though I didn't know how": ED to Louise and Frances Norcross, [summer 1874], *Letters,* 2:526.

201 "There, father, I never dared do that while you were living": WAD, quoted in Mary Lee Hall to MTB, August 5, 1933, Yale.

201 "he seemed peculiarly pleased": ED to TWH, [July 1874], *Letters,* 2:528.

201 "Mr. Bowles was with us": ED to TWH, [July 1874], *Letters,* 2:528.

201 The shops of Amherst had closed: Information about the funeral is from the *Springfield Republican,* June 20, 1874, and MDB, *Emily Dickinson Face to Face,* p. 13.

201 "Miss Vinnie told me": Mary Lee Hall to MTB, December 29, 1939, Yale.

202 "His Heart was pure and terrible": ED to TWH, [July 1874], *Letters,* 2:528.

202 "Though it is many nights": ED to Louise and Frances Norcross, [summer 1874], *Letters,* 2:526.

202 "without any body": ED to Louise and Frances Norcross, [August 1876], *Letters,* 2:559.

202 "Home is so far from Home": ED to TWH, July 1875, *Letters,* 2:542.

202 "I have wished for you"; "Your beautiful Hymn": ED to TWH, [July 1874], *Letters,* 2:528.

203 the protofeminist speaker: As Mary Loeffelholz points out in her fine article "Dickinson's 'Decoration,' " the poem was reprinted in *The Woman's Journal* just after it appeared in *Scribner's Monthly.* She also conjectures the identity of the woman as Margaret Elliott Hazard.

203 "I thought that being a Poem one's self": ED to TWH, [May 1874], *Letters,* 2:525.

203 And when "Decoration" appeared in *Scribner's Monthly*: See TWH, "Decoration," p. 234.

203 "It has assisted that Pause of Space": ED to TWH, July 1874, *Letters,* 2:528.

203 "The broadest words": ED to TWH, [late May 1874], *Letters,* 2:525.

203 "had twice seen you": ED to TWH, January 1876, *Letters,* 2:547.

203 "Mother was paralyzed Tuesday": ED to TWH, [mid-June 1875], *Letters,* 2:542.

203 "I am glad": ED to TWH, [July 1875], *Letters,* 2:542.

204 "Knowing that his fraternal love towards me": ED, quoted in *YH,* 2:237.

204 Emily named Vinnie: See *YH,* 2:261.

204 "weird & strange power": TWH to AH, November 30, 1875, Houghton.

204 "I have a little manuscript volume": HHJ to ED, March 20, 1876, Houghton.

204 "asked me for my Mind": ED to TWH, April 25, 1862, *Letters,* 2:405.

205 "My Brother and Sisters would love to see you": ED to TWH, [May 1874], *Letters,* 2:525.

205 "The last of Summer is Delight—": Fr 1380; "The Heart is the Capital of the Mind": Fr 1381C; "The Mind lives on the Heart": Fr 1384; "The Rat is the conciseset Tenant": Fr 1369; " 'Faithful to the end' amended": Fr 1386.

205 or, in an earlier version, "be lean": "The Mind lives on the Heart": Fr 1384A.

206 "the writer, when he adopts a high aim": TWH, "Literature as an Art," p. 753.

206 "I often go Home in thought to you": ED to TWH, [February 1876], *Letters,* 2:548.

206 "It makes me happy to send you the Book": ED to TWH, [February 1876], *Letters,* 2:548.

206 The one they called "Immortality"; "I believed it would": ED to TWH, [spring 1876], *Letters,* 2:551. Thomas Johnson conjectures that the poem is " 'Faithful to the end' amended." I have my doubts.

206 "You once told me": ED to TWH, [February 1876], *Letters,* 2:548.

206 "I was lonely": ED to TWH, [spring 1876], *Letters,* 2:551.

206 "I sued the News—yet feared—the News": Fr 1391.

206 "The things we thought that we should do": Fr 1279.

207 "I wish your friend had my strength": ED to TWH, [spring 1876], *Letters,* 2:551.

207 "May I cherish it twice": ED to MCH, [spring 1876], *Letters,* 2:554.

207 "I am glad to have been": ED to TWH, [spring 1876], *Letters,* 2:553.

207 "a little Granite Book you can lean upon": ED to MCH, [December 1876], *Letters,* 2:569.

207 "I am glad if I did not": ED to MCH, [August 1876], *Letters,* 2:558.

207 "Your letters always surprise me": ED to TWH, [June 1869], *Letters,* 2:186.

207 "I hoped you might show me something of your's": ED to TWH, [August 1877], *Letters,* 2:588.

207 "Thank you for having written the 'Atlantic Essays' ": ED to TWH, [November 1871], *Letters,* 2:491.

207 "I was re-reading 'Oldport' ": ED to TWH, [January 1874], *Letters,* 2:518.

208 "A Wind that woke a lone Delight": Fr 1216D.

208 "Though inaudible": ED to TWH, [spring 1876], *Letters,* 2:553.

208 "Your thought is so serious": ED to TWH, [spring 1876], *Letters,* 2:552.

208 "That it is true": ED to TWH, [January 1876], *Letters,* 2:546.

208 "Candor—my Preceptor—is the only wile": ED to TWH, [February 1876], *Letters,* 2:548. She alludes to his paragraph in the prelude to *Malbone:* "One learns, in growing older, that no fiction can be so strange nor appear so improbable as would the simple truth; and that doubtless even Shakespeare did but timidly transcribe a few of the deeds and passions he had personally known. For no man of middle age can dare trust himself to portray life in its full intensity, as he has studied or shared it; he must resolutely set aside as indescribable the things most worth describing, and must expect to be charged with exaggeration, even when he tells the rest."

208 "I almost inferred from your accent": ED to TWH, [August 1876], *Letters,* 2:559.

208 "Surely, in the shelter of such *double* anonymousness": HHJ to ED, [summer 1876], *Letters,* 2:563.

208 "I felt [li]ke a [gr]eat ox"; "Let somebody somewhere": HHJ to ED, [fall 1876], *Letters,* 2:565.

209 "I told her I was unwilling": ED to TWH, [October 1876], *Letters,* 2:563.

209 "Often, when troubled by entreaty": ED to TWH, [early 1877], *Letters,* 2:573.

209 Misunderstanding her request: Critics once read *Mercy Philbrick's Choice* as based on Helen Hunt's and Higginson's unplighted friendship; other critics find Emily Dickinson in the figure of Mercy Philbrick, a woman devoted to her art. But this latter reading is strained. However, the male protagonist, Stephen White, bears some resemblance to Higginson in that he is preternaturally devoted to an ill, cranky mother who resembles Mary. And doubtless the novel contains Helen Hunt's evaluation of the Higginson marriage: "This tyrannical woman held him chained. His submission to her would have seemed abject, if it had not been based on a sentiment and grounded in a loyalty which compelled respect" (p. 71).

209 "My dear friend": TWH to ED, [fall 1876], *Letters,* 2:564.

210 "I thought your approbation": ED to TWH, [January 1877], *Letters,* 2:572.

210 Friends of Vinnie's: See *YH,* 2:253.

211 It occupies a "special place": HHJ to ED, October 25, 1878, *Letters,* 2:626.

211 "Though we know": ED to TWH, [June 1877], *Letters,* 2:583.

211 "Lay this Laurel on the One": Fr 1428C.

211 "I have no other Playmate": ED to TWH, [August 1877], *Letters,* 2:588; "It sounded as if the streets were running": Fr 1454C; "She laid her docile Crescent down": Fr 1453C; "I have no Life but this—": Fr 1432C; "After all Birds have been investigated and laid aside": Fr 1383.

212 "the loving you" and "the love of you": See Fr, 3:1251–1253.

213 "The Wilderness is new—": ED to TWH, [September 1877], *Letters,* 2:590.

CHAPTER TWELVE: MOMENTS OF PREFACE

214 "Your Face is more joyful": ED to TWH, [October 1876], *Letters,* 2:566.

214 "How little there seems left to be done": TWH, journal, September 2, 1877, Houghton.

214 "With sorrow": ED to TWH, [September 1877], BPL.

214 "Perhaps she does not go so far": Fr 1455C; "If I could help you?": ED to TWH, [September 1877], *Letters,* 2:590.

215 "Danger is not at first": ED to TWH, [autumn 1877], *Letters,* 2:594.

215 "To be human": ED to TWH, [September 1877], *Letters,* 2:592.

215 At least one Dickinson biographer: See Taggard, *The Life and Mind of Emily Dickinson,* p. 318.

216 "I remember nothing so strong": ED to TWH, [September 1877], *Letters,* 2:592.

216 "Dear Mr Bowles found out too late": ED to Elizabeth Holland, [early 1878], *Letters,* 2:604.

216 "I felt it shelter to speak with you": ED to TWH, January 19, 1878, *Letters,* 2:599.

216 "When you have lost a friend": ED to TWH, [early June 1878], *Letters,* 2:611.

216 A military Rip Van Winkle: See TWH to AH, February 28, 1878, Houghton.

216 "inalienable muttonchop whiskers": Wilson, *Patriotic Gore,* p. 488.

216 "I began to feel fearfully bewildered": TWH to AH, February 22, 1878, Houghton.

216 "An individual seems so insignificant": TWH, journal, February 21–25, 1878, Houghton.

216 "The same sky was above her"; "I hold it utterly ungenerous": See TWH, "Some War Scenes Revisited."

217 Incensed, Higginson had denounced the . . . massacre: TWH, "Border Ruffianism in South Carolina," p. 1.

218 "The Hope of seeing you was so sweet and serious—": ED to TWH, [March 1878], *Letters,* 2:607.

218 "Is this the Hope that opens and shuts": ED to TWH, [June 1878], *Letters,* 2:611.

218 "How brittle are the Piers": Fr 1459.

218 "I have felt like a troubled Top": ED to Elizabeth Holland, [December 1877], *Letters,* 2:596.

219 Darwin looked older: See TWH, "Carlyle's Laugh," p. 465; for his travels, see also TWH, "The Road to England" and "Literary Paris Twenty Years Ago."

219 "There is no one so happy": ED to TWH, [December 1878], *Letters,* 2:627.

219 "known little of Literature": ED to TWH, [February 1879], *Letters,* 2:635.

219 she responded with typical humor: ED to TWH, [December 1879], *Letters,* 2:649.

220 "Must I lose the Friend": ED to TWH, [1879], *Letters,* 2:649.

220 Such coincident occasions: Though we don't know when Dickinson began her romance with Judge Lord, I suspect that, had she been in love with him at the time of Higginson's marriage, she would have mailed him a poem slightly less reserved than the one she did send, reiterating themes haunting her work since her father's death (I have copied the poem with the breaks that appeared in the letter to Higginson, BPL (1093):

> We knew not that
> We were to live
> Nor when — we are
> to die —
> Our ignorance our
> Cuirass is —
> We wear Mortality
> As lightly as an
> Option Gown
> till asked to take it
> off.
> By his intrusion, God
> is known —
> It is the same
> with Life —

220 "Judge Lord never seemed to coalesce": SGD, "Annals of the Evergreens," typed ms., n.d., Houghton.

221 "strong in his intellect": "Otis Phillips Lord," in Hurd, *History of Essex County, Massachusetts,* p. xliv.

221 "Calvary and May": ED to Benjamin Kimball, [1885], *Letters,* 3:861.

221 And he and she exchanged vows: Lord's letters to Dickinson were burned by the vigilant Vinnie, so we cannot be sure when the romance began. Biographers like Richard Sewall and Cynthia Wolff, following MTB, who first published evidence of the relationship, posit 1878 as the date of the earliest of these passionate fragments, but more recently — and more persuasively — Alfred Habegger has suggested that the romance began at a later time, particularly since Elizabeth Lord died only the year before. Similarly, I tend to think that the romance did not begin to flower until early 1880, though this, too, is a guess.

222 "the trespass of my rustic Love": ED to Otis Lord, [April 1882], Werner A 742e. I have followed the corrective numbering-chronology offered in Marta Werner's diligent *Emily Dickinson's Open Folios.* Those interested in Dickinson's letters to Lord should begin with this volume despite its occasional mistakes in transcription; it does offer a more convincing array of letters and suggests a better chronology than that offered by Johnson.

222 "Yet Tenderness has not a Date": ED to Otis Lord, [April 30, 1882?], Werner A 742f.

222 "Judge Lord was with us": ED to TWH, [October 1876], *Letters,* 2:566.

222 "Sweetest Name": ED to Otis Lord, n.d., Werner A 748b.

222 "You said with loved timidity": ED to Otis Lord, [December 3, 1882], Werner 749d.

222 "That was a big—sweet Story—": ED to Otis Lord, [April 30, 1882?], Werner A 742.

223 "My lovely Salem smiles at me"; "I confess that I love him—": ED to Otis Lord, n.d., Werner A 734, 735.

223 In another draft of a letter: ED to Otis Lord, n.d., Werner A 736.

223 "To lie so near your longing—": ED to Otis Lord, [1878–1879], Werner A 740.

223 "Dont you know you are happiest": ED to Otis Lord, n.d., Werner A 739.

223 "Tuesday is a deeply depressed Day": ED to Otis Lord, n.d., Werner A 757, 757a.

223 "Were Departure Separation": [ED to Otis Lord?]; see *Revelation,* p. 94, and Werner, p. 275n: the original manuscript is missing.

224 In the summer of 1878: See " 'Saxe Holm' Evolved," the *Springfield Republican,* July 25, 1878, pp. 3–4.

224 "We can only say that we happen to know": *Springfield Republican,* August 3, 1878, p. 3.

224 "an old-fashioned girl"; "exquisitely refined & dainty in all her ways": TWH to Ellen Conway, November 4, 1878, Butler.

225 his "only safety"; "I'm adrift in the universe without it": TWH to Ellen Conway, December 6, 1878, Butler.

225 "clear good-sense and . . . modest faithfulness": TWH, "Seaside and Prairie," p. 3.

225 "I shall pick 'May flowers' more furtively": ED to TWH, [spring 1880], *Letters,* 3:661. Interestingly, he waited over a year before he shared the compliments with Dickinson, or she waited to answer him.

225 "I shall no doubt": TWH to Ellen Conway, October 20, 1879, Butler.

226 "The Face in Evanescence lain": Fr 1521.

226 "Most of our Moments": ED to TWH, [spring 1880], *Letters,* 3:660.

226 "dazzling Baby": ED to TWH, [August 1880], *Letters,* 3:668.

226 "I know but little of Little Ones": ED to TWH, [summer 1881], *Letters,* 3:711.

226 " 'Go traveling with us'!": Fr 1561.

227 "It is such inexpressible happiness": TWH to AH, December 22, 1880, Houghton.

227 "The responsibility of Pathos": ED to Elizabeth Holland, [fall 1880], *Letters,* 3:675.

228 "very improper": ED to Elizabeth Holland, July 1889, *Letters,* 3:667.

228 "I have promised three Hymns": ED to TWH, [November 1880], *Letters,* 3:680.

228 "The thoughtfulness I may not accept": ED to TWH, [November 1880], *Letters,* 3:681.

228 "A Route of Evanescence": Fr 1489E.

228 "My Country's Wardrobe": "My country need not change her gown," Fr 1540; "The Savior must have been": Fr 1538.

229 "Mine Enemy is growing old—": Fr 1539B.

229 Cotton Mather would have burned her as a witch: Allen Tate, "Emily Dickinson," in Sewall, *Emily Dickinson,* p. 27.

CHAPTER THIRTEEN: THINGS THAT NEVER
CAN COME BACK

230 Hearing him scream: See MLT, journal, October 18, 1891, Yale.
230 " 'Aunt Emily, speaking of someone' ": Edward (Ned) Dickinson, quoted in MDB, *Emily Dickinson Face to Face*, p. 169.
232 "had gone back and become a young brother again": MDB, *Emily Dickinson Face to Face*, p. 171.
232 It was a privilege: See MDB, *Emily Dickinson Face to Face*, p. 45.
232 Adored by his family and fussed over: See "Death of a Promising Boy," *Amherst Record*, October 17, 1883.
232 "He gathered Hearts": ED to SGD, [October 1884], *Letters*, 3:842.
232 "Your Urchin": ED to SGD, [1880], *Letters*, 3:673.
232 A yellow wide-brimmed planter's hat: See Claude M. Fuess, *Amherst: The Story of a New England College* (Boston: Little, Brown, 1935), p. 135, and Vryling Buffum to MTB, Yale.
232 Foraging through picture galleries: See *YH*, 2:41.
233 like "meeting God face to face": SGD, "Annals of the Evergreens," typed ms., n.d., Houghton.
233 "socially ambitious"—"perhaps a little too aggressive": Burgess, *Reminiscences of an American Scholar*, p. 60.
233 "Sue saw no one as a child": MLT, "Short Character Sketches," [1882], Yale.
234 "rare hours, full of merriment": Catherine Anthon to MDB, October 8, 1914, Houghton.
234 "a really brilliant and highly cultivated woman": Burgess, *Reminiscences of an American Scholar*, p. 60.
234 "The tie between us": ED to SGD, [late 1885], *Letters*, 3:893.
234 "Dear Sue—": ED to SGD, [c. 1882], *Letters*, 3:733.
235 "One Sister have I in our house—": Fr 5A.
235 "But Susan is a stranger yet—": Fr 1433C (variant of "What mystery pervades a well!").
235 "I feel the red in my mind": ED to Elizabeth Holland, *Letters*, 2:452.
236 "The Things that never can come back, are several—": Fr 1564; also in ED to Elizabeth Holland, [fall 1881], *Letters*, 3:714, and chapter 3.
237 "I think everyone will exclaim over it": MLT, journal, [summer 1879], quoted in *Austin and Mabel*, p. 52.
237 "My little one will, I feel, be always secondary": MLT, journal, October 6, 1879, MLT Papers, Yale.
237 Having been "taken in": See MLT reminiscence, MTB Papers, Yale.
237 who "stimulates me intellectually more than any other woman": MLT to WAD, [February 17, 1883], Yale.
238 "She thinks it is such a fine thing"; "I could twist him around my little finger": MLT, journal, March 2, 1882, Yale.
238 "their little affair": MLT, journal, September 15, 1882, Yale.
239 "dear" Mr. Austin Dickinson "is so very fond of me"; "to think that out of all the splendid & noble women": MLT, journal, September 15, 1882, Yale.
239 "It nearly broke my heart": WAD to MLT, [fall 1882], Yale; "I love you,

I admire you": WAD to MLT, [1882], Yale; "The sun cannot shine without": WAD to MLT, [1882], Yale. All quoted in *Austin and Mabel,* pp. 135, 138, 145.

239   "The way in which you love me": MLT to WAD, [November 29, 1883], Yale.

239   "The greatest proof I have *ever* had": MLT, journal, August 3, 1883, Yale.

239   "Ned has been very devoted": MLT, journal, December 6, 1882, Yale.

240   "Where is the wrong in preferring sunshine to shadow!": WAD to MLT, [November 1882?], Yale.

240   It would take another year: The best analysis of the affair can be found in Gay, *The Bourgeois Experience,* pp. 71–108; for a full account of the affair, see *Austin and Mabel.*

240   "Emily always respected real emotion": MTB, diary, March 27, 1851, Yale.

240   "If anything happens to me": WAD, quoted in *Austin and Mabel,* p. 139.

240   "She has not been outside": MLT to Mary and Eben Loomis, November 6, 1881, Yale.

240   some of Emily's strange, powerful poems: See MLT, diary, February 8, 1882, Yale.

240   "All the literary men are after her": MLT, diary, March 26, 1882, Yale.

241   " 'You will not allow your husband to go there' ": *Revelation,* p. 59.

241   Before Austin would cross another Rubicon: WAD, diary, September 11, 1882, box 101, Yale.

241   "It was odd to think": MLT, journal, September 16, 1882, Yale.

241   "A Route of Evanescence": Fr 1489F.

241   "That without suspecting it": ED to MLT, [September 1882], *Letters,* 3:740. Dickinson had also sent this poem, which she clearly liked, to Helen Hunt Jackson, her Norcross cousins, and Sarah Tuckerman before sending it to Higginson for his approval in 1880 and then consenting to offer it for auction at a charity benefit.

241   "I have just had a most lovely note": MLT, journal, October 6, 1882, Yale.

242   "The great mission of pain": ED to Frances and Louise Norcross, [late November 1882], *Letters,* 3:750.

242   "We were never intimate": ED to Elizabeth Holland, [December 1882], *Letters,* 3:754.

242   A cousin recalled: Clara Newman Turner, "My Personal Acquaintance with Emily Dickinson," quoted in *YH,* 2:383.

242   "My Brother is with us so often": ED to James D. Clark, [mid-March 1883], *Letters,* 3:765.

242   "Blow has followed blow": ED to Elizabeth Holland, [mid-December 1882], *Letters,* 3:754.

242   the "coals of fire": TWH to Moncure Conway, June 9, 1882, Butler.

242   "a intimacy of many years": ED to James D. Clark, [August 1882], *Letters,* 3:737.

243   "He rang one summer evening": ED to James C. Clark, [August 1882], *Letters,* 3:738.

243   "Your Sorrow was in Winter—": ED to Otis Lord, [December 3, 1882], Werner A 749c.

243   "Further in Summer than the Birds": Fr 895D.

244 " 'Open the Door' ": ED to Elizabeth Holland, [1883], *Letters*, 3:803.

244 "Emily was devoted": LD to unknown recipients, November 16, [1883], UVA.

244 "I see him in the Star": ED to SGD, [October 1883], *Letters*, 3:799.

244 "Gilbert was his idol": MLT, journal, November 11, 1883, Yale.

244 "I kept him alive": MLT, journal, March 30, 1884, Yale.

245 "He, the youthful serious young scientist": MTB, drafts, February 27–August 30, 1927, Yale.

245 "I do not think David is": MLT, journal, February 6, 1890, Yale.

245 "beyond anything I have known": WAD to MLT, July 6, 1885, Yale.

245 Adultery, he told his daughter: See MTB, notes on an interview with her father, David Peck Todd, September 29–October 3, 1933, Yale.

245 "every one knows that he": MLT, journal, January 6, 1885, Yale.

246 "the law of God": MLT journal, March 4, 1885, Yale.

246 "Our life together is as white and unspotted": WAD to MLT, [October 1884], Yale.

246 "The whole town weeps for him": MLT, diary, August 19, 1895, Yale.

CHAPTER FOURTEEN: MONARCH OF DREAMS

247 "from a race of day-dreamers": TWH, "The Monarch of Dreams," holograph, Houghton.

247 " 'Does all dreaming without action' ": TWH, "The Monarch of Dreams," holograph, Houghton.

247 "felt himself a changed being": *Monarch*, p. 48.

248 "the lost opportunity": *Monarch*, p. 52.

248 "It is a warning": TWH to AH, December 7, 1886, Houghton.

248 "To live and die only to transfuse external nature": TWH, "Literature as an Art," p. 747.

248 this "has made me willing to vary my life": TWH, journal, frontispiece, 1873, Houghton.

249 "The trouble with me": TWH, journal, March 14, 1875, Houghton.

249 "I died for Beauty—but was scarce": Fr 448; Beauty and truth are "Kinsmen": This perplexing poem, narrated by one of Dickinson's posthumous speakers, is also a response to Elizabeth Barrett Browning's *Vision*: "These were poets true, / Who died for Beauty as martyrs do / For Truth—the ends being scarcely two" (lines 289–291); see Pollak, "Dickinson, Poe, and Barrett Browning," p. 124.

250 "as a swimmer yields his body to a strong current": TWH, "The Monarch of Dreams," holograph, Houghton.

250 "I began to doubt everything": "A Night in the Water," in *Army Life*, pp. 123–124.

250 Few of his accomplishments: See TWH to LSH, January 29, 1862, Houghton.

250 "I'm adrift in the universe without it": TWH to Ellen Conway, December 6, 1878, Butler.

250 "My favorite child": TWH to Edmund Clarence Stedman, October 24, 1887, Butler.

251 "The Pilgrims landed": "More Mingled Races" [1897], in *Book and Heart,*
p. 151.

251 "inexpedient . . . to advocate women's suffrage": Harper, *The House of
Harper,* p. 250.

251 "The Mendelssohn family had not the slightest objection": TWH, "The
Shadow of the Harem," in *W&M,* p. 251.

252 "in a literary way": TWH to Moncure Conway, [1884], Butler.

253 "no thin idealist, no coarse realist": quoted in TWH, "Margaret Fuller
Ossoli," in Parton, et al., *Eminent Women of the Age,* p. 186.

253 "I affirm that democratic society": TWH, "Americanism in Literature,"
p. 62.

253 "actual life—the life of every day": TWH, "Literature in a Republic"
(1892), in Reed et al., *Modern Eloquence,* 5:574.

253 "the aristocracy of the millionaires is only a prelude": *Part,* p. 110.

253 "Sow a victim, and you reap a socialist": *Book and Heart,* p. 173.

254 Yet he apparently said nothing: Tilden Edelstein points out that Higginson's social views were in flux: he had supported labor during the
Amesbury-Salisbury strike of 1852, but during the labor strikes of 1887
he said nothing either; see *Strange Enthusiasm,* pp. 378–379.

CHAPTER FIFTEEN: PUGILIST AND POET

255 she wrapped small gifts: The turquoise brooch is described in Barney,
"Fragments from Emily Dickinson," p. 801.

255 "The doctor calls it 'revenge of the nerves' ": ED to Louise and Frances
Norcross, [August 1884], *Letters,* 3:827.

255 For several days she seemed delirious: See SGD to Martha Dickinson,
October 22, 1884, Houghton.

255 "Biography first convinces us of the fleeing of the Biographied": ED to
TWH, [February 1885], *Letters,* 3:864.

255 "Pass to thy Rendezvous of Light": Fr 1624.

255 "I work to drive the awe away": ED to Louise and Frances Norcross,
[March 1884], *Letters,* 3:817.

256 "How *can* the sun shine": Mary Lee Hall to Genevieve Taggard, November 4, 1929, NYPL.

256 "I have not been strong for the last year": ED to Mrs. Samuel E. Mack,
[autumn 1884], *Letters,* 3:843.

256 "The Crisis of the sorrow": ED to Elizabeth Holland, [late 1883], *Letters,*
3:802.

256 "the Flood subject": ED to TWH, June 8, 1866, *Letters,* 2:454.

256 "Exterior—to Time—": In Fr 446.

256 "Circumference, thou bride": ED to Daniel Chester French, [April
1884], *Letters,* 3:822, see also Fr 1636B; "Success is dust": ED to Daniel
Chester French, [April 1884], *Letters,* 2:821.

256 "My Business is Circumference": ED to TWH, [July 1862], *Letters,* 2:412.

257 "How happy is the little Stone": Fr 1570; "Come show thy Durham
Breast to her who loves thee best": Fr 1572B; "Obtaining but our own
extent": Fr 1573; "The Moon upon her fluent route": Fr 1574B.

257 "No Brigadier throughout the Year": Fr 1596.

258 "it is a cruel wrong to your 'day & generation' ": HHJ to ED, September 5, 1884, Houghton.

258 "The kind but incredible opinion": ED to Thomas Niles, [April 1882], *Letters*, 3:725.

258 "Further in Summer than the Birds": Fr 895D; "It sifts from Leaden Sieves—": Fr 291E; see also Fr 291D.

258 "I would not for the world rob you of this very rare book": Thomas Niles to ED, March 31, 1883, *Letters*, 3:769.

258 "the Bird seemed true": Thomas Niles to ED, [April 1883], *Letters*, 3:769.

258 "The Wind begun to rock the Grass": Fr 796; "A Route of Evanescence": Fr 1489; "Ample make this Bed—": Fr 804.

259 "Pupil"; "Emblem is immeasurable—": ED to TWH, [April 1883], *Letters*, 3:773.

259 " 'And yet I live!' ": TWH, "Sunshine and Petrarch," p. 310; "Antony's remark to a friend": ED to Otis Lord, Werner A 741a. Higginson revised himself—making the passage worse—when he republished "Sunshine and Petrarch" in *Oldport Days:* " 'And yet I live!' What a pause is implied before these words! the drawing of a long breath, immeasurably long; like that vast interval of heart-beats that precedes Shakespeare's 'Since Cleopatra died.' I can think of no other passage in literature that has in it the same wide spaces of emotion." He returned to the subject in his 1888 sonnet "Since Cleopatra Died": MWH, *The Century*, June 2, 1888, p. 256.

> "Since Cleopatra died
> I have lived in such dishonor, that the world
> Doth wonder at my baseness." {*Antony and Cleopatra*}

> "Since Cleopatra died!" Long years are past,
>   In Antony's fancy, since the deed was done.
>   Love counts its epochs, not from sun to sun,
>   But by the heart-throb. Mercilessly fast
> Time has swept onward since she looked her last
>   On life, a queen. For him the sands have run
>   Whole ages through their glass, and kings have won
>   And lost their empires o'er earth's surface vast
> Since Cleopatra died. Ah! Love and Pain
>   Make their own measure of all things that be.
>   No clock's slow ticking marks their deathless strain;
> The life they own is not the life we see;
>   Love's single moment is eternity;
>   Eternity, a thought in Shakespere's brain.

259 "I hardly dare to know": ED to Louise and Frances Norcross, [March 1884], *Letters*, 3:817.

259 " 'Supernatural,' was only the Natural": ED to TWH, [late November 1862], *Letters*, 2:182.

259 "Not 'Revelation'—'tis—that waits": Fr 500.

260 "Those—dying then": Fr 1581.

260 "Faith is *Doubt*": ED to SGD, [1884], *Letters,* 3:830.

260 "What channel needs our faith": "Calm," in *Thalatta,* p. 183.

260 "next to the yearnings of human affections": *New World,* p. 177.

260 "I hear robins a great way off": ED to Louise and Frances Norcross, [April 1873], *Letters,* 2:504.

260 "The most triumphant bird": Fr 1285B.

262 "Please say it is not so": ED to TWH, August 6, 1885, *Letters,* 3:884.

262 "Not knowing when Herself may come": Fr 1647C.

262 "Of Glory not a Beam is left": Fr 1685.

262 She was breathing with difficulty: see MDB, *Emily Dickinson Face to Face,* p. 67.

262 "Emily seemed to go off": WAD, diary, May 13, 1886, Yale.

262 Bigelow diagnosed Bright's disease: I draw on the fine work of Norbert Hirschhorn and Polly Longsworth, " 'Medicine Posthumous.' "

263 "It was settled": WAD, diary, May 15, 1886, Yale.

263 "Audacity of Bliss": ED to TWH, [spring 1886], *Letters,* 3:903. See also this early poem (Fr 145):

> *A little East of Jordan,*
> *Evangelists record,*
> *A Gymnast and an Angel*
> *Did wrestle long and hard —*
>
> *Till morning touching mountain —*
> *And Jacob, waxing strong,*
> *The Angel begged permission*
> *To Breakfast — to return!*
>
> *Not so, said cunning Jacob!*
> *"I will not let thee go*
> *Except thou bless me" — Stranger!*
> *The which acceded to —*
>
> *Light swung the silver fleeces*
> *"Peniel" Hills beyond,*
> *And the bewildered Gymnast*
> *Found he had worsted God!*

CHAPTER SIXTEEN: RENDEZVOUS OF LIGHT

264 "How large a portion": TWH, journal, May 19, 1886, Houghton.

264 "but not . . . that she would die": ED to TWH, August 6, 1885, *Letters,* 3:884.

264 "bereft of Book and Thought": ED to TWH, [spring 1886], *Letters,* 3:903.

265 "to take to Judge Lord": TWH, journal, May 19, 1886, Houghton.

265 "a favorite with our friend": TWH, quoted in *Dear Preceptor,* p. 270.

265 The honorary pallbearers: For details about the funeral, I have drawn upon TWH, journal, May 19, 1886, Houghton, and MLT to Mary and Eben Loomis, May 23, 1886, Yale.

266 "It was a never to be forgotten burial": Harriet T. Jameson to John Franklin Jameson, May 23, 1886, LC.

266 "into a little deeper mystery": MLT, journal, September 1, 1886, Yale.

266 "Not disappointed with the world": *Springfield Republican,* [May 18, 1886], clipping, Houghton.

267 "What a Hazard a Letter is!": ED to TWH, August 6, 1885, *Letters,* 3:884.

267 "It is true of all of us": *Part,* p. 139.

267 "Through the solitary prowess": In Fr 790.

267 "Are you too deeply occupied to say if my Verse is alive?": ED to TWH, April 15, 1862, *Letters,* 2:403.

267 "Deity—does He live now?": ED to TWH, [May 1886], *Letters,* 3:905.

CHAPTER SEVENTEEN: POETRY OF THE PORTFOLIO

271 "I have no doubt": Harriet T. Jameson to John Franklin Jameson, May 30, 1886, LC.

272 she took her "first lessons by studying the famous fossil bird-tracks": TWH, "Emily Dickinson's Letters," p. 444.

272 "her true Flaubert was Penelope": See the groundbreaking essay "A Consideration of the Poems of Emily Dickinson, 1973," in Howard, *Paper Trail,* p. 11; see also Cameron, *Choosing Not Choosing.*

272 "I was to have compiled the poems—": SGD, quoted in *AB,* p. 115.

273 "The Wind begun to rock the Grass": Fr 796D; "Col. Higginson, Dr. Holland, 'H.H.'": SGD to Richard Watson Gilder, December 31, 1886, NYPL.

273 "I know I have the gift of expression": MLT, journal, November 10, 1887, Yale.

273 "a notice of me in *Woman's Journal*": MLT, diary, November 2, 1889, Yale.

275 Years later Vinnie would insist: See *AB,* p. 357.

275 the "wilderness" of them all: MLT to Mary and Eben Loomis, February 23, 1889, Yale.

275 By her own admission: See also Franklin, *The Editing of Emily Dickinson,* pp. 16–17, 23–25.

275 "I felt their genius": MLT, journal, November 30, 1890, Yale.

276 "They seemed to open the door": MLT, journal, November 30, 1890, Yale.

276 Together they sifted through the huge stash: MLT to WAD, November 17, 1889, Yale.

276 "He staid an hour or more": MLT, diary, November 6, 1889, Yale.

276 "But I read him nearly a dozen": MLT, journal, November 30, 1890, Yale.

276 Steadfast and unflappable: That Higginson was reluctant about publication seems Mabel's self-serving interpretation after the fact; Sewall's apotheosis of Mrs. Todd is based largely on his prejudice in favor of her version of events and his animus against Higginson. Mrs. Todd's diary— the account she made the day she met Higginson—is at variance with the journal entry that she made just after the publication of the poems

and on which Sewall and others have based their summary of events. It seems that in that journal entry, she was already fashioning a story that made her the primary mover of Dickinson's publication. See Sewall, pp. 220ff., and MLT, journal, November 30, 1890, Yale.

276 Though his hair grew thinner still: TWH to AH, November 7, 1888, Houghton; TWH, journal, November 7, 1888, Houghton.

277 "not only to that political organization": Frederick Douglass, quoted in *Strange Enthusiasm,* p. 378.

277 "internal difference—": In Fr 320.

277 "No Man can be a Poet & a Book-Keeper": Nathaniel Hawthorne to Elizabeth Hawthorne, October 31, 1820, in Hawthorne, *The Centenary Edition,* 16:132.

277 "There are many new to me": TWH to MLT, November 25, 1889, Yale.

278 "Softer than silence, stiller than still air": "The Snowing of the Pines," in *Afternoon Landscape,* p. 26.

278 "Safe in their Alabaster Chambers—": Fr 124.

278 "O lake of boyish dreams! I linger round": "Sea-Gulls at Fresh Pond," in *Afternoon Landscape,* p. 26.

279 "I cannot reach you": TWH to ED, May 11, 1869, Houghton.

279 "beyond all worlds, all space, all thought": "Astra Castra," in *Afternoon Landscape,* p. 58. The full text of "Astra Castra" reads:

> Somewhere betwixt me and the farthest star,
>   Or else beyond all worlds, all space, all thought,
>   Dwells that freed spirit, now transformed and taught
> To move in orbits where the immortals are.
> Does she rejoice or mourn? Perchance from far
>   Some earthly errand she but now has sought,
>   By instantaneous ways among us brought,
> Ways to which night and distance yield no bar.
> Could we but reach and touch that wayward will
>   On earth so hard to touch, would she be found
>   Controlled or yet impetuous, free or bound,
> Tameless as ocean, or serene and still?
>   If in her heart one eager impulse stirs,
>   Could heaven itself calm that wild mood of hers?

Edelstein, in *Strange Enthusiasm,* p. 345, rightly points out the connection between this poem and ED.

279 that "certain Slant of light": Fr 320.

279 "A contained those of most original thought": Unsigned, undated reminiscence in the MLT Papers, folder 12, box 68, Yale.

280 "My brain fairly reels": MLT to WAD, November 17, 1889, Yale.

280 "Emily Dickinson's poems": TWH, journal, November 20, 1889, Houghton.

280 "My confidence in their *availability*": TWH, quoted in *AB,* p. 35.

280 "Perhaps you can suggest more subdivisions": TWH to MLT, November 25, 1889, Yale.

280 "I am at work with many interruptions on the poems": TWH to MLT, December 19, 1889, Yale.

280 "You are acting for me & *not* yourself": LD to MLT, March 4, 1890, Yale.

280 he had "selected and arranged": TWH to LD, April 8, 1890, quoted in *AB,* p. 51. Mabel Todd's daughter, Millicent Todd Bingham, copied and arranged the letters, now at Yale, for her publication of them; I have not located the originals.

281 Houghton Mifflin thought he had lost his mind: see *AB,* p. 51.

281 "unwise to perpetuate": Thomas Niles, quoted in MLT, journal, November 30, 1890, Yale.

281 "which shall be exempt from copyright": Thomas Niles to TWH, June 10, 1889, quoted in *AB,* p. 53.

281 "came very near to that indefinable quality": Arlo Bates, quoted in *AB,* p. 52.

281 "I changed words here and there": MLT, journal, November 30, 1890, Yale.

282 "I find with dismay": TWH to MLT, July 6, 1890, Yale; " 'I shall know why, when time is over' ": Fr 215.

282 "I died for Beauty—": Fr 448. See *AB,* p. 41, though Bingham did not evidently know which poem the editors discussed.

282 "These are the days when Birds come back—": Fr 122.

282 "The Grass so little has to do": Fr 379.

282 "It cannot go in so": TWH, quoted in *AB,* p. 58. Since I cannot find the original letter and Higginson seldom used exclamation marks, I do wonder if Mabel Todd performed some of what her daughter called "creative editing" on Higginson.

282 "Further in Summer than the Birds": Fr 895D; "It sifts from Leaden Sieves—": Fr 291E; "My Cricket and the Snow": ED to Thomas Niles, [March 1883], *Letters,* 3:768.

283 "not believe, myself, in naming them": MLT, journal, November 30, 1890, Yale.

283 "was exceedingly loath to assign titles to any of them": MLT, quoted in *AB,* p. 57.

283 "Almost!": "Within my reach!" Fr 69; "The Secret": "Some things that fly there be—," Fr 68; "Dawn": "When Night is almost done—," Fr 679; "Real": "I like a look of Agony," Fr 339; "Setting Sail": "Exultation is the going," Fr 143; "Too Late": "Delayed till she had ceased to know—," Fr 67; "Why?": "The Bumble of a Bee—," Fr 217.

283 "Presentiment is": "Presentiment—is that long shadow—on the Lawn—," Fr 487; "A wounded deer": "A *wounded* Deer—leaps highest—," Fr 181; "The brain": "The Brain, within it's Groove," Fr 563; "I've seen": "I've seen a Dying Eye,": Fr 648; "I reason": "I reason, Earth is short—," Fr 403.

283 "Because I could not stop for Death": Fr 479.

283 "Two swimmers wrestled on the spar—": Fr 227.

284 "Death and Life": See "Apparently with no surprise," Fr 1668.

285 "I dare say you are aware": LD, quoted in *AB,* p. 60.

285 "I have her letter to Mr. Higginson": MLT, diary, July 20, 1890, Yale.

285 "There came a day": "There came a Day—at Summer's full—," Fr 325.

285 "Your name should appear somewhere": TWH to MLT, September 12, 1890, Yale.

285 "It is proper": TWH to MLT, September 17, 1890, Yale.

285 "Emerson said, many years since": TWH, "An Open Portfolio," *Christian Union,* September 25, 1890, p. 392. Subsequent quotations and poems are from this article.

286 "delineate, by a few touches": TWH, preface to *Poems,* First Series.

286 "Glee—": "Glee—The great storm is over—," Fr 685; "I never saw": "I never saw a Moor," Fr 800; "Soul, wilt thou": See also "Soul, Wilt thou toss again?" Fr 89.

286 "I died": "I died for Beauty—but was scarce," Fr 448.

286 "Safe in their Alabaster Chambers—": Fr 124.

287 "I am *astounded*": TWH to MLT, November 12, 1890, Yale.

287 "No Brigadier throughout the Year": Fr 1596; "A Route of Evanescence": Fr 1489; "Dare you see a Soul at the 'White Heat'?": Fr 401; "The nearest Dream recedes—unrealized—": Fr 304; "When I hoped I feared—": Fr 594; "Before I got my eye put out—": Fr 336B; "It sifts from Leaden Sieves": Fr 291D; "A Bird, came down the Walk—": Fr 359.

287 "Your riches taught me poverty": In Fr 418B.

287 "This shows we *must* have another volume": TWH to MLT, November 12, 1890, Yale.

287 "the only person who can feel as I do"; "I feel . . . as if we had climbed": TWH to MLT, December 15, 1890, Yale.

CHAPTER EIGHTEEN: ME — COME! MY DAZZLED FACE

288 Fed for years: See Stedman, *Poets of America,* pp. 457–461; see also Stedman, *An American Anthology,* pp. xv–xxiv.

288 "A poet, most of all, should not believe in limitations": Stedman, *Poets of America,* p. 461.

289 "bitch-goddess success": See Richardson, *William James,* p. 306.

289 "at the head of all American fiction": TWH to Edith Wharton, December 5, 1905, Beinecke Rare Book and Manuscript Library, Yale University, New Haven, Conn.

289 "Nobody reads Thoreau": TWH, journal, December 23, 1866, Houghton; see also *Malbone,* pp. 99–100.

289 "irresistible needle-touch": [TWH], Recent Poetry, *Nation,* November 27, 1890, p. 423.

290 if "nothing else had come out of our life": [Howells], Editor's Study, p. 320.

290 "I have hoped and hoped": MLT, diary, December 31, 1890, Yale.

290 Apprised of some internecine warfare: See TWH to MLT, December 23, 1890, Yale.

291 And to her great satisfaction: It is not clear whether she kept the money or gave it to Lavinia, but it seems she kept it; she also kept one hundred dollars from book royalties, the same amount paid Higginson.

291 "I think there is in literary history": TWH to Brander Matthews, March 24, 1891, Butler.

291 "the *art* of composition": *New World,* p. 16; see Thoreau, "The Last Days of John Brown," in *A Yankee in Canada,* p. 284.

291 "Let us alter as little as possible": TWH to MLT, April 21, 1891, Yale.

292 "put so in order to have the rhyme perfect": MLT to TWH, July 18, 1891, BPL.

292 "Whose are the little beds—I asked": Fr 85.

292 when Todd wanted to replace: See MLT to TWH, July 13, 1891, BPL; "Dare you see a Soul at the 'White Heat'?": Fr 401.

292 "One poem only I dread a little to print": TWH to MLT, April 21, 1891, Yale; " 'Wild Nights' ": "Wild nights—Wild nights!" Fr 269.

292 "Further in Summer than the Birds—": Fr 895; "They dropped like Flakes—": Fr 545.

292 "It was not Death, for I stood up": *Poems,* Second Series; the poem is Fr 355.

294 "it might do well for you to suggest": TWH to MLT, August 4, 1891, Yale.

294 "all interference not absolutely inevitable": This and the subsequent quotation is from MLT, preface to *Poems,* Second Series.

295 "It would seem that at first I tried a little": This and subsequent quotations are from TWH, "Emily Dickinson's Letters."

296 "Essential oils": "Essential Oils—are wrung," Fr 772; "Wild nights!": "Wild nights—Wild nights!" Fr 269; "Going to him!": "Going to Him! Happy letter!" Fr 277; "Their height": "Their Hight in Heaven comforts not—," Fr 725.

296 the more they balked: Quotations in *AB,* pp. 174–175.

296 "I honestly think his mind unbalanced": Thomas Bailey Aldrich, quoted in Lubbers, *Emily Dickinson,* p. 202.

296 "I fail to detect in her work": [Aldrich], "The Contributors' Club," p. 144.

296 "It is reassuring to hear the English": Alice James, *The Diary of Alice James,* p. 227.

297 "I had expected to leave the letters entirely to you": TWH to MLT, May 13, 1893, BPL.

298 "give the copyright of Emily's mind to anyone": LD, quoted in TWH to MLT, May 30, 1893, BPL.

298 it "will be the last, I suppose": TWH to MLT, August 27, 1893, Yale.

298 "I wish as I always do": TWH to MLT, September 27, 1895, Yale.

298 "mystic and bizarre Emily": TWH to MLT, November 29, 1894, Yale.

298 "I think she can trust my honor": LD, quoted in *AB,* p. 297.

299 "It is noticeable, also, that in a few of the poems": [TWH], Recent Poetry, *Nation,* October 8, 1896, p. 275.

299 "Her vogue has passed": Literary Notes, *New York Tribune,* [August 23, 1896], quoted in *AB,* p. 345.

299 "often like that of Emily Dickinson": [TWH], Recent Poetry, *Nation,* December 11, 1902, p. 465.

300 "best for now": WAD, quoted in *Austin and Mabel,* p. 297.

300 "moral quicksand": *Austin and Mabel,* p. 412.

300 Evidently Mrs. Todd had forgotten: Later commentators see Sue maliciously guiding the suit from a discreet distance in order to take revenge on the woman who wrecked her home.

301 "I shall die standing up": MLT, diary, December 31, 1898, Yale.

301 "blight of self-interest and self-glorification": MTB, notes, February 27–August 30, 1927, Yale.

301 "Me—Come! My dazzled face": Fr 389.

CHAPTER NINETEEN: BECAUSE I COULD NOT STOP

302 "American literature is not": *New World,* p. 34.

302 "the mixture of nationalities is constantly coining": TWH, "Letter to a Young Contributor," p. 406.

302 "the art of composition is as simple": Henry David Thoreau, quoted in *New World,* p. 16.

303 "Mr. James has no doubt placed himself": *New World,* pp. 65–66.

303 "Let the picture only be well drawn": *Book and Heart,* p. 43.

303 "in case I were going to prison": "The Biography of Browning's Fame," Boston Browning Society Papers, 1886–1897, quoted in Hintz, "Thomas Wentworth Higginson," p. 483.

303 "in attempting to enforce . . . [fixed] laws": TWH, preface to TWH and Bigelow, *American Sonnets,* p. iii. He included sonnets by Poe, Edwin Markham, Henry Timrod, Jones Very, Whittier, and Ellery Channing as well as a large number of women sonneteers, including his wife, Minnie, Emma Lazarus, Maria Lowell, Harriet Monroe, Louise Brooks, and Edith Wharton.

303 the "American poet of passion is yet to come": TWH, "Americanism in Literature," p. 59.

304 "She is to be tested": [TWH], Recent Poetry, *Nation,* October 8, 1896, p. 275.

304 "We take for granted": "Leading Figures in American Literature," *Dial,* November 1, 1903, p. 314.

304 "She died,—*this* was the way she died": Fr 154.

304 "a strange, solitary, morbidly sensitive": TWH and Boynton, *A Reader's History of American Literature,* p. 131.

305 "stands at the opposite remove": TWH and Boynton, *A Reader's History of American Literature,* p. 131.

305 "an admiring Bog": In "I'm Nobody! Who are you?" Fr 260.

305 "It would be easy to make up a long list of authors": *Book and Heart,* p. 208.

305 "Perhaps the more we are destined": *Book and Heart,* p. 210.

305 "Few of us now remain who were baptized": TWH to Edna Dow Cheney, December 27, 1893, Smith.

306 "just as near slavery as possible": TWH, "The Case of the Carpet Baggers," *Nation,* March 2, 1899, pp. 162–163.

306 "To those who were living": *CY,* p. 363.

307 "Freedom is freedom": TWH, "Where Liberty Is Not, There Is My Country," *Harper's Bazaar,* August 12, 1899, p. 671.

307 "These people have a right to the freedom of civilization": TWH, quoted in *Strange Enthusiasm,* p. 389.

307 "must cut adrift from every organization": TWH, "Address to the Colored People of the United States," September 26, 1900, Houghton. Iron-

ically, racism fueled the anti-imperialism of the Democratic candidates, who wished to steer clear of "brown" Filipinos.

307 "I have yours of Nov. 23rd": TWH to William Jennings Bryan, copy marked "private," November 27, 1901, Houghton.

308 "a freedom tempered by chain-gangs, lynching, and the lash": TWH's essay "Intensely Human," originally published in the *Atlantic Monthly* in 1904, was collected in *Part*, p. 114.

308 "Was any white man ever lynched": "Intensely Human," in *Part*, p. 121.

308 "As the memories of the slave period fade away": "Intensely Human," in *Part*, p. 136.

309 "I am a man old enough to recall": TWH, introduction to William Sinclair, *The Aftermath of Slavery*, p. xi.

309 "the fact of colorphobia": TWH to Brander Matthews, September 14, 1906, Butler.

309 "it is important for this race to produce": "Intensely Human," in *Part*, p. 130.

309 "They saved you": TWH, from "Now and Then," *Harvard Graduates Magazine*, September 1904, p. 47.

309 "No white community will ever consent": TWH, *Boston Evening Transcript*, June 1, 1909.

310 *Cheerful Yesterdays* is indeed, in spite of its cheer": Henry James, "American Letter," p. 677.

311 "He is too much of a moralist": Theodore Tilton, *The Golden Age* (1871), pasted into TWH's *Atlantic Essays* scrapbook, Houghton.

311 "There are so many younger writers to be recognized & encouraged": TWH to Edmund Clarence Stedman, August 6, 1905, Butler.

311 "The old trees must fall in order to give the younger growth a chance": *Book and Heart*, p. 189.

311 "but for some inches of space": *TWH*, p. 388.

312 "All teaches us": TWH, "The Favorites of a Day," *Independent*, November 19, 1896, p. 2.

312 "was prized as having gained a second place": *CY*, p. 183.

312 "occupied intensely in practical affairs": Santayana, *The Genteel Tradition*, pp. 39–40.

312 "sicklied o'er with T. W. Higginson": Alice James, *The Diary of Alice James*, p. 227.

312 "There is not, to my mind": Amy Lowell, quoted in Damon, *Amy Lowell*, p. 611.

313 "uncertain certainty": In Fr 1421.

313 "unconscious and uncatalogued": Quoted in Monroe, "The Single Hound," p. 138.

313 "dug out of her native granite": Quoted in Elizabeth Shepley Sergeant, "An Early Imagist," *New Republic*, [August 14, 1915]; quoted in Blake and Wells, *The Recognition of Emily Dickinson*, p. 89.

313 "Once adjust oneself to the spinsterly angularity": Conrad Aiken, introduction to *Selected Poems of Emily Dickinson*, quoted in Blake and Wells, *The Recognition of Emily Dickinson*, p. 117.

313 the "hero of a hundred *Atlantic* paragraphs": Taggard, *The Life and Mind of Emily Dickinson*, p. 172.

313 the dull "Cambridge" group: See Macy, *American Writers on American Literature,* p. 178.

314 " 'Half-cracked' to Higginson": Adrienne Rich, "I Am in Danger—Sir—," in Rich, *Necessities of Life,* p. 33.

314 "one should not demand more acumen": Lubbers, *Emily Dickinson,* pp. 201–202.

314 "we must choose between the past forms": TWH, *Things New and Old,* p. 5.

314 "It is remarkable": Hawthorne, *The Centenary Edition,* 1:164.

314 " 'George Washington was the Father of his Country',": ED to Elizabeth Holland, [late autumn 1884], *Letters,* 3:849.

315 "very good for elder years": *TWH,* p. 393.

315 "I wish we had automobiles when I was a boy": TWH, quoted in "Colonel Higginson," *Hartford Courant,* [May 11, 1911], p. 8.

315 "Best of all, is to lead": TWH, "The Unforlorn Hope," *Independent,* [April 14, 1892], p. 6.

315 "Joy! shipmate—joy!": Whitman, *Leaves of Grass,* in *Complete Poetry and Collected Prose,* p. 608.

316 "that I am glad we live in a universe large enough": TWH, "Immortality," *Radical,* (May 1869), p. 385

317 "Because I could not stop for Death—": Fr 479.

Selected Bibliography

Aaron, Daniel. *The Unwritten War: American Writers and the Civil War.* New York: Alfred A. Knopf, 1973.

[Adams, Henry]. "Frothingham's Transcendentalism." *North American Review,* October 1876.

[Aldrich, Thomas Bailey]. The Contributors' Club. *Atlantic Monthly,* January 1892.

Anderson, Charles. *Emily Dickinson's Poetry: Stairway of Surprise.* New York: Anchor Books, 1966.

Barney, Margaret Higginson, ed. "Fragments from Emily Dickinson." *Atlantic Monthly,* June 1927.

Benfey, Christopher. *Emily Dickinson and the Problem of Others.* Amherst: University of Massachusetts Press, 1984.

———. *Emily Dickinson: Lives of a Poet.* New York: George Braziller, 1986.

Berkove, Lawrence I. " 'A Slash of Blue!': An Unrecognized Emily Dickinson War Poem." *Emily Dickinson Journal* 10, no. 1 (Spring 2001): 1–8.

Berlin, Ira, Joseph P. Reidy, and Leslie S. Rowland, eds. *The Black Military Experience.* Cambridge: Cambridge University Press, 1983.

Bianchi, Martha Dickinson. *Emily Dickinson Face to Face: Unpublished Letters with Notes and Reminiscences.* Boston: Houghton Mifflin, 1932.

———. *The Life and Letters of Emily Dickinson.* Boston: Houghton Mifflin, 1924.

Bingham, Millicent Todd. *Ancestors' Brocades: The Literary Debut of Emily Dickinson.* New York: Harper & Brothers, 1945.

———. *Emily Dickinson: A Revelation.* New York: Harper & Row, 1954.

———, ed. *Emily Dickinson's Home: Letters of Edward Dickinson and His Family.* New York: Harper & Brothers, 1955; reprint, Mineola, N.Y.: Dover Publications, 1967.

Bishop, Elizabeth. "Unseemly Deductions." Review of *The Riddle of Emily Dickinson,* by Rebecca Patterson. *New Republic,* August 18, 1952.

Black, David. "Discipline and Pleasure: Or, Sports and the Wild in the Writings of Thomas Wentworth Higginson." *Aethlon* 8, no. 2 (Spring 1991): 1–13.

Blake, Caesar R., and Carlton F. Wells, eds. *The Recognition of Emily Dickinson: Selected Criticism since 1890.* Ann Arbor: University of Michigan Press, 1964.

Brennan, Sister T. C. "Thomas Wentworth Higginson: Reformer and Man of Letters." PhD diss., University of Michigan, 1958.

Brill, Leonard. "Thomas Wentworth Higginson and *The Atlantic Monthly.*" PhD diss., University of Minnesota, 1969.

Brooks, Van Wyck. *New England: Indian Summer, 1865–1915.* New York: E. P. Dutton, 1940.

Burgess, John W. *Reminiscences of an American Scholar: The Beginnings of Columbia University.* New York: Columbia University Press, 1934.

Burr, George Lincoln, ed. *Narratives of New England Witchcraft Cases.* 1914; reprint, Mineola, N.Y.: Dover Publications, 2002.

Cabell, James Branch, and A. J. Hanna. *The St. Johns: A Parade of Diversities.* New York: Farrar & Rinehart, 1943.

Cameron, Sharon. *Choosing Not Choosing: Dickinson's Fascicles.* Chicago: University of Chicago Press, 1992.

———. *Lyric Time: Dickinson and the Limits of Genre.* Baltimore: Johns Hopkins University Press, 1979.

Cipper, Charles. "A Little Beyond: The Problem of the Transcendalist Movement in American History." *Journal of American History* (September 1998): 502–539.

Cody, John. *After Great Pain: The Inner Life of Emily Dickinson.* Cambridge, Mass.: Belknap Press / Harvard University Press, 1971.

Cornish, Dudley Taylor. *The Sable Arm: Black Troops in the Union Army, 1861–1865.* 1956; reprint, Lawrence: University of Kansas Press, 1987.

Damon, S. Foster. *Amy Lowell: A Chronicle with Extracts from Her Correspondence.* Boston: Houghton Mifflin, 1935.

Dana, Richard Henry. *The Journal.* 3 vols. Edited by Robert Lucid. Cambridge, Mass.: Belknap Press / Harvard University Press, 1968.

Dandurand, Karen. "New Dickinson Civil War Publications." *American Literature* 56, no. 1 (March 1984): 18–27.

Dickinson, Emily. *The Letters of Emily Dickinson.* 3 vols. Edited by Thomas H. Johnson with Theodora Ward. Cambridge, Mass.: Belknap Press / Harvard University Press, 1955.

———. *The Master Letters of Emily Dickinson.* Edited by R. W. Franklin. Amherst, Mass.: Amherst College Press, 1986.

———. *Open Me Carefully: Emily Dickinson's Intimate Letters to Susan Huntington Dickinson.* Edited by Martha Nell Smith and Ellen Louise Hart. Ashfield, Mass.: Paris Press, 1998.

———. *Poems.* Edited by Mabel Loomis Todd and Thomas Wentworth Higginson. Boston: Roberts Brothers, 1890.

———. *Poems.* Second Series. Edited by Thomas Wentworth Higginson and Mabel Loomis Todd. Boston: Roberts Brothers, 1891.

———. *The Poems of Emily Dickinson.* Reading Edition. Edited by R. W. Franklin. Cambridge, Mass.: Belknap Press / Harvard University Press, 1999.

————. *The Poems of Emily Dickinson.* Variorum Edition 3 vols. Edited by R. W. Franklin. Cambridge, Mass.: Belknap Press / Harvard University Press, 1998.

————. *The Poems of Emily Dickinson.* 3 vols. Edited by Thomas H. Johnson. Cambridge, Mass.: Belknap Press / Harvard University Press, 1955.

————. *The Single Hound: Poems of a Lifetime.* Edited by Martha Dickinson Bianchi. Boston: Little, Brown, 1914; reprint, London: Hesperus Press, 2005.

[Dickinson, Susan Gilbert]. "Harriet Prescott's Early Work." *Springfield Republican,* February 1, 1903.

Diehl, Joanne Feit. *Dickinson and the Romantic Imagination.* Princeton, N.J.: Princeton University Press, 1981.

Drake, Ross. "The Law That Ripped America in Two." *Smithsonian,* May 2004.

Du Bois, W. E. B. *John Brown.* 1909; reprint, New York: Modern Library, 2001.

Eberwein, Jane D. *Dickinson: Strategies of Limitation.* Amherst: University of Massachusetts Press, 1985.

Edelstein, Tilden G. *Strange Enthusiasm: A Life of Thomas Wentworth Higginson.* New Haven, Conn.: Yale University Press, 1968.

Elbert, Monika M., ed. *Separate Spheres No More: Gender Convergence in American Literature, 1830–1930.* Tuscaloosa: University of Alabama Press, 2000.

Elliott, Maud Howe. *This Was My Newport.* 1944; reprint, New York: Arno Press, 1975.

Emerson, Dorothy, ed. *Standing before Us: Unitarian Universalist Women and Social Reform, 1776–1936.* Boston: Skinner House Books, 1999.

Emerson, Ralph Waldo. *Essays and Poems.* Edited by Joel Porte. New York: Library of America, 1983.

Erkkila, Betsy. "Emily Dickinson and Class." *American Literary History* 4 (1992): 1–27.

Farr, Judith. *The Passion of Emily Dickinson.* Cambridge, Mass.: Harvard University Press, 1992.

Fast, Robin R., and Christine M. Gordon, eds. *Approaches to Teaching Dickinson's Poetry.* New York: Modern Language Association, 1989.

Flexner, Eleanor. *Century of Struggle: The Woman's Rights Movement in the United States.* 1959; enl. ed., Cambridge, Mass.: Belknap Press / Harvard University Press, 1996.

Foner, Eric. *Reconstruction: America's Unfinished Revolution, 1863–1877.* New York: Harper Perennial, 1989.

Ford, Worthington Chauncy, ed. *A Cycle of Adams Letters, 1861–1865.* Boston: Houghton Mifflin, 1920.

Franklin, Ralph, ed. *The Editing of Emily Dickinson: A Reconsideration.* Madison: University of Wisconsin Press, 1967.

Frederickson, George M. *The Black Image in the White Mind: The Debate on Afro-American Character and Destiny, 1817–1914.* New York: Harper & Row, 1971.

————. *The Inner Civil War: Northern Intellectuals and the Crisis of the Union.* New York: Harper & Row, 1965.

Gay, Peter. *The Bourgeois Experience: Victoria to Freud.* Vol. 1, *Education of the Senses.* New York: W. W. Norton, 1999.

Gelpi, Albert J. *Emily Dickinson: The Mind of the Poet*. Cambridge, Mass.: Harvard University Press, 1965.

Giantvalley, Scott. " 'Strict, Straight Notions of Literary Propriety': Thomas Wentworth Higginson's Gradual Unbending to Walt Whitman." *Walt Whitman Quarterly Review* 4, no. 4 (Spring 1987): 17–27.

Gornick, Vivian. *The Solitude of Self: Thinking about Elizabeth Cady Stanton*. New York: Farrar, Straus & Giroux, 2005.

Green, Clara Bellinger. "A Reminiscence of Emily Dickinson." *Bookman*, November 1924.

Grimké, Charlotte Forten. *The Journals of Charlotte Forten Grimké*. Edited by Brenda Stevenson. New York: Oxford University Press, 1988.

———. "Life on the Sea Islands," pt. 2. *Atlantic Monthly*, June 1864, pp. 666–676.

Gurstein, Rochelle. "The Importance of Being Earnest." *New Republic*, March 12, 2001.

Habegger, Alfred. *My Wars Are Laid Away in Books: The Life of Emily Dickinson*. New York: Random House, 2001.

Hall, Florence Howe. *The Story of "The Battle Hymn of the Republic."* New York: Harper & Brothers, 1916.

Hallowell, Norwood P. *The Negro as a Soldier in the War of the Rebellion: Read before the Military Historical Society of Massachusetts, January 5, 1892*. Boston: Little, Brown, 1897.

Harper, J. Henry. *The House of Harper: A Century of Publishing in Franklin Square*. New York: Harper & Brothers, 1912.

Hart, Ellen Louise. "The Encoding of Homoerotic Desire: Emily Dickinson's Letters and Poems to Susan Dickinson, 1850–1886." *Tulsa Studies in Women's Literature* 9, no. 2 (Fall 1990): 251–272.

Hawthorne, Nathaniel. *The Centenary Edition of the Works of Nathaniel Hawthorne*. Vol. 1, *The Scarlet Letter*. Edited by William Charvat, Roy Harvey Pearce, and Claude M. Simpson. Columbus: Ohio State University Press, 1962.

———. *The Centenary Edition of the Works of Nathaniel Hawthorne*. Vol. 16, *The Letters, 1843–1853*. Edited by Thomas Woodson, L. Neal Smith, and Norman Holmes Pearson. Columbus: Ohio State University Press, 1985.

———. *The Centenary Edition of the Works of Nathaniel Hawthorne*. Vol. 23, *Miscellaneous Prose and Verse*. Edited by Thomas Woodson, Claude M. Simpson, and L. Neal Smith. Columbus: Ohio State University Press, 1994.

———. "Chiefly about War-Matters, by a Peaceable Man." *Atlantic Monthly*, July 1862, pp. 43–62.

Higginson, Mary Thacher. *Thomas Wentworth Higginson: The Story of His Life*. Boston: Houghton Mifflin, 1914; reprint, Port Washington, N.Y.: Kennikat Press, 1971.

Higginson, Thomas Wentworth. *The Afternoon Landscape: Poems and Translations*. New York: Longmans, Green, 1889.

———. "Americanism in Literature." *Atlantic Monthly*, January 1870, pp. 56–64.

———. "April Days." *Atlantic Monthly*, April 1861, pp. 385–395.

———. *Army Life in a Black Regiment*. Boston: Fields, Osgood, 1870;

reprinted in *Army Life in a Black Regiment, and Other Writings*. New York: Penguin Classics, 1997.

———. "An Artist's Dream." *Atlantic Monthly,* July 1867, pp. 100–108.

———. *Book and Heart: Essays on Literature and Life*. New York: Harper & Brothers, 1897.

———. "Border Ruffianism in South Carolina." *Independent,* August 10, 1876.

———. "Carlyle's Laugh." *Atlantic Monthly,* October 1881, pp. 463–466.

———. *Carlyle's Laugh, and Other Surprises*. Boston: Houghton Mifflin, 1909.

———. "Charlotte Prince Hawes." *The Radical,* January 1867, p. 283.

———. *Cheerful Yesterdays*. Boston: Houghton Mifflin, 1898.

———. *Common Sense about Women*. Boston: Lea and Shepard, 1882.

———. *The Complete Civil War Journal and Selected Letters of Thomas Wentworth Higginson*. Edited by Christopher Looby. Chicago: University of Chicago Press, 1999.

———. *Contemporaries*. Boston: Houghton Mifflin, 1900.

———. "Decoration." *Scribner's Monthly,* June 1874, pp. 234–235.

———. *Descendants of the Reverend Francis Higginson*. Cambridge, Mass.: privately printed, 1910; reprint, Orange Park, Fla.: Quintin Publications, 2002.

———. "Emily Dickinson's Letters." *Atlantic Monthly,* October 1891, pp. 444–456.

———. "Fair Play the Best Policy." *Atlantic Monthly,* May 1865, pp. 623–631.

———. "The First Black Regiment." *Outlook,* July 2, 1898, pp. 521–531.

———. "Gabriel's Defeat." *Atlantic Monthly,* September 1862, pp. 337–345.

———. "Going to Mount Katahdin." *Putnam's Monthly Magazine,* September 1856, pp. 242–256.

———. "Gymnastics." *Atlantic Monthly,* March 1861, pp. 283–302.

———. "The Haunted Window." *Atlantic Monthly,* April 1867, pp. 429–437.

———. "Helen Hunt: Short Studies of American Authors." *Literary World,* October 25, 1879.

———. "Immortality." *The Radical,* May 1869, p. 385.

———. "Leaves from an Officer's Journal." *Atlantic Monthly,* November 1864, pp. 521–530.

———. *Letters and Journals of Thomas Wentworth Higginson, 1846–1906*. Edited by Mary Thacher Higginson. Boston: Houghton Mifflin, 1921.

———. "Letter to a Young Contributor." *Atlantic Monthly,* April 1862, pp. 401–411.

———. "The Life of Birds." *Atlantic Monthly,* September 1862, pp. 368–377.

———. "Literary Paris Twenty Years Ago." *Atlantic Monthly,* January 1898, pp. 81–90.

———. "Literature as an Art." *Atlantic Monthly,* December 1867, pp. 745–755.

———. "Madam Delia's Expectations." *Atlantic Monthly,* January 1871, pp. 40–50.

———. *The Magnificent Activist: The Writings of Thomas Wentworth Higginson*. Edited by Howard N. Meyer. Cambridge, Mass.: Da Capo Press, 2000.

———. *Malbone: An Oldport Romance*. Boston: Fields, Osgood, 1869.

————. "The Maroons of Surinam." *Atlantic Monthly,* May 1860, pp. 549–558.

————. "Massachusetts in Mourning! A Sermon." *Massachusetts Spy,* June 8, 1854.

————. *Massachusetts in the Army and Navy during the War of 1861–1865.* Vol. 1. Boston: Wright & Potter, 1896.

————. *The Monarch of Dreams.* Boston: Lee and Shepard, 1887.

————. "Mrs. Helen Jackson (H.H.)." *Century,* December 1885, pp. 251–255.

————. "My Out-Door Study." *Atlantic Monthly,* September 1861, pp. 302–309.

————. "Nathaniel Hawthorne and His Wife." *Atlantic Monthly,* February 1885, pp. 259–265.

————. "Nat Turner's Insurrection." *Atlantic Monthly,* August 1861, pp. 302–310.

————. *The New World and the Book.* Boston: Lee and Shepard, 1892.

————. "The Ordeal of Battle." *Atlantic Monthly,* July 1861, pp. 88–95.

————. "Ought Women to Learn the Alphabet?" *Atlantic Monthly,* February 1859, pp. 137–150.

————. "Our Future Militia System." *Atlantic Monthly,* September 1865, pp. 371–379.

————. *Part of a Man's Life.* Boston: Houghton Mifflin, 1905.

————. "Physical Courage." *Atlantic Monthly,* November 1858, p. 728.

————. "A Plea for Culture." *Atlantic Monthly,* January 1867, pp. 29–38.

————. "Procession of the Flowers." *Atlantic Monthly,* December 1862, pp. 649–657.

[————]. Recent Poetry. *Nation,* November 27, 1890.

[————]. Recent Poetry. *Nation,* October 8, 1896.

[————]. Recent Poetry. *Nation,* December 11, 1902.

————. "The Road to England." *Atlantic Monthly,* October 1899, pp. 521–529.

————. "Safety Matches." *Independent,* September 21, 1865.

————. "Saints and Their Bodies." *Atlantic Monthly,* March 1858, pp. 582–595.

————. "Sappho." *Atlantic Monthly,* July 1871, pp. 83–93.

————. "Seaside and Prairie." *The Woman's Journal,* November 18, 1876.

————. "A Shadow." *Atlantic Monthly,* July 1870, pp. 4–10.

————. "The Shaw Memorial and the Sculptor St. Gaudens." Pt. 3, "Colored Troops under Fire." *The Century,* June 1897, pp. 194–200.

————. "Some War Scenes Revisited." *Atlantic Monthly,* July 1878, pp. 1–10.

————. "The Sunny Side of the Transcendental Era." *Atlantic Monthly,* January 1904, pp. 6–14.

————. "Sunshine and Petrarch." *Atlantic Monthly,* September 1867, pp. 307–311.

————. *The Sympathy of Religions.* Boston: Free Religious Association, 1876.

————. Thanksgiving Day Sermon, November 30, 1848. *National Era,* January 25, 1849.

————. *Things New and Old: An Installation Sermon.* Worcester, Mass.: Earle & Drew, 1852.

————. "Two Antislavery Leaders." *International Review,* August 1880.

————. "Water-Lilies." *Atlantic Monthly,* September 1858, pp. 465–474.

————. *Woman and Her Wishes: An Essay Inscribed to the Massachusetts Constitutional Convention.* Boston: Robert F. Wallcut, 1853.

————. *Woman and the Alphabet: A Series of Essays.* Boston: Houghton Mifflin, 1900.

————. "The Woman Who Most Influenced Me." *Ladies' Home Journal,* October 1895.

————. *Women and Men.* New York: Harper & Brothers, 1887.

————, trans. *The Works of Epictetus: Consisting of His Discourses, in Four Books, 'The Enchiridion,' and Fragments.* Boston: Little, Brown, 1865.

———— and E. H. Bigelow, eds. *American Sonnets.* Boston: Houghton Mifflin, 1890.

———— and Henry Walcott Boynton. *A Reader's History of American Literature.* Boston: Houghton Mifflin, 1903.

Hintz, Howard. "Thomas Wentworth Higginson: The Disciple of the New." PhD diss. New York University, 1937.

Hirschhorn, Norbert, and Polly Longsworth. " 'Medicine Posthumous': A New Look at Emily Dickinson's Medical Conditions." *New England Quarterly* 69, no. 2 (June 1996): 299–316.

Howard, Richard. *Paper Trail: Selected Prose, 1965–2003.* New York: Farrar, Straus & Giroux, 2004.

Howe, Susan. *My Emily Dickinson.* Berkeley, Calif.: North Atlantic Books, 1985.

[Howells, William Dean]. Editor's Study. *Harper's New Monthly Magazine,* January 1891, pp. 318–320.

Hurd, Duane Hamilton, comp. *History of Essex County, Massachusetts, with Biographical Sketches of Many of Its Pioneers and Prominent Men.* Philadelphia: J. W. Lewis, 1888.

Jackson, Helen Hunt. *Mercy Philbrick's Choice.* Boston: Roberts Brothers, 1877.

James, Alice. *The Diary of Alice James.* Edited by Leon Edel. New York: Dodd, Mead, 1964.

James, Garth Wilkinson. "Memoir of Garth Wilkinson James." In *War Papers, Read before the State of Wisconsin, Military Order of the Loyal Legion of the United States.* Milwaukee: Burdick, Armitage & Allen, 1891.

James, Henry. "American Letter." *Literature* 2 (June 11, 1898).

————. *Literary Criticism.* Vol. 1, *Essays on Literature, American Writers, English Writers.* Edited by Leon Edel. New York: Library of America, 1984.

————. *Notes of a Son and Brother.* New York: Charles Scribner's Sons, 1914.

Jenkins, MacGregor. *Emily Dickinson: Friend and Neighbor.* Boston: Little, Brown, 1930.

Koscher, William P. "The Evolution, Tone, and Milieu of New England's Greatest Newspaper: *The Springfield Republican,* 1824–1920." *Historical Journal of Western Massachusetts* 5, no. 1 (Spring 1976).

Lease, Benjamin. *Emily Dickinson's Reading of Men and Books: Sacred Soundings.* New York: St. Martin's Press, 1990.

Le Duc, Thomas. *Piety and Intellect at Amherst College, 1865–1912.* New York: Columbia University Press, 1946.

Lee, Maurice S. "Writing through the War: Melville and Dickinson after the Renaissance." *PMLA* 115, no. 5 (October 2000): 1124–1128.

Leyda, Jay. *The Years and Hours of Emily Dickinson.* 2 vols. New Haven, Conn.: Yale University Press, 1960.

Ljungquist, Kent P., and Anthony Conti. " 'Near My Heart' after Fifty Years: Thomas Wentworth Higginson's Reminiscence of Worcester." *Concord Saunterer* 3 (Fall 1995).

Loeffelholz, Mary. "Dickinson's 'Decoration.' " *ELH* 72, no. 3 (Fall 2005): 663–689.

Longfellow, Samuel, and Thomas Wentworth Higginson, comps. *Thalatta: A Book for the Sea-side.* Boston: Ticknor, Reed & Fields, 1853.

Longsworth, Polly. *Austin and Mabel: The Amherst Affair and Love Letters of Austin Dickinson and Mabel Loomis Todd.* New York: Farrar, Straus & Giroux, 1984.

———. *The World of Emily Dickinson.* New York: W. W. Norton, 1990.

Looby, Christopher. "Flowers of Manhood: Race, Sex, and Floriculture from Thomas Wentworth Higginson to Robert Mapplethorpe." *Criticism* 37 (Winter 1995): 109–156.

Lowell, Robert. *Life Studies and For the Union Dead.* New York: Farrar, Straus & Giroux, 1964.

Lubbers, Karl. *Emily Dickinson: The Critical Revolution.* Ann Arbor: University of Michigan Press, 1986.

McCormick, Edgar L. "Higginson, Emerson, and a National Literature." *ESQ: A Journal of the American Renaissance* 37 (1964).

———. "Thomas Wentworth Higginson as a Literary Critic." PhD diss. University of Michigan, 1958.

McPherson, James. *The Battle Cry of Freedom: The Civil War Era.* New York: Oxford University Press, 1988.

———. *The Struggle for Equality: Abolitionists and the Negro in the Civil War and Reconstruction.* Princeton, N.J.: Princeton University Press, 1964.

Macy, John, ed. *American Writers on American Literature, by Thirty-seven Contemporary Writers.* New York: Horace Liveright, 1931.

Marcellin, Leigh-Anne Urbanowicz. " 'Singing off the Charnel Steps': Soldiers and Mourners in Emily Dickinson's Poetry." *Emily Dickinson Journal* 9, no. 2 (Fall 2000): 64–74.

Marchalonis, Shirley, ed. *Patrons and Protégées: Gender, Friendship, and Writing in Nineteenth-Century America.* New Brunswick, N.J.: Rutgers University Press, 1988.

Mayer, Henry. *All on Fire: William Lloyd Garrison and the Abolition of Slavery.* New York: St. Martin's Press, 1998.

Merriam, George S. *The Life and Times of Samuel Bowles.* 2 vols. New York: Century, 1885.

Meyer, Howard N. "Thomas Wentworth Higginson Checklist." *Higginson Journal* 43 (December 1985).

Miller, Cristanne. *Emily Dickinson: A Poet's Grammar.* Cambridge, Mass.: Harvard University Press, 1987.

Miller, Paul M. "The Relevance of the Rev. Charles Wadsworth to the Poet Emily Dickinson." *Higginson Journal* 61 (June 1991).

Mitchell, Domhnall. *Emily Dickinson: Monarch of Perception.* Amherst: University of Massachusetts Press, 2000.

———. "Revising the Script: Emily Dickinson's Manuscripts." *American Literature* 70, no. 4 (December 1998): 705–737.

Monroe, Harriet. "The Single Hound." *Poetry* 5 (December 1914).

Monteiro, George. "Higginson on Melville." *Melville Society Extracts* 57 (February 1984): 15.

Moore, Frank, ed. *The Rebellion Record: A Diary of American Events.* Vol. 6, *December 17, 1860–April 30, 1864.* New York: D. Van Nostrand, 1864.

Morison, Samuel Eliot. *Three Centuries of Harvard, 1636–1936.* Cambridge, Mass.: Harvard University Press, 1936.

Morse, Jonathan. "Emily Dickinson and the Spasmodic School: A Note on Thomas Wentworth Higginson's Esthetics." *New England Quarterly* 50, no. 3 (September 1977): 505–509.

Myerson, Joel, ed. *The Transcendentalists: A Review of Research and Criticism.* New York: Modern Language Association, 1984.

Nathan, Rhoda B., ed. *Nineteenth-Century Women Writers of the English-Speaking World.* New York: Greenwood Press, 1986.

Nelson, Robert K., and Kenneth M. Price. "Debating Manliness: Thomas Wentworth Higginson, William Sloane Kennedy, and the Question of Whitman." *American Literature* 73, no. 3 (September 2001): 497–524.

Nevins, Allan. *Ordeal of the Union.* Vol. 2, *A House Dividing, 1852–1857.* New York: Charles Scribner's Sons, 1947.

———. *The War for the Union.* 4 vols. New York: Charles Scribner's Sons, 1959–1971.

Oberhaus, Dorothy Huff. *Emily Dickinson's Fascicles: Method and Meaning.* University Park: Pennsylvania State University Press, 1995.

Olpin, Larry. "In Defense of the Colonel: Col. Higginson and a Problem of Literary Evaluation." *Higginson Journal* 42 (June 1985).

Parton, James, Horace Greeley, Thomas Wentworth Higginson, J. S. C. Abbott, James M. Hoppin, William Winter, Theodore Tilton, et al. *Eminent Women of the Age, Being Narratives of the Lives and Deeds of the Most Prominent Women of the Present Generation.* Hartford, Conn.: S. M. Betts, 1869.

Pearson, Elizabeth Ware, ed. *Letters from Port Royal, 1862–1868.* Boston: W. B. Clarke, 1906.

Phillips, Kate. *Helen Hunt Jackson: A Literary Life.* Berkeley: University of California Press, 2003.

Picker, John M. "The Union of Music and Text in Whitman's *Drum-Taps* and Higginson's *Army Life in a Black Regiment.*" *Walt Whitman Quarterly Review* 12, no. 4 (Summer 1995): 23.

Pollak, Vivian R. "Dickinson, Poe, and Barrett Browning: A Clarification." *New England Quarterly* 54, no. 1 (March 1981): 121–124.

———. *Dickinson: The Anxiety of Gender.* Ithaca, N.Y.: Cornell University Press, 1984.

———, ed. *A Poet's Parents: The Courtship Letters of Emily Norcross and Edward Dickinson.* Chapel Hill: University of North Carolina Press, 1988.

Poole, W. Scott. "Memory and the Abolitionist Heritage: Thomas Wentworth Higginson and the Uncertain Meaning of the Civil War." *Civil War History* 51, no. 2 (June 2005): 202–217.

Potter, David M. *The Impending Crisis, 1848–1861.* Compiled and edited by Don E. Fehrenbacher. New York: Harper Perennial, 1976.

Quarles, Benjamin. *The Negro in the Civil War.* 1953; reprint, Boston: Da Capo Press, 1989.

Reed, Thomas B., Justin McCarthy, Rossiter Johnson, and Albert Ellery Bergh, eds. *Modern Eloquence.* 15 vols. Philadelphia: J. D. Morris, 1900–1903.

Renehan, Edward J., Jr. *The Secret Six: The True Tale of the Men Who Conspired with John Brown.* Columbia: University of South Carolina Press, 1996.

Reynolds, David. *John Brown, Abolitionist: The Man Who Killed Slavery, Sparked the Civil War, and Seeded Civil Rights.* New York: Alfred A. Knopf, 2005.

Rich, Adrienne. *Necessities of Life: Poems, 1962–1965.* New York: W. W. Norton, 1966.

Richards, Laura Elizabeth Howe, and Maude Howe Elliott. *Julia Ward Howe, 1819–1910.* Boston: Houghton Mifflin, 1916.

Richardson, Robert D. *Emerson: The Mind on Fire; A Biography.* Berkeley: University of California Press, 1995.

———. *William James: In the Maelstrom of American Modernism.* Boston: Houghton Mifflin, 2006.

Rodier, Katharine. " 'What Is Inspiration?': Emily Dickinson, T. W. Higginson, and Maria White Lowell." *Emily Dickinson Journal* 4, no. 2 (1995): 20–43.

Rogers, Seth. "Letters of Dr. Seth Rogers." *Proceedings of the Massachusetts Historical Society* 43 (February 1910).

Rose, Willie Lee. *Rehearsal for Reconstruction: The Port Royal Experiment.* 1964; reprint, New York: Oxford University Press, 1976.

St. Armand, Barton Levi. *Emily Dickinson and Her Culture: The Soul's Society.* Cambridge: Cambridge University Press, 1984.

———. "Fine Fitnesses: Dickinson, Higginson, and Literary Luminism." *Prospects* 14 (1989).

Sánchez-Eppler, Karen. *Touching Liberty: Abolition, Feminism, and the Politics of the Body.* Berkeley: University of California Press, 1993.

Santayana, George. *The Genteel Tradition: Nine Essays.* Edited by Douglas L. Wilson, 1911; reprint, Lincoln: University of Nebraska Press, 1967.

Schama, Simon. *Dead Certainties, Unwarranted Speculations.* New York: Vintage, 1992.

Scharnhorst, Gary. "A Glimpse of Dickinson at Work." *American Literature* 57, no. 3 (October 1985): 483–485.

Sewall, Richard, ed. *Emily Dickinson: A Collection of Critical Essays.* Englewood Cliffs, N.J.: Prentice Hall, 1963.

———. *The Life of Emily Dickinson.* 2 vols. New York: Farrar, Straus & Giroux, 1974.

———, ed. *The Lyman Letters: New Light on Emily Dickinson and Her Family.* Amherst: University of Massachusetts Press, 1965.

Shaw, Robert Gould. *Blue-Eyed Child of Fortune: The Civil War Letters of Robert Gould Shaw.* Edited by Russell Duncan. Athens: University of Georgia Press, 1999.

Sinclair, William. *The Aftermath of Slavery: A Study of the Condition and Environment of the American Negro,* with an introduction by Thomas Wentworth Higginson. Boston: Small, Maynard, 1905.

Smith, John David, ed. *Black Soldiers in Blue: African American Troops in the Civil War Era.* Chapel Hill: University of North Carolina Press, 2002.

Smith, Martha Nell. *Rowing in Eden: Rereading Emily Dickinson.* Austin: University of Texas Press, 1992.

Spofford, Harriet. "Pomegranate-Flowers." *Atlantic Monthly,* May 1861, pp. 573–579.

Stanton, Elizabeth Cady. *Elizabeth Cady Stanton as Revealed in Her Letters, Diary, and Reminiscences.* Edited by Theodore Stanton and Harriot Stanton Blatch. New York: Harper & Brothers, 1922.

———, Susan B. Anthony, and Matilda Joslyn Gage. *History of Woman Suffrage.* Vol. 2. 1887; reprint, New York: Arno Press, 1969.

Stauffer, John. *The Black Hearts of Men: Radical Abolitionists and the Transformation of Race.* Cambridge, Mass.: Harvard University Press, 2002.

Stecopoulos, Harry, and Michael Uebel, eds. *Race and the Subject of Masculinities.* Durham, N.C.: Duke University Press, 1997.

Stedman, Edmund Clarence, ed. *An American Anthology, 1787–1900: Selections Illustrating the Editor's Critical Review of American Poetry in the Nineteenth Century.* Boston: Houghton Mifflin, 1900.

———, ed. *Poets of America.* Boston: Houghton Mifflin, 1885.

Strachey, J. W. "The Man of Letters as Reformer." *Spectator,* March 29, 1902.

Taggard, Genevieve. *The Life and Mind of Emily Dickinson.* New York: Alfred A. Knopf, 1930.

Taylor, Susie King. *Reminiscences of My Life in Camp with the 33rd United States Colored Troops (Late 1st S.C. Volunteers).* Boston: Susie King Taylor, 1902.

Thoreau, Henry David. *Walden, and Civil Disobedience.* Edited by Sherman Paul. Cambridge, Mass.: Riverside Press, 1960.

———. *A Yankee in Canada, with Anti-slavery and Reform Papers.* Boston: Ticknor & Fields, 1866.

Tuttleton, James W. *Thomas Wentworth Higginson.* Boston: Twayne, 1978.

Vendler, Helen. *Poets Thinking: Pope, Whitman, Dickinson, Yeats.* Cambridge, Mass.: Harvard University Press, 2004.

Von Frank, Albert. "John Brown, James Redpath, and the Idea of Revolution." *Civil War History* 52, no. 2 (June 2006): 142–160.

———. *The Trials of Anthony Burns: Freedom and Slavery in Emerson's Boston.* Cambridge, Mass.: Harvard University Press, 1998.

Wadsworth, Charles. "The Gospel Call." In *Sermons.* New York: A. Roman, 1869.

———. *Religion in Politics: A Sermon Preached in the Arch Street Presbyterian Church.* Philadelphia: W. S. Martien, 1853.

Ward, Theodora Van Wagenen. "Emily Dickinson and T. W. Higginson." *Boston Public Library Quarterly* 5, no. 1 (January 1953).

Wardrop, Daneen. "The Poetics of Political Involvement and Non-Involvement." *Emily Dickinson Journal* 10, no. 2 (Fall 2001): 52–67.

Wells, Anna Mary. *Dear Preceptor: The Life and Times of Thomas Wentworth Higginson.* Boston: Houghton Mifflin, 1963.

———. "Note on Higginson's Reputation." *Dickinson Studies* 51 (1984): 20–21.

Werner, Marta L. *Emily Dickinson's Open Folios: Scenes of Reading, Surfaces of Writing.* Ann Arbor: University of Michigan Press, 1995.

Whicher, George. *This Was a Poet*. New York: Charles Scribner's Sons, 1938.

Whitman, Walt. *Complete Poetry and Collected Prose*. Edited by Justin Kaplan. New York: Library of America, 1984.

Whittier, John Greenleaf. *Justice and Expediency; or, Slavery Considered with a View to Its Rightful and Effectual Remedy, Abolition*. Haverhill, Mass.: C. P. Thayer, 1833.

Wilentz, Sean. *The Rise of American Democracy: Jefferson to Lincoln*. New York: W. W. Norton, 2005.

Williams, Donald H. "T. W. Higginson on Thoreau and Maine." *Colby Library Quarterly* 7 (March 1965).

Wilson, Edmund. *Patriotic Gore: Studies in the Literature of the American Civil War*. New York: Oxford University Press, 1962.

Wolff, Cynthia Griffin. *Emily Dickinson*. New York: Alfred A. Knopf, 1986.

Wolosky, Shira. *Dickinson: A Voice of War*. New Haven, Conn.: Yale University Press, 1984.

Wyman, Lillie Buffum Chase, and Arthur Crawford Wyman. *Elizabeth Buffum Chase, 1806–1899: Her Life and Its Environment*. 2 vols. Boston: W. B. Clarke, 1914.

Emily Dickinson Poems Known to Have Been Sent to Thomas Wentworth Higginson

Safe in their Alabaster Chambers—, Fr 124
I'll tell you how the Sun rose—, Fr 204
We play at Paste—, Fr 282A
The nearest Dream recedes—unrealized—, Fr 304
There came a Day at Summer's full, Fr 325D
Of all the Sounds despatched abroad, Fr 334B
South Winds jostle them—, Fr 98E
As if I asked a common Alms, Fr 14
Of Tribulation—these are They, Fr 328
Your Riches, taught me, poverty—, Fr 418B
Some keep the Sabbath going to Church—, Fr 236
It sifts from Leaden Sieves., Fr 291B&D
Success—is counted sweetest, Fr 112D
Before I got my eye put out—, Fr 336B
I cannot dance upon my Toes—, Fr 381A
A Bird, came down the Walk—, Fr 359
Dare you see a Soul at the "White Heat"?, Fr 401
That after Horror—that 'twas *us*—, Fr 243B
The Soul unto itself, Fr 579A
Best Gains—must have the Losses' test—, Fr 499
Not "Revelation"—'tis—that waits, Fr 500
The Robin is the One, Fr 501
I did not deem that Planétary forces, Fr 568A
The only News I know, Fr 820B
Further in Summer than the Birds, Fr 895D

Blazing in Gold and quenching in Purple, Fr 321
Except the smaller size, Fr 606
A Death blow is a Life blow to Some, Fr 966
Paradise is of the Option—, Fr 1125A
A narrow Fellow in the Grass, Fr 1096
They say that "Time assuages"—, Fr 861B
Ample make this Bed—, Fr 804C
To undertake is to achieve, Fr 991
As imperceptibly as Grief, Fr 935D
The Luxury to apprehend, Fr 819
Trust adjusts her "Peradventure"—, Fr 1177
When I hoped I feared—, Fr 594
The Days that we can spare, Fr 1229B
Step lightly on this narrow Spot—, Fr 1227
Remembrance has a Rear and Front., Fr 1234
Immortal is an ample word, Fr 1223B
To disappear enhances—The Man that runs away, Fr 1239C
He preached opon "Breadth" till it argued him narrow—, Fr 1266
Our own Possessions though our own, Fr 1267
The Show is not the Show, Fr 1270C
The Sea said "Come" to the Brook—, Fr 1275
Not any higher stands the Grave, Fr 1214
Longing is like the Seed, Fr 1298A
Dominion lasts until obtained—, Fr 1299
The Wind begun to rock the Grass, Fr 796D
Who were "the Father and the Son", Fr 1280
Because that you are going, Fr 1314
To his simplicity, Fr 1387
A Wind that woke a lone Delight, Fr 1216D
Presuming on that lone result, Fr 1242B
The mushroom—, is the Elf of Plants— Fr 1350E
Of Life to own—, Fr 1327
Pink—small—and punctual—, Fr 1350D
The last of Summer is Delight—, Fr 1380
The Heart is the Capital of the Mind., Fr 1381C
The Mind lives on the Heart, Fr 1384
The Rat is the concisest Tenant, Fr 1369
"Faithful to the end" amended, Fr 1386
Take all away—, Fr 1390
I sued the News—yet feared—the News, Fr 1391
The things we thought that we should do, Fr 1279
The long sigh of the Frog, Fr 1394A
The Treason of an accent, Fr 1388
Of their peculiar light, Fr 1396A
How know it from a Summer's Day?, Fr 1412, to MCH
The Flake the Wind exasperate, Fr 1410, to MCH
Summer laid her supple Glove, Fr 1411E
After all Birds have been investigated and laid aside—, Fr 1383
To wane without disparagement, Fr 1416B

Emily Dickinson Poems Cited

Index

Page numbers in *italics* refer to illustrations.

"A *wounded* deer leaps highest"
(Dickinson), 283

"Barbarism and Civilization"
(Higginson), 93
"Barefoot Boy" (Whittier), 165
Batchelder, James, 83, 84, 336*n*
Bates, Arlo, 281, 288
"Battle-Field, The" ("They dropped
like Flakes—") (Dickinson),
107
"Battle Hymn of the Republic"
(J. W. Howe), 110
Beaufort, S.C., 123, *124, 128,* 133,
138, 143, 216, 217, 227, 303,
314, 317
"Because I could not stop for
Death—" (Dickinson), 75,
317–18
"Because that you are going"
(Dickinson), 195–6
Beecher, Henry Ward, 71, 88, 233
Beecher, Lyman, 41
"Before I got my eye put out—"
(Dickinson), 72, 287
Bellamy, Edward, 253
"Bereavement in their death to feel"
(Dickinson), 151
"Best Gains—must have the Losses'
test—" (Dickinson), 154
Bianchi, Martha Dickinson "Mattie"
(niece), 43, 52, 72, 201, *231,*
232, 234, 238, 291, 301, 313,
334*n*
Bigelow, Otis, 262, 370*n*
Bingham, Millicent Todd, 224, 245,
276, 301, 367*n*
Birds, The (Aristophanes), 315
Bishop, Elizabeth, 52
Blackmur, R. P., 69
black regiments, 12, 123, 125–36,
138–41, 143–5, 170, 227, 250,
307, 311–12, 316, 317, 349*n*
cruel and unfair treatment of,
136–7, 139, 140, 141, 144,
173, 174
Massachusetts Fifty-fourth, 12,
123, 134–6, 139–43, *142,* 311
successes of, 132, 135

see also First South Carolina
Volunteers regiment
Blackwell, Henry, 187
Blake, William, 12, 286
"Blazing in Gold and quenching in
Purple" ("The Sunset")
(Dickinson), 149–50, 167
"Bliss is the sceptre of the child"
(Dickinson), 42
Blithedale Romance, The (Hawthorne),
24
Booth, Mary, 251
Boston, Mass., 18, 22, 30, 31, 46,
52, 60, 63, 88, 90, 134, 158,
162, 197, 198, 199, 200, 201,
204, 262, 276, 310, 311
Burns affair in, 4, 81–6, *85,* 87,
96, 97, 127, 134, 305, 336*n,*
337*n*
Boston Evening Transcript, 307
Boston Library, 315, 317
Boston Post, 150
Boston Woman's Club, 204
Boutwell, George, 307
Bowles, Mary, 79–80, 147
Bowles, Samuel, 71, 78–80, *78,* 107,
113, 166, 201, 245
death of, 216, 219
Brannan, John M., 173
Bright's disease, 262
Brisbane, William Henry, 129–30
Brontë, Emily, 112, 265, 316
Brontë sisters, 56, 66, 258
Brook Farm, 21–2, 27
Brooklyn Daily Eagle, 150
Brooks, Louise, 370*n*
Brown, Antoinette, 34
Brown, John, 4, 9, 88, 89–93, 95,
125, 133, 188, 225, 248, 302
Brown, William Wells, 28
Browne, Thomas, 7
Browning, Elizabeth Barrett, 7, 35,
56, 112, 185, 193, 249, 303,
361*n*
Browning, Robert, 7, 21, 35, 108,
112, 199, 266
Bryan, William Jennings, 307–8
Bryant, William Cullen, 149, 312
Buchanan, James, 89